Elvira J. Bradshaw

Dec 14 1859

POEMS,

PLAYS AND ESSAYS,

BY

OLIVER GOLDSMITH, M. B

WITH

A CRITICAL DISSERTATION ON HIS POETRY,

BY

BY JOHN AIKIN, M. D.

AND

AN INTRODUCTORY ESSAY,

BY

HENRY T. TUCKERMAN, ESQ

BOSTON:
PHILLIPS, SAMPSON AND COMPANY.
1857.

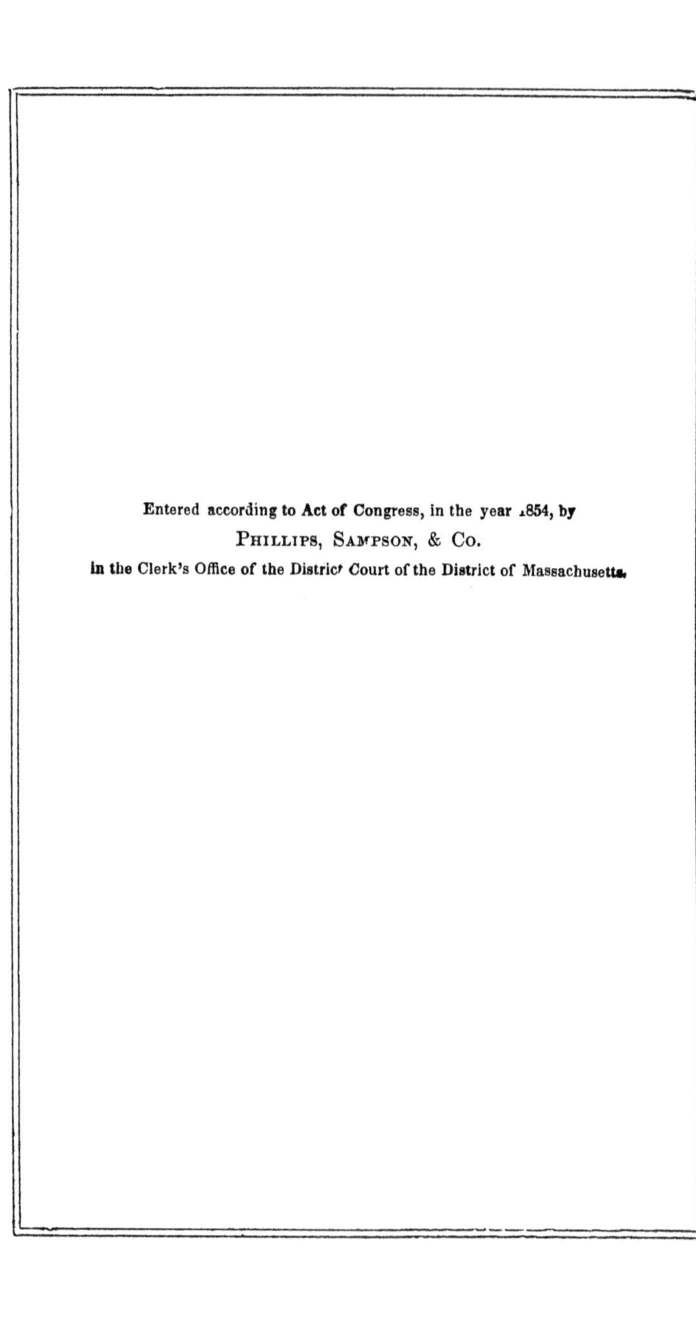

CONTENTS.

POEMS.

PLAYS.

ESSAYS.

INTRODUCTORY ESSAY.*

BY HENRY T. TUCKERMAN.

It is sometimes both pleasing and profitable to recur to those characters in literary history who are emphatically favorites, and to glance at the causes of their popularity. Such speculations frequently afford more important results than the mere gratification of curiosity. They often lead to a clearer perception of the true tests of genius, and indicate the principle and methods by which the common mind may be most successfully addressed. The advantage of such retrospective inquiries is still greater at a period like the present, when there is such an obvious tendency to innovate upon some of the best established theories of taste; when the passion for novelty seeks for such unlicensed indulgence, and invention seems to exhaust itself rather upon forms than ideas. In literature, especially, we appear to be daily losing one of the most valuable elements — simplicity. The prevalent taste is no longer gratified with the natural. There is a growing appetite for what is startling and peculiar, seldom accompanied by any discriminating demand for the true and original; and yet, experience has fully proved that these last are the only permanent elements of literature; and no healthy mind, cognizant of its own history, is unaware that the only intellectual aliment

* From "Thoughts on the Poets," by H. T. T.

which never palls upon the taste, is that which is least indebted to extraneous accompaniments for its relish.

It is ever refreshing to revert to first principles. The study of the old masters may sometimes make the modern artist despair of his own efforts; but if he have the genius to discover, and follow out the great principle upon which they wrought, he will not have contemplated their works in vain. He will have learned that devotion to Nature is the grand secret of progress in Art, and that the success of her votaries depends upon the singleness, constancy, and intelligence of their worship. If there is not enthusiasm enough to kindle this flame in its purity, nor energy sufficient to fulfil the sacrifice required at that high altar, let not the young aspirant enter the priesthood of art. When the immortal painter of the Transfiguration was asked to embody his ideal of perfect female loveliness, he replied — there would still be an infinite distance between his work and the existent original. In this profound and vivid perception of the beautiful in nature, we perceive the origin of those lovely creations, which, for more than three hundred years, have delighted mankind. And it is equally true of the pen as the pencil, that what is drawn from life and the heart, alone bears the impress of immortality. Yet the practical faith of our day is diametrically opposed to this truth. The writers of our times are constantly making use of artificial enginery. They have, for the most part, abandoned the integrity of purpose and earnest directness of earlier epochs. There is less faith, as we before said, in the natural; and when we turn from the midst of the forced and hot-bed products of the modern school, and ramble in the garden of old English literature, a cool and calm refreshment invigorates the spirit, like the first breath of mountain air to the weary wayfarer.

There are few writers of the period more generally beloved than Dr. Goldsmith. Of his contemporaries, Burke excelled him in splendor of diction, and Johnson in depth of thought. The former continues to enjoy a larger share of admiration, and the latter of respect, but the labors of their less pretending companion have secured him a far richer heritage of love. Of all posthumous tributes to genins, this seems the most truly desirable. It recognizes the man as well as the author. It is called forth by more interesting characteristics than talent. It bespeaks a greater than ordinary association of the individual with his works, and looking beyond the mere embodiment of his intellect, it gives assurance of an attractiveness in his character which has made itself felt even through the artificial medium of writing. The authors are comparatively few, who have awakened this feeling of personal interest and affection. It is common, indeed, for any writer of genius to inspire emotions of gratitude in the breasts of those susceptible to the charm, but the instances are rare in which this sentiment is vivified and elevated into positive affection. And few, I apprehend, among the wits and poets of old England, have more widely awakened it than Oliver Goldsmith. I have said this kind of literary fame was eminently desirable. There is, indeed, something inexpressibly touching in the thought of one of the gifted of our race, attaching to himself countless hearts by the force of a charm woven in by-gone years, when environed by neglect and discouragement. Though a late, it is a beautiful recompense, transcending mere critical approbation, or even the reverence men offer to the monuments of mind. We can conceive of no motive to effort which can be presented to a man of true feeling, like the hope of winning the love of his kind by the faithful exhibition of himself. It is a nobler purpose than that entertained by heartless ambition. The appeal is not merely to the judgment and imagination, it is to the universal heart of mankind. Such fame is emphatically rich. It gains its possessor warm friends instead of mere admirers. To establish such an inheritance in the breast of humanity, were indeed worthy of sacrifice and toil. It is an offering not only to intellectual but to moral graces, and its possession argues for the sons of fame holier qualities than genius itself. It eloquently indicates that its subject is not only capable of interesting the general mind by the power of his creations, but of captivating the feelings by the earnest beauty of his nature. Of all oblations, therefore, we deem it the most valuable. It is this sentiment with which the lovers of painting regard the truest interpreters of the art. They wonder at Michael Angelo but love Raphael, and gaze upon the pensively beautiful delineation he has left us of himself, with the regretful tenderness with which we look upon the portrait of a departed friend. The devotees of music, too, dwell with glad astonishment upon the celebrated operas of Rosini and some of the German composers, but the memory of Bellini is absolutely loved. It is well remarked by one of Goldsmith's biographers, that the very fact of his being spoken of always with the epithet "poor" attached to his name, is sufficient evidence of the kind of fame he enjoys. Whence, then, the peculiar attraction of his writings, and wherein consists the spell which has so long rendered his works the favorites of so many and such a variety of readers?

The primary and all pervading charm of Goldsmith is his truth. It is interesting to trace this delightful characteristic, as it exhibits itself not less in his life than in his writings. We see it displayed in the remarkable frankness which distinguished his intercourse with others, and in that winning simplicity which so frequently excited the contemptuous laugh of the worldly-wise, but failed not to draw towards him the more valuable sympathies of less perverted natures. All who have sketched his biography unite in declaring, that he could not dissemble; and we have a good illustration of his want of tact in concealing a defect, in the story which is related of him at the time of his unsuccessful attempt at medical practice in Edinburgh — when, his only velvet coat being deformed by a huge patch on the right breast, he was accustomed, while in the drawing-room, to cover it in the most awkward manner with his hat. It was his natural truthfulness which led him to so candid and habitual a confession of his faults. Johnson ridiculed him for so freely describing the state of his feelings during the representation of his first play; and, throughout his life, the perfect honesty of his spirit made him the subject of innumerable practical jokes. Credulity is perhaps a weakness almost inseparable from eminently truthful characters Yet, if such is the case, it does not in the least diminish our faith in the superiority and value of such characters. Waiving all moral considerations, we believe it can be demonstrated that truth is one of the most essential elements of real greatness, and surest means of eminent success. Management, chicanery and cunning, may advance men in the career of the world; it may forward the views of the politician, and clear the way of the diplomatist. But when humanity is to be addressed in the universal language of genius; when, through the medium of literature and art, man essays to reach the heart of his kind, the more sincere the appeal, the surer its effect; the more direct the call, and deeper the response. In a word, the more largely truth enters into a work, the more certain the fame of its author. But a few months since, I saw the Parisian populace crowding around the church where the remains of Talleyrand lay in state, but the fever of curiosity alone gleamed from their eyes, undimmed by tears. When Goldsmith died, Reynolds, then in the full tide of success, threw his pencil aside in sorrow, and Burke turned from the fast-brightening vision of renown, to weep.

Truth is an endearing quality. None are so beloved as the ingenuous. We feel in approaching them that the look of welcome is unaffected — that the friendly grasp is from the heart, and we regret their departure as an actual loss. And not less winningly shines this high and sacred principle through the labors of genius. It immortalizes history — it is the true origin of eloquence, and constitutes the living charm of poetry. When Goldsmith penned the lines —

> " To me more dear, congenial to my heart,
> One native charm than all the gloss of art,"

he furnished the key to his peculiar genius, and recorded the secret which has embalmed his memory. It was the clearness of his own soul which reflected so truly the imagery of life. He did but transcribe the unadorned convictions that glowed in his mind, and faithfully traced the pictures which nature threw upon the mirror of his fancy. Hence the unrivalled excellence of his descriptions. Rural life has never found a sweeter eulogist. To countless memories have his village landscapes risen pleasantly, when the " murmnr " rose at eventide. Where do we not meet with a kind-hearted philosopher delighting in some speculative hobby, equally dear as the good Vicar's theory of Monogamy ? The vigils of many an ardent student have been beguiled by his portraiture of a country clergyman — brightening the dim vista of futurity as his own ideal of destiny; and who has not, at times, caught the very solace of retirement from his sweet apostrophe ?

The genius of Goldsmith was chiefly fertilized by observation. He was not one of those who regard books as the only, or even the principal sources of knowledge. He recognized and delighted to study the unwritten lore so richly spread over the volume of nature, and shadowed forth so variously from the scenes of every-day life and the teachings of individual experience. There is a class of minds, second to none in native acuteness and reflective power, so constituted as to flourish almost exclusively by observation. Too impatient of restraint to endure the long vigils of the scholar, they are yet keenly alive to every idea and truth which is evolved from life. Without a tithe of that spirit of application that binds the German student for years to his familiar tomes, they suffer not a single impression which events or character leave upon their memories to pass unappreciated. Unlearned, in a great measure, in the history of the past, the present is not allowed to pass without eliciting their intelligent comment. Unskilled in the technicalities of learning, they contrive to appropriate, with surprising facility, the wisdom born of the passing moment. No striking trait of character — no remarkable effect in nature — none of the phenomena of social existence, escape them. Like Hogarth, they are constantly enriching themselves with sketches from life; and as he drew street-wonders upon his thumb-nail, they note and remember, and afterwards elaborate and digest whatever of interest experience affords. Goldsmith was a true specimen of this class. He vindicated, indeed, his claim to the title of scholar, by research and study; but the field most congenial to his taste, was the broad universe of nature and man. It was his love of observation which gave zest to the roving life he began so early to indulge. His boyhood was passed in a constant succession of friendly visits. He was ever migrating from the house of one kinsman or friend to that of another; and on these occasions, as well as when at home, he was silently but faithfully observing. The result is easily traced in his writings. Few authors, indeed, are so highly indebted to personal observation for their materials. It is well known that the original of the Vicar of Wakefield was his own father. Therein has he embodied in a charming manner his early recollections of his parent, and the picture is rendered still more complete in his papers on the "Man in Black." The inimitable description, too, of the "Village Schoolmaster," is drawn from the poet's early teacher; and the veteran who "shouldered his crutch and told how fields were won," had often shared the hospitality of his father's roof. The leading incident in "She Stoops to Conquer," was his own adventure; and, there is little question, that, in the quaint tastes of Mr. Burchell, he aimed to exhibit many of his peculiar traits. But it is not alone in the leading characters of his novel, plays and poems, that we discover Goldsmith's observing power. It is equally discernible throughout his essays and desultory papers. Most of his illustrations are borrowed from personal experience, and his opinions are generally founded upon experiment. His talent for fresh and vivid delineation, is ever most prominently displayed when he is describing what he actually witnessed, or drawing from the rich fund of his early impressions or subsequent adventures. No appeal to humor, curiosity, or imagination, was unheeded; and it is the blended pictures he contrived to combine from these cherished associations, that impart so lively an interest to his pages. One moment we find him noting, with philosophic sympathy, the pastimes of a foreign peasantry; and another, studying the operations of a spider at his garret window, — now busy in nomenclating the peculiarities of the Dutch, and anon, alluding to the exhibition of Cherokee Indians. The natural effect of this thirst for experimental knowledge, was to beget a love for foreign travel. Accordingly, we find that Goldsmith, after exhausting the narrow circle which his limited means could compass at home, projected a continental tour, and long cherished the hope of visiting the East. Indeed, we could scarcely have a stronger proof of his enthusiasm, than the long journey he undertook and actually accomplished on foot. The remembrance of his romantic wanderings over Holland, France, Germany, and Italy, imparts a singular interest to his writings. It was, indeed, worthy of a true poet that, enamored of nature and delighting in the observation of his species, he should thus manfully go forth, with no companion but his flute, and wander over these fair lands hallowed by past associations and existent beauty. A rich and happy era, despite its moments of discomfort, to such a spirit, was that year of solitary pilgrimage. Happy and proud must have been the imaginative pedestrian, as he reposed his weary frame in the peasant's cottage "beside the murmuring Loire;" and happier still when he stood amid the green valleys of Switzerland, and looked around upon her snow-capt hills, hailed the old towers of Verona, or entered the gate of Florence — the long-anticipated goals to which his weary footsteps had so patiently tended. If anything could enhance the pleasure of musing amid these scenes of poetic interest, it must have been the consciousness of having reached them by so gradual and self-denying a progress. There is, in truth, no more characteristic portion of Goldsmith's biography, than that which records this remarkable tour; and there are few more striking instances of the available worth of talent. Unlike the bards of old, he won not his way to shelter and hospitality by appealing to national feeling; for the lands through which he roamed were not his own, and the lay of the last minstrel had long since died away in oblivion. But he gained the ready kindness of the peasantry by playing the flute, as they danced in the intervals of toil; and won the favor of the learned by successful disputation at the convents and universities — a method of rewarding talent which was extensively practised in Europe at that period. Thus, solely befriended by his wits, the roving poet rambled over the continent, and, notwithstanding the vicissitudes incident to so precarious a mode of seeing the world, to a mind like his, there was ample compensation in the superior opportunities for observation thus afforded. He mingled frankly with the people, and saw things as they were. The scenery which environed him flitted not before his senses, like the shifting scenes of a panorama, but became familiar to his eye under the changing aspects of time and season. Manners and customs he quietly studied, with the advantage of sufficient opportunity to institute just comparisons and draw fair inferences. In short, Goldsmith was no tyro in the philosophy of travel; and, although the course he pursued was dictated by necessity, its superior results are abundantly evidenced throughout his works. We have, indeed, no formal narrative of his journeyings; but what is better, there is scarcely a page thrown off, to supply the pressing wants of the moment, which is not enriched by some pleasing reminiscence or sensible thought, garnered from the recollection and scenes of that long pilgrimage. Nor did he fail to embody the prominent impressions of so interesting an epoch of his checkered life, in a more en during and beautiful form. The poem of "The Traveller," originally sketched in Switzerland, was subsequently revised and extended. It was the foundation of Goldsmith's poetical fame. The subject evinces the taste of the author. The unpretending vein of enthusiasm which runs through it, is only equalled by the force and simplicity of the style. The rapid sketches of the several countries it presents, are vigorous and pleasing; and the reflections interspersed, abound with that truly humane spirit, and that deep sympathy with the good, the beautiful, and the true, which distinguishes the poet. This production may be regarded as the author's first deliberate attempt in the career of genius. It went through nine editions during his life, and its success contributed, in a great measure, to encourage and sustain him in future and less genial efforts.

The faults which are said to have deformed the character of Goldsmith, belong essentially to the class of foibles rather than absolute and positive errors. Recent biographers agree in the opinion, that his alleged devotion to play has either been grossly exaggerated, or was but a temporary mania; and we should infer from his own allusion to the subject, that he had, with the flexibility of disposition that belonged to him, yielded only so far to its seductions as to learn from experience the supreme folly of the practice. It is at all events certain, that his means were too restricted, and his time, while in London, too much occupied, to allow of his enacting the part of a regular and professed gamester; and during the latter and most busy years of his life, we have the testimony of the members of the celebrated club to which he was attached, to the temperance and industry of his habits. Another, and in the eyes of the world, perhaps, greater weakness recorded of him, was a mawkish vanity, sometimes accompanied by jealousy of more successful competitors for the honors of literature. Some anecdotes, illustrative of this unamiable trait, are preserved, which would amuse us, were they associated with less noble endowments or a more uninteresting character. As it is, however, not a few of them challenge credulity, from their utter want of harmony with certain dispositions which he is universally allowed to have possessed. But it is one of the greatest and most common errors in judging of character, to take an isolated and partial, instead of a broad and comprehensive view of the various qualities which go to form the man, and the peculiar circumstances that have influenced their development. Upon a candid retrospect of Goldsmith's life, it appears to us that the display of vanity, which in the view of many are so demeaning, may be easily and satisfactorily explained. Few men possess talent of any kind unconsciously. It seems designed by the Creator, that the very sense of capacity should urge genius to fulfil its mission, and support its early and lonely efforts by the earnest conviction of ultimate success. To beings thus endowed, the neglect and contumely of the world — the want of sympathy — the feeling of misappreciation, is often a keen sorrow felt precisely in proportion to the susceptibility of the individual, and expressed according as he is ingenuous and frank.

In the case of Goldsmith, his long and solitary struggle with poverty — his years of obscure toil — his ill-success in every scheme for support, coupled as they were with an intuitive and deep consciousness of mental power and poetic gifts, were calculated to render him painfully alive to the superior consideration bestowed upon less deserving but more presumptuous men, and the unmerited and unjust disregard to his own claims. Weak it undoubtedly was, for him to give vent so childishly to such feelings, but this sprung from the spontaneous honesty of his nature. He felt as thousands have felt under similar circumstances, but, unlike the most of men, "he knew not the art of concealment." Indeed, this free-spoken and candid disposition was inimical to his success in more than one respect. He was ever a careless talker, unable to play the great man, and instinctively preferring the spontaneous to the formal, and "thinking aloud" to studied and circumspect speech. The "exquisite sensibility to contempt," too, which he confesses belonged to him, frequently induced an appearance of conceit, when no undue share existed. The truth is, the legitimate pride of talent, for want of free and natural scope, often exhibited itself in Goldsmith greatly to his disadvantage. The fault was rather in his destiny than himself. He ran away from college with the design of embarking for America, because he was reproved by an unfeeling tutor before a convivial party of his friends; and descended to a personal rencontre with a printer, who impudently delivered Dodsley's refusal that he should undertake an improved edition of Pope. He concealed his name when necessity obliged him to apply for the office of Usher; and received visits and letters at a fashionable coffee-house, rather than expose the poorness of his lodgings. He joined the crowd to hear his own ballads sung when a student; and openly expressed his wonder at the stupidity of people, in preferring the tricks of a mountebank to the society of a man like himself. While we smile at, we cannot wholly deride such foibles, and are constrained to say of Goldsmith as he said of the Village Pastor—

"And e'en his failings leaned to virtue's side."

It is not easy to say, whether the improvidence of our poet arose more from that recklessness of the future, characteristic of the Irish temperament, or the singular confidence in destiny which is so common a trait in men of ideal tendencies. It would naturally be supposed, that the stern lesson of severe experience would have eventually corrected this want of foresight. It was but the thoughtlessness of youth which lured him to forget amid the convivialities of a party, the vessel on board which he had taken passage and embarked his effects, on his first experiment in travelling; but later in life, we find him wandering out on the first evening of his arrival in Edinburgh, without noting the street or number of his lodgings; inviting a party of strangers in a public garden to take tea with him, without a sixpence in his pocket; and obstinately persisting, during his last illness, in taking a favorite medicine, notwithstanding it aggravated his disease. A life of greater vicissitude it would be difficult to find in the annals of literature. Butler and Otway were, indeed, victims of indigence, and often perhaps, found themselves, like our bard, "in a garret writing for bread, and expecting every moment to be dunned for a milk-score," but the biography of Goldsmith displays a greater variety of shifts resorted to for subsistence. He was successively an itinerant musician, a half-starved usher, a chemist's apprentice, private tutor, law-student, practising physician, eager disputant, hack-writer, and even, for a week or two, one of a company of strolling players. In the History of George Primrose, he is supposed to have described much of his personal experience prior to the period when he became a professed *litterateur*. We cannot but respect the independent spirit he maintained through all these struggles with adverse fortune. Notwithstanding his poverty, the attempt to chain his talents to the service of a political faction by mercenary motives was indignantly spurned, and when his good genius proved triumphant, he preferred to inscribe its first acknowledged offspring to his brother, than, according to the servile habits of the day, dedicate it to any aristocratic patron, "that thrift might follow fawning." With all his incapacity for assuming dignity, Goldsmith never seems to have forgotten the self-respect becoming one of nature's nobility.

The high degree of excellence attained by Goldsmith in such various and distinct species of literary effort, is worthy of remark. As an essayist he has contributed some of the most pure and graceful specimens of English prose discoverable in the whole range of literature. His best comedy continues to maintain much of its original popularity, notwithstanding the revolutions which public taste has undergone since it was first produced; and "The Hermit" is still an acknowledged model in ballad-writing. If from his more finished works, we turn to those which were thrown off under the pressing exigencies of his life, it is astonishing what a contrast of subjects employed his pen. During his college days, he was constantly writing ballads on popular events, which he disposed of at five shillings each, and subsequently, after his literary career had fairly commenced, we find him sedulously occupied in preparing prefaces, historical compilations, translations, and reviews for the booksellers; one day throwing off a pamphlet on the Cock-lane Ghost, and the next inditing Biographical Sketches of Beau Nash; at one moment, busy upon a festive song, and at another deep in composing the words of an Oratorio. It is curious, with the intense sentiment and finished pictures of fashionable life with which the fictions of our day abound, fresh in the memory, to open the Vicar of Wakefield. We seem to be reading the memoirs of an earlier era, instead of a different sphere of life. There are no wild and improbable incidents, no startling views, and with the exception of Burchell's incognito, no attempt to excite interest through the attraction of mystery. And yet, few novels have enjoyed such extensive and permanent favor. It is yet the standard work for introducing students on the continent to a knowledge of our language, and although popular taste at present demands quite a different style of entertainment, yet Goldsmith's novel is often reverted to with delight, from the vivid contrast it presents to the reigning school; while the attractive picture it affords of rural life and humble virtue, will ever render it intrinsically dear and valuable.

But the "Deserted Village" is, of all Goldsmith's productions, unquestionably the favorite. It carries back the mind to the early seasons of life, and re-asserts the power of unsophisticated tastes. Hence, while other poems grow stale, this preserves its charm. Dear to the heart and sacred to the imagination, are those sweet delineations of unperverted existence. There is true pathos in that tender lament over the superseded sports and ruined haunts of rustic enjoyment, which never fails to find a response in every feeling breast. It is an elaborate and touching epitaph, written in the cemetery of the world, over what is dear to all humanity. There is a truth in the eloquent defence of agricultural pursuits and natural pastimes, that steals like a well-remembered strain over the heart immersed in the toil and crowds of cities. There is an unborn beauty in the similes of the bird and her "unfledged offspring," the hare that "pants to the place from whence at first he flew," and the "tall cliff that lifts its awful form," which, despite their familiarity, retain their power to delight. And no clear and susceptible mind can ever lose its interest in the unforced, unexaggerated and heart-stirring numbers, which animate with pleasure the pulses of youth, gratify the mature taste of manhood, and fall with soothing sweetness upon the ear of age.

We are not surprised at the exclamation of a young lady who had been accustomed to say, that our poet was the homeliest of men, after reading the "Deserted Village" — "I shall never more think Dr. Goldsmith ugly!" This poem passed through five editions in as many months, and from its domestic character became immediately popular throughout England. Its melodious versification is doubtless, in a measure, to be ascribed to its author's musical taste, and the fascinating ease of its flow is the result of long study and careful revision. Nothing is more deceitful than the apparent facility observable in poetry. No poet exhibits more of this characteristic than Ariosto, and yet his manuscripts are filled with erasures and repetitions. Few things appear more negligently graceful than the well-arranged drapery of a statue, yet how many experiments must the artist try before the desired effect is produced. So thoroughly did the author revise the "Deserted Village," that not a single original line remained. The clearness and warmth of his style is, to my mind, as indicative of Goldsmith's truth, as the candor of his character or the sincerity of his sentiments. It has been said of Pitt's elocution, that it had the effect of impressing one with the idea that the man was greater than the orator. A similar influence it seems to me is produced by the harmonious versification and elegant diction of Goldsmith.

It is not, indeed, by an analysis, however critical, of the intellectual distinctions of any author, that we can arrive at a complete view of his genius. It is to the feelings that we must look for that earnestness which gives vigor to mental efforts, and imparts to them their peculiar tone and coloring. And it will generally be found that what is really and permanently attractive in the works of genius, independent of mere diction, is to be traced rather to the heart than the head. We may admire the original conception, the lofty imagery or winning style of a popular author, but what touches us most deeply is the sentiment of which these are the vehicles. The fertile invention of Petrarch, in displaying under such a variety of disguises the same favorite subject, is not so moving as the unalterable devotion which inspires his fancy and quickens his muse. The popularity of Mrs. Hemans is more owing to the delicate and deep enthusiasm than to the elegance of her poetry, and Charles Lamb is not less attractive for his kindly affections than for his quaint humor. Not a little of the peculiar charm of Goldsmith, is attributable to the excellence of his heart. Mere talent would scarcely have sufficed to interpret and display so enchantingly the humble characters and scenes to which his most brilliant efforts were devoted. It was his sincere and ready sympathy with man, his sensibility to suffering in every form, his strong social sentiment and his amiable interest in all around, which brightened to his mind's eye. what to the less susceptible is unheeded and obscure. Naturally endowed with free and keen sensibilities, his own experience of privation prevented them from indurating through age or prosperity. He cherished throughout his life an earnest faith in the better feelings of our nature. He realized the universal beauty and power of Love; and neither the solitary pursuits of literature, the elation of success, nor the blandishments of pleasure or society, ever banished from his bosom the generous and kindly sentiments which adorned his character. He was not the mere creature of attainment, the reserved scholar or abstracted dreamer. Pride of intellect usurped not his heart. Pedantry congealed not the fountains of feeling. He rejoiced in the exercise of all those tender and noble sentiments which are so much more honorable to man than the highest triumphs of mind. And it is these which make us love the man not less than admire the author. Goldsmith's early sympathy with the sufferings of the peasantry, is eloquently expressed in both his poems and frequently in his prose writings. How expressive that lament for the destruction of the 'Ale-House'—that it would

> 'No more impart
> An hour's importance to the poor man's heart.'

There is more true benevolence in the feeling which prompted such a thought, than in all the cold and calculating philosophy with which so many expect to elevate the lower classes in these days of ultra-reform. When shall we learn that we must sympathize with those we would improve? At college, we are told, one bitter night Goldsmith encountered a poor woman and her infants shivering at the gate, and having no money to give them, bringing out all his bed-clothes, and to keep himself from freezing, cut open his bed and slept within it. When hard at work earning a scanty pittance in his garret, he spent every spare penny in cakes for the children of his poorer neighbors, and when he could do nothing else, taught them dancing by way of cheering their poverty. Notwithstanding his avowed antipathy to Baretti, he visited and relieved him in prison; and when returning home with the 100*l.* received from his bookseller for the 'Deserted Village, upon being told by an acquaintance he fell in with, that it was a great price for so little a thing, replied, 'Perhaps it is more than he can afford,' and returning, offered to refund a part. To his poor countrymen he was a constant benefactor, and while he had a shilling was ready to share it with them, so that they familiarly styled him 'our doctor.' In Leyden, when on the point of commencing his tour, he stripped himself of all his funds to send a collection of flower-roots to an uncle who was devoted to botany; and on the first occasion that patronage was offered him, declined aid for himself, to bespeak a vacant living for his brother. In truth, his life abounds in anecdotes of a like nature. We read one day of his pawning his watch for Pilkington, another of his bringing home a poor foreigner from Temple gardens to be his amanuensis, and again of his leaving the card-table to relieve a poor woman, whose tones as she chanted some ditty in passing, came to him above the hum of gaiety and *indicated to his ear distress.* Though the frequent and undeserved subject of literary abuse, he was never known to write severely against any one.

His talents were sacredly devoted to the cause of virtue and humanity. No malignant satire ever came from his pen. He loved to dwell upon the beautiful vindications in Nature of the paternity of God, and expatiate upon the noblest and most universal attributes of man. 'If I were to love you by rule,' he writes to his brother, 'I dare say I never could do it sincerely.' There was in his nature, an instinctive aversion to the frigid ceremonial and meaningless professions which so coldly imitate the language of feeling. Goldsmith saw enough of the world, to disrobe his mind of that scepticism born of custom which 'makes dotards of us all.' He did not wander among foreign nations, sit at the cottage fire-side, nor mix in the thoroughfare and gay saloon, in vain. Travel liberalized his views and demolished the barriers of local prejudice. He looked around upon his kind with the charitable judgment and interest born of an observing mind and a kindly heart—with an infinite love, an infinite pity.' He delighted in the delineation of humble life, because he knew it to be the most unperverted. Simple pleasures warmed his fancy because he had learned their preëminent truth. Childhood with its innocent playfulness, intellectual character with its tutored wisdom, and the uncultivated but 'bold peasantry,' interested him alike. He could enjoy an hour's friendly chat with his fellow-lodger — the watchmaker in Green Arbor Court — not less than a literary discussion with Dr. Johnson. 'I must own,' he writes, 'I should prefer the title of the ancient philosopher, namely, a Citizen of the World — to that of an Englishman, a Frenchman, an European, or that of any appellation whatever.' And this title he has nobly earned, by the wide scope of his sympathies and the beautiful pictures of life and nature universally recognized and universally loved, which have spread his name over the world. Pilgrims to the supposed scene of the Deserted Village have long since carried away every vestige of the hawthorn at Lissoy, but the laurels of Goldsmith will never be garnered by the hand of time, or blighted by the frost of neglect, as long as there are minds to appreciate, or hearts to reverence the household lore of English literature.

MEMOIRS

OF

OLIVER GOLDSMITH, M.B.

BY DR. AIKIN.

It cannot be said of this ornament of British literature, as has been observed of most authors, that the memoirs of his life comprise little more than a history of his writings. Goldsmith's life was full of adventure; and a due consideration of his conduct, from the outset to his death, will furnish many useful lessons to those who live after him.

Our Author, the third son of Mr. Charles Goldsmith, was born at Elphin, in the county of Roscommon, Ireland, on the 29th of November, 1728. His father, who had been educated at Dublin College, was a clergyman of the established church, and had married Anne, daughter of the Rev. Oliver Jones, master of the diocesan school of Elphin. Her mother's brother, the Rev. Mr. Green, then rector of Kilkenny West, lent the young couple the house in which our author was born; and at his death Mr. Green was succeeded in his benefice by his clerical *protégée.*

Mr. Charles Goldsmith had five sons and two daughters.

Henry, the eldest son (to whom the poem of 'The Traveller' is dedicated), distinguished himself greatly both at school and at college; but his marriage at nineteen years of age appears to have been a bar to his preferment in the church; and we believe that he never ascended above a curacy.

The liberal education which the father bestowed upon Henry had deducted so much from a narrow income that, when Oliver was born, after an interval of seven years from the birth of the former child, no prospect in life appeared for him, but a mechanical or mercantile occupation.

The rudiments of instruction he acquired from a schoolmaster in the village, who had served in Queen Anne's wars as a quarter-master in that detachment of the army which was sent to Spain. Being of a communicative turn, and finding a ready hearer in young Oliver, this man used frequently to entertain him with what he called his adventures; nor is it without probability supposed, that these laid the foundation of that wandering disposition which became afterwards so conspicuous in his pupil.

At a very early age Oliver began to exhibit indications of genius; for, when only seven or eight years old, he would often amuse his father and mother with poetical attempts, which attracted much notice from them and their friends; but his infant mind does not appear to have been much elated by their approbation; for after his verses had been admired, they were, without regret, committed by him to the flames.

He was now taken from the tuition of the quondam soldier, to be put under that of the Rev. Mr. Griffin, schoolmaster of Elphin; and was at the same time received into the house of his father's brother, John Goldsmith, Esq., of Ballyoughter, near that town.

Our author's eldest sister, Catharine, (afterwards married

to Daniel Hodson, Esq., of Lishoy, near Ballymahon,) relates, that one evening, when Oliver was about nine years of age, a company of young people of both sexes being assembled at his uncle's, the boy was required to dance a hornpipe, a youth undertaking to play to him on the fiddle. Being but lately out of the small-pox, which had much disfigured his countenance, and his bodily proportions being short and thick, the young musician thought to show his wit by comparing our hero to Æsop dancing; and having harped a little too long, as the caperer thought, on this bright idea, the latter suddenly stopped, and said,

Our herald hath proclaim'd this saying,
'See Æsop dancing,'—and his Monkey playing.

This instance of early wit, we are told, decided his fortune; for, from that time, it was determined to send him to the university; and some of his relations, who were in the church, offered to contribute towards the expense, particularly the Rev. Thomas Contarine, rector of Kilmore, near Carrick-upon-Shannon, who had married an aunt of Oliver's. The Rev. Mr. Green also, whom we have before mentioned, liberally assisted in this friendly design.

To further the purpose intended, he was now removed to Athlone, where he continued about two years under the Rev. Mr. Campbell; who being then obliged by ill-health to resign the charge, Oliver was sent to the school of the Rev. Patrick Hughes, at Edgeworthstown, in the county of Longford.*

* We are told, that in his last journey to this school, he had an adventure, which is thought to have suggested the plot of his comedy of 'She stoops to conquer.'—Some friend had given him a guinea; and in his way to Edgeworthstown, which was about twenty miles

Under this gentleman he was prepared for the university; and on the 11th of June, 1744, was admitted a Sizer of Trinity college, Dublin,* under the tuition of the Rev. Mr. Wilder, one of the Fellows, who was a man of harsh temper and violent passions; and Oliver being of a thoughtless and gay turn, it cannot be surprising that they should soon be dissatisfied with each other.

Oliver, it seems, had one day imprudently invited a party of both sexes to a supper and ball in his rooms; which coming to the ears of his tutor, the latter entered the place in the midst of their jollity, abused the whole company, and inflicted manual correction on Goldsmith in their presence.

This mortification had such an effect on the mind of Oliver, that he resolved to seek his fortune in some place where he should be unknown: accordingly he sold his books and clothes, and quitted the university; but loitered about the streets,

from his father's house, he had amused himself the whole day with viewing the gentlemen's seats on the road; and at nightfall found himself in the small town of Ardagh. Here he inquired for the best house in the place, meaning the best *inn;* but his informant, taking the question in its literal sense, shewed him to the house of a private gentleman; where, calling for somebody to take his horse to the stable, our hero alighted, and was shown into the parlor, being supposed to have come on a visit to the master, whom he found sitting by the fire. This gentleman soon discovered Oliver's mistake; but being a man of humor, and learning from him the name of his father, (whom he knew), he favored the deception. Oliver ordered a good supper, and invited his landlord and landlady, with their daughters, to partake of it; he treated them with a bottle or two of wine, and, at going to bed, ordered a hot cake to be prepared for his breakfast: nor was it till he was about to depart, and called for his bill, that he discovered his mistake.

* The celebrated Edmund Burke was at the same time a collegian there.

considering of a destination, till his money was exhausted. With a solitary shilling in his pocket he at last left Dublin; by abstinence he made this sum last him three days, and then was obliged to part, by degrees, with the clothes off his back: in short, to such an extremity was he reduced, as to find a handful of gray-peas, given him by a girl at a wake, the most comfortable repast that he had ever made.

After numberless adventures in this vagrant state, he found his way home, and was replaced under his morose and merciless tutor; by whom he was again exposed to so many mortifications, as induced an habitual despondence of mind, and a total carelessness about his studies; the consequence of which was, that he neither obtained a scholarship, nor became a candidate for the premiums. On the 25th of May, 1747, he received a public admonition, for having assisted other collegians in a riot occasioned by a scholar having been arrested, *quod seditioni favisset, et tumultuantibus opem tulisset:* in this case, however, he appears to have fared better than some of his companions, who were expelled the university. On the 15th of June following he was elected one of the exhibitioners on the foundation of Erasmus Smyth; but was not admitted to the degree of Bachelor of Arts till February, 1749, which was two years after the usual period.

Oliver's father being now dead, his uncle Contarine undertook to supply his place, and wished him to prepare for holy orders. This proposal not meeting with the young man's inclination, Mr. Contarine next resolved on sending him to London, that he might study law in the temple. Whilst at Dublin, however, on his way to England, he fell in with a sharper, who cheated him at play of 50*l.*, which had been provided for his carriage, etc. He returned, and received his uncle's forgiveness: it was now finally settled that he should make physic his profession; and he departed for Edinburgh, where he settled about the latter end of the year 1752. Here he attended the lectures of Dr. Monroe and the other medical professors; but his studies were by no means regular; and an indulgence in dissipated company, with a ready hand to administer to the necessities of whoever asked him, kept him always poor.

Having, however, gone through the usual courses of physic and anatomy in the Scottish university, Goldsmith was about to remove to Leyden to complete his studies; and his departure was hastened by a debt to Mr. Barclay, a tailor in Edinburgh, which he had imprudently made his own by becoming security for a fellow student who, either from want of principle or of means, had failed to pay it: for this debt he was arrested; but was released by the kindness of Dr. Sleigh and Mr. Laughlin Maclaine, whose friendship he had acquired at the college.

He now embarked for Bourdeaux, on board a Scotch vessel called the St. Andrew's, Capt. John Wall, master. The ship made a tolerable appearance; and, as another inducement to our hero, he was informed that six agreeable passengers were to be his company. They had been but two days at sea, however, when a storm drove them into Newcastle-upon-Tyne, and the passengers went ashore to refresh after the fatigue of their voyage. 'Seven men and I, (says Goldsmith) were on shore the following evening; but as we were all very merry, the room door burst open, and there entered a sergeant and twelve grenadiers, with their bayonets screwed, who put us all under the King's arrest. It seems, my company were Scotchmen in the French service, and had been in Scotland to enlist soldiers for Louis XV. I endeavored all I could to prove my innocence ; however, I remained in prison with the rest a fortnight, and with difficulty got off even then. But hear how Providence interposed in my favor : the ship, which had set sail for Bourdeaux before I got from prison, was wrecked at the mouth of the Garonne, and every one of the crew drowned.'—Fortunately, there was a ship now ready at Newcastle, for Holland, on board of which he embarked, and in nine days reached Rotterdam ; whence he travelled by land to Leyden.

Here he resided about a year, studying anatomy under Albinus, and chemistry under Gambius ; but here, as formerly, his little property was destroyed by play and dissipation ; and he is actually believed to have set out on his travels with only one clean shirt, and not a guilder in his purse, trusting wholly to Providence for a subsistence.

It is generally understood, that in the history of his Philosophic Vagabond, (Vicar of Wakefield, chap. xx.) he has related many of his own adventures ; and that when on his pedestrian tour through Flanders and France, as he had some knowledge of music, he turned what had formerly been his amusement into a present means of subsistence. 'I passed, (says he) among the harmless peasants of Flanders, and among such of the French as were poor enough to be very merry ; for I ever found them sprightly in proportion to their wants. Whenever I approached a peasant's house towards nightfall, I played on my German flute one of my most merry tunes, and that procured me not only a lodging, but subsistence for the next day. I once or twice attempted to play for people of fashion ; but they always thought my performance odious, and never rewarded me even with a trifle. This was to me the more extraordinary; as whenever I used in better days to play for company, when playing was my amusement, my music never failed to throw them into raptures, and the ladies especially; but as it was now my only means, it was received with contempt: a proof how ready the world is to underrate those talents by which a man is supported!' At the different monasteries in his tour, especially those of his own nation, his learning generally procured him temporary entertainment; and thus he made his way to Switzerland, in which country he first cultivated his poetical talents with any particular effect; for here we find he wrote about two hundred lines of his 'Traveller.'

The story which has commonly been told, of his having acted as travelling tutor to a young miser, is now thought to have been too hastily adopted from the aforesaid History of a Philosophic Vagabond, and never to have been the real situation of the author of that history. From Switzerland, Goldsmith proceeded to Padua, where he stayed six months, and is by some supposed to have taken there his degree of Bachelor of Physic; though others are of opinion, that if ever he really took any medical degree abroad, it was at Louvain.*

After visiting all the northern part of Italy, he travelled, still on foot, through France; and, embarking at Calais, landed at Dover in the summer of 1756, unknown, as he supposed, to a single individual, and with not a guinea in his pocket.

His first endeavors were, to procure employment as an usher in some school; but the want of a recommendation as to character and ability rendered his efforts for some time fruit-

* In 1769, it is certain, he was admitted M. B. at Oxford, which university he visited in February, in company with Dr. Johnson.

less; and how he subsisted is not easy to guess. At length, however, it appears he procured an usher's place; but in what part the school was situated, or how long he continued in it, we do not learn; though we may form some idea of the uncongeniality of the place to his mind, from the following passage in the Philosophic Vagabond: 'I have been an usher at a boarding-school; and may I die but I would rather be an under-turnkey in Newgate. I was up early and late; I was brow-beat by the master, hated for my ugly face by my mistress, worried by the boys within, and never permitted to stir out to meet civility abroad.'

When in a fit of disgust he had quitted this academy, his pecuniary necessities soon became pressing; to relieve which he applied to several apothecaries and chemists for employment as a journeyman; but here his threadbare appearance, awkward manners, and the want of a recommendation, operated sorely to his prejudice;* till at last a chemist near Fish-street-hill, probably moved by compassion, gave him employment in his laboratory, where he continued till he learned that his old friend Dr. Sleigh, of Edinburgh, was in town: on him (who had, as we have seen, formerly relieved him from embarrassment,) Goldsmith waited, was kindly received, and invited to share his purse during his continuance in London.

This timely assistance enabled our author to commence medical practice at Bankside, in Southwark, whence he after-

* In a letter, dated Dec. 1757, he writes thus:—'At London, you may easily imagine what difficulties I had to encounter; without friends, recommendations, money or impudence; and that in a country where being born an Irishman was sufficient to keep me unemployed. Many in such circumstances would have had recourse to the friar's cord or the suicide's halter. But with all my follies I had principle to resist the one, and resolution to combat the other.

ward removed to the neighborhood of the Temple; his success as a physician is not known, but his income was very small; for, as he used to say, he got very few fees, though he had abundance of patients. Some addition, however, he now began to derive from the efforts of his pen; and it appears that he was for awhile with the celebrated Samuel Richardson as corrector of the press.

About this time he renewed his acquaintance with one of the young physicians whom he had known at Edinburgh. This was a son of the Rev. Dr. John Milner, a dissenting minister, who kept a classical school of eminence at Peckham, in Surrey. Mr. Milner, observing Goldsmith's uncertain mode of living, invited him to take the charge of his father's school, the Doctor being then confined by illness: to this he consented; and Dr. Milner, in return, promised to exert his interest with the India Directors to procure for him some medical establishment in the Company's service. This promise he faithfully performed, and Goldsmith was actually appointed physician to one of the factories in India in 1758. It appears, however, that our author never availed himself of this post,* but continued in Dr. Milner's academy; and in this very year sold to Mr. Edward Dilly, for twenty guineas, 'The Memoirs of a Protestant condemned to the Galleys of France for his Religion. Written by Himself. Translated from the Original, just published at the Hague, by James Willington.' 2 vols. 12mo.

Towards the latter end of 1758, Goldsmith happened to

* Though it is certain, that, in contemplation of going to India, he circulated Proposals to print by Subscription 'An essay on the Present State of Taste and Literature in Europe,' as a means of defraying the expenses of his fitting out for the voyage.

dine at Dr. Milner's table with Mr. Ralph Griffiths, the proprietor of The Monthly Review, who invited him to write articles of criticism for that respectable publication, on the terms of a liberal salary, besides board and lodging. By a written agreement this engagement was to last for a year; but at the end of seven or eight months it was dissolved by mutual consent, and Goldsmith took a miserable apartment in Green-Arbor-court, Little Old Bailey.* In this wretched hovel our author completed his 'Inquiry into the Present State of Polite Literature in Europe,' which was published in 1759, by Dodsley, and was well received. In October of the same year he began 'The Bee,' a weekly publication, which terminated at the eighth number. About this time, also, he contributed some articles to The Critical Review, one of which (we believe a review of 'Ovid's Epistles translated into English verse, by a Mr. Barrett, Master of the Grammar School at Ashford, in Kent,) introduced him to the acquaintance of Dr. Smollett, who was then editor of The British Magazine; and for that work Goldsmith wrote most of those 'Essays,' which were afterwards collected and published in a separate volume. By Dr. Smollett too he was recommended to some respectable booksellers, particularly to Mr. John Newbery, who well deserved the eulogium bestowed by Warburton on the trade in general, as one of 'the best judges and most liberal rewarders of literary merit.' By Mr. Newbery, Goldsmith was engaged at a salary of 100*l.* a-year, to write for The Public Ledger a series of periodical papers. These he called 'Chinese Letters;' and they were afterwards collected in two volumes, under the title of 'The Citizen of the

* An engraving of the house, illustrated by a description, was given in 'The European Magazine,' vol. xliii. pp. 7, 8.

World.' It was soon after this that he commenced his acquaintance with Dr. Johnson.

The important engagement with Newbery for a hundred pounds a year, encouraged Goldsmith to descend Break-neck-steps,* and to hire a decent apartment in Wine-Office-court, Fleet-street. Here he dropped the humble *Mister*, and dubbed himself *Doctor* Goldsmith. Here also he put the finishing hand to his excellent novel called 'The Vicar of Wakefield,' but was, when he had done, extremely embarrassed in his circumstances, dunned by his landlady for arrears of rent, and not daring to stir abroad for fear of arrest: in fact, she herself at length had him arrested; he then summoned resolution to send a message to Dr. Johnson; stating that he was in great distress, and begging that he would come to him as soon as possible. Johnson sent him a guinea, and promised to follow almost immediately. When he arrived, he found Goldsmith in a violent passion with the woman of the house, but consoling himself as well as he could with a bottle of Madeira, which he had already purchased with part of the guinea. Johnson, corking the bottle, desired Goldsmith would be calm, and consider in what way he could extricate himself. The latter then produced his novel as ready for the press. The Doctor looked into it, saw its merit, and went away with it to Mr. Newbery, who gave him 60*l.* for it; with this sum he returned to Goldsmith, who, with many invectives, paid his landlady her rent. Newbery, however, seems not to have been very sanguine in his hopes of this novel; for he kept the MS. by him near three years unprinted: his ready purchase of it, probably, was in the way of a benefaction to its

* A steep flight of stairs (commonly so termed) leading from the door of his lodging-house in Green-Arbor-court to Fleet-market.

distressed author, rather than under any idea of profit by the publication.

Early in the year 1763, Goldsmith removed to lodgings at Canonbury-house, Islington, where he compiled several works for Mr. Newbery; among which were, 'The Art of Poetry,' 2 vols. 12mo.; a 'Life of Nash;' and a 'History of England, in a Series of Letters from a Nobleman to his Son.' This latter book was for a long time attributed to George Lord Lyttleton.

In the following year he took chambers on the upper story of the Library stair-case in the Inner Temple, and began to live in a genteel style. Still, however, he was little known, except among the booksellers, till the year 1765, when he produced his poem called 'The Traveller; or, A Prospect of Society,' which had obtained high commendation from Dr. Johnson, who declared 'that there had not been so fine a poem since the time of Pope;' yet such was Goldsmith's diffidence, that, though he had completed it some years before, he had not courage enough to publish, till urged to it by Johnson's suggestions. This poem heightened his literary character with the booksellers, and introduced him to several persons of superior rank and talents, as Lord Nugent (afterwards earl of Clare), Mr. Burke, Sir Joshua Reynolds, Dr. Nugent, Mr. Bennet Langton, Mr Topham Beauclerc, etc., and he was elected one of the first members of 'The Literary Club,' which had been just instituted by Johnson, Burke, and Sir Joshua, and met at the Turk's-head, Gerard-street, Soho, every Friday evening.

His pathetic ballad of 'The Hermit,' which was also published in 1765, recommended him to the Countess (afterwards Duchess) of Northumberland, who was a generous patroness of merit. In the following year his 'Vicar of Wakefield' was printed, and universally read and admired.

His reputation being now fairly established as a novelist, a poet, and a critic, Goldsmith turned his thoughts to the drama, and set about his comedy called 'The Good-natured Man.' This he first offered to Garrick, who, after a long fluctuation between doubt and encouragement, at length declined bringing it forward at Drury-lane theatre; it was therefore taken to Covent-garden, accepted by Mr. Colman, and presented for the first time on the 29th of January, 1768. It was acted nine times; and by the profits of the author's three third-nights, with the sale of the copyright, a clear 500*l.* was produced.

With this, and some money which he had reserved out of the produce of a 'Roman History,' in 2 vols. 8vo., and other works, he was enabled to descend from his attic story in the Inner Temple, and to purchase for 400*l.*, and furnish elegantly, a spacious set of chambers on the first floor, at No. 2, Brick-court, Middle Temple.

On the establishment of the Royal Academy, in 1769, Sir Joshua Reynolds recommended Goldsmith to his Majesty for the Honorary Professorship of History, which was graciously conferred on him. In the following year he produced that highly-finished poem called 'The Deserted Village.' Previous to its publication, we are told, the bookseller (Mr. Griffin, of Catharine street, Strand) had given him a note of a hundred guineas for the copy. This circumstance Goldsmith mentioned soon afterwards to a friend, who observed that it was a large sum for so small a performance. 'In truth' replied Goldsmith, 'I think so too; it is near five shillings a couplet, which is much more than the honest man can afford, and, indeed, more than any modern poetry is worth. I have not been easy since I received it; I will, therefore, go back and return him his note;' which he actually did; but the sale was so rapid, that the bookseller soon paid him the hundred guineas with proper acknowledgments for the generosity of his conduct.

Soon after the appearance of the Deserted Village, our author paid a tribute to the memory of Dr. Parnell, in a Life prefixed to a new edition of his 'Poems on several Occasions.' In the year 1771 he produced his 'History of England, from the earliest Times to the Death of George II.,' in 4 vols. 8vo.; for which Mr. Thomas Davies, the bookseller, paid him 500*l.*

The Earl of Lisburne, one day at a dinner of the Royal Academicians, lamented to Goldsmith that he should neglect the muses to compile histories, and write novels, instead of penning poetry with which he was sure to charm his readers. 'My lord,' replied cur author, 'in courting the muses I should starve; but by my other labors I eat, drink, wear good clothes, and enjoy the luxuries of life.'

Goldsmith had, besides his regular works, much of the other business of an author by profession; such as penning Prefaces and Introductions to the books of other writers; some of these have been published among his prose works; but, no doubt, many remain at this day unknown.

His second dramatic effort, being a comedy called 'She Stoops to Conquer; or, The Mistakes of a Night,' was first presented at Covent-garden theatre, March 15, 1773, and received with an applause fully adequate to the author's sanguine hopes, and contrary to the expectations of Mr. Coiman, who had not consented to receive the piece but at the earnest and reiterated instances of many friends. What was called sentimental comedy had at that time got an unaccountable hold of the public taste; Kelly was subserving this un-British propensity by his 'False Delicacy,' etc., and Goldsmith's piece (which was designed by him to bring back the town to a relish of humor) being certainly in the opposite extreme, and hardly anything else than a farce of five acts instead of two, Colman, and his actors from him, had predestined the play to condemnation: when, therefore, towards the conclusion of the first performance, the author expressed some apprehension lest one of the jokes put into the mouth of Tony Lumpkin should not be relished by the audience, the manager, who had been in fear through the whole piece, replied, 'D—n it, Doctor, don't be terrified at a squib; why, we have been sitting these two hours on a barrel of gunpowder.' Goldsmith's pride was so hurt at this remark, that the friendship which had till then subsisted between him and Colman, was thenceforth annihilated.

The piece had a great run, and its author cleared by the third-nights, and the sale of the copy, upwards of 800*l.* Dr. Johnson said of it, 'That he knew of no comedy for many years that had so much exhilarated an audience, that had answered so much the great end of comedy — the making an audience merry.' It certainly added much to the author's reputation, and is still, with his 'Good-natured Man,' on the list of acting plays; but it brought on him the envy and malignity of some of his contemporaries; and in the London Packet of Wednesday, March 24, 1773, printed for T. Evans, in Paternoster-row, appeared the following scurrilous epistle, evidently designed to injure his third-night (being the ninth representation):—

'TO DR. GOLDSMITH.

'*Vous vous noyez en vanité.*

'Sir.—The happy knack which you have learnt of puffing your own compositions, provokes me to come forth. You have not been the editor of newspapers and magazines, not to discover the trick of literary *humbug*. But the gauze is so thin, that the very foolish part of the world see through it, and discover the Doctor's monkey face and cloven foot. Your poetic vanity is as unpardonable as your personal. Would man believe it, and will woman bear it, to be told that for hours the *great* Goldsmith will stand surveying his grotesque Oranhotan's figure in a pier-glass? Was but the lovely H—k as much enamored, you would not sigh, my gentle swain, in vain. But your vanity is preposterous. How will this same bard of Bedlam ring the changes in praise of Goldy! But what has he to be either proud or vain of? The "Traveller" is a flimsy poem, built upon false principles; principles diametrically opposite to liberty. What is "The Good-natured Man," but a poor, water-gruel, dramatic dose? What is "The Deserted Village," but a *pretty* poem of easy numbers, without fancy, dignity, genius, or fire? And pray what may be the last speaking pantomime,* so praised by the Doctor himself, but an incoherent piece of stuff, the figure of a woman with a fish's tail, without plot, incident, or intrigue? We are made to laugh at stale, dull jokes, wherein we mistake pleasantry for wit, and grimace for humor: wherein every scene is unnatural, and inconsistent with the rules, the laws of nature, and of the drama; viz. Two gentlemen come to a man of fortune's house, eat, drink, sleep, etc., and take it for an

* Meaning 'She Stoops to Conquer.'

inn. The one is intended as a lover to the daughter; he talks with her for some hours, and when he sees her again in a different dress, he treats her as a bar-girl, and swears she squinted. He abuses the master of the house, and threatens to kick him out of his own doors. The 'Squire, whom we are told is to be a fool, proves to be the most sensible being of the piece; and he makes out a whole act by bidding his mother lie close behind a bush, persuading her that his father, her own husband, is a highwayman, and that he is come to cut their throats; and to give his cousin an opportunity to go off, he drives his mother over hedges, ditches, and through ponds. There is not, sweet, sucking Johnson, a natural stroke in the whole play, but the young fellow's giving the stolen jewels to the mother, supposing her to be the landlady. That Mr. Colman did no justice to this piece, I honestly allow; that he told all his friends it would be damned, I positively aver; and from such ungenerous insinuations, without a dramatic merit, it rose to public notice; and it is now the *ton* to go to see it, though I never saw a person that either liked it or approved it, any more than the absurd plot of *the Home's* tragedy of Alonzo. Mr. Goldsmith, correct your arrogance, reduce your vanity, and endeavor to believe, as a man, you are of the plainest sort; and as an author, but a mortal piece of mediocrity.'

> '*Brisez le miroir infidele,*
> *Qui vous cache la verité.*

'Tom Tickle.'

By one of those 'd——d good-natured friends,' who are described by Sir Fretful Plagiary, the newspaper containing the foregoing offensive letter was eagerly brought to Goldsmith, who otherwise, perhaps, had never seen or heard of it. Our hero went to the shop brimfull of ire, and finding Evans behind his counter, thus addressed him: 'You have published a thing in your paper (my name is Goldsmith) reflecting upon a young lady. As for myself, I do not mind it.'— Evans at this moment stooped down, intending probably to look for a paper, that he might see what the enraged author meant; when Goldsmith, observing his back to present a fair mark for his cane, laid it on lustily. The bibliopolist, however, soon defended himself, and a scuffle ensued, in which our author got his full share of blows. Dr. Kenrick, who was sitting in Evans's counting-house (and who was strongly suspected to have been the writer of the letter), now came forward, parted the combatants, and sent Goldsmith home in a coach, grievously bruised.

This attack upon a man, in his own house, furnished matter of discussion for some days to the newspapers; and an action at law was threatened to be brought for the assault; but by the interposition of friends the affair was compromised; and on Wednesday, the 31st of March, Goldsmith inserted the following Address in the Daily Advertiser:—

'TO THE PUBLIC.

'Lest it should be supposed that I have been willing to correct in others an abuse of which I have been guilty myself, I beg leave to declare that in all my life I never wrote, or dictated, a single paragraph, letter, or essay, in a newspaper, except a few moral essays, under the character of a Chinese, about ten years ago, in the Ledger; and a letter, to which I signed my name, in the St. James's Chronicle. If the liberty of the press, therefore, has been abused, I have had no hand in it.

'I have always considered the press as the protector of our freedom, as a watchful guardian, capable of uniting the weak against the encroachments of power. What concerns the public most properly admits of a public discussion. But, of late, the press has turned from defending public interest, to making inroads upon private life; from combating the strong, to overwhelming the feeble. No condition is now too obscure for its abuse, and the protector is become the tyrant of the people. In this manner the freedom of the press is beginning to sow the seeds of its own dissolution; the great must oppose it from principle, and the weak from fear; till at last every rank of mankind shall be found to give up its benefits, content with security from its insults.

'How to put a stop to this licentiousness, by which all are indiscriminately abused, and by which vice consequently escapes in the general censure, I am unable to tell; all I could wish is, that, as the law gives us no protection against the injury, so it should give calumniators no shelter after having provoked correction. The insults which we receive before the public, by being more open, are the more distressing. By treating them with silent contempt we do not pay a sufficient deference to the opinion of the world. By recurring to legal redress, we too often expose the weakness of the law, which only serves to increase our mortification by failing to relieve us. In short, every man should singly consider himself as a guardian of the liberty of the press, and, as far as his influence can extend, should endeavor to prevent its licentiousness becoming at last the grave of its freedom.

OLIVER GOLDSMITH.'

Mr. Boswell having intimated to Dr. Johnson his suspicions

that *he* was the real writer of this Address, the latter said, 'Sir, Dr. Goldsmith would no more have asked me to have written such a thing as that for him, than he would have asked me to feed him with a spoon, or to do anything else that denoted his imbecility. I as much believe that he wrote it, as if I had seen him do it. Sir, had he shewn it to any one friend, he would not have been allowed to publish it. He has indeed done it very well; but it is a foolish thing well done. I suppose he has been so much elated with the success of his new comedy, that he has thought everything that concerns him must be of importance to the public.'

About a month after this, to oblige Mr. Quick, the commedian, who had very successfully exerted himself in the character of Tony Lumpkin, Goldsmith, we believe, reduced Sedley's 'Grumbler' to a farce; and it was performed for Mr. Quick's benefit on the 8th of May, but was never printed: indeed, some persons doubt whether Goldsmith did more than revise an alteration which had been made by some other person.

Our author now, oddly enough, took it into his head to reject the title of *Doctor* (with which he had been self-invested), and to assume the plain address of *Mr.* Goldsmith; but whatever his motive to this might be, he could not effect it with the public, who to the day of his death called him Doctor; and the same title is usually annexed to his name even now, though the degree of Bachelor of Physic was the highest ever actually conferred upon him.

After having compiled a History of Rome, and two Histories of England, he undertook, and completed in 1773, '*A History of the Earth and Animated Nature*,' in 8 vols. 8vo., which was printed in 1774, and he received for it 850*l*.

The emoluments which he had derived from his writings for some few years past were, indeed, very considerable; but were rendered useless in effect, by an incautious liberality, which prevented his distinguishing proper from improper objects of his bounty; and also by an unconquerable itch for gaming, a pursuit in which his impatience of temper, and his want of skill, wholly disqualified him for succeeding.

His last production, '*Retaliation*,' was written for his own amusement and that of his friends who were the subjects of it. That he did not live to finish it, is to be lamented; for it is supposed that he would have introduced more characters. What he has left, however, is nearly perfect in its kind; with wonderful art he has traced all the leading features of his several portraits, and given with truth the characteristic peculiarities of each; no man is lampooned, no man is flattered. The occasion of the poem was a circumstance of festivity. A literary party with which he occasionally dined at the St. James's coffe-house, one day proposed to write epitaphs on him. In these, his person, dialect, etc., were good-humoredly ridiculed: and as Goldsmith could not disguise his feelings on the occasion, he was called upon for a Retaliation, which he produced at the next meeting of the party; but this, with his '*Haunch of Venison*,' and some other short poems, were not printed till after his death.

He had at this time ready for the press, 'The Grecian History, from the earliest State to the Death of Alexander the Great,' which was afterwards printed in 2 vols. 8vo. He had also formed a design of compiling a 'Universal Dictionary of Arts and Sciences,' a prospectus of which he printed and sent to his friends, many of whom had promised to furnish him with articles on different subjects. The booksellers, however, though they had a high opinion of his abilities, were startled at the bulk, importance, and expense of so great an undertaking, the execution of which was to depend upon a man with whose indolence of temper, and method of procrastination, they had long been acquainted : the coldness with which they met his proposals was lamented by Goldsmith to the hour of his death ; which seems to have been accelerated by a neglect of his health, occasioned by continual vexation of mind, on account of his frequently involved circumstances, although the last year's produce of his labor is generally believed to have amounted to 1800*l.*

In the spring of 1774 he was attacked in a very severe manner by the stranguary, a disease of which he had often experienced slight symptoms. It now induced a nervous fever, which required medical assistance ; and on the 25th of March he sent for his friend Mr. (afterwards Dr.) Hawes, to whom he related the symptoms of his malady, expressing at the same time a disgust with life, and a despondency which did not well become a man of his understanding. He told Mr. Hawes that he had taken two ounces of ipecacuanha wine as an emetic, and that it was his intention to take Dr. James's fever powders, which he desired he would send him. Mr. Hawes represented to his patient the impropriety of taking the medicine at that time ; but no argument could induce him to relinquish his intention. Finding this, and justly apprehensive of the fatal consequences of his putting this rash resolve in execution, he requested permission to send for Dr. Fordyce, of whose medical abilities he knew that Goldsmith had the highest opinion. Dr. Fordyce came, and corroborated the apothecary's assertion, adding every argument that he could think of to dissuade him from using the powders in the present case ; but, deaf to all the remonstrances of his physician and his friend, he obstinately persisted in his resolution.

The next day Mr. Hawes again visited his patient, and inquiring of him how he did, Goldsmith sighed deeply, and in a dejected tone said, 'I wish I had taken your friendly advice last night.' Dr. Fordyce came, and, finding the alarming symptoms increase, desired Mr. Hawes to propose sending for Dr. Turton : to this Goldsmith readily consented. The two physicians met, and held consultations twice a day till Monday, April 4th, when their patient died.

Warmth of affection induced Sir Joshua Reynolds and other friends of Goldsmith to lay a plan for a sumptuous public funeral : according to which he was to have been interred in Westminster Abbey, and his pall to have been supported by Lord Shelburne (afterwards Marquis of Lansdowne), Lord Louth, Sir Joshua Reynolds, Mr. Edmund Burke, the Hon. Topham Beauclerc, and Mr. Garrick ; but on a slight inspection of his affairs, it was found that, so far from having left property to justify so expensive a proceeding, he was about 2000*l.* in debt. The original intention, therefore, was abandoned ; and he was privately interred in the Temple burial-ground at five o'clock on Saturday evening, April 9th, attended by the Rev. Joseph Palmer (nephew of Sir Joshua Reynolds, and afterwards Dean of Cashel in Ireland), Mr Hugh Kelly, Mr. (afterwards Dr.) Hawes, Messrs. John and Robert Day, and Mr. Etherington.

A subscription, however, was speedily raised among Goldsmith's friends, but chiefly by the Literary Club ; and a marble monumental stone, executed by Nollekens, consisting of a large medallion, exhibiting a good resemblance of our author, in profile, embellished with appropriate ornaments, was placed in Westminster Abbey, between those of Gay the poet, and the Duke of Argyle, in Poet's Corner; having underneath, on a tablet of white marble, the following inscription, from the pen of his friend, Dr. Johnson:—

OLIVARII GOLDSMITH,
Poetæ, Physici, Historici,
Qui nullum ferè scribendi genus
Non tetigit;
Nullum quod tetigit non ornavit:
Sive risus essent movendi
Sive lacrymæ,
Affectuum potens et lenis dominator:
Ingenio sublimis, vividus, versatilis,
Oratione grandis, nitidus, venustus;
Hoc monumento memoriam coluit
Sodalium amor,
Amicorum fides,
Lectorum veneratio.
Natus in Hibernià, Forneiæ Longfordiensis,
In loco cui nomen Pallas,
Nov. XXIX, MDCCXXXI.*
Eblanæ literis institutus,
Obiit Londini,
Apr. IV. MDCCLXXIV.

Of which the following is a translation:—

By the love of his associates,
The fidelity of his friends,
And the veneration of his readers,
This monument is raised

* Johnson had been misinformed in these particulars: it has been since ascertained that he was born at Elphin, in the county of Roscommon, Nov. 29, 1728.

To the memory of
OLIVER GOLDSMITH,
A poet, a natural philosopher, and an historian,
Who left no species of writing untouched by his pen;
Nor touched any that he did not embellish:
Whether smiles or tears were to be excited,
He was a powerful yet gentle master
Over the affections;
Of a genius at once sublime, lively, and
equal to every subject;
In expression at once lofty, elegant, and graceful.
He was born in the kingdom of Ireland,
At a place called Pallas, in the parish of Forney,
And county of Longford,
29th Nov. 1731.*
Educated at Dublin,
And died in London,
4th April, 1774.

Beside this Latin epitaph, Dr. Johnson honored the memory of Goldsmith with the following short one in Greek:—

Τὸν τάφον εἰσορἀας τον Ολιβαρίοιο, κονίην
Ἀφροσι μὴ σεμνην, Ξεῖνε, πόδεσσι πάτει·
Οἶσι μεμηλε φυσις, μὲτρων χάρις, ἔργα παλαιοῦν
Κλαίετε ποιητην, ἱστόρικον, φυσικον.

Mr. Boswell, who was very intimately acquainted with Goldsmith, thus speaks of his person and character:—

'The person of Goldsmith was short; his countenance coarse and vulgar; his deportment that of a scholar, awkwardly affecting the complete gentleman. No man had the art of displaying, with more advantage, whatever literary acquisitions he made. His mind resembled a fertile but thin soil; there was a quick but not a strong vegetation of whatever chanced

* See the Note on the preceding page.

to be thrown upon it. No deep root could be struck. The oak of the forest did not grow there; but the elegant shrubbery, and the fragrant parterre, appeared in gay succession. It has been generally circulated, and believed, that he was a mere fool in conversation. In allusion to this, Mr. Horatio Walpole, who admired his writings, said, he was "an inspired idiot;" and Garrick describes him as one,—

> "—————— for shortness called Noll,
> Who wrote like an angel, and talk'd like poor Poll."

But in reality these descriptions are greatly exaggerated. He had no doubt a more than common share of that hurry of ideas which we often find in his countrymen, and which sometimes introduces a laughable confusion in expressing them. He was very much what the French call *un étourdi:* and from vanity, and an eager desire of being conspicuous wherever he was, he frequently talked carelessly, without any knowledge of the subject, or even without thought. Those who were any ways distinguished, excited envy in him to so ridiculous an excess, that the instances of it are hardly credible. He, I am told, had no settled system of any sort, so that his conduct must not be too strictly criticised; but his affections were social and generous; and when he had money, he bestowed it liberally. His desires of imaginary consequence frequently predominated over his attention to truth.

'His prose has been admitted as the model of perfection, and the standard of the English language. Dr. Johnson says, "Goldsmith was a man of such variety of powers, and such felicity of performance, that he seemed to excel in whatever he attempted; a man who had the art of being minute without tediousness, and generally without confusion; whose language was capacious without exuberance; exact without restraint; and easy without weakness."

'His merit as a poet is universally acknowledged. His writings partake rather of the elegance and harmony of Pope, than the grandeur and sublimity of Milton; and it is to be lamented that his poetical productions are not more numerous; for though his ideas flowed rapidly, he arranged them with great caution, and occupied much time in polishing his periods, and harmonizing his numbers.

'His most favorite poems are, "The Traveller," "Deserted Village," "Hermit," and "Retaliation." These productions may be justly ranked with the most admired works in English poetry.

'"The Traveller" delights us with a display of charming imagery, refined ideas, and happy expressions. The characteristics of the different nations are strongly marked, and the predilection of each inhabitant in favor of his own ingeniously described.

'"The Deserted Village" is generally admired; the characters are drawn from the life. The descriptions are lively and picturesque; and the whole appears so easy and natural, as to bear the semblance of historical truth more than poetical fiction. The description of the parish priest, (probably intended for a character of his brother Henry) would have done honor to any poet of any age. In this description, the simile of the bird teaching her young to fly, and of the mountain that rises above the storm, are not easily to be paralleled. The rest of the poem consists of the character of the village schoolmaster, and a description of the village alehouse; both drawn with admirable propriety and force; a descant on the mischiefs of luxury and wealth; the variety of artificial pleasures; the miseries of those who, for want of employment at home, are driven to settle new colonies abroad; and concludes with a beautiful apostrophe to poetry.

'"The Hermit" holds equal estimation with the rest of his poetical productions.

'His last poem, of "Retaliation," is replete with humor, free from spleen, and forcibly exhibits the prominent features of the several characters to which it alludes. Dr. Johnson sums up his literary character in the following concise manner: "Take him [Goldsmith] as a poet, his 'Traveller' is a very fine performance; and so is his 'Deserted Village,' were it not sometimes too much the echo of his 'Traveller.' Whether we take him as a poet, as a comic writer, or as an historian, he stands in the first class."'

We have before observed, that his poem of 'RETALIATION' was provoked by several jocular epitaphs written upon him by the different members of a dinner club to which he belonged. Of these we subjoin a part of that which was produced by Garrick:—

'Here, Hermes, says Jove, who with nectar was mellow,
Go, fetch me some clay—I will make an odd fellow.
Right and wrong shall be jumbled; much gold, and some dross;
Without cause be he pleased, without cause be he cross;
Be sure, as I work, to throw in contradictions;
A great lover of truth, yet a mind turned to fictions.
Now mix these ingredients, which, warm'd in the baking,
Turn to learning and gaming, religion and raking;
With the love of a wench, let his writings be chaste,
Tip his tongue with strange matter, his pen with fine taste;
That the rake and the poet o'er all may prevail,
Set fire to his head, and set fire to his tail;
For the joy of each sex on the world I'll bestow it,
This scholar, rake, christian, dupe, gamester, and poet.

Though a mixture so odd, he shall merit great fame,
And among other mortals be Goldsmith his name.
When on earth this strange meteor no more shall appear,
You, Hermes, shall fetch him, to make us sport here.'

To these we shall add another sketch of our author (by way of Epitaph), written by a friend as soon as he heard of his death: —

'Here rests from the cares of the world and his pen,
A poet whose like we shall scarce meet again;
Who, though form'd in an age when corruptions ran high,
And folly alone seem'd with folly to vie;
When Genius with traffic too commonly train'd,
Recounted her merits by what she had gain'd,
Yet spurn'd at those walks of debasement and pelf,
And in poverty's spite dared to think for himself.
Thus freed from those fetters the muses oft bind,
He wrote from the heart to the hearts of mankind;
And such was the prevalent force of his song,
Sex, ages, and parties, he drew in a throng.
'The lovers —'t was theirs to esteem and commend,
For his Hermit had proved him their tutor and friend.
The statesman, his politic passions on fire,
Acknowledged repose from the charms of his lyre.
The moralist too had a feel for his rhymes,
For his Essays were curbs on the rage of the times.
Nay, the critic, all school'd in grammatical sense,
Who looked in the glow of description for *tense*,
Reform'd as he read, fell a dupe to his art,
And confess'd by his eyes what he felt at his heart.
'Yet, bless'd with original powers like these,
His principal forte was on paper to please;
Like a fleet-footed hunter, though first in the chase,
On the road of plain sense he oft slackened his pace;
Whilst Dulness and Cunning, by whipping and goring.

Their hard-footed hackneys paraded before him.
Compounded likewise of such primitive parts,
That his manners alone would have gain'd him our hearts.
So simple in truth, so ingenuously kind,
So ready to feel for the wants of mankind;
Yet praise but an author of popular quill,
This lux of philanthropy quickly stood still;
Transform'd from himself, he grew meanly severe,
And rail'd at those talents he ought not to fear.
  'Such then were his foibles; but though they were such
As shadow'd the picture a little too much,
The style was all graceful, expressive, and grand,
And the whole the result of a masterly hand.
  'Then hear me, blest spirit! now seated above,
Where all is beatitude, concord, and love,
If e'er thy regards were bestow'd on mankind,
THY MUSE AS A LEGACY LEAVE US BEHIND.
I ask it by proxy for letters and fame,
As the pride of our heart and the old English name.
I demand it as such for virtue and truth,
As the solace of age and the guide of our youth.
Consider what poets surround us—how dull!
From Minstrelsy B——e to Rosamond H—ll!
Consider what K—ys *enervate* the stage;
Consider what K——cks may *poison* the age;
O! protect us from such, nor let it be said,
That in Goldsmith the last British poet lies dead!'

ON THE

POETRY OF DR. GOLDSMITH.

BY DR. AIKIN.

AMONG those false opinions which, having once obtained currency, have been adopted without examination, may be reckoned the prevalent notion, that, notwithstanding the improvement of this country in many species of literary composition, its poetical character has been on the decline ever since the supposed Augustan age of the beginning of this [the 18th] century. No one poet, it is true, has fully succeeded to the laurel of Dryden or Pope; but if without prejudice we compare the minor poets of the present age (*minor*, I mean, with respect to the *quantity*, not the *quality*, of their productions), with those of any former period, we shall, I am convinced, find them greatly superior not only in taste and correctness, but in every other point of poetical excellence. The works of many late and present writers might be confidently appealed to in proof of this assertion; but it will suffice to instance the author who is the subject of the present Essay; and I cannot for a moment hesitate to place the name of GOLDSMITH as a poet, above that of Addison, Parnell, Tickell, Congreve, Lansdown, or any of those who fill the greater part of the voluminous collection of the *English Poets*. Of these, the main body has obtained a prescriptive right to the honor of classical writers; while their works, ranged on the shelves as necessary appendages to a modern library, are rarely taken down, and contribute very little to the stock of literary amusement. Whereas the pieces of GOLDSMITH are our familiar companions; and supply passages for recollection, when our minds are either composed to moral reflection, or warmed by strong emotions and elevated conceptions. There is, I acknowledge, much of habit and accident in the attachments we form to particular writers; yet I have little doubt, that if the lovers of English poetry were confined to a small selection of authors, GOLDSMITH would find a place in the favorite list of a great majority. And it is, I think, with much justice that a great modern critic has ever regarded this concurrence of public favor, as one of the least equivocal tests of uncommon merit. Some kinds of excellence, it is true, will more readily be recognized than others; and this will not always be in proportion to the degree of mental power employed in the respective productions: but he who obtains general and lasting applause in any work of art, must have happily executed a design judiciously formed. This remark is of fundamental consequence in estimating the poetry of GOLDSMITH; because it will enable us to hold the balance steady, when it might be disposed to incline to the superior claims of a style of loftier pretension, and more brilliant reputation.

Compared with many poets of deserved eminence, GOLDSMITH will appear characterized by his *simplicity*. In his language will be found few of those figures which are supposed *of themselves* to constitute poetry; — no violent transpositions;

no uncommon meanings and constructions; no epithets drawn from abstract and remote ideas; no coinage of new words by the ready mode of turning nouns into verbs; no bold prosopopœia, or audacious metaphor:—it scarcely contains an expression which might not be used in eloquent and descriptive prose. It is replete with imagery; but that imagery is drawn from obvious sources, and rather enforces the simple idea, than dazzles by new and unexpected ones. It rejects not common words and phrases; and, like the language of Dryden and Otway, is thereby rendered the more forcible and pathetic. It is eminently nervous and concise; and hence affords numerous passages which dwell on the memory. With respect to his matter, it is taken from human life, and the objects of nature. It does not body forth things unknown, and create new beings. Its humbler purpose is to represent manners and characters as they really exist; to impress strongly on the heart moral and political sentiments; and to fill the imagination with a variety of pleasing or affecting objects selected from the stores of nature. If this be not the highest department of poetry, it has the advantage of being the most universally agreeable. To receive delight from the sublime fictions of Milton, the allegories of Spenser, the learning of Gray, and the fancy of Collins, the mind must have been prepared by a course of particular study; and perhaps, at a certain period of life, when the judgment exercises a severer scrutiny over the sallies of the imagination, the relish for artificial beauties will always abate, if not entirely desert us. But at every age, and with every degree of culture, correct and well-chosen representations of nature must please. We admire them when young; we recur to them when old; and they charm us till nothing longer can charm. Farther, in forming a scale of excellence for artists, we are not only to consider who works upon the noblest design, but who fills his design best. It is, in reality, but a poor excuse for a slovenly performer to say '*magnis tamen excidit ausis;*' and the addition of one master-piece of any kind to the stock of art, is a greater benefit, than that of a thousand abortive and mis-shapen wonders.

If GOLDSMITH then be referred to the class of *descriptive poets*, including the description of moral as well as of physical nature, it will next be important to inquire by what means he has attained the rank of a master in his class. Let us then observe how he has selected, combined, and contrasted his objects, with what truth and strength of coloring he has expressed them, and to what end and purpose.

As poetry and eloquence do not describe by an exact enumeration of every circumstance, it is necessary to *select* certain particulars which may excite a sufficiently distinct image of the thing to be represented. In this *selection*, the great art is to give *characteristic marks*, whereby the object may at once be recognized, without being obscured in a mass of common properties, which belong equally to many others. Hence the great superiority of *particular* images to *general* ones in description: the former identify, while the latter disguise. Thus, all the hackneyed representations of the country in the works of ordinary versifiers, in which groves, and rills, and flowery meads are introduced just as the rhyme and measure require, present nothing to the fancy but an indistinct daub of coloring, in which all the diversity of nature is lost and confounded. To catch the discriminating features, and present them bold and prominent, by few, but decisive strokes, is the talent of a master; and it will not be easy to produce a superior to GOLDSMITH in this respect. The mind is never in doubt as to the meaning of his figures, nor does it languish over the survey of trivial and unappropriated circumstances. All is alive — all is filled — yet all is clear.

The proper *combination* of objects refers to the impression they are calculated to make on the mind ; and requires that they should harmonize, and reciprocally enforce and sustain each other's effect. They should unite in giving one leading tone to the imagination ; and without a sameness of form, they should blend in an uniformity of hue. This, too, has very successfully been attended to by GOLDSMITH, who has not only sketched his single figures with truth and spirit, but has combined them into the most harmonious and impressive groups. Nor has any descriptive poet better understood the great force of *contrast*, in setting off his scenes, and preventing any approach to wearisomeness by repetition of kindred objects. And, with great skill, he has contrived that both parts of his contrast should conspire in producing one intended moral effect. Of all these excellences, examples will be pointed out as we take a cursory view of the particular pieces.

In addition to the circumstances already noted, the *force* and *clearness* of representation depend also on the diction. It has already been observed, that GOLDSMITH's language is remarkable for its general simplicity, and the direct and proper use of words. It has ornaments, but these are not far-fetched. The epithets employed are usually qualities strictly belonging to the subject, and the true coloring of the simple figure They are frequently contrived to express a necessary circumstance in the description, and thus avoid the usual imputation of being expletive. Of this kind are 'the *rattling* terrors of the *vengeful* snake ; '*indurated* heart ;' 'shed *intolerable* day ;' *matted* woods ;' '*ventrous* ploughshare ;' '*equinoctial* fervors.'

The examples are not few of that indisputable mark of true poetic language, where a single word conveys an image; as in these instances: 'resignation gently *slopes* the way;' '*scoops out* an empire;' 'the vessel, idly waiting, *flaps* with every gale;' 'to *winnow* fragrance;' 'murmurs *fluctuate* in the gale.' All metaphor, indeed, does this in some degree; but where the accessory idea is either indistinct or incongruous, as frequently happens when it is introduced as an artifice to force language up to poetry, the effect is only a gaudy obscurity.

The *end* and *purpose* to which description is directed is what distinguishes a well-planned piece from a loose effusion; for though a vivid representation of striking objects will ever afford some pleasure, yet if aim and design be wanting, to give it a basis, and stamp it with the dignity of meaning, it will in a long performance prove flat and tiresome. But this is a want which cannot be charged on GOLDSMITH; for both the *Traveller* and the *Deserted Village* have a great moral in view, to which the whole of the description is made to tend. I do not now inquire into the legitimacy of the conclusions he has drawn from his premises; it is enough to justify his plans, that such a purpose is included in them.

The *versification* of GOLDSMITH is formed on the general model that has been adopted since the refinement of English poetry, and especially since the time of Pope. To manage rhyme couplets so as to produce a pleasing effect on the ear, has since that period been so common an attainment, that it merits no particular admiration. GOLDSMITH may, I think, be said to have come up to the usual standard of proficiency in this respect, without having much surpassed it. A musical ear, and a familiarity with the best examples, have enabled him, without much apparent study, almost always to avoid defect, and very often to produce excellence. It is no censure of this poet to say that his versification presses less on the attention than his matter. In fact he has none of those peculiarities of versifying, whether improvements or not, that some who aim at distinction in this point have adopted. He generally suspends or closes the sense at the end of the line or of the couplet; and therefore does not often give examples of that greater compass and variety of melody which is obtained by longer clauses, or by breaking the coincidences of the cadence of sound and meaning. He also studiously rejects triplets and alexandrines. But allowing for the want of these sources of variety, he has sufficiently avoided monotony; and in the usual flow of his measure, he has gratified the ear with as much change, as judiciously shifting the line-pause can produce.

Having made these general observations on the nature of GOLDSMITH's poetry, I proceed to a survey of his principal pieces.

The *Traveller, or Prospect of Society*, was first sketched out by the author during a tour in Europe, great part of which he performed on foot, and in circumstances which afforded him the fullest means of becoming acquainted with the most numerous class in society, peculiarly termed *the people.* The date of the first edition is 1765. It begins in the gloomy mood natural to genius in distress, when wandering alone,

'Remote, unfriended, melancholy, slow.'

After an affectionate and regretful glance to the peaceful seat of fraternal kindness, and some expressions of self-pity, the Poet sits down amid Alpine solitudes to spend a pensive hour in meditating on the state of mankind. He finds that the natives of every land regard their own with preference; whence he is led to this proposition, — that if we impartially compare the advantages belonging to different countries, we shall conclude that an equal portion of good is dealt to all the human race. He farther supposes, that every nation, having in view one peculiar species of happiness, models life to that alone; whence this favorite kind, pushed to an extreme, becomes a source of peculiar evils. To exemplify this by instances, is the business of the subsequent descriptive part of the piece.

Italy is the first country that comes under review. Its general landscape is painted by a few characteristic strokes, and the felicity of its climate is displayed in appropriate imagery. The revival of arts and commerce in Italy, and their subsequent decline, are next touched upon; and hence is derived the present disposition of the people — easily pleased with splendid trifles, the wrecks of their former grandeur; and sunk into an enfeebled moral and intellectual character, reducing them to the level of children.

From these he turns with a sort of disdain, to view a nobler race, hardened by a rigorous climate, and by the necessity of unabating toil. These are the *Swiss*, who find, in the equality of their condition, and their ignorance of other modes of life, a source of content which remedies the natural evils of their lot. There cannot be a more delightful picture than the poet has drawn of the Swiss peasant, going forth to his morning's labor, and returning at night to the bosom of domestic happiness. It sufficiently accounts for that *patriot passion* for which they have ever been so celebrated, and which is here described in lines that reach the heart, and is illustrated by a beautiful simile. But this state of life has also its disadvantages. The sources of enjoyment being few, a vacant listlessness is apt to creep upon the breast; and if nature urges to throw this off by occasional bursts of pleasure, no stimulus can reach the purpose but gross sensual debauch. Their morals, too, like their enjoyments, are of a coarse texture. Some sterner virtues hold high dominion in their breast, but all the gentler and more refined qualities of the heart, which soften and sweeten life, are exiled to milder climates.

To the more genial climate of *France* the traveller next repairs, and in a very pleasing rural picture he introduces himself in the capacity of musician to a village party of dancers beside the murmuring Loire. The leading feature of this nation he represents as being the love of praise; which passion, while it inspires sentiments of honor, and a desire of pleasing, also affords a free course to folly, and nourishes vanity and ostentation. The soul, accustomed to depend for its happiness on foreign applause, shifts its principles with the change of fashion, and is a stranger to the value of self-approbation.

The strong contrast to this national character is sought in *Holland*; a most graphical description of the scenery presented by that singular country introduces the moral portrait of the people. From the necessity of unceasing labor, induced by their peculiar circumstances, a habit of industry has been formed, of which the natural consequence is a love of gain. The possession of exuberant wealth has given rise to the arts and conveniences of life; but at the same time has introduced a crafty, cold, and mercenary temper, which sets everything, even liberty itself, at a price. How different, exclaims the poet, from their Belgian ancestors! how different from the present race of Britain!

To Britain, then, he turns, and begins with a slight sketch of the country, in which, he says, the mildest charms of creation are combined.

'Extremes are only in the master's mind.'

He then draws a very striking picture of a stern, thoughtful independent freeman, a creature of reason, unfashioned by the common forms of life, and loose from all its ties; — and this he gives as the representative of the English character. A society formed by such unyielding, self-dependent beings, will naturally be a scene of violent political contests, and ever in a ferment with party. And a still worse fate awaits it; for the ties of nature, duty, and love, failing, the fictitious bonds of wealth and law must be employed to hold together such a reluctant association; whence the time may come, that valor, learning, and patriotism, may all lie levelled in one sink of avarice. These are the ills of freedom; but the Poet, who would only repress to secure, goes on to deliver his ideas of the cause of such mischiefs, which he seems to place in the usurpations of aristocratical upon regal authority; and with great energy he expresses his indignation at the oppressions the poor suffer from their petty tyrants. This leads him to a kind of anticipation of the subject of his 'Deserted Village,' where, laying aside the politician, and resuming the poet, he describes, by a few highly pathetic touches, the depopulated fields, the ruined village, and the poor, forlorn inhabitants, driven from their beloved home, and exposed to all the perils of the transatlantic wilderness. It is by no means my intention to enter into a discussion of GOLDSMITH's political opinions, which bear evident marks of confused notions and a heated imagination. I shall confine myself to a remark upon the English national character, which will apply to him in common with various other writers, native and foreign.

This country has long been in the possession of more unrestrained freedom of thinking and acting than any other perhaps that ever existed; a consequence of which has been, that all those peculiarities of character, which in other nations remain concealed in the general mass, have here stood forth prominent and conspicuous; and these being from their nature calculated to draw attention, have by superficial observers been mistaken for the general character of the people. This has been particularly the case with political distinction. From the publicity of all proceedings in the legislative part of our constitution and the independence with which many act, all party differences are strongly marked, and public men take their side with openness and confidence. Public topics, too, are discussed by all ranks; and whatever seeds there are in any part of the society of spirit and activity, have full opportunity of germinating. But to imagine that these busy and high-spirited characters compose a majority of the community, or perhaps a much greater proportion than in other countries, is a delusion. This nation, as a body, is, like all others, characterized by circumstances of its situation; and a rich commercial people, long trained to society, inhabiting a climate where many things are necessary to the comfort of life, and under a government abounding with splendid distinctions, cannot possibly be a knot of philosophers and patriots.

To return from this digression. Though it is probable that few of GOLDSMITH'S readers will be convinced, even from the instances he has himself produced, that the happiness of mankind is everywhere equal; yet all will feel the force of the truly philosophical sentiment which concludes the piece — that man's chief bliss is ever seated in his mind; and that but a small part of real felicity consists in what human governments can either bestow or withhold.

The *Deserted Village*, first printed in 1769, is the companion-piece of the Traveller, formed, like it, upon a plan which unites description with sentiment, and employs both in inculcating a political moral. It is a view of the prosperous and ruined state of a country village, with reflections on the causes of both. Such it may be defined in prose; but the disposition, management, and coloring of the piece, are all calculated for poetical effect. It begins with a delightful picture of *Auburn* when inhabited by a happy people. The view of the village itself, and the rural occupations and pastimes of its simple natives, is in the best style of painting, by a selection of characteristic circumstances. Is is immediately contrasted by a similar bold sketch of its ruined and desolated condition. Then succeeds an imaginary state of England, in a kind of golden age of equality; with its contrast likewise. The apostrophe that follows, the personal complaint of the poet, and the portrait of a sage in retirement, are sweetly sentimental touches, that break the continuity of description.

He returns to *Auburn*, and having premised another masterly sketch of its two states, in which the images are chiefly drawn from sounds, he proceeds to what may be called the interior history of the village. In his first figure he has tried his strength with Dryden. The *parish priest* of that great poet, improved from Chaucer, is a portrait full of beauty, but drawn in a loose, unequal manner, with the flowing vein of digressive thought and imagery that stamps his style. The subject of the draught, too, is considerably different from that of GOLDSMITH, having more of the ascetic and mortified cast in conformity to the saintly model of the Roman Catholic priesthood. The pastor of *Auburn* is more *human*, but is not on that account a less venerable and interesting figure; though I know not whether all will be pleased with his familiarity with vicious characters, which goes beyond the purpose of mere reformation. The description of him in his professional character is truly admirable; and the similes of the bird instructing his young to fly, and the tall cliff rising above the storm, have been universally applauded. The first, I believe, is original;—the second is not so, though it has probably never been so well drawn and applied. The subsequent sketches of the village schoolmaster and alehouse, are close imitations of nature in low life, like the pictures of Teniers and Hogarth. Yet even these humorous scenes slide imperceptibly into sentiment and pathos; and the comparison of the simple pleasures of the poor, with the splendid festivities of the opulent, rises to the highest style of moral poetry. Who has not felt the force of that reflection,

'The heart distrusting asks, if this be joy?'

The writer then falls into a strain of reasoning against luxury and superfluous wealth, in which the sober inquirer will find much serious truth, though mixed with poetical exaggeration. The description of the contrasted scenes of magnificence and misery in a great metropolis, closed by the pathetic figure of the forlorn, ruined female, is not to be surpassed.

Were not the subjects of GOLDSMITH'S description so skilfully varied, the uniformity of manner, consisting in an enumeration of single circumstances, generally depicted in single lines, might tire; but, where is the reader who can avoid being hurried along by the swift current of imagery, when to such a passage as the last succeeds a landscape fraught with all the sublime terrors of the torrid zone;—and then, an exquisitely tender history-piece of the departure of the villagers: concluded with a group (slightly touched indeed) of allegorical personages? A noble address to the Genius of Poetry, in which is compressed the moral of the whole, gives a dignified finishing to the work.

If we compare these two principal poems of GOLDSMITH, we may say, that the 'Traveller' is formed upon a more regular plan, has a higher purpose in view, more abounds in thought, and in the expression of moral and philosophical ideas; the 'Deserted Village' has more imagery, more variety, more pathos, more of the peculiar character of poetry. In the first, the moral and natural descriptions are more general and elevated; in the second, they are more particular and interesting. Both are truly original productions; but the 'Deserted Village' has less peculiarity, and indeed has given rise to imitations which may stand in some parallel with it; while the 'Traveller' remains an *unique*.

With regard to GOLDSMITH's other poems, a few remarks will suffice. The 'Hermit,' printed in the same year with the 'Traveller,' has been a very popular piece, as might be expected of a tender tale prettily told. It is called a 'Ballad,' but I think with no correct application of that term, which properly means a story related in language either naturally or affectedly rude and simple. It has been a sort of a fashion to admire these productions; yet in the really ancient ballads, for one stroke of beauty, there are pages of insipidity and vulgarity; and the imitations have been pleasing in proportion as they approached more finished compositions. In GOLDSMITH'S 'Hermit,' the language is always polished, and often ornamented. The best things in it are some neat turns of moral and pathetic sentiment, given with a simple conciseness that fits them for being retained in the memory. As to the story, it has little fancy or contrivance to recommend it.

We have already seen that GOLDSMITH possessed humor; and, exclusively of his comedies, pieces professedly humorous form a part of his poetical remains. His imitations of Swift are happy, but they *are* imitations. His tale of the 'Double Transformation' may vie with those of Prior. His own natural vein of easy humor flows freely in his 'Haunch of Venison' and 'Retaliation;' the first, an admirable specimen of a very ludicrous story made out of a common incident by the help of conversation and character; the other, an original thought, in which his talent at drawing portraits, with a mixture of the serious and the comic, is most happily displayed.

POEMS.

VERSES

ON THE

DEATH OF DR. GOLDSMITH.

EXTRACT FROM A POEM

WRITTEN BY COURTNEY MELMOTH, ESQ.

ON THE DEATH OF EMINENT ENGLISH POETS.

THE TEARS OF GENIUS.

THE village bell tolls out the note of death,
And through the echoing air the length'ning sound,
With dreadful pause, reverberating deep,
Spreads the sad tidings o'er fair Auburn's vale.
There, to enjoy the scenes her bard had praised
In all the sweet simplicity of song,
GENIUS, in pilgrim garb, sequester'd sat,
And herded jocund with the harmless swains;
But when she heard the fate-foreboding knell,
With startled step, precipitate and swift,
And look pathetic, full of dire presage,
The church-way walk beside the neigb'ring green,
Sorrowing she sought; and there, in black array,
Borne on the shoulders of the swains he loved,
She saw the boast of Auburn moved along.

Touch'd at the view, her pensive breast she struck,
And to the cypress, which incumbent hangs,
With leaning slope and branch irregular,
O'er the moss'd pillars of the sacred fane,
The brier-bound graves shadowing with funeral gloom,
Forlorn she hied; and there the crowding wo
(Swell'd by the parent) press'd on bleeding thought,
Big ran the drops from her maternal eye,
Fast broke the bosom-sorrow from her heart,
And pale Distress sat sickly on her cheek,
As thus her plaintive Elegy began:—

'And must my children all expire?
Shall none be left to strike the lyre?
Courts Death alone a learned prize?
Falls his shafts only on the wise?
Can no fit marks on earth be found,
From useless thousands swarming round?
What crowding ciphers cram the land.
What hosts of victims, at command!
Yet shall the ingenious drop alone?
Shall Science grace the tyrant's throne?
Thou murd'rer of the tuneful train,
I charge thee with my children slain!
Scarce has the sun thrice urged his annual tour,
Since half my race have felt thy barbarous power;
Sore hast thou thinn'd each pleasing art,
And struck a muse with every dart;
Bard after bard obey'd thy slaughtering call,
Till scarce a poet lives to sing a brother's fall.
Then let a widow'd mother pay
The tribute of a parting lay;

Tearful, inscribe the monumental strain,
And speak aloud her feelings and her pain!
'And first, farewell to thee, my son,' she cried,
'Thou pride of Auburn's dale — sweet bard, farewell!
Long for thy sake the peasant's tear shall flow,
And many a virgin bosom heave with woe;
For thee shall sorrow sadden all the scene,
And every pastime perish on the green;
The sturdy farmer shall suspend his tale,
The woodman's ballad shall no more regale,
No more shall Mirth each rustic sport inspire,
But every frolic, every feat, shall tire.
No more the evening gambol shall delight,
Nor moonshine-revels crown the vacant night;
But groups of villagers (each joy forgot)
Shall form a sad assembly round the cot.
Sweet bard, farewell! — and farewell, Auburn's bliss,
The bashful lover, and the yielded kiss:
The evening warble Philomela made,
The echoing forest, and the whispering shade,
The winding brook, the bleat of brute content,
And the blithe voice that "whistled as it went:"
These shall no longer charm the ploughman's care,
But sighs shall fill the pauses of despair.
'GOLDSMITH, adieu; the "book-learn'd priest" for thee
Shall now in vain possess his festive glee,
The oft-heard jest in vain he shall reveal,
For now, alas! the jest he cannot feel.
But ruddy damsels o'er thy tomb shall bend,
And conscious weep for their and virtue's friend;

The milkmaid shall reject the shepherd's song,
And cease to carol as she toils along:
All Auburn shall bewail the fatal day,
When from her fields their pride was snatch'd away.
And even the matron of the cressy lake,
In piteous plight, her palsied head shall shake,
While all adown the furrows of her face
Slow shall the lingering tears each other trace.
'And, oh, my child! severer woes remain
To all the houseless and unshelter'd train!
Thy fate shall sadden many an humble guest,
And heap fresh anguish on the beggar's breast;
For dear wert thou to all the sons of pain,
To all that wander, sorrow or complain:
Dear to the learned, to the simple dear,
For daily blessing mark'd thy virtuous year;
The rich received a moral from thy head,
And from thy heart the stranger found a bed:
Distress came always smiling from thy door;
For God had made thee agent to the poor,
Had form'd thy feelings on the noblest plan,
To grace at once the poet and the man.'

EXTRACT FROM A MONODY.

Dark as the night, which now in dunnest robe
Ascends her zenith o'er the silent globe,
Sad Melancholy wakes, a while to tread,

With solemn step, the mansions of the dead:
Led by her hand, o'er this yet recent shrine
I sorrowing bend; and here essay to twine
The tributary wreath of laureat bloom,
With artless hands, to deck a poet's tomb, —
The tomb where Goldsmith sleeps. Fond hopes, adieu!
No more your airy dreams shall mock my view;
Here will I learn ambition to control,
And each aspiring passion of the soul:
E'en now, methinks, his well-known voice I hear,
When late he meditated flight from care,
When, as imagination fondly hied
To scenes of sweet retirement, thus he cried: —
'Ye splendid fabrics, palaces, and towers,
Where dissipation leads the giddy hours,
Where pomp, disease, and knavery reside,
And folly bends the knee to wealthy pride;
Where luxury's purveyors learn to rise,
And worth, to want a prey, unfriended dies;
Where warbling eunuchs glitter in brocade,
And hapless poets toil for scanty bread:
Farewell! to other scenes I turn my eyes,
Embosom'd in the vale where Auburn lies —
Deserted Auburn, those now ruin'd glades,
Forlorn, yet ever dear and honor'd shades,
There, though the hamlet boasts no smiling train,
Nor sportful pastime circling on the plain,
No needy villains prowl around for prey,
No slanderers, no sycophants betray;
No gaudy foplings scornfully deride
The swain, whose humble pipe is all his pride,—

There will I fly to seek that soft repose,
Which solitude contemplative bestows.
Yet, oh, fond hope! perchance there still remains
One lingering friend behind, to bless the plains;
Some hermit of the dale, enshrined in ease,
Long lost companion of my youthful days;
With whose sweet converse in his social bower,
I oft may chide away some vacant hour;
To whose pure sympathy I may impart
Each latent grief that labors at my heart,
Whate'er I felt, and what I saw, relate,
The shoals of luxury, the wrecks of state,—
Those busy scenes, where science wakes in vain,
In which I shared, ah! ne'er to share again.
But whence that pang? does nature now rebel?
Why falters out my tongue the word farewell?
Ye friends! who long have witness'd to my toil,
And seen me ploughing in a thankless soil,
Whose partial tenderness hush'd every pain,
Whose approbation made my bosom vain,—
'Tis you to whom my soul divided hies
With fond regret, and half unwilling flies;
Sighs forth her parting wishes to the wind,
And lingering leaves her better half behind.
Can I forget the intercourse I shared,
What friendship cherish'd, and what zeal endear'd?
Alas! remembrance still must turn to you,
And, to my latest hour, protract the long adieu.
Amid the woodlands, wheresoe'er I rove,
The plain, or secret covert of the grove,
Imagination shall supply her store

Of painful bliss, and what she can restore;
Shall strew each lonely path with flow'rets gay,
And wide as is her boundless empire stray;
On eagle pinions traverse earth and skies,
And bid the lost and distant objects rise.
Here, where encircled o'er the sloping land
Woods rise on woods, shall Aristotle stand;
Lyceum round the godlike man rejoice,
And bow with reverence to wisdom's voice.
There, spreading oaks shall arch the vaulted dome,
The champion, there, of liberty and Rome,
In Attic eloquence shall thunder laws,
And uncorrupted senates shout applause.
Not more ecstatic visions rapt the soul
Of Numa, when to midnight grots he stole,
And learnt his lore, from virtue's mouth refined,
To fetter vice, and harmonize mankind.
Now stretch'd at ease beside some fav'rite stream
Of beauty and enchantment will I dream;
Elysium, seats of arts, and laurels won,
The Graces three, and Japhet's* fabled son;
Whilst Angelo shall wave the mystic rod,
And see a new creation wait his nod;
Prescribe his bounds to Time's remorseless power,
And to my arms my absent friends restore;
Place me amidst the group, each well known face,
The sons of science, lords of human race;
And as oblivion sinks at his command,
Nature shall rise more finish'd from his hand.

* Prometheus

Thus some magician, fraught with potent skill,
Transforms and moulds each varied mass at will;
Calls animated forms of wondrous birth,
Cadmean offspring, from the teeming earth,
Unceres the ponderous tombs, the realms of night,
And calls their cold inhabitants to light;
Or, as he traverses a dreary scene,
Bids every sweet of nature there convene,
Huge mountains skirted round with wavy woods,
The shrub-deck'd lawns, and silver-sprinkled floods,
Whilst flow'rets spring around the smiling land,
And follow on the traces of his wand.
'Such prospects, lovely Auburn! then, be thine,
And what thou canst of bliss impart be mine;
Amid thy humble shades, in tranquil ease,
Grant me to pass the remnant of my days.
Unfetter'd from the toil of wretched gain,
My raptured muse shall pour her noblest strain,
Within her native bowers the notes prolong,
And, grateful, meditate her latest song.
Thus, as adown the slope of life I bend,
And move, resign'd, to meet my latter end,
Each worldly wish, each worldly care repress'd,
A self-approving heart alone possess'd,
Content, to bounteous Heaven I 'll leave the rest.'
Thus spoke the Bard: but not one friendly power
With nod assentive crown'd the parting hour;
No eastern meteor glared beneath the sky,
No dextral omen: Nature heaved a sigh
Prophetic of the dire, impending blow,
The presage of her loss, and Britain's woe.

Already portion'd, unrelenting fate
Had made a pause upon the number'd date;
Behind stood Death, too horrible for sight,
In darkness clad, expectant, pruned for flight;
Pleased at the word, the shapeless monster sped,
On eager message to the humble shed,
Where, wrapt by soft poetic visions round,
Sweet slumbering, Fancy's darling son he found.
At his approach the silken pinion'd train,
Affrighted, mount aloft, and quit the brain,
Which late they fann'd. Now other scenes than dales
Of woody pride, succeed, or flowery vales:
As when a sudden tempest veils the sky,
Before serene, and streaming lightnings fly,
The prospect shifts, and pitchy volumes roll
Along the drear expanse, from pole to pole;
Terrific horrors all the void invest,
Whilst the arch spectre issues forth confest.
The Bard beholds him beckon to the tomb
Of yawning night, eternity's dread womb;
In vain attempts to fly, th' impassive air
Retards his steps, and yields him to despair;
He feels a gripe that thrills through every vein,
And panting struggles in the fatal chain.
Here paused the fell destroyer, to survey
The pride, the boast of man, his destined prey;
Prepared to strike, he pois'd aloft the dart,
And plunged the steel in Virtue's bleeding heart;
Abhorrent, back the springs of life rebound,
And leave on Nature's face a ghastly wound,
A wound enroll'd among Britannia's woes,

That ages yet to follow cannot close.
O Goldsmith! how shall Sorrow now essay
To murmur out her slow, incondite lay?
In what sad accents mourn the luckless hour,
That yielded thee to unrelenting power;
Thee, the proud boast of all the tuneful train
That sweep the lyre, or swell the polish'd strain?
Much-honored Bard! if my untutor'd verse
Could pay a tribute worthy of thy hearse,
With fearless hands I'd build the fane of praise,
And boldly strew the never-fading bays.
But, ah! with thee my guardian genius fled,
And pillow'd in thy tomb his silent head:
Pain'd Memory alone behind remains,
And pensive stalks the solitary plains,
Rich in her sorrows; honors without art
She pays in tears redundant from the heart.
And say, what boots it o'er thy hallow'd dust
To heap the graven pile, or laurell'd bust;
Since by thy hands already raised on high,
We see a fabric tow'ring to the sky;
Where, hand in hand with Time, the sacred lore
Shall travel on, till Nature is no more?

LINES BY W. WOTTY.

Adieu, sweet Bard! to each fine feeling true,
Thy virtues many, and thy foibles few,—

Those form'd to charm e'en vicious minds, and these
With harmless mirth the social soul to please.
Another's woe thy heart could always melt;
None gave more free, for none more deeply felt.
Sweet Bard, adieu! thy own harmonious lays
Have sculptured out thy monument of praise:
Yes, these survive to Time's remotest day;
While drops the bust, and boastful tombs decay.
Reader, if number'd in the Muse's train,
Go, tune the lyre, and imitate his strain;
But, if no poet thou, reverse the plan,
Depart in peace, and imitate the man.

THE TRAVELLER;

OR,

A PROSPECT OF SOCIETY.

DEDICATION.

TO THE REV. HENRY GOLDSMITH.

DEAR SIR,—I am sensible that the friendship between us can acquire no new force from the ceremonies of a dedication; and perhaps it demands an excuse thus to prefix your name to my attempts, which you decline giving with your own. But as a part of this poem was formerly written to you from Switzerland, the whole can now, with propriety, be only inscribed to you. It will also throw a light upon many parts of it, when the reader understands, that it is addressed to a man who, despising fame and fortune, has retired early to happiness and obscurity, with an income of forty pounds a-year.

I now perceive, my dear brother, the wisdom of your humble choice. You have entered upon a sacred office, where the harvest is great, and the laborers are but few; while you have left the field of ambition, where the laborers are many and the harvest not worth carrying away. But of all kinds of ambition — what from the refinement of the times, from different systems of criticism, and from the divisions of party — that which pursues poetical fame is the wildest.

Poetry makes a principal amusement among unpolished nations; but in a country verging to the extremes of refinement, painting and music come in for a share. As these offer the feeble mind a less laborious entertainment, they at first rival poetry, and at length supplant her; they engross all that favor once shown to her, and though but younger sisters, seize upon the elder's birthright.

Yet, however this art may be neglected by the powerful, it is still in greater danger from the mistaken efforts of the learned to improve it. What criticisms have we not heard of late in favor of blank verse and Pindaric odes, choruses, anapests and iambics, alliterative care and happy negligence! Every absurdity has now a champion to defend it; and as he is generally much in the wrong, so he has always much to say; for error is ever talkative.

But there is an enemy to this art still more dangerous, — I mean party. Party entirely distorts the judgment, and destroys the taste. When the mind is once infected with this disease, it can only find pleasure in what contributes to increase the distemper. Like the tiger, that seldom desists from pursuing man after having once preyed upon human flesh, the reader, who has once gratified his appetite with calumny, makes ever after the most agreeable feast upon murdered reputation. Such readers generally admire some half-witted thing, who wants to be thought a bold man, having lost the character of a wise one. Him they dignify with the name of poet: his tawdry lampoons are called satires; his turbulence is said to be force, and his frenzy fire.

What reception a poem may find, which has neither abuse,

party, nor blank verse to support it, I cannot tell, nor am I solicitous to know. My aims are right. Without espousing the cause of any party, I have attempted to moderate the rage of all. I have endeavored to shew that there may be equal happiness in states that are differently governed from our own; that every state has a particular principle of happiness, and that this principle in each may be carried to a mischievous excess. There are few can judge better than yourself how far these positions are illustrated in this poem. I am, dear Sir, your most affectionate brother,

OLIVER GOLDSMITH.

THE TRAVELLER.

REMOTE, unfriended, melancholy, slow,
Or by the lazy Sheld, or wandering Po,
Or onward, where the rude Carinthian boor
Against the houseless stranger shuts the door;
Or where Campania's plain forsaken lies,
A weary waste expanding to the skies:
Where'er I roam, whatever realms to see,
My heart untravell'd fondly turns to thee;
Still to my brother turns, with ceaseless pain,
And drags at each remove a lengthening chain.
Eternal blessings crown my earliest friend,
And round his dwelling guardian saints attend!
Blest be that spot, where cheerful guests retire
To pause from toil, and trim their evening fire!
Blest that abode, where want and pain repair,
And every stranger finds a ready chair!
Blest be those feasts with simple plenty crown'd,
Where all the ruddy family around
Laugh at the jests or pranks that never fail,
Or sigh with pity at some mournful tale;
Or press the bashful stranger to his food,
And learn the luxury of doing good!

But me, not destined such delights to share,
My prime of life in wandering spent, and care;
Impell'd, with steps unceasing, to pursue
Some fleeting good, that mocks me with the view,
That like the circle bounding earth and skies,
Allures from far, yet, as I follow, flies:
My fortune leads to traverse realms alone,
And find no spot of all the world my own.
E'en now, where Alpine solitudes ascend,
I sit me down a pensive hour to spend;
And, placed on high above the storm's career,
Look downward where a hundred realms appear:
Lakes, forests, cities, plains extending wide,
The pomp of kings, the shepherd's humbler pride.
When thus Creation's charms around combine,
Amidst the store should thankless pride repine?
Say, should the philosophic mind disdain
That good which makes each humbler bosom vain?
Let school-taught pride dissemble all it can,
These little things are great to little man;
And wiser he, whose sympathetic mind
Exults in all the good of all mankind.
Ye glittering towns, with wealth and splendor crown'd;
Ye fields, where summer spreads profusion round;
Ye lakes, whose vessels catch the busy gale;
Ye bending swains, that dress the flowery vale;
For me your tributary stores combine,
Creation's heir, the world — the world is mine!
As some lone miser, visiting his store,
Bends at his treasure, counts, recounts it o'er,
Hoards after hoards his rising raptures fill,

Yet still he sighs, for hoards are wanting still.
Thus to my breast alternate passions rise,
Pleased with each good that Heaven to man supplies;
Yet oft a sigh prevails, and sorrows fall,
To see the sum of human bliss so small:
And oft I wish, amidst the scene to find
Some spot to real happiness consign'd,
Where my worn soul, each wandering hope at rest,
May gather bliss to see my fellows blest.
But where to find that happiest spot below
Who can direct, when all pretend to know?
The shuddering tenant of the frigid zone
Boldly proclaims that happiest spot his own;
Extols the treasures of his stormy seas,
And his long nights of revelry and ease:
The naked negro, panting at the Line,
Boasts of his golden sands and palmy wine,
Basks in the glare, or stems the tepid wave,
And thanks his gods for all the good they gave.
Such is the patriot's boast where'er we roam,
His first, best country, ever is at home.
And yet, perhaps, if countries we compare,
And estimate the blessings which they share,
Though patriots flatter, still shall wisdom find
An equal portion dealt to all mankind;
As different good, by art or nature given,
To different nations makes their blessings even.
Nature, a mother kind alike to all,
Still grants her bliss at labor's earnest call;
With food as well the peasant is supplied
On Idra's cliffs as Arno's shelvy side;

And though the rocky-crested summits frown,
These rocks by custom turn to beds of down.
From art more various are the blessings sent,—
Wealth, commerce, honor, liberty, content.
Yet these each other's power so strong contest,
That either seems destructive of the rest.
Where wealth and freedom reign, contentment fails,
And honor sinks, where commerce long prevails.
Hence every state, to one loved blessing prone,
Conforms and models life to that alone.
Each to the favorite happiness attends,
And spurns the plan that aims at other ends,
Till carried to excess in each domain,
This Favorite good begets peculiar pain.
But let us try these truths with closer eyes,
And trace them through the prospect as it lies;
Here, for a while, my proper cares resign'd,
Here let me sit in sorrow for mankind;
Like yon neglected shrub at random cast,
That shades the steep, and sighs at every blast.
Far to the right, where Apennine ascends,
Bright as the summer, Italy extends;
Its uplands sloping deck the mountain's side,
Woods over woods in gay theatric pride,
While oft some temple's mouldering tops between,
With venerable grandeur mark the scene.
Could Nature's bounty satisfy the breast,
The sons of Italy were surely blest:
Whatever fruits in different climes are found,
That proudly rise, or humbly court the ground;
Whatever blooms in torrid tracts appear,

Whose bright succession decks the varied year;
Whatever sweets salute the northern sky
With vernal lives, that blossom but to die;
These here disporting own the kindred soil,
Nor ask luxuriance from the planter's toil;
While sea-born gales their gelid wings expand,
To winnow fragrance round the smiling land.
  But small the bliss that sense alone bestows,
And sensual bliss is all this nation knows.
In florid beauty groves and fields appear,
Man seems the only growth that dwindles here.
Contrasted faults through all his manners reign:
Though poor, luxurious; though submissive, vain;
Though grave, yet trifling; zealous, yet untrue!
And e'en in penance planning sins anew.
All evils here contaminate the mind,
That opulence departed leaves behind:
For wealth was theirs; not far removed the date,
When commerce proudly flourish'd through the state;
At her command the palace learn'd to rise,
Again the long fall'n column sought the skies;
The canvas glow'd beyond e'en nature warm,
The pregnant quarry teem'd with human form:
Till, more unsteady than the southern gale,
Commerce on other shores display'd her sail;
While nought remain'd, of all that riches gave,
But towns unmann'd, and lords without a slave:
And late the nation found, with fruitless skill,
Its former strength was but plethoric ill.
  Yet, still the loss of wealth is here supplied
By arts, the splendid wrecks of former pride;

From these the feeble heart and long-fall'n mind
An easy compensation seem to find.
Here may be seen in bloodless pomp array'd,
The pasteboard triumph and the cavalcade;
Processions form'd for piety and love,
A mistress or a saint in every grove.
By sports like these are all their cares beguil'd;
The sports of children satisfy the child:
Each nobler aim repress'd by long control,
Now sinks at last, or feebly mans the soul;
While low delights succeeding fast behind,
In happier meanness occupy the mind;
As in those dooms where Cæsars once bore sway,
Defaced by time, and tottering in decay,
There in the ruin, heedless of the dead,
The shelter-seeking peasant builds his shed;
And, wondering man could want the larger pile,
Exults, and owns his cottage with a smile.
My soul, turn from them! turn we to survey
Where rougher climes a nobler race display,
Where the bleak Swiss their stormy mansion tread,
And force a churlish soil for scanty bread:
No product here the barren hills afford,
But man and steel, the soldier and his sword;
No vernal blooms their torpid rocks array,
But winter lingering chills the lap of May;
No zephyr fondly sues the mountain's breast,
But meteors glare, and stormy glooms invest.
Yet still, even here, content can spread a charm,
Redress the clime, and all its rage disarm.
Though poor the peasant's hut, his feast though small,

He sees his little lot the lot of all;
Sees no contiguous palace rear its head,
To shame the meanness of his humble shed;
No costly lord the sumptuous banquet deal
To make him loathe his vegetable meal;
But calm, and bred in ignorance and toil,
Each wish contracting, fits him to the soil.
Cheerful, at morn, he wakes from short repose,
Breathes the keen air, and carols as he goes;
With patient angle trolls the finny deep,
Or drives his vent'rous ploughshare to the steep;
Or seeks the den where snow-tracks mark the way,
And drags the struggling savage into day.
At night returning, every labor sped,
He sits him down the monarch of a shed;
Smiles by a cheerful fire, and round surveys
His children's looks that brighten to the blaze,
While his loved partner, boastful of her hoard,
Displays her cleanly platter on the board;
And haply too some pilgrim, thither led,
With many a tale repays the nightly bed.
  Thus every good his native wilds impart,
Imprints the patriot passion on his heart;
And e'en those ills that round his mansion rise,
Enhance the bliss his scanty fund supplies.
Dear is that shed to which his soul conforms,
And dear that hill that lifts him to the storms;
And as a child, when scaring sounds molest,
Clings close and closer to the mother's breast,
So the loud torrent, and the whirlwind's roar,
But bind him to his native mountains more.

Such are the charms to barren states assign'd:
Their wants but few, their wishes all confined;
Yet let them only share the praises due,—
If few their wants, their pleasures are but few;
For every want that stimulates the breast,
Becomes a source of pleasure when redrest.
Hence from such lands each pleasing science flies,
That first excites desire, and then supplies;
Unknown to them, when sensual pleasures cloy,
To fill the languid pause with finer joy;
Unknown those powers that raise the soul to flame,
Catch every nerve, and vibrate through the frame.
Their level life is but a smouldering fire,
Nor quench'd by want, nor fann'd by strong desire;
Unfit for raptures, or, if raptures cheer
On some high festival of once a-year,
In wild excess the vulgar breast takes fire,
Till, buried in debauch, the bliss expire.
But not their joys alone thus coarsely flow,—
Their morals, like their pleasures, are but low;
For, as refinement stops, from sire to son
Unalter'd, unimproved the manners run;
And love's and friendship's finely pointed dart
Fall blunted from each indurated heart.
Some sterner virtues o'er the mountain's breast
May sit like falcons cowering on the nest;
But all the gentler morals,— such as play
Through life's more cultured walks, and charm the way,—
These, far dispersed, on timorous pinions fly,
To sport and flutter in a kinder sky.
To kinder skies, where gentler manners reign,

I turn; and France displays her bright domain.
Gay, sprightly land of mirth and social ease,
Pleased with thyself, whom all the world can please,
How often have I led thy sportive choir,
With tuneless pipe beside the murmuring Loire!
Where shading elms along the margin grew,
And freshen'd from the wave, the zephyr flew;
And haply, though my harsh touch flatt'ring still,
But mock'd all tune, and marr'd the dancer's skill;
Yet would the village praise my wondrous power,
And dance, forgetful of the noontide hour.
Alike all ages: dames of ancient days
Have led their children through the mirthful maze;
And the gay grandsire, skill'd in gestic lore,
Has frisk'd beneath the burden of threescore.
So blest a life these thoughtless realms display;
Thus idly busy rolls their world away:
Theirs are those arts that mind to mind endear,
For honor forms the social temper here:
Honor, that praise which real merit gains,
Or e'en imaginary worth obtains,
Here passes current; paid from hand to hand,
It shifts in splendid traffic round the land;
From courts to camps, to cottages it strays,
And all are taught an avarice of praise:
They please, are pleased; they give to get esteem;
Till, seeming blest, they grow to what they seem.
But while this softer art their bliss supplies,
It gives their follies also room to rise;
For praise too dearly loved, or warmly sought,
Enfeebles all internal strength of thought:

And the weak soul, within itself unblest,
Leans for all pleasure on another's breast.
Hence Ostentation here, with tawdry art,
Pants for the vulgar praise which fools impart;
Here Vanity assumes her pert grimace,
And trims her robes of frieze with copper lace;
Here beggar Pride defrauds her daily cheer,
To boast one splendid banquet once a-year:
The mind still turns where shifting fashion draws,
Nor weighs the solid worth of self-applause.
To men of other minds my fancy flies,
Embosom'd in the deep where Holland lies.
Methinks her patient sons before me stand,
Where the broad ocean leans against the land,
And, sedulous to stop the coming tide,
Lift the tall rampire's artificial pride.
Onward, methinks, and diligently slow,
The firm connected bulwark seems to grow,
Spreads its long arms amidst the watery roar,
Scoops out an empire, and usurps the shore;
While the pent Ocean, rising o'er the pile,
Sees an amphibious world beneath him smile;
The slow canal, the yellow-blossom'd vale,
The willow-tufted bank, the gliding sail,
The crowded mart, the cultivated plain,
A new creation rescued from his reign.
Thus, while around the wave-subjected soil
Impels the native to repeated toil,
Industrious habits in each bosom reign,
And industry begets a love of gain.
Hence all the good from opulence that springs,

With all those ills superflous treasure brings,
Are here display'd. Their much-loved wealth imparts
Convenience, plenty, elegance, and arts;
But view them closer, craft and fraud appear;
Even liberty itself is barter'd here;
At gold's superior charms all freedom flies,
The needy sell it, and the rich man buys.
A land of tyrants, and a den of slaves,
Here wretches seek dishonorable graves,
And, calmly bent, to servitude conform,
Dull as their lakes that slumber in the storm.
  Heavens! how unlike their Belgic sires of old!
Rough, poor, content, ungovernably bold,
War in each breast, and freedom on each brow;
How much unlike the sons of Britain now!
  Fired at the sound, my genius spreads her wing,
And flies where Britain courts the western spring;
Where lawns extend that scorn Arcadian pride,
And brighter streams than famed Hydaspes glide.
There all around the gentlest breezes stray,
There gentle music melts on every spray;
Creation's mildest charms are there combined,
Extremes are only in the master's mind!
Stern o'er each bosom Reason holds her state,
With daring aims irregularly great,
Pride in their port, defiance in their eye,
I see the lords of human kind pass by;
Intent on high designs, a thoughtful band,
By forms unfashion'd, fresh from nature's hand,
Fierce in their native hardiness of soul,
True to imagined right above control, —

While e'en the peasant boasts these rights to scan,
And learns to venerate himself as man.
Thine, Freedom, thine the blessings pictured here,
Thine are those charms that dazzle and endear!
Too blest indeed were such without alloy;
But, fostered e'en by Freedom, ills annoy;
That independence Britons prize too high,
Keeps man from man, and breaks the social tie;
The self-dependent lordlings stand alone,
All claims that bind and sweeten life unknown;
Here, by the bonds of nature feebly held,
Minds combat minds, repelling and repell'd;
Ferments arise, imprison'd factions roar,
Represt ambition struggles round her shore;
Till, overwrought, the general system feels
Its motion stop, or frenzy fire the wheels.
Nor this the worst. As Nature's ties decay,
As duty, love, and honor fail to sway,
Fictitious bonds, the bonds of wealth and law,
Still gather strength, and force unwilling awe.
Hence all obedience bows to these alone,
And talent sinks, and merit weeps unknown;
Till time may come, when stript of all her charms,
The land of scholars, and the nurse of arms,
Where noble stems transmit the patriot flame,
Where kings have toil'd, and poets wrote for fame,
One sink of level avarice shall lie,
And scholars, soldiers, kings, unhonor'd die.
But think not, thus when Freedom's ills I state,
I mean to flatter kings, or court the great:
Ye powers of truth, that bid my soul aspire,

Far from my bosom drive the low desire!
And thou, fair Freedom, taught alike to feel
The rabble's rage, and tyrant's angry steel;
Thou transitory flower, alike undone
By proud contempt, or favor's fostering sun —
Still may thy blooms the changeful clime endure!
I only would repress them to secure:
For just experience tells, in every soil,
That those that think must govern those that toil;
And all that Freedom's highest aims can reach,
Is but to lay proportion'd loads on each.
Hence, should one order disproportion'd grow,
Its double weight must ruin all below.
  Oh, then, how blind to all that truth requires,
Who think it freedom when a part aspires!
Calm is my soul, nor apt to rise in arms,
Except when fast approaching danger warms:
But when contending chiefs blockade the throne,
Contracting regal power to stretch their own;
When I behold a factious band agree
To call it freedom when themselves are free,
Each wanton judge new penal statutes draw,
Laws grind the poor, and rich men rule the law;
The wealth of climes, where savage nations roam,
Pillaged from slaves to purchase slaves at home, —
Fear, pity, justice, indignation, start,
Tear off reserve, and bare my swelling heart;
Till, half a patriot, half a coward grown,
I fly from petty tyrants to the throne.
  Yes, brother, curse with me that baleful hour,
When first ambition struck at regal power;

And thus, polluting honor in its source,
Gave wealth to sway the mind with double force.
Have we not seen, round Britain's peopled shore,
Her useful sons exchanged for useless ore?
Seen all her triumphs but destruction haste,
Like flaring tapers brightening as they waste?
Seen Opulence, her grandeur to maintain,
Lead stern Depopulation in her train,
And over fields, where scatter'd hamlets rose,
In barren, solitary pomp repose?
Have we not seen, at Pleasure's lordly call,
The smiling, long-frequented village fall?
Beheld the duteous son, the sire decay'd,
The modest matron, and the blushing maid,
Forced from their homes, a melancholy train,
To traverse climes beyond the western main,
Where wild Oswego spreads her swamps around,
And Niagara stuns with thundering sound?
  E'en now, perhaps, as there some pilgrim strays
Through tangled forests, and through dangerous ways,
Where beasts with man divided empire claim,
And the brown Indian marks with murderous aim;
There, while above the giddy tempest flies,
And all around distressful yells arise,
The pensive exile, bending with his woe,
To stop too fearful, and too faint to go,
Casts a long look where England's glories shine,
And bids his bosom sympathize with mine.
  Vain, very vain, my weary search to find
That bliss which only centres in the mind:
Why have I stray'd from pleasure and repose,

To seek a good each government bestows?
In every government, though terrors reign,
Though tyrant kings, or tyrant laws restrain,
How small, of all that human hearts endure,
That part which laws or kings can cause or cure?
Still to ourselves in every place consign'd,
Our own felicity we make or find:
With secret course which no loud storms annoy,
Glides the smooth current of domestic joy.
The lifted axe, the agonizing wheel,
Luke's iron crown, and Damien's bed of steel,
To men remote from power but rarely known,
Leave reason, faith, and conscience, all our own.

THE

DESERTED VILLAGE.

TO SIR JOSHUA REYNOLDS.

DEAR SIR. — I can have no expectations, in an address of this kind, either to add to your reputation, or to establish my own. You can gain nothing from my admiration, as I am ignorant of that art in which you are said to excel; and I may lose much by the severity of your judgment, as few have a juster taste in poetry than you. Setting interest, therefore, aside, to which I never paid much attention, I must be indulged at present in following my affections. The only dedication I ever made, was to my brother, because I loved him better than most other men. He is since dead. Permit me to inscribe this Poem to you.

How far you may be pleased with the versification and mere mechanical parts of this attempt, I do not pretend to inquire: but I know you will object (and, indeed, several of our best and wisest friends concur in the opinion), that the depopulation it deplores is no where to be seen, and the disorders it laments are only to be found in the poet's own imagination. To this I can scarcely make any other answer, than that I sincerely believe what I have written; that I have taken all possible pains, in my country excursions, for these four or five years past, to be certain of what I allege;

and that all my views and inquiries have led me to believe those miseries real, which I here attempt to display. But this is not the place to enter into an inquiry whether the country be depopulating or not: the discussion would take up much room, and I should prove myself, at best, an indifferent politician, to tire the reader with a long preface, when I want his unfatigued attention to a long poem.

In regretting the depopulation of the country, I inveigh against the increase of our luxuries; and here also I expect the shout of modern politicians against me. For twenty or thirty years past, it has been the fashion to consider luxury as one of the greatest national advantages; and all the wisdom of antiquity in that particular as erroneous. Still, however, I must remain a professed ancient on that head, and continue to think those luxuries prejudicial to states by which so many vices are introduced, and so many kingdoms have been undone. Indeed, so much has been poured out of late on the other side of the question, that merely for the sake of novelty and variety, one would sometimes wish to be in the right.

I am, dear Sir,

Your sincere friend, and ardent admirer,

OLIVER GOLDTMITH.

THE DESERTED VILLAGE.*

Sweet Auburn! loveliest village of the plain,
Where health and plenty cheer'd the laboring swain,
Where smiling spring its earliest visit paid,
And parting summer's lingering blooms delay'd:
Dear lovely bowers of innocence and ease,
Seats of my youth, when every sport could please,
How often have I loiter'd o'er thy green,
Where humble happiness endear'd each scene!
How often have I paused on every charm,
The shelter'd cot, the cultivated farm,
The never-failing brook, the busy mill,
The decent church that topt the neighboring hill,
The hawthorn bush, with seats beneath the shade,
For talking age and whispering lovers made!
How often have I blest the coming day,

* The locality of this poem is supposed to be Lissoy, near Ballymahan, where the poet's brother Henry had his living. As usual in such cases, the place afterwards became the fashionable resort of poetical pilgrims, and paid the customary penalty of furnishing relics for the curious. The *hawthorn bush* has been converted into snuff-boxes, and now adorns the cabinets of poetical virtuosi.

When toil remitting lent its turn to play,
And all the village train, from labor free,
Led up their sports beneath the spreading tree;
While many a pastime circled in the shade,
The young contending as the old survey'd;
And many a gambol frolick'd o'er the ground,
And slights of art and feats of strength went round;
And still as each repeated pleasure tired,
Succeeding sports the mirthful band inspired;
The dancing pair that simply sought renown
By holding out to tire each other down;
The swain mistrustless of his smutted face,
While secret laughter titter'd round the place;
The bashful virgin's sidelong looks of love,
The matron's glance that would those looks reprove:
These were thy charms, sweet village! sports, like these
With sweet succession, taught e'en toil to please;
These round thy bowers their cheerful influence shed,
These were thy charms — but all these charms are fled.
   Sweet smiling village, loveliest of the lawn,
Thy sports are fled, and all thy charms withdrawn!
Amidst thy bowers the tyrant's hand is seen,
And desolation saddens all thy green:
One only master grasps the whole domain,
And half a tillage stints thy smiling plain.
No more the grassy brook reflects the day,
But, choked with sedges, works its weedy way;
Along thy glades, a solitary guest,
The hollow-sounding bittern guards its nest;
Amidst thy desert walks the lapwing flies,
And tires their echoes with unvaried cries:

Sunk are thy bowers in shapless ruin all,
And the long grass o'ertops the mouldering wall;
And, trembling, shrinking from the spoiler's hand,
Far, far away thy children leave the land.
Ill fares the land, to hastening ills a prey,
Where wealth accumulates, and men decay;
Princes and lords may flourish, or may fade;
A breath can make them, as a breath has made;
But a bold peasantry, their country's pride,
When once destroyed, can never be supplied.
A time there was, ere England's griefs began,
When every rood of ground maintain'd its man:
For him light Labor spread her wholesome store,
Just gave what life required, but gave no more;
His best companions, innocence and health,
And his best riches, ignorance of wealth.
But times are alter'd: trade's unfeeling train
Usurp the land, and dispossess the swain;
Along the lawn, where scatter'd hamlets rose,
Unwieldy wealth and cumbrous pomp repose,
And every want to luxury allied,
And every pang that folly pays to pride.
Those gentle hours that plenty bade to bloom,
Those calm desires that ask'd but little room,
Those healthful sports that graced the peaceful scene,
Lived in each look, and brighten'd all the green,—
These, far departing, seek a kinder shore,
And rural mirth and manners are no more.
Sweet Auburn! parent of the blissful hour,
Thy glades forlorn confess the tyrant's power.
Here as I take my solitary rounds,

Amidst thy tangling walks and ruined grounds,
And, many a year elapsed, return to view
Where once the cottage stood, the hawthorn grew,
Remembrance wakes with all her busy train,
Swells at my breast, and turns the past to pain.
In all my wanderings round this world of care,
In all my griefs — and God has given my share —
I still had hopes, my latest hours to crown,
Amidst these humble bowers to lay me down;
To husband out life's taper at the close,
And keep the flame from wasting by repose:
I still had hopes — for pride attends us still —
Amidst the swains to shew my book-learn'd skill,
Around my fire an evening group to draw,
And tell of all I felt and all I saw;
And as a hare, whom hounds and horns pursue,
Pants to the place from whence at first she flew,
I still had hopes, my long vexations past,
Here to return and die at home at last.
O blest retirement, friend to life's decline,
Retreat from cares, that never must be mine!
How blest is he who crowns in shades like these,
A youth of labor with an age of ease;
Who quits a world where strong temptations try,
And, since 'tis hard to combat, learns to fly!
For him no wretches, born to work and weep,
Explore the mine, or tempt the dangerous deep;
No surly porter stands in guilty state,
To spurn imploring famine from the gate;
But on he moves to meet his latter end,
Angels around befriending virtue's friend;

Sinks to the grave with unperceived decay,
While resignation gently slopes the way;
And, all his prospects brightening to the last,
His heaven commences ere the world be past.
Sweet was the sound, when oft at evening's close,
Up yonder hill the village murmur rose;
There, as I past with careless steps and slow,
The mingling notes came soften'd from below;
The swain responsive as the milk-maid sung,
The sober herd that low'd to meet their young;
The noisy geese that gabbled o'er the pool,
The playful children just let loose from school;
The watch-dog's voice that bay'd the whispering wind,
And the loud laugh that spoke the vacant mind,—
These all in sweet confusion sought the shade,
And fill'd each pause the nightingale had made.
But now the sounds of population fail;
No cheerful murmurs fluctuate in the gale,
No busy steps the grass-grown footway tread,
But all the bloomy flush of life is fled:
All but yon widow'd, solitary thing,
That feebly bends beside the plashy spring;
She, wretched matron, forced in age, for bread,
To strip the brook with mantling cresses spread,
To pick her wintry fagot from the thorn,
To seek her nightly shed, and weep till morn;
She only left of all the harmless train,
The sad historian of the pensive plain.
Near yonder copse, where once the garden smiled,
And still where many a garden-flower grows wild,
There, where a few torn shrubs the place disclose,

The village preacher's modest mansion rose.
A man he was to all the country dear,
And passing rich with forty pounds a-year:
Remote from towns he ran his godly race,
Nor e'er had changed, nor wish'd to change, his place;
Unskilful he to fawn, or seek for power,
By doctrines fashion'd to the varying hour;
Far other aims his heart had learn'd to prize,
More bent to raise the wretched than to rise.
His house was known to all the vagrant train,
He chid their wanderings, but relieved their pain;
The long-remember'd beggar was his guest,
Whose beard descending swept his aged breast;
The ruin'd spendthrift, now no longer proud,
Claim'd kindred there, and had his claims allow'd;
The broken soldier, kindly bade to stay,
Sat by his fire, and talk'd the night away,
Wept o'er his wounds, or, tales of sorrow done,
Shoulder'd his crutch, and show'd how fields were won.
Pleased with his guests, the good man learn'd to glow,
And quite forgot their vices in their woe:
Careless their merits or their fautls to scan,
His pity gave ere charity began.
  Thus to relieve the wretched was his pride,
And e'en his failings lean'd to virtue's side;
But in his duty prompt at every call,
He watch'd and wept, he pray'd and felt, for all;
And, as a bird each fond endearment tries
To tempt its new-fledged offspring to the skies,
He tried each art, reproved each dull delay,
Allured to brighter worlds, and led the way.

Beside the bed where parting life was laid,
And sorrow, guilt, and pain, by turns dismay'd,
The reverend champion stood. At his control,
Despair and anguish fled the struggling soul;
Comfort came down the trembling wretch to raise,
And his last faltering accents whisper'd praise.
At church, with meek and unaffected grace,
His looks adorn'd the venerable place;
Truth from his lips prevail'd with double sway,
And fools who came to scoff, remain'd to pray.
The service past, around the pious man,
With ready zeal, each honest rustic ran;
E'en children follow'd, with endearing wile,
And pluck'd his gown, to share the good man's smile;
His ready smile a parent's warmth express'd;
Their welfare pleased him, and their cares distress'd;
To them his heart, his love, his griefs, were given,
But all his serious thoughts had rest in heaven.
As some tall cliff that lifts its awful form,
Swells from the vale, and midway leaves the storm,
Though round its breast the rolling clouds are spread,
Eternal sunshine settles on its head.
Beside yon straggling fence that skirts the way,
With blossom'd furze, unprofitably gay,
There in his noisy mansion, skill'd to rule,
The village master taught his little school.
A man severe he was, and stern to view;
I knew him well, and every truant knew:
Well had the boding tremblers learn'd to trace
The day's disasters in his morning face;
Full well they laugh'd, with countefeited glee,

At all his jokes, for many a joke had he;
Full well the busy whisper, circling round,
Convey'd the dismal tidings when he frown'd:
  Yet he was kind, or, if severe in aught,
The love he bore to learning was in fault.
The village all declared how much he knew,
'T was certain he could write and cipher too;
Lands he could measure, terms and tides presage,
And e'en the story ran — that he could gauge:
In arguing, too, the parson own'd his skill,
For e'en though vanquish'd, he could argue still;
While words of learned length and thund'ring sound,
Amazed the gazing rustics ranged around;
And still they gazed, and still the wonder grew,
That one small head could carry all he knew.
But past is all his fame. The very spot
Where many a time he triumph'd, is forgot.
  Near yonder thorn, that lifts its head on high,
Where once the sign-post caught the passing eye,
Low lies that house where nut-brown draughts inspired,
Where graybeard mirth, and smiling toil, retired,
Where village statesmen talk'd with looks profound,
And news much older than their ale went round.
Imagination fondly stoops to trace
The parlor splendors of that festive place:
The white-wash'd wall, the nicely-sanded floor,
The varnish'd clock that click'd behind the door;
The chest, contrived a double debt to pay,
A bed by night, a chest of draws by day;
The pictures placed for ornament and use,
The twelve good rules, the royal game of goose;

The hearth, except when winter chill'd the day,
With aspen boughs, and flowers, and fennel gay;
While broken tea cups, wisely kept for show,
Ranged o'er the chimney, glisten'd in a row.
Vain, transitory splendors! Could not all
Reprieve the tottering mansion from its fall?
Obscure it sinks, nor shall it more impart
An hour's importance to the poor man's heart:
Thither no more the peasant shall repair,
To sweet oblivion of his daily care;
No more the farmer's news, the barber's tale,
No more the woodman's ballad shall prevail;
No more the smith his dusky brow shall clear,
Relax his pond'rous strength, and learn to hear;
The host himself no longer shall be found
Careful to see the mantling bliss go round;
Nor the coy maid, half willing to be prest,
Shall kiss the cup to pass it to the rest.
Yes! let the rich deride, the proud disdain,
These simple blessings of the lowly train;
To me more dear, congenial to my heart,
One native charm, than all the gloss of art.
Spontaneous joys, where nature has its play,
The soul adopts, and owns their first-born sway;
Lightly they frolic o'er the vacant mind,
Unenvied, unmolested, unconfined:
But the long pomp, the midnight masquerade,
With all the freaks of wanton wealth array'd, —
In these, ere triflers half their wish obtain,
The toiling pleasure sickens into pain;
And, e'en while fashion's brightest arts decoy,

The heart, distrusting, asks if this be joy?
  Ye friends to truth, ye statesmen, who survey
The rich man's joys increase, the poor's decay,
'T is yours to judge how wide the limits stand
Between a splendid and a happy land.
Proud swells the tide with loads of freighted ore,
And shouting Folly hails them from her shore;
Hoards, e'en beyond the miser's wish, abound,
And rich men flock from all the world around.
Yet count our gains: this wealth is but a name
That leaves our useful products still the same.
Not so the loss: the man of wealth and pride
Takes up a space that many poor supplied;
Space for his lake, his park's extended bounds,
Space for his horses, equipage, and hounds:
The robe that wraps his limbs in silken sloth,
Has robb'd the neighboring fields of half their growth:
His seat, where solitary sports are seen,
Indignant spurns the cottage from the green;
Around the world each needful product flies,
For all the luxuries the world supplies:—
While thus the land, adorn'd for pleasure all,
In barren splendor feebly waits its fall.
  As some fair female, unadorn'd and plain,
Secure to please while youth confirms her reign,
Slights every borrow'd charm that dress supplies,
Nor shares with art the triumph of her eyes;
But when those charms are past — for charms are frail —
When time advances, and when lovers fail,
She then shines forth, solicitous to bless,
In all the glaring impotence of dress:

Thus fares the land, by luxury betray'd;
In nature's simplest charms at first array'd:
But verging to decline, its splendors rise,
Its vistas strike, its palaces surprise;
While, scourged by famine from the smiling land,
The mournful peasant leads his humble band;
And while he sinks, without one arm to save,
The country blooms — a garden and a grave.
Where, then, ah! where shall poverty reside,
To 'scape the pressure of contiguous pride?
If to some common's fenceless limits stray'd,
He drives his flock to pick the scanty blade,
Those fenceless fields the sons of wealth divide,
And e'en the bare-worn common is denied.
If to the city sped, what waits him there?
To see profusion that he must not share;
To see ten thousand baneful arts combined
To pamper luxury, and thin mankind;
To see each joy the sons of pleasure know
Extorted from his fellow-creatures' wo.
Here while the courtier glitters in brocade,
There the pale artist plies his sickly trade;
Here while the proud their long-drawn pomps display,
There the black gibbet glooms beside the way.
The dome where Pleasure holds her midnight reign,
Here, richly deck'd, admits the gorgeous train;
Tumultuous grandeur crowds the blazing square,
The rattling chariots clash, the torches glare.
Sure scenes like these no troubles e'er annoy!
Sure these denote one universal joy!
Are these thy serious thoughts? — Ah, turn thine eyes

Where the poor houseless shivering female lies:
She once, perhaps, in village plenty blest,
Has wept at tales of innocence distrest:
Her modest looks the cottage might adorn,
Sweet as the primrose peeps beneath the thorn:
Now lost to all — her friends, her virtue fled,
Near her betrayer's door she lays her head,
And, pinch'd with cold, and shrinking from the shower,
With heavy heart deplores that luckless hour,
When idly first, ambitious of the town,
She left her wheel, and robes of country brown.
Do thine, sweet Auburn, thine, the loveliest train,
Do thy fair tribes participate her pain?
E'en now, perhaps, by cold and hunger led,
At proud men's doors they ask a little bread!
Ah, no. To distant climes, a dreary scene,
Where half the convex-world intrudes between,
Through torrid tracts with fainting steps they go,
Where wild Altama * murmurs to their wo.
Far different there from all that charm'd before,
The various terrors of that horrid shore;
Those blazing suns that dart a downward ray,
And fiercely shed intolerable day;
Those matted woods where birds forget to sing,
But silent bats in drowsy clusters cling;
Those poisonous fields with rank luxuriance crown'd,
Where the dark scorpion gathers death around;
Where at each step the stranger fears to wake

* The Altama (or Altamaha) is a river in the province of Georgia, United States.

9

The rattling terrors of the vengeful snake;
Where crouching tigers wait their hapless prey,
And savage men, more murd'rous still than they;
While oft in whirls the mad tornado flies,
Mingling the ravaged landscape with the skies.
Far different these from every former scene,
The cooling brook, the grassy-vested green,
The breezy covert of the warbling grove,
That only shelter'd thefts of harmless love.
  Good Heaven! what sorrows gloom'd that parting day
That call'd them from their native walks away;
When the poor exiles, every pleasure past,
Hung round the bowers, and fondly look'd their last,
And took a long farewell, and wish'd in vain
For seats like these beyond the western main;
And shuddering still to face the distant deep,
Return'd and wept, and still return'd to weep!
The good old sire the first prepared to go
To new-found worlds, and wept for others' wo;
But for himself, in conscious virtue brave,
He only wish'd for worlds beyond the grave:
His lovely daughter, lovelier in her tears,
The fond companion of his helpless years,
Silent went next, neglectful of her charms,
And left a lover's for her father's arms:
With louder plaints the mother spoke her woes,
And blest the cot where every pleasure rose,
And kiss'd her thoughtless babes with many a tear,
And clasp'd them close, in sorrow doubly dear,
Whilst her fond husband strove to lend relief
In all the silent manliness of grief.

O luxury! thou curst by Heaven's decree,
How ill exchanged are things like these for thee!
How do thy potions, with insidious joy,
Diffuse their pleasures only to destroy!
Kingdoms by thee, to sickly greatness grown,
Boast of a florid vigor not their own:
At every draught more large and large they grow,
A bloated mass of rank unwieldy wo;
Till, sapp'd their strength, and every part unsound,
Down, Down they sink, and spread a ruin round.
E'en now the devastation is begun,
And half the business of destruction done;
E'en now, methinks, as pondering here I stand,
I see the rural Virtues leave the land.
Down where yon anchoring vessel spreads the sail
That idly waiting flaps with every gale,
Downward they move a melancholy band,
Pass from the shore and darken all the strand.
Contented Toil, and hospitable Care,
And kind connubial Tenderness, are there;
And Piety with wishes placed above,
And steady Loyalty, and faithful Love.
And thou, sweet Poetry, thou loveliest maid,
Still first to fly where sensual joys invade;
Unfit, in these degenerate times of shame,
To catch the heart, or strike for honest fame;
Dear charming nymph, neglected and decried,
My shame in crowds, my solitary pride;
Thou source of all my bliss, and all my woe,
That found'st me poor at first, and keep'st me so;
Thou guide, by which the nobler arts excel,

Thou nurse of every virtue, fare thee well!
Farewell; and oh! where'er thy voice be tried,
On Torno's cliffs, or Pambamarca's side,
Whether where equinoctial fervors glow,
Or winter wraps the polar world in snow,
Still let thy voice, prevailing over time,
Redress the rigors of th' inclement clime;
Aid slighted truth with thy persuasive strain;
Teach erring man to spurn the rage of gain;
Teach him, that states of native strength possest,
Though very poor, may still be very blest;
That trade's proud empire hastes to swift decay,
As ocean sweeps the labor'd mole away;
While self-dependent power can time defy,
As rocks resist the billows and the sky.

THE

THE HERMIT;

A BALLAD.

The following letter, addressed to the printer of the St. James's Chronicle, appeared in that paper in June, 1767.

Sir,—As there is nothing I dislike so much as newspaper controversy, particularly upon trifles, permit me to be as concise as possible in informing a correspondent of yours, that I recommended Blainville's Travels, because I thought the book was a good one, and I think so still. I said I was told by the bookseller that it was then first published; but in that, it seems, I was misinformed, and my reading was not extensive enough to set me right.

Another correspondent of yours accuses me of having taken a ballad I published some time ago, from one* by the ingenious Mr. Percy. I do not think there is any great resemblance between the two pieces in question. If there be any, his ballad is taken from mine. I read it to Mr. Percy some years ago; and he (as we both considered these things as trifles at best) told me with his usual good humor, the next time I saw him, that he had taken my plan to form the fragments of Shakspeare into a ballad of his own. He then read me his little Cen-

* Friar of Orders Gray. *Reliques of Ancient Poetry*, vol. i, book 2, No. 17.

to, if I may so call it, and I highly approved it. Such petty anecdotes as these are scarcely worth printing; and, were it not for the busy disposition of some of your correspondents, the public should never have known that he owes me the hint of his ballad, or that I am obliged to his frendship and learning for communications of a much more important nature.—I am, Sir, yours, etc. OLIVER GOLDSMITH.

THE HERMIT.

'TURN, gentle Hermit of the dale,
  And guide my lonely way,
To where yon taper cheers the vale
  With hospitable ray.

'For here forlorn and lost I tread,
  With fainting steps and slow,
Where wilds, immeasurably spread,
  Seem length'ning as I go.'

'Forbear, my son,' the Hermit cries,
  'To tempt the dangerous gloom;
For yonder faithless phantom flies
  To lure thee to thy doom.

'Here to the houseless child of want
  My door is open still;
And though my portion is but scant,
  I give it with good will.

'Then turn to-night, and freely share
  Whate'er my cell bestows;
My rushy couch and frugal fare,
  My blessing and repose.

'No flocks that range the valley free,
To slaughter I condemn;
'Taught by that Power that pities me,
I learn to pity them:

'But from the mountain's grassy side,
A guiltless feast I bring;
A scrip with herbs and fruits supplied,
And water from the spring.

'Then, pilgrim, turn, thy cares forego;
All earth-born cares are wrong:
Man wants but little here below,
Nor wants that little long.'

Soft as the dew from heaven descends,
His gentle accents fell:
The modest stranger lowly bends,
And follows to the cell.

Far in a wilderness obscure,
The lonely mansion lay,
A refuge to the neighb'ring poor,
And strangers led astray.

No stores beneath its humble thatch
Required a master's care;
The wicket, opening with a latch,
Received the harmless pair.

And now, when busy crowds retire
To take their evening rest,
The Hermit trimm'd his little fire,
And cheer'd his pensive guest:

And spread his vegetable store,
And gaily press'd and smiled;
And, skill'd in legendary lore,
The lingering hours beguiled.

Around, in sympathetic mirth,
Its tricks the kitten tries,
The cricket chirrups on the hearth,
The crackling fagot flies.

But nothing could a charm impart
To soothe the stranger's woe;
For grief was heavy at his heart,
And tears began to flow.

His rising cares the Hermit spied,
With answering care oppress'd:
And, 'Whence unhappy youth,' he cried,
'The sorrows of thy breast?

'From better habitations spurn'd,
Reluctant dost thou rove?
Or grieve for friendship unreturn'd,
Or unregarded love?

'Alas! the joys that fortune brings,
Are trifling, and decay;
And those who prize the paltry things,
More trifling still than they.

'And what is friendship but a name,
A charm that lulls to sleep;
A shade that follows wealth or fame,
But leaves the wretch to weep?

'And love is still an emptier sound,
The modern fair one's jest;
'On earth unseen, or only found
To warm the turtle's nest.

'For shame, fond youth, thy sorrows hush,
And spurn the sex,' he said;
But while he spoke, a rising blush
His love-lorn guest betray'd.

Surprised, he sees new beauties rise,
Swift mantling to the view;
Like colors o'er the morning skies,
As bright, as transient too.

The bashful look, the rising breast,
Alternate spread alarms:
The lovely stranger stands confess'd,
A maid in all her charms.

And, 'Ah! forgive a stranger rude —
A wretch forlorn,' she cried:
'Whose feet unhallow'd thus intrude
Where heaven and you reside.

'But let a maid thy pity share,
Whom love has taught to stray;
Who seeks for rest, but finds despair
Companion of her way.

'My father lived beside the Tyne,
A wealthy lord was he:
And all his wealth was mark'd as mine,
He had but only me.

'To win me from his tender arms,
Unnumber'd suitors came,
Who praised me for imputed charms,
And felt, or feign'd, a flame.

'Each hour a mercenary crowd
With richest proffers strove;
Amongst the rest young Edwin bow'd,
But never talk'd of love.

'In humble, simplest habit clad,
No wealth nor power had he;
Wisdom and worth were all he had,
But these were all to me.

'And when, beside me in the dale,
He caroll'd lays of love,
His breath lent fragrance to the gale,
And music to the grove. *

The blossom opening to the day,
The dews of heaven refined,
Could nought of purity display
To emulate his mind.

'The dew, the blossom on the tree,
With charms inconstant shine;
Their charms were his, but, wo to me,
Their constancy was mine.

* This stanza was preserved by Richard Archdale, Esq., a member of the Irish Parliament, to whom it was given by Goldsmith, and was first inserted after the author's death.

'For still I tried each fickle art,
  Importunate and vain;
And while his passion touch'd my heart,
  I triumph'd in his pain;

'Till, quite dejected with my scorn,
  He left me to my pride;
And sought a solitude forlorn,
  In secret, where he died.

'But mine the sorrow, mine the fault,
  And well my life shall pay;
I'll seek the solitude he sought,
  And stretch me where he lay.

'And there forlorn, despairing, hid,
  I'll lay me down and die;
'Twas so for me that Edwin did,
  And so for him will I.'

'Forbid it, Heaven!' the Hermit cried,
  And clasp'd her to his breast;
The wondering fair one turn'd to chide —
  'Twas Edwin's self that press'd!

'Turn, Angelina, ever dear,
  My charmer, turn to see
Thy own, thy long-lost Edwin here,
  Restored to love and thee.

'Thus let me hold thee to my heart,
  And every care resign:
And shall we never, never part,
  My life — my all that's mine.

No, never from this hour to part
  We'll live and love so true,
The sigh that rends thy constant heart
  Shall break thy Edwin's too.

THE HAUNCH OF VENISON.*

A POETICAL EPISTLE TO LORD CLARE.

THANKS, my lord, for your venison, for finer or fatter
Ne'er ranged in a forest, or smoked in a platter.
The haunch was a picture for painters to study,
The fat was so white, and the lean was so ruddy;
Though my stomach was sharp, I could scarce help
regretting
To spoil such a delicate picture by eating:
I had thoughts, in my chamber to place it in view,
To be shewn to my friends as a piece of virtu;
As in some Irish houses, where things are so so,
One gammon of bacon hangs up for a show;
But for eating a rasher of what they take pride in,
They'd as soon think of eating the pan it is fried in.
But hold—let me pause—don't I hear you pronounce,
This tale of the bacon's a damnable bounce?
Well, suppose it a bounce—sure a poet may try,
By a bounce now and then, to get courage to fly.
But, my lord, it's no bounce: I protest, in my turn,

* The description of the dinner party in this poem is imitated from Boileau's fourth Satire. Boileau himself took the hint from Horace, Lib. ii. Sat. 8, which has also been imitated by Regnier, Sat. 10.

It's a truth, and your lordship may ask Mr. Burn.*
To go on with my tale: as I gazed on the haunch,
I thought of a friend that was trusty and staunch,
So I cut it, and sent it to Reynolds undrest,
To paint it, or eat it, just as he liked best.
Of the neck and the breast I had next to dispose —
'Twas a neck and a breast that might rival Munroe's;
But in parting with these I was puzzled again,
With the how, and the who, and the where, and the
when.
There's H—d, and C—y, and H—rth, and H—ff,
I think they love venison — I know they love beef;
There's my countryman, Higgins — oh, let him alone
For making a blunder, or picking a bone:
But, hang it! to poets who seldom can eat
Your very good mutton's a very good treat;
Such dainties to them their health it might hurt;
It's like sending them ruffles, when wanting a shirt.
While thus I debated, in reverie centred,
An acquaintance — a friend, as he call'd himself —
enter'd;
An under-bred, fine-spoken fellow was he,
And he smiled as he looked at the venison and me, —
'What have you got here? — Why, this is good eating!
Your own, I suppose — or is it in waiting?'
'Why, whose should it be?' cried I, with a flounce,
'I get these things often' — but that was a bounce:
'Some lords, my acquaintance, that settle the nation,
Are pleased to be kind — but I hate ostentation.'

* Lord Clare's nephew.

'If that be the case, then,' cried he, very gay,
'I'm glad I have taken this house in my way:
To-morrow you take a poor dinner with me;
No words — I insist on't — precisely at three;
We'll have Johnson, and Burke, — all the wits will be
there:
My acquaintance is slight, or I'd ask my Lord Clare.
And, now that I think on't, as I am a sinner,
We wanted this venison to make out a dinner.
What say you — a pasty? it shall, and it must,
And my wife, little Kitty, is famous for crust.
Here, porter — this venison with me to Mile-end:
No stirring, I beg — my dear friend, — my dear friend!
Thus, snatching his hat, he brush'd off like the wind,
And the porter and eatables follow'd behind.
Left alone to reflect, having emptied my shelf,
And 'nobody with me at sea but myself;'*
Though I could not help thinking my gentleman hasty,
Yet Johnson, and Burke, and a good venison pasty,
Were things that I never disliked in my life,
Though clogg'd with a coxcomb, and Kitty his wife.
So next day, in due splendour to make my approach,
I drove to his door in my own hackney-coach.
When come to the place where we all were to dine,
(A chair-lumbered closet, just twelve feet by nine),
My friend bade me welcome, but struck me quite dumb
With tidings that Johnson and Burke would not come;
'For I knew it,' he cried, 'both eternally fail,

* See the letters that passed between his Royal Highness Henry Duke of Cumberland, and Lady Grosvenor. 12mo. 1769.

The one with his speeches, and t'other with Thrale: *
But no matter, I'll warrant we'll make up the party
With two full as clever, and ten times as hearty.
The one is a Scotchman, the other a Jew:
They're both of them merry, and authors like you:
The one writes the Snarler, the other the Scourge;
Some thinks he writes Cinna — he owns to Panurge.'
While thus he described them, by trade and by name,
They enter'd, and dinner was served as they came.
  At the top, a fried liver and bacon were seen;
At the bottom, was tripe in a swinging tureen;
At the sides, there was spinage, and pudding made hot;
In the middle, a place where the pasty — was not.
Now, my lord, as for tripe, it's my utter aversion,
And your bacon I hate like a Turk or a Persian;
So there I sat stuck like a horse in a pound,
While the bacon and liver went merrily round:
But what vex'd me most was that d——'d Scottish rogue,
With his long-winded speeches, his smiles, and his brogue;
And, 'Madam,' quoth he, 'may this bit be my poison,
A prettier dinner I never set eyes on:
Pray, a slice of your liver, though may I be curst,
But I've ate of your tripe till I'm ready to burst.'
'The tripe!' quoth the Jew, with his chocolate cheek,
'I could dine on this tripe seven days in a week:
I like these here dinners, so pretty and small;

* An eminent London brewer, M. P. for the borough of Southwark, at whose table Dr. Johnson was a frequent guest.

But your friend there, the Doctor, eats nothing at all.
'O ho!' quoth my friend, 'he'll come on in a trice.
He's keeping a corner for something that's nice:
There's a pasty.' — 'A pasty!' repeated the Jew,
'I don't care if I keep a corner for't too.'
'What the deil mon, a pasty!' re-echoed the Scot,
'Though splitting, I'll still keep a corner for that.'
'We'll all keep a corner,' the lady cried out;
'We'll all keep a corner,' was echo'd about.
While thus we resolved, and the pasty delay'd,
With looks that quite petrified, enter'd the maid:
A visage so sad, and so pale with affright,
Waked Priam, in drawing his curtains by night.
But we quickly found out — for who could mistake her? —
That she came with some terrible news from the baker:
And so it fell out; for that negligent sloven
Had shut out the pasty on shutting his oven.
Sad Philomel thus — but let similes drop —
And now that I think on't, the story may stop.
To be plain, my good lord, it's but labor misplaced,
To send such good verses to one of your taste:
You've got an odd something — a kind of discerning,
A relish — a taste — sicken'd over by learning;
At least it's your temper, as very well known,
That you think very slightly of all that's your own.
So, perhaps, in your habits of thinking amiss,
You may make a mistake, and think slightly of this.

RETALIATION.

Dr. Goldsmith and some of his friends occasionally dined at the St. James's Coffeehouse. One day, it was proposed to write epitaphs on him. His country, dialect, and person, furnished subjects of witticism. He was called on for *Retaliation*, and, at their next meeting, produced the following poem.

Of old, when Scarron his companions invited,
Each guest brought his dish, and the feast was united;
If our landlord * supplies us with beef and with fish,
Let each guest bring himself, and he brings the best dish;
Our Dean † shall be venison, just fresh from the plains;
Our Burke ‡ shall be tongue, with a garnish of brains;
Our Will § shall be wild-fowl of excellent flavor,
And Dick ‖ with his pepper shall heighten the savor;

* The master of the St. James's Coffeehouse, where the Doctor and the friends he has characterized in this poem, occasionally dined.

† Doctor Barnard, Dean of Derry, in Ireland, afterwards Bishop of Killaloe.

‡ The Right Hon. Edmund Burke.

§ Mr. William Burke, formerly secretary to General Conway, and member for Bedwin.

‖ Mr. Richard Burke, collector of Granada.

Our Cumberland's * sweetbread its place shall obtain,
And Douglas † is pudding, substantial and plain;
Our Garrick's ‡ a salad, for in him we see
Oil, vinegar, sugar, and saltness agree:
To make out the dinner, full certain I am,
That Ridge § is anchovy, and Reynolds ‖ is lamb;
That Hickey's ¶ a capon, and, by the same rule,
Magnanimous Goldsmith a gooseberry fool.
At a dinner so various — at such a repast,
Who'd not be a glutton, and stick to the last?
Here, waiter, more wine, let me sit while I'm able,
Till all my companions sink under the table;
Then, with chaos and blunders encircling my head,
Let me ponder, and tell what I think of the dead.
Here lies the good Dean, reunited to earth,
Who mixed reason with pleasure, and wisdom with
mirth:
If he had any faults, he has left us in doubt —
At least, in six weeks I could not find 'em out;
Yet some have declared, and it can't be denied 'em,
That sly-boots was cursedly cunning to hide 'em.

* Mr. Richard Cumberland, author of *The West Indian*, *The Jew*, and other dramatic works.

† Doctor Douglas, Canon of Windsor, and afterwards Bishop of Salisbury, was himself a natvie of Scotland, and obtained considerable reputation by his detection of the forgeries of his countrymen, Lauder and Bower.

‡ David Garrick, Esq.

§ Counsellor John Ridge, a gentleman belonging to the Irish bar.

‖ Sir Joshua Reynolds.

¶ An eminent attorney.

Here lies our good Edmund, whose genius was such,
We scarcely can praise it or blame it too much;
Who, born for the universe, narrow'd his mind,
And to party gave up what was meant for mankind:
Though fraught with all learning, yet straining his throat,
To persuade Tommy Townshend * to lend him a vote;
Who, too deep for his hearers, still went on refining,
And thought of convincing, while they thought of
dining: †
Though equal to all things, for all things unfit;
Too nice for a statesman, too proud for a wit;
For a patriot, too cool; for a drudge disobedient;
And too fond of the *right* to pursue the *expedient*.
In short, 'twas his fate, unemploy'd or in place, sir,
To eat mutton cold, and cut blocks with a razor.
Here lies honest William, whose heart was a mint,
While the owner ne'er knew half the good that was in't:
The pupil of impulse, it forced him along,
His conduct still right, with his argument wrong;
Still aiming at honor, yet fearing to roam,
The coachman was tipsy, the chariot drove home.
Would you ask for his merits? alas! he had none;
What was good was spontaneous, his faults were his own.

* Mr. T. Townshend, member for Whitchurch, afterwards Lord Sydney.

† Mr. Burke's speeches in Parliament, though distinguished by all the force of reasoning and eloquence of their highly-gifted author, were not always listened to with patience by his brother members, who not unfrequently took the opportunity of retiring to dinner when he rose to speak. To this circumstance, which procured for the orator the *sobriquet* of the *Dinner Bell*, allusion is here made.

Here lies honest Richard, whose fate I must sigh at;
Alas, that such frolic should now be so quiet!
What spirits were his! what wit and what whim!
Now breaking a jest, and now breaking a limb! *
Now wrangling and grumbling to keep up the ball!
Now teasing and vexing, yet laughing at all!
In short, so provoking a devil was Dick,
That we wish'd him full ten times a-day at Old Nick.
But missing his mirth and agreeable vein,
As often we wish'd to have Dick back again.
Here Cumberland lies, having acted his parts,
The Terence of England, the mender of hearts;
A flattering painter, who made it his care
To draw men as they ought to be, not as they are.
His gallants are all faultless, his women divine,
And Comedy wonders at being so fine;
Like a tragedy queen he has dizen'd her out,
Or rather like Tragedy giving a rout.
His fools have their follies so lost in a crowd
Of virtues and feelings, that Folly grows proud;
And coxcombs, alike in their failings alone,
Adopting his portraits, are pleased with their own.
Say, where has our poet this malady caught,
Or wherefore his characters thus without fault?
Say, was it, that vainly directing his view
To find out men's virtues, and finding them few,
Quite sick of pursuing each troublesome elf,

* Mr. Richard Burke having slightly fractured an arm and a leg at different times, the Doctor has rallied him on these accidents, as a kind of retributive justice, for breaking jests upon other people.

He grew lazy at last, and drew from himself?
Here Douglas retires from his toils to relax,
The scourge of impostors, the terror of quacks:
Come, all ye quack bards, and ye quacking divines,
Come, and dance on the spot where your tyrant reclines:
When satire and censure encircled his throne,
I fear'd for your safety, I fear'd for my own;
But now he is gone, and we want a detector,
Our Dodds * shall be pious, our Kenricks † shall lecture;
Macpherson ‡ write bombast, and call it a style;
Our Townshend make speeches, and I shall compile:
New Lauders § and Bowers ‖ the Tweed shall cross over,
No countryman living their tricks to discover;
Detection her taper shall quench to a spark,
And Scotchman meet Scotchman, and cheat in the dark.
Here lies David Garrick, describe him who can,

* The Rev. Dr. Dodd, who was executed for forgery.

† Dr. Kenrick, who read lectures at the Devil Tavern, under the title of 'The School of Shakspeare.' He was a well-known writer, of prodigious versatility, and some talent. Dr. Johnson observed of him, 'He is one of the many who have made themselves *public*, without making themselves known.'

‡ James Macpherson, Esq., who from the mere force of his style, wrote down the first poet of all antiquity.

§ William Lauder, who, by interpolating certain passages from the Adamus Exul of Grotius, with translations from Paradise Lost, endeavored to fix on Milton a charge of plagiarism from the modern Latin poets. Dr. Douglas detected and exposed this imposture, and extorted from the author a confession and apology.

‖ Archibald Bower, a Scottish Jesuit, and author of a History of the Popes from St. Peter to Lambertini. Dr. Douglas convicted Bower of gross imposture, and totally destroyed the credit of his history.

An abridgment of all that was pleasant in man;
As an actor, confess'd without rival to shine,
As a wit, if not first, in the very first line:
Yet, with talents like these, and an excellent heart
The man had his failings, a dupe to his art.
Like an ill-judging beauty, his colors he spread,
And beplaster'd with rouge his own natural red.
On the stage he was natural, simple, affecting;
'Twas only that when he was off he was acting.
With no reason on earth to go out of his way,
He turn'd and he varied full ten times a day:
Though secure of our hearts, yet confoundedly sick
If they were not his own by finessing and trick:
He cast off his friends, as a huntsman his pack,
For he knew when he pleased he could whistle them back.
Of praise a mere glutton, he swallow'd what came,
And the puff of a dunce he mistook it for fame;
Till his relish, grown callous almost to disease,
Who pepper'd the highest was surest to please.
But let us be candid, and speak out our mind,
If dunces applauded, he paid them in kind.
Ye Kenricks, ye Kellys,* and Woodfalls † so grave,
What a commerce was yours, while you got and you
gave!
How did Grub-street re-echo the shouts that you raised,
While he was be-Roscius'd, and you were be-praised!
But peace to his spirit, wherever it flies,
To act as an angel and mix with the skies:

* Mr. Hugh Kelley, originally a staymaker, afterwards a newspaper editor and dramatist, and latterly a barrister.

† Mr. William Woodfall, printer of the *Morning Chronicle.*

Those poets who owe their best fame to his skill,
Shall still be his flatterers, go where he will;
Old Shakspeare receive him with praise and with love,
And Beaumonts and Bens be his Kelleys above.
  Here Hickey reclines, a most blunt, pleasant creature,
And slander itself must allow him good nature;
He cherish'd his friend, and he relish'd a bumper;
Yet one fault he had, and that one was a thumper.
Perhaps you may ask if the man was a miser?
I answer, No, no, for he always was wiser.
Too courteous, perhaps, or obligingly flat?
His very worst foe can't accuse him of that.
Perhaps he confided in men as they go,
And so was too foolishly honest? Ah, no!
Then what was his failing? come tell it, and burn ye:
He was, could he help it? a special attorney.
  Here Reynolds is laid, and, to tell you my mind,
He has not left a wiser or better behind;
His pencil was striking, resistless, and grand,
His manners were gentle, complying, and bland:
Still born to improve us in every part,
His pencil our faces, his manners our heart.
To coxcombs averse, yet most civilly steering,
When they judged without skill, he was still hard of hearing:
When they talked of their Raphaels, Corregios, and stuff,
He shifted his trumpet,* and only took snuff.

* Sir Joshua Reynolds was so deaf as to be under the necessity of using an ear-trumpet in company.

POSTSCRIPT.

After the fourth edition of this poem was printed, the publisher received the following epitaph on Mr. Whitefoord,* from a friend of the late Dr. Goldsmith.

Here Whitefoord reclines, and, deny it who can,
Though he merrily lived, he is now a grave man: †
Rare compound of oddity, frolic, and fun!
Who relish'd a joke, and rejoiced in a pun;
Whose temper was generous, open, sincere;
A stranger to flattery, a stranger to fear;
Who scatter'd around wit and humor at will;
Whose daily *bon mots* half a column might fill:
A Scotchman, from pride and from prejudice free;
A scholar, yet surely no pedant was he.
What pity, alas! that so liberal a mind
Should so long be to newspaper essays confined!
Who perhaps to the summit of science could soar,
Yet content if 'the table he set in a roar:'
Whose talents to fill any station were fit,
Yet happy if Woodfall ‡ confess'd him a wit.
Ye newspaper witlings, ye pert scribbling folks!
Who copied his squibs, and re-echoed his jokes;
Ye tame imitators, ye servile herd, come,
Still follow your master, and visit his tomb;
To deck it, bring with you festoons of the vine,

* Mr. Caleb Whitefoord, author of many humorous essays.

† Mr. Whitefoord was so notorious a punster, that Dr. Goldsmith used to say it was impossible to keep him company, without being infected with the itch of punning.

‡ Mr. H. S. Woodfall, printer of the *Public Advertiser*.

And copious libations bestow on his shrine;
Then strew all around it (you can do no less)
Cross Readings, *Ship News*, and *Mistakes of the Press.**
  Merry Whitefoord, farewell! for thy sake I admit
That a Scot may have humor, I had almost said wit;
This debt to thy memory I cannot refuse,
'Thou best-humor'd man with the worst-humor'd Muse.'

THE

DOUBLE TRANSFORMATION.

A TALE.

SECLUDED from domestic strife,
Jack Book-worm led a college life;
A fellowship at twenty-five
Made him the happiest man alive;
He drank his glass, and cracked his joke,
And freshmen wonder'd as he spoke.
  Such pleasures, unalloy'd with care,
Could any accident impair?
Could Cupid's shaft at length transfix
Our swain, arrived at thirty-six?
  Oh, had the archer ne'er come down
To ravage in a country town!
Or Flavia been content to stop

* Mr. Whitefoord had frequently indulged the town with humorous pieces under those titles in the *Public Advertiser*.

At triumphs in a Fleet Street shop!
Oh, had her eyes forgot to blaze!
Or Jack had wanted eyes to gaze!
Oh! — but let exclamation cease,
Her presence banished all his peace;
So with decorum all things carried,
Miss frown'd, and blush'd, and then was — married
  Need we expose to vulgar sight
The raptures of the bridal night?
Need we intrude on hallow'd ground,
Or draw the curtains closed around?
Let it suffice that each had charms:
He clasped a goddess in his arms;
And though she felt his usage rough,
Yet in a man 'twas well enough.
  The honey-moon like lightning flew,
The second brought its transports too;
A third, a fourth, were not amiss,
The fifth was friendship mixed with bliss:
But, when a twelvemonth passed away,
Jack found his goddess made of clay;
Found half the charms that deck'd her face
Arose from powder, shreds, or lace;
But still the worst remain'd behind, —
That very face had robb'd her mind.
  Skill'd in no other arts was she,
But dressing, patching, repartee;
And, just as humor rose or fell,
By turns a slattern or a belle.
'Tis true she dressed with modern grace,
Half naked, at a ball or race;

But when at home, at board or bed,
Five greasy nightcaps wrapp'd her head.
Could so much beauty condescend
To be a dull, domestic friend?
Could any curtain-lectures bring
To decency so fine a thing!
In short, by night, 'twas fits or fretting;
By day, 'twas gadding or coquetting.
Fond to be seen, she kept a bevy
Of powder'd coxcombs at her levee;
The squire and captain took their stations,
And twenty other near relations:
Jack suck'd his pipe, and often broke
A sigh in suffocating smoke;
While all their hours were pass'd between
Insulting repartee and spleen.
  Thus, as her faults each day were known,
He thinks her features coarser grown;
He fancies every vice she shews,
Or thins her lips, or points her nose:
Whenever rage or envy rise,
How wide her mouth, how wild her eyes!
He knows not how, but so it is,
Her face is grown a knowing phiz;
And, though her fops are wondrous civil,
He thinks her ugly as the devil.
  Now, to perplex the ravell'd noose,
As each a different way pursues,
While sullen or loquacious strife
Promised to hold them on for life,
That dire disease, whose ruthless power

Withers the beauty's transient flower,—
Lo! the small pox, with horrid glare,
Levell'd its terrors at the fair;
And, rifling every youthful grace,
Left but the remnant of a face.
  The glass, grown hateful to her sight,
Reflected now a perfect fright:
Each former art she vainly tries
To bring back lustre to her eyes;
In vain she tries her paste and creams
To smooth her skin, or hide its seams;
Her country beaux and city cousins,
Lovers no more, flew off by dozens;
The squire himself was seen to yield,
And e'en the captain quit the field.
  Poor madam, now condemn'd to hack
The rest of life with anxious Jack,
Perceiving others fairly flown,
Attempted pleasing him alone.
Jack soon was dazzled to behold
Her present face surpass the old:
With modesty her cheeks are dyed,
Humility displaces pride;
For tawdry finery is seen
A person ever neatly clean;
No more presuming on her sway,
She learns good nature every day:
Serenely gay, and strict in duty,
Jack finds his wife a perfect beauty.

THE GIFT.*

TO IRIS, IN BOW STREET, COVENT GARDEN.

Say, cruel Iris, pretty rake,
  Dear mercenary beauty,
What annual offering shall I make
  Expressive of my duty?

My heart, a victim to thine eyes,
  Should I at once deliver,
Say, would the angry fair one prize
  The gift, who slights the giver?

A bill, a jewel, watch, or toy,
  My rivals give — and let 'em:
If gems, or gold, impart a joy,
  I'll give them — when I get 'em.

I'll give — but not the full-blown rose,
  Or rose-bud more in fashion;
Such short-lived offerings but disclose
  A transitory passion —

I'll give thee something yet unpaid,
  Not less sincere than civil, —
I'll give thee — ah! too charming maid! —
  I'll give thee — to the Devil!

* Imitated from Grecourt, a witty French poet.

AN ELEGY ON THE DEATH OF A MAD DOG.

Good people all, of every sort,
  Give ear unto my song,
And if you find it wondrous short,
  It cannot hold you long.

In Islington there was a man,
  Of whom the world might say,
That still a godly race he ran,
  Whene'er he went to pray.

A kind and gentle heart he had,
  To comfort friends and foes:
The naked every day he clad,
  When he put on his clothes.

And in that town a dog was found,
  As many dogs there be,
Both mongrel, puppy, whelp, and hound,
  And curs of low degree.

This dog and man at first were friends;
  But when a pique began,
The dog, to gain his private ends,
  Went mad, and bit the man.

Around from all the neighboring streets
  The wond'ring neighbors ran,
And swore the dog had lost his wits,
  To bite so good a man.

The wound it seem'd both sore and sad
  To every Christian eye;
And while they swore the dog was mad,
  They swore the man would die.

But soon a wonder came to light,
  That show'd the rogues they lied:
The man recover'd of the bite —
  The dog it was that died.

THE LOGICIANS REFUTED.*

IN IMITATION OF DEAN SWIFT.

LOGICIANS have but ill defined
As rational the human mind:
Reason, they say, belongs to man,
But let them prove it if they can.
Wise Aristotle and Smiglesius,
By ratiocinations specious,
Have strove to prove with great precision,
With definition and division,
Homo est ratione preditum;
But for my soul I cannot credit 'em;
And must in spite of them maintain,
That man and all his ways are vain;
And that this boasted lord of nature
Is both a weak and erring creature;

* This happy imitation was adopted by his Dublin publisher, as a genuine poem of Swift, and as such it has been reprinted in almost every edition of the Dean's works. Even Sir Walter Scott has inserted it without any remark in his edition of Swift's Works.

That instinct is a surer guide
Than reason, boasting mortals' pride;
And that brute beasts are far before 'em —
Deus est anima brutorum.
Who ever knew an honest brute
At law his neighbor prosecute,
Bring action for assault and battery?
Or friend beguile with lies and flattery?
O'er plains they ramble unconfined,
No politics disturb their mind;
They eat their meals, and take their sport,
Nor know who's in or out at court:
They never to the levee go
To treat as dearest friend a foe;
They never importune his grace,
Nor ever cringe to men in place;
Nor undertake a dirty job,
Nor draw the quill to write for Bob.*
Fraught with invective they ne'er go
To folks at Paternoster Row:
No judges, fiddlers, dancing-masters,
No pickpockets, or poetasters,
Are known to honest quadrupeds;
No single brute his fellow leads.
Brutes never meet in bloody fray,
Nor cut each other's throats for pay.
Of beasts, it is confess'd, the ape
Comes nearest us in human shape:
Like man, he imitates each fashion,

* Sir Robert Walpole.

And malice is his ruling passion:
But both in malice and grimaces,
A courtier any ape surpasses.
Behold him humbly cringing wait
Upon the minister of state;
View him soon after to inferiors
Aping the conduct of superiors:
He promises with equal air,
And to perform takes equal care.
He in his turn finds imitators;
At court the porters, lacqueys, waiters,
Their masters' manners still contract,
And footmen, lords and dukes can act.
Thus at the court, both great and small
Behave alike, for all ape all.

A NEW SIMILE.

IN THE MANNER OF SWIFT.

Long had I sought in vain to find
A likeness for the scribbling kind —
The modern scribbling kind, who write
In wit, and sense, and nature's spite —
Till reading — I forgot what day on —
A chapter out of Tooke's Pantheon,
I think I met with something there
To suit my purpose to a hair.
But let us not proceed too furious, —
First please to turn to god Mercurius;
You'll find him pictured at full length,

In book the second, page the tenth;
The stress of all my proofs on him I lay,
And now proceed we to our simile.
Imprimis, pray observe his hat,
Wings upon either side — mark that.
Well! what is it from thence we gather?
Why, these denote a brain of feather.
A brain of feather! very right;
With wit that's flighty, learning light;
Such as to modern bard's decreed:
A just comparison — proceed.
In the next place, his feet peruse,
Wings grow again from both his shoes;
Design'd, no doubt, their part to bear,
And waft his godship through the air:
And here my simile unites;
For in a modern poet's flights,
I'm sure it may be justly said,
His feet are useful as his head.
Lastly, vouchsafe t' observe his hand,
Fill'd with a snake-encircled wand,
By classic authors term'd caduceus,
And highly famed for several uses:
To wit, — most wondrously endued,
No poppy-water half so good;
For let folks only get a touch,
Its soporific virtue's such,
Though ne'er so much awake before,
That quickly they begin to snore;
Add, too, what certain writers tell,
With this he drives men's souls to hell.

Now, to apply, begin we then:—
His wand's a modern author's pen;
The serpents round about it twin'd
Denote him of the reptile kind,
Denote the rage with which he writes,
His frothy slaver, venom'd bites;
An equal semblance still to keep,
Alike, too, both conduce to sleep;
This difference only, as the god
Drove souls to Tart'rus with his rod,
With his goose-quill the scribbling elf,
Instead of others, damns himself.
And here my simile almost tript,
Yet grant a word by way of postcript.
Moreover, Merc'ry had a failing;
Well! what of that? out with it — stealing
In which all modern bards agree,
Being each as great a thief as he.
But e'en this deity's existence
Shall lend my simile assistance:
Our modern bards! why, what a pox,
Are they but senseless stones and blocks?

DESCRIPTION OF AN AUTHOR'S BED-CHAMBER.

Where the Red Lion, staring o'er the way,
Invites each passing stranger that can pay;
Where Calvert's butt, and Parson's black champagne,

Regale the drabs and bloods of Drury-lane:
There, in a lonely room, from bailiffs snug,
The Muse found Scroggen stretch'd beneath a rug;
A window, patch'd with paper, lent a ray,
That dimly show'd the state in which he lay;
The sanded floor that grits beneath the tread;
The humid wall with paltry pictures spread;
The royal game of goose was there in view,
And the twelve rules the Royal Martyr drew;
The Seasons, framed with listing, found a place,
And brave Prince William show'd his lamp-black face.
The morn was cold; he views with keen desire
The rusty grate unconscious of a fire:
With beer and milk arrears the frieze was scored,
And five crack'd tea-cups dress'd the chimney-board;
A nightcap deck'd his brows instead of bay,
A cap by night—a stocking all the day!*

A PROLOGUE,

WRITTEN AND SPOKEN BY THE POET LABERIUS, A ROMAN KNIGHT, WHOM CÆSAR FORCED UPON THE STAGE.

[Preserved by Macrobius.]

WHAT! no way left to shun th' inglorious stage,
And save from infamy my sinking age!
Scarce half alive, oppress'd with many a year,
What in the name of dotage drives me here?

* The author has given, with a very slight alteration, a similar description of the alehouse. in the Deserted Village.

A time there was, when glory was my guide,
Nor force nor fraud could turn my steps aside;
Unawed by power, and unappall'd by fear,
With honest thrift I held my honor dear:
But this vile hour disperses all my store,
And all my hoard of honor is no more;
For, ah! too partial to my life's decline,
Cæsar persuades, submission must be mine;
Him I obey, whom Heaven itself obeys,
Hopeless of pleasing, yet inclined to please.
Here then at once I welcome every shame,
And cancel, at threescore, a life of fame:
No more my titles shall my children tell,
The old buffoon will fit my name as well:
This day beyond its term my fate extends,
For life is ended when our honor ends.

AN ELEGY ON THE GLORY OF HER SEX, MRS. MARY BLAIZE.

Good people all, with one accord,
  Lament for Madam Blaize,
Who never wanted a good word —
  From those who spoke her praise.

The needy seldom pass'd her door,
  And always found her kind;
She freely lent to all the poor —
  Who left a pledge behind.

She strove the neighborhood to please
With manners wondrous winning;
And never follow'd wicked ways —
Unless when she was sinning.

At church, in silks and satin new,
With hoop of monstrous size,
She never slumber'd in her pew —
But when she shut her eyes.

Her love was sought, I do aver,
By twenty beaux and more;
The king himself has follow'd her —
When she has walk'd before.

But now, her wealth and finery fled,
Her hangers-on cut short all:
The doctors found, when she was dead —
Her last disorder mortal.

Let us lament in sorrow sore,
For Kent Street well may say,
That had she lived a twelvemonth more —
She had not died to-day.

ON A BEAUTIFUL YOUTH

STRUCK BLIND BY LIGHTNING.

SURE, 'twas by Providence design'd,
Rather in pity than in hate,
That he should be, like Cupid, blind,
To save him from Narcissus' fate.

THE CLOWN'S REPLY.

John Trott was desired by two witty peers
To tell them the reason why asses had ears;
'An't please you,' quoth John, 'I'm not given to letters,
Nor dare I pretend to know more than my betters;
Howe'er from this time, I shall ne'er see your graces —
As I hope to be saved! — without thinking on asses.'

EPITAPH ON DR. PARNELL.

This tomb, inscribed to gentle Parnell's name,
May speak our gratitude, but not his fame.
What heart but feels his sweetly moral lay,
That leads to truth through pleasure's flowery way?
Celestial themes confess'd his tuneful aid;
And Heaven, that lent him genius, was repaid.
Needless to him the tribute we bestow,
The transitory breath of fame below:
More lasting rapture from his works shall rise,
While converts thank their poet in the skies.

EPITAPH ON EDWARD PURDON.*

Here lies Ned Purdon, from misery freed,
Who long was a bookseller's hack:
He led such a damnable life in this world,
I don't think he'll wish to come back.

* This gentleman was educated at Trinity College, Dublin; but having wasted his patrimony, he enlisted as a foot soldier. Growing tired of that employment, he obtained his discharge, and became a scribbler in the newspapers. He translated Voltaire's *Henriade.*

STANZAS ON THE TAKING OF QUEBEC.

Amidst the clamor of exulting joys,
  Which triumph forces from the patriot heart,
Grief dares to mingle her soul-piercing voice,
  And quells the raptures which from pleasure start.

O Wolfe!* to thee a streaming flood of woe
  Sighing we pay, and think e'en conquest dear;
Quebec in vain shall teach our breast to glow,
  Whilst thy sad fate extorts the heart-wrung tear.

Alive, the foe thy dreadful vigor fled,
  And saw thee fall with joy-pronouncing eyes:
Yet they shall know thou conquerest, though dead!
  Since from thy tomb a thousand heroes rise.

STANZAS ON WOMAN.

When lovely woman stoops to folly,
  And finds too late that men betray,
What charm can soothe her melancholy?
  What art can wash her guilt away?

The only art her guilt to cover,
  To hide her shame from every eye,
To give repentance to her lover,
  And wring his bosom, is — to die.

* Goldsmith claimed relationship with this gallant soldier, whose character he greatly admired.

A SONNET.*

WEEPING, murmuring, complaining,
  Lost to every gay delight,
Myra, too sincere for feigning,
  Fears th' approaching bridal night.

Yet why impair thy bright perfection,
  Or dim thy beauty with a tear?
Had Myra followed my direction,
  She long had wanted cause of fear

SONG.

From the Oratorio of the *Captivity.*

THE wretch condemned with life to part,
  Still, still on hope relies;
And every pang that rends the heart
  Bids expectation rise.

Hope, like the glimmering taper's light,
  Adorns and cheers the way;
And still, as darker grows the night,
  Emits a brighter ray.

SONG.

From the Oratorio of the *Captivity.*

O MEMORY! thou fond deceiver,
  Still importunate and vain,
To former joys recurring ever,
  And turning all the past to pain.

* This sonnet is imitated from a French madrigal of St. Pavier.

Thou, like the world, the oppress'd oppressing,
Thy smiles increase the wretch's woe;
And he who wants each other blessing,
In thee must ever find a foe.

SONG.

Intended to have been sung in the Comedy of *She Stoops to Conquer*, but omitted, because Mrs. Bulkley, who acted the part of Miss Hardcastle, could not sing.

Ah me! when shall I marry me?
Lovers are plenty, but fail to relieve me;
He, fond youth, that could carry me,
Offers to love, but means to deceive me.

But I will rally, and combat the ruiner:
Not a look, nor a smile, shall my passion discover.
She that gives all to the false one pursuing her,
Makes but a penitent, and loses a lover.

PROLOGUE TO ZOBEIDE, A TRAGEDY;

WRITTEN BY JOSEPH CRADOCK, ESQ., ACTED AT THE THEATRE ROYAL, COVENT GARDEN, 1772.

SPOKEN BY MR. QUICK.

In these bold times, when Learning's sons explore
The distant climates and the savage shore;
When wise astronomers to India steer,
And quit for Venus many a brighter here;
While botanists, all cold to smiles and dimpling,

Forsake the fair, and patiently — go simpling:
Our bard into the general spirit enters,
And fits his little frigate for adventures.
With Scythian stores, and trinkets deeply laden,
He this way steers his course, in hopes of trading;
Yet ere he lands he's ordered me before,
To make an observation on the shore.
Where are we driven? our reckoning sure is lost!
This seems a rocky and a dangerous coast.
Lord, what a sultry climate am I under!
Yon ill-foreboding cloud seems big with thunder:
[*Upper Gallery.*
There mangroves spread, and larger than I've seen 'em — [*Pit.*
Here trees of stately size — and billing turtles in 'em.
[*Balconies.*
Here ill-condition'd oranges abound — [*Stage.*
And apples, bitter apples, strew the ground:
[*Tasting them.*
The inhabitants are cannibals, I fear;
I heard a hissing — there are serpents here!
Oh, there the people are — best keep my distance:
Our Captain, gentle natives, craves assistance;
Our ship's well stored — in yonder creek we've laid her,
His Honor is no mercenary trader.
This is his first adventure: lend him aid,
And we may chance to drive a thriving trade.
His goods, he hopes, are prime, and brought from far,
Equally fit for gallantry and war..
What! no reply to promises so ample?
I'd best step back — and order up a sample.

EPILOGUE

TO THE COMEDY OF THE SISTERS.*

WHAT! five long acts — and all to make us wiser!
Our authoress sure has wanted an adviser.
Had she consulted me, she should have made
Her moral play a speaking masquerade:
Warm'd up each bustling scene, and in her rage,
Have emptied all the green-room on the stage.
My life on't this had kept her play from sinking,
Have pleased our eyes, and saved the pain of thinking.
Well, since she thus has shown her want of skill,
What if *I* give a masquerade? — I will.
But how? ay, there's the rub! [*pausing*] I've got my
cue:
The world's a masquerade! the masquers, you, you, you.
[*To Boxes, Pit, and Gallery.*
Lud! what a group the motley scene discloses!
False wits, false wives, false virgins, and false spouses!
Statesmen with bridles on; and, close beside 'em,
Patriots in party-color'd suits that ride 'em:
There Hebes, turn'd of fifty, try once more
To raise a flame in Cupids of threescore;
These in their turn, with appetites as keen,
Deserting fifty, fasten on fifteen:

* By Mrs. Charlotte Lennox, author of the *Female Quixote*, *Shakspeare Illustrated*, etc. It was performed one night only at Covent Garden, in 1769. This lady was praised by Dr. Johnson, as the cleverest female writer of her age.

Miss, not yet full fifteen, with fire uncommon,
Flings down her sampler, and takes up the woman;
The little urchin smiles, and spreads her lure,
And tries to kill, ere she 's got power to cure.
Thus 't is with all: their chief and constant care
Is to seem everything — but what they are.
Yon broad, bold, angry spark, I fix my eye on,
Who seems t' have robb'd his vizor from the lion;
Who frowns, and talks, and swears, with round parade,
Looking, as who should say, Damme! who 's afraid?
[*Mimicking.*

Strip but this vizor off, and, sure I am,
You 'll find his lionship a very lamb:
Yon politician, famous in debate,
Perhaps, to vulgar eyes, bestrides the state;
Yet, when he deigns his real shape t' assume,
He turns old woman, and bestrides a broom.
Yon patriot, too, who presses on your sight,
And seems, to every gazer, all in white,
If with a bribe his candor you attack,
He bows, turns round, and whip — the man 's in black!
Yon critic, too — but whither do I run?
If I proceed, our bard will be undone!
Well, then, a truce, since she requests it too:
Do you spare her, and I 'll for once spare you.

EPILOGUE,

SPOKEN BY

MRS. BULKLEY AND MISS CATLEY.

Enter Mrs. Bulkley, who courtesies very low, as beginning to speak. Then enter Miss Catley, who stands full before her, and courtesies to the audience.

Mrs. Bulkley. HOLD, Ma'am, your pardon. What 's your business here?

Miss Catley. The Epilogue.

Mrs. B. The Epilogue?

Miss C. Yes, the Epilogue, my dear.

Mrs. B. Sure, you mistake, Ma'am. The Epilogue! *I* bring it.

Miss C. Excuse me, Ma'am. The author bid *me* sing it.

Recitative.

Ye beaux and belles, that form this splendid ring,
Suspend your conversation while I sing.

Mrs. B. Why, sure, the girl 's beside herself! an Epilogue of singing?
A hopeful end, indeed, to such a blest beginning.
Besides, a singer in a comic set —
Excuse me, Ma'am, I know the etiquette.

Miss C. What if we leave it to the house?

Mrs. B. The house? — Agreed.

Miss C. Agreed.

Mrs. B. And she whose party 's largest shall proceed.

And first, I hope you 'll readily agree
I 've all the critics and the wits for me.
They, I am sure, will answer my commands:
Ye candid judging few, hold up your hands.
What! no return? I find too late, I fear,
That modern judges seldom enter here.

Miss C. I'm for a different set:—Old men, whose trade is
Still to gallant and dangle with the ladies.

Recitative.

Who mump their passion, and who, grimly smiling,
Still thus address the fair with voice beguiling:

AIR.—*Cotillon.*

Turn, my fairest, turn, if ever
  Strephon caught thy ravish'd eye,
Pity take on your swain so clever,
  Who without your aid must die.
    Yes, I shall die, hu, hu, hu, hu!
    Yes, I must die, ho, ho, ho, ho!

Da Capo.

Mrs. B. Let all the old pay homage to your merit;
Give me the young, the gay, the men of spirit.
Ye travell'd tribe, ye macaroni train,
Of French friseurs and nosegays justly vain,
Who take a trip to Paris once a-year,

To dress, and look like awkward Frenchmen here,—
Lend me your hands: O, fatal news to tell,
Their hands are only lent to the Heinelle.
Miss C. Ay, take your travellers — travellers indeed!
Give me my bonny Scot, that travels from the Tweed.
Where are the chiels? Ah, ah, I well discern
The smiling looks of each bewitching bairn.

AIR.— *A bonnie young lad is my Jockey.*

I'll sing to amuse you by night and by day,
And be unco merry when you are but gay;
When you with your bagpipes are ready to play,
My voice shall be ready to carol away
With Sandy, and Sawney, and Jockey,
With Sawnie, and Jarvie, and Jockey.

Mrs. B. Ye gamesters, who, so eager in pursuit,
Make but of all your fortune one *va toute:*
Ye jockey tribe, whose stock of words are few,
'I hold the odds — Done, done, with you, with you!'
Ye barristers, so fluent with grimace,
'My Lord, your Lordship misconceives the case:'
Doctors, who answer every misfortuner,
'I wish I'd been call'd in a little sooner:'
Assist my cause with hands and voices hearty,
Come, end the contest here, and aid my party.

AIR.— *Ballinamony.*

Miss C. Ye brave Irish lads, hark away to the crack,
Assist me, I pray, in this woeful attack;
For — sure, I don't wrong you — you seldom are slack,

When the ladies are calling, to blush and hang back.
For you are always polite and attentive,
Still to amuse us inventive,
And death is your only preventive;
Your hands and voices for me.

Mrs. B. Well, Madam, what if, after all this sparring,
We both agree, like friends, to end our jarring?
Miss C. And that our friendship may remain unbroken,
What if we leave the Epilogue unspoken?
Mrs. B. Agreed.
Miss C. Agreed.
Mrs. B. And now with late repentance,
Un-epilogued the Poet waits his sentence.
Condemn the stubborn fool, who can't submit
To thrive by flattery, though he starves by wit.
Exeunt.

AN EPILOGUE

INTENDED FOR MRS. BULKLEY.

There is a place — so Ariosto sings —
A treasury for lost and missing things,
Lost human wits have places there assign'd them,
And they who lose their senses, there may find them.
But where 's this place, this storehouse of the age?
The Moon, says he; but I affirm, the Stage —
At least, in many things, I think I see
His lunar and our mimic world agree:
Both shine at night, for, but at Foote's alone,
We scarce exhibit till the sun goes down;

Both prone to change, no settled limits fix,
And sure the folks of both are lunatics.
But in this parallel my best pretence is,
That mortals visit both to find their senses;
To this strange spot, Rakes, Macaronies, Cits,
Come thronging to collect their scatter'd wits.
The gay coquette, who ogles all the day,
Comes here at night, and goes a prude away.
Hither th' affected city dame advancing,
Who sighs for Operas, and doats on dancing,
Taught by our art, her ridicule to pause on,
Quits the *Ballet*, and calls for *Nancy Dawson.*
The Gamester, too, whose wit's all high or low,
Oft risks his fortune on one desperate throw,
Comes here to saunter, having made his bets,
Finds his lost senses out, and pays his debts.
The Mohawk, too, with angry phrases stored —
As, 'Damme, Sir!' and 'Sir, I wear a sword!'
Here lesson'd for a while, and hence retreating,
Goes out, affronts his man, and takes a beating.
Here comes the sons of scandal and of news,
But find no sense — for they had none to lose.
Of all the tribe here wanting an adviser,
Our Author 's the least likely to grow wiser;
Has he not seen how you your favor place
On sentimental queens, and lords in lace?
Without a star, a coronet, or garter,
How can the piece expect or hope for quarter?
No high-life scenes, no sentiment: the creature
Still stoops among the low to copy Nature.
Yes, he 's far gone: and yet some pity fix,
The English laws forbid to punish lunatics.

EPILOGUE,

SPOKEN BY MR. LEE LEWES, IN THE CHARACTER OF HARLEQUIN, AT HIS BENEFIT.

HOLD! Prompter, hold! a word before your nonsense
I'd speak a word or two, to ease my conscience.
My pride forbids it ever should be said
My heels eclipsed the honors of my head;
That I found humor in a piebald vest,
Or ever thought that jumping was a jest.
[*Takes off his mask.*
Whence, and what art thou, visionary birth?
Nature disowns, and reason scorns thy mirth:
In thy black aspect every passion sleeps,
The joy that dimples, and the wo that weeps.
How hast thou fill'd the scene with all thy brood
Of fools pursuing and of fools pursued!
Whose ins and outs no ray of sense discloses,
Whose only plot it is to break our noses;
Whilst from below the trap-door *demons* rise,
And from above the dangling deities:
And shall I mix in this unhallow'd crew?
May rosin'd lightning blast me if I do!
No — I will act — I'll vindicate the stage:
Shakspeare himself shall feel my tragic rage.
Off! off! vile trappings! a new passion reigns!
The madd'ning monarch revels in my veins.
Oh! for a Richard's voice to catch the theme, —

'Give me another horse! bind up my wounds! —soft —
'twas but a dream.'
Ay, 'twas but a dream, for now there's no retreating,
If I cease Harlequin, I cease from eating.
'Twas thus that Æsop's stag, a creature blameless,
Yet something vain, like one that shall be nameless,
Once on the margin of a fountain stood
And cavill'd at his image in the flood:
'The deuce confound,' he cries, 'these drumstick shanks,
They never have my gratitude nor thanks;
They're perfectly disgraceful! strike me dead!
But for a head, yes, yes, I have a head:
How piercing is that eye! how sleek that brow!
My horns! — I'm told that horns are the fashion now.'
Whilst thus he spoke, astonish'd, to his view,
Near, and more near, the hounds and huntsmen drew;
'Hoicks! hark forward!' came thund'ring from behind:
He bounds aloft, outstrips the fleeting wind;
He quits the woods, and tries the beaten ways;
He starts, he pants, he takes the circling maze:
At length, his silly head, so prized before,
Is taught his former folly to deplore;
Whilst his strong limbs conspire to set him free,
And at one bound he saves himself — like me.
[*Taking a jump through the stage door*

THRENODIA AUGUSTALIS.*

SACRED TO THE MEMORY OF HER LATE ROYAL HIGHNESS THE

PRINCESS DOWAGER OF WALES.

SPOKEN AND SUNG IN THE GREAT ROOM IN SOHO-SQUARE,

Thursday, the 20th day of February, 1772.

ADVERTISEMENT.

THE following may more properly be termed a compilation than a poem. It was prepared for the composer in little more than two days: and may therefore rather be considered as an industrious effort of gratitude than of genius.

In justice to the composer, it may likewise be right to inform the public, that the music was adapted in a period of time equally short.

SPEAKERS—*Mr. Lee and Mrs. Bellamy.*

SINGERS—*Mr. Champnes, Mr. Dine, and Miss Jameson.*

THE MUSIC PREPARED AND ADAPTED BY SIGNIOR VENTO.

* This poem was first printed in Chalmers' edition of the *English Poets*, from a copy given by Goldsmith to his friend, Joseph Cradock, Esq., author of the tragedy of *Zobeide.*

THRENODIA AUGUSTALIS.

OVERTURE — A SOLEMN DIRGE.

AIR — TRIO.

Arise, ye sons of worth, arise,
And waken every note of woe!
When truth and virtue reach the skies
'Tis ours to weep the want below.

CHORUS.

When truth and virtue, etc.

MAN SPEAKER.

The praise attending pomp and power,
The incense given to kings,
Are but the trappings of an hour,
Mere transitory things.
The base bestow them; but the good agree
To spurn the venal gifts as flattery.
But when to pomp and power are join'd
An equal dignity of the mind;
When titles are the smallest claim;
When wealth and rank, and noble blood,
But aid the power of doing good:
Then all their trophies last — and flattery turns to fame.
Blest spirit, thou, whose fame, just born to bloom,
Shall spread and flourish from the tomb,
How hast thou left mankind for Heaven!
Even now reproach and faction mourn,
And, wondering how their rage was born,

Request to be forgiven!
Alas! they never had thy hate;
Unmoved, in conscious rectitude,
Thy towering mind self-centred stood,
Nor wanted man's opinion to be great.
In vain, to charm the ravish'd sight,
A thousand gifts would fortune send;
In vain, to drive thee from the right,
A thousand sorrows urged thy end:
Like some well-fashion'd arch thy patience stood,
And purchased strength from its increased load.
Pain met thee like a friend to set thee free,
Affliction still is virtue's opportunity!
Virtue, on herself relying,
Every passion hushed to rest,
Loses every pain of dying
In the hopes of being blest.
Every added pang she suffers
Some increasing good bestows,
And every shock that malice offers
Only rocks her to repose.

SONG. BY A MAN — AFFETUOSO.

Virtue, on herself relying, etc.
to
Only rocks her to repose.

WOMAN SPEAKER.

Yet ah! what terrors frown'd upon her fate,
Death, with its formidable band,
Fever, and pain, and pale consumptive care,

Determined took their stand.
Nor did the cruel ravagers design
To finish all their efforts at a blow:
But, mischievously slow,
They robb'd the relic and defaced the shrine.
With unavailing grief,
Despairing of relief,
Her weeping children round
Beheld each hour
Death's growing pow'r,
And trembled as he frown'd.
As helpless friends who view from shore
The laboring ship, and hear the tempest roar,
While winds and waves their wishes cross,—
They stood, while hope and comfort fail,
Not to assist, but to bewail
The inevitable loss.
Relentless tyrant, at thy call
How do the good, the virtuous fall!
Truth, beauty, worth, and all that most engage,
But wake thy vengeance and provoke thy rage.

SONG. BY A MAN — BASSO, STOCCATO, SPIRITUOSO.

When vice my dart and scythe supply,
How great a King of Terrors I!
If folly, fraud, your hearts engage,
Tremble, ye mortals, at my rage!
Fall, round me fall, ye little things,
Ye statesmen, warriors, poets, kings,
If virtue fail her counsel sage,
Tremble, ye mortals, at my rage!

MAN SPEAKER.

Yet let that wisdom, urged by her example,
Teach us to estimate what all must suffer:
Let us prize death as the best gift of nature,
As a safe inn where weary travellers,
When they have journey'd through a world of cares,
May put off life, and be at rest forever.
Groans, weeping friends, indeed, and gloomy sables,
May oft distract us with their sad solemnity:
The preparation is the executioner.
Death, when unmask'd, shows me a friendly face,
And is a terror only at a distance:
For as the line of life conducts me on
To Death's great court, the prospect seems more fair;
'Tis Nature's kind retreat, that's always open
To take us in when we have drained the cup
Of life, or worn our days to wretchedness.
In that secure, serene retreat,
Where all the humble, all the great,
  Promiscuously recline;
Where wildly huddled to the eye,
The beggar's pouch, and prince's purple lie:
  May every bliss be thine!
And, ah! blest spirit, wheresoe'er thy flight,
Through rolling worlds, or fields of liquid light,
May cherubs welcome their expected guest!
May saints with songs receive thee to their rest!
May peace, that claim'd while here, thy warmest love,
May blissful, endless peace be thine above!

SONG. BY A WOMAN — AMOROSO.

Lovely, lasting Peace, below,
Comforter of every woe,
Heavenly born, and bred on high,
To crown the favorites of the sky!
Lovely, lasting Peace, appear!
This world itself, if thou art here,
Is once again with Eden blest,
And man contains it in his breast.

WOMAN SPEAKER.

Our vows are heard! Long, long to mortal eyes,
Her soul was fitting to its kindred skies:
Celestial like her bounty fell,
Where modest Want and patient Sorrow dwell;
Want pass'd for Merit at her door,
  Unseen the modest were supplied,
Her constant pity fed the poor, —
  Then only poor, indeed, the day she died.
And, oh! for this, while sculpture decks thy shrine,
  And art exhausts profusion round,
The tribute of a tear be mine,
  A simple song, a sigh profound.
There faith shall come — a pilgrim gray,
To bless the tomb that wraps thy clay!
And calm Religion shall repair
To dwell a weeping hermit there.
Truth, Fortitude, and Friendship, shall agree
To blend their virtues while they think of thee.

AIR — CHORUS POMPOSO.

Let us — let all the world agree,
To profit by resembling thee.

PART II.

OVERTURE — PASTORALE.

MAN SPEAKER.

Fast by that shore where Thames' translucent stream
Reflects new glories on his breast,
Where, splendid as the youthful poet's dream,
He forms a scene beyond Elysium blest;
Where sculptured elegance and native grace
Unite to stamp the beauties of the place;
While, sweetly blending, still are seen
The wavy lawn, the sloping green;
While novelty, with cautious cunning,
Through every maze of fancy running,
From China borrows aid to deck the scene:
There, sorrowing by the river's glassy bed,
Forlorn, a rural band complain'd,
All whom Augusta's bounty fed,
All whom her clemency sustain'd;
The good old sire, unconscious of decay,
The modest matron, clad in home-spun gray,
The military boy, the orphan'd maid,
The shatter'd veteran now first dismay'd, —
These sadly join beside the murmuring deep,
And, as they view the towers of Kew,
Call on their mistress — now no more — and weep.

CHORUS.— AFFETUOSO, LARGO.

Ye shady walks, ye waving greens,
Ye nodding towers, ye fairy scenes,
Let all your echoes now deplore,
That she who form'd your beauties is no more.

MAN SPEAKER.

First of the train the patient rustic came,
 Whose callous hand had form'd the scene,
Bending at once with sorrow and with age,
 With many a tear, and many a sigh between:
'And where,' he cried, 'shall now my babes have bread,
 Or how shall age support its feeble fire?
No lord will take me now, my vigor fled,
 Nor can my strength perform what they require:
Each grudging master keeps the laborer bare,
A sleek and idle race is all their care.
My noble mistress thought not so:
 Her bounty, like the morning dew,
Unseen, though constant, used to flow,
 And as my strength decay'd, her bounty grew.'

WOMAN SPEAKER.

In decent dress, and coarsely clean,
The pious matron next was seen,
Clasp'd in her hand a godly book was borne,
By use and daily meditation worn;
That decent dress, this holy guide,
Augusta's cares had well supplied.
'And ah!' she cries, all wobegone,

'What now remains for me?
Oh! where shall weeping want repair
To ask for charity?
Too late in life for me to ask,
And shame prevents the deed,
And tardy, tardy are the times
To succor, should I need.
But all my wants, before I spoke,
Were to my mistress known;
She still relieved, nor sought my praise,
Contented with her own.
But every day her name I'll bless,
My morning prayer, my evening song,
I'll praise her while my life shall last,
A life that cannot last me long.'

SONG.— BY A WOMAN.

Each day, each hour, her name I'll bless,
My morning and my evening song,
And when in death my vows shall cease,
My children shall the note prolong.

MAN SPEAKER.

The hardy veteran after struck the sight,
Scarr'd, mangled, maim'd in every part,
Lopp'd of his limbs in many a gallant fight,
In nought entire — except his heart:
Mute for a while, and sullenly distrest,
At last th' impetuous sorrow fired his breast:—
Wild is the whirlwind rolling
O'er Afric's sandy plain,

And wide the tempest howling
Along the billow'd main:
But every danger felt before,
The raging deep, the whirlwind's roar,
Less dreadful struck me with dismay
Than what I feel this fatal day.
Oh, let me fly a land that spurns the brave,
Oswego's dreary shores shall be my grave;
I'll seek that less inhospitable coast,
And lay my body where my limbs were lost.

SONG.—BY A MAN.—BASSO SPIRITUOSO.

Old Edward's sons, unknown to yield,
Shall crowd from Cressy's laurell'd field,
To do thy memory right:
For thine and Britain's wrongs they feel,
Again they snatch the gleamy steel,
And wish th' avenging fight.

WOMAN SPEAKER.

In innocence and youth complaining,
Next appear'd a lovely maid;
Affliction, o'er each feature reigning,
Kindly came in beauty's aid:
Every grace that grief dispenses,
Every glance that warms the soul,
In sweet succession charms the senses,
While Pity harmonized the whole.
'The garland of beauty,' 'tis thus she would say,
'No more shall my crook or my temples adorn;
I'll not wear a garland — Augusta's away —

I'll not wear a garland until she return.
But, alas! that return I never shall see:
The echoes of Thames shall my sorrows proclaim,
There promised a lover to come — but, ah me!
'Twas death — 'twas the death of my mistress that came.
But ever, for ever, her image shall last,
I'll strip all the Spring of its earliest bloom;
On her grave shall the cowslip and primrose be cast,
And the new-blossom'd thorn shall whiten her tomb.

SONG.— BY A WOMAN.— PASTORALE.

With garlands of beauty the Queen of the May
No more will her crook or her temples adorn;
For who'd wear a garland when she is away,
When she is removed, and shall never return?

On the grave of Augusta these garlands be placed,
We'll rifle the Spring of its earliest bloom,
And there shall the cowslip and primrose be cast,
And the new-blossom'd thorn shall whiten her tomb.

CHORUS.— ALTRO MODO.

On the grave of Augusta this garland be placed,
We'll rifle the Spring of its earliest bloom,
And there shall the cowslip and primrose be cast,
And the tears of her country shall water her tomb.

THE CAPTIVITY: AN ORATORIO.*

THE PERSONS.

First Jewish Prophet.	*First Chaldean Priest.*
Second Jewish Prophet.	*Second Chaldean Priest.*
Israelitish Woman.	*Chaldean Woman.*

Chorus of Youths and Virgins.

SCENE — *The Banks of the River Euphrates near Babylon.*

ACT THE FIRST.

FIRST PROPHET.

YE captive tribes that hourly work and weep
Where flows Euphrates murmuring to the deep,
Suspend your woes a while, the task suspend,
And turn to God, your father and your friend:
Insulted, chain'd, and all the world our foe,
Our God alone is all we boast below.

Air.

FIRST PROPHET.

Our God is all we boast below,
To him we turn our eyes;

* This was first printed from the original, in Dr. Goldsmith's own hand-writing, in the 8vo. edition of his *Miscellaneous Works*, published in 1820.

And every added weight of wo
  Shall make our homage rise.

SECOND PROPHET.

And though no temple richly dress'd,
  Nor sacrifice is here,
We'll make his temple in our breast,
  And offer up a tear.
[*The first stanza repeated by the* CHORUS.

ISRAELITISH WOMAN.

That strain once more! it bids remembrance rise,
And brings my long-lost country to mine eyes:
Ye fields of Sharon, dress'd in flowery pride,
Ye plains where Kedron rolls its glassy tide,
Ye hills of Lebanon, with cedars crown'd,
Ye Gilead groves, that fling perfumes around, —
How sweet those groves! that plain how wondrous fair!
How doubly sweet when Heaven was with us there!

Air.

O Memory! thou fond deceiver,
  Still importunate and vain;
To former joys recurring ever,
  And turning all the past to pain.

Hence, intruder most distressing!
  Seek the happy and the free:
The wretch who wants each other blessing,
  Ever wants a friend in thee.

SECOND PROPHET.

Yet why complain? What though by bonds confined?

Should bonds repress the vigor of the mind?
Have we not cause for triumph, when we see
Ourselves alone from idol worship free?
Are not, this very morn, those feasts begun
Where prostrate error hails the rising sun?
Do not our tyrant lords this day ordain
For superstitious rites and mirth profane?
And should we mourn? Should coward virtue fly,
When vaunting folly lifts her head on high?
No! rather let us triumph still the more,
And as our fortune sinks, our spirits soar.

Air.

The triumphs that on vice attend
Shall ever in confusion end;
The good man suffers but to gain,
And every virtue springs from pain:
As aromatic plants bestow
No spicy fragrance while they grow;
But crush'd, or trodden to the ground,
Diffuse their balmy sweets around.

FIRST PROPHET.

But hush, my sons, our tyrant lords are near,
The sounds of barbarous pleasure strike mine ear;
Triumphant music floats along the vale,
Near, nearer still, it gathers on the gale:
The growing sound their swift approach declares —
Desist, my sons, nor mix the strain with theirs.

Enter CHALDEAN PRIESTS *attended.*

Air.

FIRST PRIEST.

Come on, my companions, the triumph display,
  Let rapture the minutes employ;
The sun calls us out on this festival day,
  And our monarch partakes in the joy.

SECOND PRIEST.

Like the sun, our great monarch all rapture supplies,
  Both similar blessings bestow:
The sun with his splendor illumines the skies,
  And our monarch enlivens below.

Air.

CHALDEAN WOMAN.

Haste, ye sprightly sons of pleasure,
Love presents the fairest treasure,
  Leave all other joys for me.

A CHALDEAN ATTENDANT.

Or rather, love's delights despising,
Haste to raptures ever rising,
  Wine shall bless the brave and free.

FIRST PRIEST.

Wine and beauty thus inviting,
Each to different joys exciting,
  Whither shall my choice incline.

SECOND PRIEST.

I'll waste no longer thought in choosing,
But, neither this nor that refusing,
I'll make them both together mine.

FIRST PRIEST.

But whence, when joy should brighten o'er the land,
This sullen gloom in Judah's captive band?
Ye sons of Judah, why the lute unstrung?
Or why those harps on yonder willows hung?
Come, take the lyre, and pour the strain along;
The day demands it: sing us Sion's song,
Dismiss your griefs, and join our warbling choir,
For who like you can wake the sleeping lyre?

Air.

Every moment as it flows,
Some peculiar pleasure owes:
Come then, providently wise,
Seize the debtor e'er it flies.

SECOND PRIEST.

Think not to-morrow can repay
The debt of pleasure lost to-day:
Alas! to-morrow's richest store
Can but pay its proper score.

SECOND PROPHET.

Chain'd as we are, the scorn of all mankind,
To want, to toil, and every ill consign'd,
Is this a time to bid us raise the strain,

Or mix in rites that Heaven regards with pain?
No, never! may this hand forget each art
That wakes to finest joys the human heart,
Ere I forget the land that gave me birth,
Or join to sounds profane its sacred mirth!

SECOND PRIEST.

Rebellious slaves! if soft persuasion fail,
More formidable terrors shall prevail.

FIRST PROPHET.

Why, let them come, one good remains to cheer—
We fear the Lord, and scorn all other fear.
[*Exeunt* CHALDEANS.

CHORUS OF ISRAELITES.

Can chains or tortures bend the mind
On God's supporting breast reclined?
Stand fast, and let our tyrants see
That fortitude is victory. [*Exeunt.*

ACT THE SECOND.

ISRAELITES *and* CHALDEANS, *as before.*

Air.

FIRST PROPHET.

O peace of mind, angelic guest,
Thou soft companion of the breast,
Dispense thy balmy store!

Wing all our thoughts to reach the skies,
Till earth, receding from our eyes,
Shall vanish as we soar!

FIRST PRIEST.

No more. Too long has justice been delay'd,
The king's commands must fully be obey'd;
Compliance with his will your peace secures,
Praise but our gods, and every good is yours.
But if, rebellious to his high command,
You spurn the favors offer'd from his hand,
Think, timely think, what terrors are behind;
Reflect, nor tempt to rage the royal mind.

Air.

Fierce is the tempest howling
Along the furrow'd main,
And fierce the whirlwind rolling
O'er Afric's sandy plain.

But storms that fly
To rend the sky,
Every ill presaging,
Less dreadful show
To worlds below
Than angry monarchs raging.

ISRAELITISH WOMAN.

Ah me! what angry terrors round us grow!
How shrinks my soul to meet the threaten'd blow.
Ye prophets, skill'd in Heaven's eternal truth,

Forgive my sex's fears, forgive my youth!
Ah! let us one, one little hour obey;
To-morrow's tears may wash the stain away.

Air.

Fatigued with life, yet loath to part,
On hope the wretch relies;
And every blow that sinks the heart
Bids the deluder rise.

Hope, like the taper's gleamy light
Adorns the wretch's way;
And still, as darker grows the night,
Emits a brighter ray.

SECOND PRIEST.

Why this delay? At length for joy prepare:
I read your looks, and see compliance there.
Come on, and bid the warbling rapture rise;
Our monarch's fame the noblest theme supplies.
Begin, ye captive bands, and strike the lyre;
The time, the theme, the place, and all conspire.

Air.

CHALDEAN WOMAN.

See the ruddy morning smiling,
Hear the grove to bliss beguiling;
Zephyrs through the woodland playing,
Streams along the valley straying.

FIRST PRIEST.

While these a constant revel keep,

Shall reason only teach to weep?
Hence, intruder! we'll pursue
Nature, a better guide than you.

SECOND PRIEST.

But hold! see, foremost of the captive choir,
The master prophet grasps his full-toned lyre.
Mark where he sits, with executing art,
Feels for each tone, and speeds it to the heart.
See, how prophetic rapture fills his form,
Awful as clouds that nurse the growing storm!
And now his voice, accordant to the string,
Prepares our monarch's victories to sing.

Air.

FIRST PROPHET.

From north, from south, from east, from west,
Conspiring nations come:
Tremble, thou vice-polluted breast!
Blasphemers, all be dumb.

The tempest gathers all around,
On Babylon it lies;
Down with her! down, down to the ground
She sinks, she groans, she dies.

SECOND PROPHET.

Down with her, Lord, to lick the dust,
Before yon setting sun;
Serve her as she hath served the just!
'Tis fix'd — it shall be done

FIRST PRIEST.

No more! when slaves thus insolent presume,
The king himself shall judge and fix their doom.
Unthinking wretches! have not you and all
Beheld our power in Zedekiah's fall?
To yonder gloomy dungeon turn your eyes:
See where dethroned your captive monarch lies,
Deprived of sight, and rankling in his chain;
See where he mourns his friends and children slain.
Yet know, ye slaves, that still remain behind
More ponderous chains, and dungeons more confined.

CHORUS OF ALL.

Arise, all potent ruler, rise,
  And vindicate the people's cause,
Till every tongue in every land
  Shall offer up unfeigned applause.

[*Exeunt.*

ACT THE THIRD.

FIRST PRIEST.

Yes, my companions, Heaven's decrees are pass'd,
And our fix'd empire shall for ever last:
In vain the madd'ning prophet threatens woe,
In vain rebellion aims her secret blow;
Still shall our name and growing power be spread,
And still our justice crush the traitor's head.

Air.

Coeval with man
Our empire began,
And never shall fall
Till ruin shakes all.
When ruin shakes all,
Then shall Babylon fall.

SECOND PROPHET.

'Tis thus the proud triumphant rear the head,—
A little while and all their power is fled.
But, ha! what means yon sadly plaintive train,
That onward slowly bends along the plain?
And now, behold, to yonder bank they bear
A pallid corse, and rest the body there.
Alas! too well mine eyes indignant trace
The last remains of Judah's royal race:
Fall'n is our king, and all our fears are o'er,
Unhappy Zedekiah is no more.

Air.

Ye wretches, who, by fortune's hate,
In want and sorrow groan,
Come, ponder his severer fate,
And learn to bless your own.

FIRST PROPHET.

Ye vain, whom youth and pleasure guide,
Awhile the bliss suspend;
Like yours, his life began in pride,
Like his, your lives shall end.

SECOND PROPHET.

Behold his wretched corse with sorrow worn,
His squalid limbs by ponderous fetters torn;
Those eyeless orbs that shook with ghastly glare,
Those unbecoming rags, that matted hair!
And shall not Heaven for this avenge the foe,
Grasp the red bolt, and lay the guilty low?
How long, how long, Almighty God of all,
Shall wrath vindictive threaten ere it fall?

Air.

ISRAELITISH WOMAN.

As panting flies the hunted hind,
  Where brooks refreshing stray;
And rivers through the valley wind,
  That stop the hunter's way:

Thus we, O Lord, alike distress'd,
  For streams of mercy long;
Streams which cheer the sore oppress'd,
  And overwhelm the strong.

FIRST PROPHET.

But whence that shout? Good Heavens! Amazement all!
See yonder tower just nodding to the fall:
Behold, an army covers all the ground,
'Tis Cyrus here that pours destruction round:
And now, behold, the battlements recline —
O God of hosts, the victory is thine!

CHORUS OF CAPTIVES.

Down with them, Lord, to lick the dust;
Thy vengeance be begun;
Serve them as they have served the just,
And let thy will be done.

FIRST PRIEST.

All, all is lost! The Syrian army fails,
Cyrus, the conqueror of the world, prevails.
The ruin smokes, the torrent pours along—
How low the proud, how feeble are the strong!
Save us, O Lord! to Thee, though late, we pray;
And give repentance but an hour's delay.

Air.

FIRST AND SECOND PRIEST.

O happy, who in happy hour
To God their praise bestow,
And own his all-consuming power
Before they feel the blow!

SECOND PROPHET.

Now, now 's our time! ye wretches, bold and blind,
Brave but to God, and cowards to mankind,
Ye seek in vain the Lord unsought before,
Your wealth, your lives, your kingdom, are no more!

Air.

O Lucifer, thou son of morn,
Of Heaven alike, and man the foe,—
Heaven, men, and all,

Now press thy fall,
And sink thee lowest of the low.

FIRST PROPHET.

O Babylon, how art thou fallen!
Thy fall more dreadful from delay!
Thy streets forlorn,
To wilds shall turn,
Where toads shall pant and vultures prey.

SECOND PROPHET.

Such be her fate. But hark! how from afar
The clarion's note proclaims the finish'd war!
Our great restorer, Cyrus, is at hand,
And this way leads his formidable band.
Give, give your songs of Sion to the wind,
And hail the benefactor of mankind:
He comes, pursuant to divine decree,
To chain the strong, and set the captive free.

CHORUS OF YOUTHS.

Rise to transports past expressing,
Sweeter by remember'd woes;
Cyrus comes, our wrongs redressing,
Comes to give the world repose.

CHORUS OF VIRGINS.

Cyrus comes, the world redressing,
Love and pleasure in his train;
Comes to heighten every blessing,
Comes to soften every pain.

SEMI-CHORUS.

Hail to him with mercy reigning,
Skill'd in every peaceful art;
Who, from bonds our limbs unchaining,
Only binds the willing heart.

THE LAST CHORUS.

But chief to thee, our God, defender, friend,
Let praise be given to all eternity;
O Thou, without beginning, without end,
Let us, and all, begin and end in Thee!

LINES ATTRIBUTED TO DR. GOLDSMITH.

INSERTED IN THE MORNING CHRONICLE, OF APRIL 3, 1800

E'EN have you seen, bathed in the morning dew,
The budding rose its infant bloom display;
When first its virgin tints unfold to view,
It shrinks, and scarcely trusts the blaze of day:

So soft, so delicate, so sweet she came,
Youth's damask glow just dawning on her cheek;
I gazed, I sigh'd, I caught the tender flame,
Felt the fond pang, and droop'd with passion weak.

THE

GOOD-NATURED MAN:

A COMEDY.

This admirable comedy was represented, for the first time, at Covent Garden, January 29, 1768. It kept possession of the stage for nine nights, but was considered by the author's friends, not to have met with all the success it deserved. Dr. Johnson said it was the best comedy which had appeared since '*The Provoked Husband*,' and Burke estimated its merits still higher.

PREFACE.

When I undertook to write a comedy, I confess I was strongly prepossessed in favor of the poets of the last age, and strove to imitate them. The term genteel comedy, was then unknown amongst us, and little more was desired by an audience, than nature and humor, in whatever walks of life they were most conspicuous. The author of the following scenes never imagined that more would be expected of him, and therefore to delineate character has been his principal aim. Those who know anything of composition, are sensible that in pursuing humor, it will sometimes lead us into the recesses of the mean: I was even tempted to look for it in the master of a sponging-house; but, in deference to the public taste — grown of late, perhaps, too delicate — the scene of the bailiffs was retrenched in the representation. In deference also to the judgment of a few friends, who think in a particular way, the scene is here restored. The author submits it to the reader in his closet; and hopes that too much refinement will not banish humor and character from ours, as it has already done from the French theatre. Indeed, the French comedy is now become so very elevated and sentimental, that it has not only banished humor and Moliere from the stage, but it has banished all spectators too.

Upon the whole, the author returns his thanks to the public, for the favorable reception which the *Good-Natured Man* has met with; and to Mr. Colman in particular, for his kindness to it. It may not also be improper to assure any who shall hereafter write for the theatre, that merit, or supposed merit, will ever be a sufficient passport to his protection.

DRAMATIS PERSONÆ.

MEN.

Mr. Honeywood.
Croaker.
Lofty.
Sir William Honeywood.
Leontine.
Jarvis.
Butler.
Bailiff.
Dubardieu.
Postboy.

WOMEN.

Miss Richland.
Olivia.
Mrs. Croaker.
Garnet.
Landlady.

Scene — LONDON.

THE

GOOD-NATURED MAN.

PROLOGUE,

WRITTEN BY DR. JOHNSON, SPOKEN BY MR. BENSLEY

Press'd by the load of life, the weary mind
Surveys the general toil of human kind,
With cool submission joins the lab'ring train,
And social sorrow loses half its pain:
Our anxious bard, without complaint, may share
This bustling season's epidemic care,
Like Cæsar's pilot, dignified by fate,
Toss'd in one common storm with all the great;
Distress'd alike, the statesman and the wit,
When one a Borough courts, and one the Pit.
The busy candidates for power and fame
Have hopes, and fears, and wishes, just the same:
Disabled both to combat or to fly,
Must hear all taunts, and hear without reply;
Uncheck'd, on both loud rabbles vent their rage,
As mongrels bay the lion in a cage.
Th' offended burgess hoards his angry tale,
For that blest year when all that vote may rail;

Their schemes of spite the poet's foes dismiss,
Till that glad night when all that hate may hiss.
'This day, the powder'd curls and golden coat,'
Says swelling Crispin, 'begg'd a cobbler's vote.'
'This night our wit,' the pert apprentice cries,
'Lies at my feet — I hiss him, and he dies.'
The great, 'tis true, can charm th' electing tribe:
The bard may supplicate, but cannot bribe.
Yet, judged by those whose voices ne'er were sold,
He feels no want of ill-persuading gold;
But confident of praise, if praise be due,
Trusts without fear to merit and to you.

ACT FIRST.

Scene — AN APARTMENT IN YOUNG HONEYWOOD'S HOUSE.

Enter Sir William Honeywood and Jarvis.

Sir William. GOOD Jarvis, make no apologies for this honest bluntness. Fidelity, like yours, is the best excuse for every freedom.

Jarvis. I can't help being blunt, and being very angry too, when I hear you talk of disinheriting so good, so worthy a young gentleman as your nephew, my master. All the world loves him.

Sir William. Say rather, that he loves all the world; that is his fault.

Jarvis. I am sure there is no part of it more dear to him than you are, though he has not seen you since he was a child.

Sir William. What signifies this affection to me? or how can I be proud of a place in a heart, where every sharper and coxcomb find an easy entrance?

Jarvis. I grant you that he is rather too good-natured; that he's too much every man's man; that he laughs this minute with one, and cries the next with another: but whose instructions may he thank for all this?

Sir William. Not mine, sure. My letters to him during my employment in Italy, taught him only that philosophy which might prevent, not defend, his errors.

Jarvis. Faith, begging your honor's pardon, I'm sorry they taught him any philosophy at all: it has only served to spoil him. This same philosophy is a good horse in a stable, but an arrant jade on a journey. For my own part, whenever I hear him mention the name on't, I'm always sure he's going to play the fool.

Sir William. Don't let us ascribe his faults to his philosophy, I entreat you. No, Jarvis, his good-nature arises rather from his fears of offending the importunate, than his desire of making the deserving happy.

Jarvis. What it arises from, I don't know; but, to be sure, everybody has it that asks for it.

Sir William. Ay, or that does not ask it. I have been now for some time a concealed spectator of his follies, and find them as boundless as his dissipation.

Jarvis. And yet, faith, he has some fine name or other for them all. He calls his extravagance, generosity; and his trusting everybody, universal benevolence. It was but last week he went security for a fellow whose face he scarce knew, and that he called an act of exalted mu — mu — munificence; ay, that was the name he gave it.

16

Sir William. And upon that I proceed, as my last effort, though with very little hopes, to reclaim him. That very fellow has just absconded, and I have taken up the security. Now, my intention is to involve him in fictitious distress, before he has plunged himself into real calamity: to arrest him for that very debt, to clap an officer upon him, and then let him see which of his friends will come to his relief.

Jarvis. Well, if I could but any way see him thoroughly vexed, every groan of his would be music to me; yet, faith, I believe it impossible. I have tried to fret him myself every morning these three years; but instead of being angry, he sits as calmly to hear me scold, as he does to his hair dresser.

Sir William. We must try him once more, however, and I'll go this instant to put my scheme into execution: and I don't despair of succeeding, as, by your means, I can have frequent opportunities of being about him without being known. What a pity it is, Jarvis, that any man's good-will to others should produce so much neglect of himself, as to require correction! Yet we must touch his weaknesses with a delicate hand. There are some faults so nearly allied to excellence, that we can scarce weed out the vice without eradicating the virtue. [*Exit.*

Jarvis. Well, go thy ways, Sir William Honeywood. It is not without reason, that the world allows thee to be the best of men. But here comes his hopeful nephew — the strange, good-natured, foolish, open-hearted — And yet, all his faults are such, that one loves him still the better for them.

Enter Honeywood.

Honeywood. Well, Jarvis, what messages from my friends this morning?

Jarvis. You have no friends.

Honeywood. Well, from my acquaintance then?

Jarvis. (*Pulling out bills.*) A few of our usual cards of compliment, that's all. This bill from your tailor; this from your mercer; and this from the little broker in Crooked-lane. He says he has been at a great deal of trouble to get back the money you borrowed.

Honeywood. That I don't know; but I am sure we were at a great deal of trouble in getting him to lend it.

Jarvis. He has lost all patience.

Honeywood. Then he has lost a very good thing.

Jarvis. There's that ten guineas you were sending to the poor gentleman and his children in the Fleet. I believe they would stop his mouth for a while at least.

Honeywood. Ay, Jarvis, but what will fill their mouths in the mean time? Must I be cruel, because he happens to be importunate; and, to relieve his avarice, leave them to insupportable distress?

Jarvis. 'Sdeath! sir, the question now is how to relieve yourself — yourself. Haven't I reason to be out of my senses, when I see things going at sixes and sevens?

Honeywood. Whatever reason you may have for being out of your senses, I hope you'll allow that I'm not quite unreasonable for continuing in mine.

Jarvis. You are the only man alive in your present situation that could do so. Every thing upon the waste.

There 's Miss Richland and her fine fortune gone already, and upon the point of being given to your rival.

Honeywood. I 'm no man's rival.

Jarvis. Your uncle in Italy preparing to disinherit you ; your own fortune almost spent ; and nothing but pressing creditors, false friends, and a pack of drunken servants that your kindness has made unfit for any other family.

Honeywood. Then they have the more occasion for being in mine.

Jarvis. Soh! What will you have done with him that I caught stealing your plate in the pantry ? In the fact — I caught him in the fact.

Honeywood. In the fact? If so, I really think that we should pay him his wages, and turn him off.

Jarvis. He shall be turned off at Tyburn, the dog ; we 'll hang him, if it be only to frighten the rest of the family.

Honeywood. No, Jarvis : it 's enough that we have lost what he has stolen ; let us not add to it the loss of a fellow creature !

Jarvis. Very fine ! well, here was the footman just now, to complain of the butler : he says he does most work, and ought to have most wages.

Honeywood. That 's but just ; though perhaps here comes the butler to complain of the footman.

Jarvis. Ay, it 's the way with them all, from the scullion to the privy-councillor. If they have a bad master, they keep quarrelling with him ; if they have a good master, they keep quarrelling with one another.

Enter Butler, drunk.

Butler. Sir, I 'll not stay in the family with Jonathan; you must part with him, or part with me, that 's the ex — ex — exposition of the matter, sir.

Honeywood. Full and explicit enough. But what 's his fault, good Philip?

Butler. Sir, he 's given to drinking, sir, and I shall have my morals corrupted by keeping such company.

Honeywood. Ha! ha! he has such a diverting way —

Jarvis. Oh, quite amusing.

Butler. I find my wine 's a-going, sir; and liquors do n't go without mouths, sir — I hate a drunkard, sir.

Honeywood. Well, well, Philip, I 'll hear you upon that another time; so go to bed now.

Jarvis. To bed! let him go to the devil.

Butler. Begging your honor's pardon, and begging your pardon, master Jarvis, I 'll not go to bed nor to the devil neither. I have enough to do to mind my cellar. I forgot, your honor, Mr. Croaker is below. I came on purpose to tell you.

Honeywood. Why did n't you show him up, blockhead.

Butler. Show him up, sir? With all my heart, sir. Up or down, all 's one to me. [*Exit.*

Jarvis. Ay, we have one or other of that family in this house from morning till night. He comes on the old affair, I suppose. The match between his son, that 's just returned from Paris, and Miss Richland, the young lady he 's guardian to.

Honeywood. Perhaps so. Mr. Croaker, knowing my

friendship for the young lady, has got it into his head that I can persuade her to what I please.

Jarvis. Ah! if you loved yourself but half as well as she loves you, we should soon see a marriage that would set all things to rights again.

Honeywood. Love me! Sure, Jarvis, you dream. No, no; her intimacy with me never amounted to more than friendship — mere friendship. That she is the most lovely woman that ever warmed the human heart with desire, I own: but never let me harbor a thought of making her unhappy, by a connection with one so unworthy her merits as I am. No, Jarvis, it shall be my study to serve her, even in spite of my wishes; and to secure her happiness, though it destroys my own.

Jarvis. Was ever the like? I want patience.

Honeywood. Besides, Jarvis, though I could obtain Miss Richland's consent, do you think I could succeed with her guardian, or Mrs. Croaker, his wife? who, though both very fine in their way, are yet a little opposite in their dispositions, you know.

Jarvis. Opposite enough, Heaven knows! the very reverse of each other: she all laugh, and no joke; he always complaining, and never sorrowful — a fretful poor soul, that has a new distress for every hour in the four-and-twenty —

Honeywood. Hush, hush! he 's coming up, he 'll hear you.

Jarvis. One whose voice is a passing bell —

Honeywood. Well, well; go, do.

Jarvis. A raven that bodes nothing but mischief — a coffin and cross-bones — a bundle of rue — a sprig of deadly nightshade — a — (*Honeywood, stopping his mouth, at last pushes him off.*) [*Exit Jarvis.*

Honeywood. I must own my old monitor is not entirely wrong. There is something in my friend Croaker's conversation that quite depresses me. His very mirth is an antidote to all gaiety, and his appearance has a stronger effect on my spirits than an undertaker's shop — Mr. Croaker, this is such a satisfaction —

Enter Croaker.

Croaker. A pleasant morning to Mr. Honeywood, and many of them. How is this? you look most shockingly to-day, my dear friend. I hope this weather does not affect your spirits. To be sure, if this weather continues — I say nothing; but God send we be all better this day three months!

Honeywood. I heartily concur in the wish, though, I own, not in your apprehensions.

Croaker. May be not. Indeed, what signifies what weather we have in a country going to ruin like ours? taxes rising and trade falling: money flying out of the kingdom, and Jesuits swarming into it. I know, at this time, no less than a hundred and twenty-seven Jesuits between Charing Cross and Temple Bar.

Honeywood. The Jesuits will scarce pervert you or me, I should hope.

Croaker. May be not. Indeed, what signifies whom they pervert, in a country that has scarce any religion to lose? I 'm only afraid for our wives and daughters.

Honeywood. I have no apprehensions for the ladies, I assure you.

Croaker. May be not. Indeed, what signifies whether they be perverted or no? The women in my time were good for something. I have seen a lady drest from top to toe in her own manufactures formerly; but now-a-days, the devil a thing of their own manufacture 's about them, except their faces.

Honeywood. But, however these faults may be practised abroad, you don 't find them at home, either with Mrs. Croaker, Olivia, or Miss Richland?

Croaker. The best of them will never be canonized for a saint when she 's dead.—By the by, my dear friend, I do n't find this match between Miss Richland and my son much relished, either by one side or t' other.

Honeywood. I thought otherwise.

Croaker. Ah! Mr. Honeywood, a little of your fine serious advice to the young lady might go far: I know she has a very exalted opinion of your understanding.

Honeywood. But would not that be usurping an authority, that more properly belongs to yourself?

Croaker. My dear friend, you know but little of my authority at home. People think, indeed, because they see me come out in the morning thus, with a pleasant face, and to make my friends merry, that all 's well within. But I have cares that would break a heart of stone. My wife has so encroached upon every one of my privileges, that I 'm now no more than a mere lodger in my own house.

Honeywood. But a little spirit exerted on your side might perhaps restore your authority.

Croaker. No, though I had the spirit of a lion! I do rouse sometimes; but what then? always haggling and haggling. A man is tired of getting the better, before his wife is tired of losing the victory.

Honeywood. It's a melancholy consideration, indeed, that our chief comforts often produce our greatest anxieties, and that an increase of our possessions is but an inlet to new disquietudes.

Croaker. Ah! my dear friend, these were the very words of poor Dick Doleful to me, not a week before he made away with himself. Indeed, Mr. Honeywood, I never see you but you put me in mind of poor Dick. Ah! there was merit neglected for you; and so true a friend! we loved each other for thirty years, and yet he never asked me to lend him a single farthing.

Honeywood. Pray what could induce him to commit so rash an action at last?

Croaker. I do n't know: some people were malicious enough to say it was keeping company with me; because we used to meet now and then, and open our hearts to each other. To be sure, I loved to hear him talk, and he loved to hear me talk; poor dear Dick! He used to say that Croaker rhymed to joker; and so we used to laugh — Poor Dick! [*Going to cry.*

Honeywood. His fate affects me.

Croaker. Ah! he grew sick of this miserable life, where we do nothing but eat and grow hungry, dress and undress, get up and lie down; while reason, that should watch like a nurse by our side, falls as fast asleep as we do.

Honeywood. To say a truth, if we compare that part of life which is to come, by that which we have past, the prospect is hideous.

Croaker. Life, at the greatest and best, is but a froward child, that must be humored and coaxed a little till it falls asleep, and then all the care is over.

Honeywood. Very true, sir, nothing can exceed the vanity of our existence, but the folly of our pursuits. We wept when we came into the world, and every day tells us why.

Croaker. Ah! my dear friend, it is a perfect satisfaction to be miserable with you. My son Leontine shan't lose the benefit of such fine conversation. I'll just step home for him. I am willing to show him so much seriousness in one scarce older than himself. And what if I bring my last letter to the Gazetteer, on the increase and progress of earthquakes? It will amuse us, I promise you. I there prove how the late earthquake is coming round to pay us another visit — from London to Lisbon — from Lisbon to the Canary Islands — from the Canary Islands to Palmyra — from Palmyra to Constantinople, and so from Constantinople back to London again. [*Exit.*

Honeywood. Poor Croaker! his situation deserves the utmost pity. I shall scarce recover my spirits these three days. Sure, to live upon such terms, is worse than death itself. And yet, when I consider my own situation — a broken fortune, a hopeless passion, friends in distress, the wish, but not the power to serve them ——

[*Pausing and sighing.*

Enter Butler.

Butler. More company below, sir; Mrs. Croaker and Miss Richland; shall I show them up? — but they're showing up themselves. [*Exit.*

Enter Mrs. Croaker and Miss Richland.

Miss Richland. You 're always in such spirits.

Mrs. Croaker. We have just come, my dear Honeywood, from the auction. There was the old deaf dowager, as usual, bidding like a fury against herself. And then so curious in antiquities! herself, the most genuine piece of antiquity in the whole collection.

Honeywood. Excuse me, ladies, if some uneasiness from friendship makes me unfit to share in this good humor: I know you 'll pardon me.

Mrs. Croaker. I vow he seems as melancholy as if he had taken a dose of my husband this morning. Well, if Richland here can pardon you, I must.

Miss Richland. You would seem to insinuate, madam, that I have particular reasons for being disposed to refuse it.

Mrs. Croaker. Whatever I insinuate, my dear, do n't be so ready to wish an explanation.

Miss Richland. I own I should be sorry Mr. Honeywood's long friendship and mine should be misunderstood.

Honeywood. There 's no answering for others, madam. But I hope you 'll never find me presuming to offer more than the most delicate friendship may readily allow.

Miss Richland. And I shall be prouder of such a tribute from you, than the most passionate professions from others.

Honeywood. My own sentiments, madam: friendship is a disinterested commerce between equals; love, an abject intercourse between tyrants and slaves.

Miss Richland. And without a compliment, I know

none more disinterested, or more capable of friendship, than Mr. Honeywood.

Mrs. Croaker. And, indeed, I know nobody that has more friends, at least among the ladies. Miss Fruzz, Miss Oddbody, and Miss Winterbottom, praise him in all companies. As for Miss Biddy Bundle, she 's his professed admirer.

Miss Richland. Indeed! an admirer! — I did not know, sir, you were such a favorite there. But is she seriously so handsome? Is she the mighty thing talked of?

Honeywood. The town, madam, seldom begins to praise a lady's beauty, till she 's beginning to lose it. [*Smiling.*

Mrs. Croaker. But she 's resolved never to lose it, it seems. For as her natural face decays, her skill improves in making the artificial one. Well, nothing diverts me more than one of those fine, old, dressy things, who thinks to conceal her age by every where exposing her person; sticking herself up in the front of a side-box; trailing through a minuet at Almack's, and then, in the public gardens — looking, for all the world, like one of the painted ruins of the place.

Honeywood. Every age has its admirers, ladies. While you, perhaps, are trading among the warmer climates of youth, there ought to be some to carry on a useful commerce in the frozen latitudes beyond fifty.

Miss Richland. But, then, the mortifications they must suffer, before they can be fitted out for traffic. I have seen one of them fret a whole morning at her hairdresser, when all the fault was her face.

Honeywood. And yet, I'll engage, has carried that face at last to a very good market. This good-natured town, madam, has husbands, like spectacles, to fit every age from fifteen to fourscore.

Mrs. Croaker. Well, you're a dear good-natured creature. But you know you're engaged with us this morning upon a strolling party. I want to show Olivia the town, and the things: I believe I shall have business for you the whole day.

Honeywood. I am sorry, madam, I have an appointment with Mr. Croaker, which it is impossible to put off.

Mrs. Croaker. What! with my husband? then I'm resolved to take no refusal. Nay, I protest you must. You know I never laugh so much as with you.

Honeywood. Why, if I must, I must. I'll swear you have put me into such spirits. Well, do you find jest, and I'll find laugh, I promise you. We'll wait for the chariot in the next room. [*Exeunt.*

Enter Leontine and Olivia.

Leontine. There they go, thoughtless and happy. My dearest Olivia, what would I give to see you capable of sharing in their amusements, and as cheerful as they are!

Olivia. How, my Leontine, how can I be cheerful, when I have so many terrors to oppress me? The fear of being detected by this family, and the apprehensions of a censuring world, when I must be detected ——

Leontine. The world, my love! what can it say? At worst it can only say, that, being compelled by a mercenary guardian to embrace a life you disliked, you formed a resolution of flying with the man of your choice; that you confided in his honor, and took refuge in my father's house, — the only one where yours could remain without censure.

Olivia. But consider, Leontine, your disobedience, and my indiscretion; your being sent to France to bring home a sister, and, instead of a sister, bringing home ——

Leontine. One dearer than a thousand sisters. One that I am convinced will be equally dear to the rest of the family, when she comes to be known.

Olivia. And that, I fear, will shortly be.

Leontine. Impossible, till we ourselves think proper to make the discovery. My sister, you know, has been with her aunt, at Lyons, since she was a child, and you find every creature in the family takes you for her.

Olivia. But may n't she write, may n't her aunt write?

Leontine. Her aunt scarce ever writes, and all my sister's letters are directed to me.

Olivia. But won't your refusing Miss Richland, for whom you know the old gentleman intends you, create a suspicion?

Leontine. There, there 's my master-stroke. I have resolved not to refuse her; nay, an hour hence I have consented to go with my father to make her an offer of my heart and fortune.

Olivia. Your heart and fortune?

Leontine. Do n't be alarmed, my dearest. Can Olivia think so meanly of my honor, or my love, as to suppose I could ever hope for happiness from any but her? No, my Olivia, neither the force, nor, permit me to add, the delicacy of my passion, leave any room to suspect me. I only offer Miss Richland a heart I am convinced she will refuse; as I am confident, that, without knowing it, her affections are fixed upon Mr. Honeywood.

Olivia. Mr. Honeywood! You 'll excuse my apprehensions; but when your merits come to be put in the balance ——

Leontine. You view them with too much partiality. However, by making this offer, I show a seeming compliance with my father's command; and perhaps, upon her refusal, I may have his consent to choose for myself.

Olivia. Well, I submit. And yet, my Leontine, I own, I shall envy her even your pretended addresses. I consider every look, every expression of your esteem, as due only to me. This is folly, perhaps; I allow it; but it is natural to suppose, that merit which has made an impression on one's own heart may be powerful over that of another.

Leontine. Do n't, my life's treasure, do n't let us make imaginary evils, when you know we have so many real ones to encounter. At worst, you know, if Miss Richland should consent, or my father refuse his pardon, it can but end in a trip to Scotland; and ——

Enter Croaker.

Croaker. Where have you been, boy? I have been seeking you. My friend Honeywood here has been saying such comfortable things! Ah! he 's an example indeed. Where is he? I left him here.

Leontine. Sir, I believe you may see him, and hear him too, in the next room: he 's preparing to go out with the ladies.

Croaker. Good gracious! can I believe my eyes or

my ears; I 'm struck dumb with his vivacity, and stunned with the loudness of his laugh. Was there ever such a transformation! *(a laugh behind the scenes, Croaker mimics it.)* Ha! ha! ha! there it goes; a plague take their balderdash! yet I could expect nothing less, when my precious wife was of the party. On my conscience, I believe she could spread a horse-laugh through the pews of a tabernacle.

Leontine. Since you find so many objections to a wife, sir, how can you be so earnest in recommending one to me?

Croaker. I have told you, and tell you again, boy, that Miss Richland's fortune must not go out of the family; one may find comfort in the money, whatever one does in the wife.

Leontine. But, sir, though in obedience to your desire, I am ready to marry her, it may be possible she has no inclination to me.

Croaker. I 'll tell you once for all how it stands. A good part of Miss Richland's large fortune consists in a claim upon government, which my good friend, Mr. Lofty, assures me the Treasury will allow. One half of this she is to forfeit, by her father's will, in case she refuses to marry you. So, if she rejects you, we seize half her fortune; if she accepts you, we seize the whole, and a fine girl into the bargain.

Leontine. But, sir, if you will listen to reason ——

Croaker. Come, then, produce your reasons. I tell you, I 'm fixed, determined — so now produce your reasons. When I am determined, I always listen to reason because it can then do no harm.

Leontine. You have alleged that a mutual choice was the first requisite in matrimonial happiness.

Croaker. Well, and you have both of you a mutual choice. She has her choice, — to marry you or lose half her fortune; and you have your choice, — to marry her, or pack out of doors without any fortune at all.

Leontine. An only son, sir, might expect more indulgence.

Croaker. An only father, sir, might expect more obedience; besides, has not your sister here, that never disobliged me in her life, as good a right as you? He 's a sad dog, Livy, my dear, and would take all from you. But he shan't, I tell you he shan't; for you shall have your share.

Olivia. Dear sir, I wish you 'd be convinced, that I can never be happy in any addition to my fortune, which is taken from his.

Croaker. Well, well, it 's a good child, so say no more; but come with me, and we shall see something that will give us a great deal of pleasure, I promise you, — old Ruggins, the currycomb maker, lying in state; I am told he makes a very handsome corpse, and becomes his coffin prodigiously. He was an intimate friend of mine, and these are friendly things we ought to do for each other.

[*Exeunt.*

ACT SECOND.

SCENE — *Croaker's House.*

Miss Richland, Garnet.

Miss Richland. Olivia not his sister! Olivia not Leontine's sister? You amaze me.

Garnet. No more his sister than I am; I had it all from his own servant: I can get anything from that quarter.

Miss Richland. But how? Tell me again, Garnet.

Garnet. Why, madam, as I told you before, instead of going to Lyons to bring home his sister, who has been there with her aunt these ten years, he never went farther than Paris; there he saw and fell in love with this young lady — by the by, of a prodigious family.

Miss Richland. And brought her home to my guardian as his daughter?

Garnet. Yes, and his daughter she will be. If he don't consent to their marriage, they talk of trying what a Scotch parson can do.

Miss Richland. Well, I own they have deceived me. And so demurely as Olivia carried it too! — Would you believe it, Garnet, I told her all my secrets; and yet the sly cheat concealed all this from me!

Garnet. And, upon my word, madam, I don't much blame her: she was loath to trust one with her secrets, that was so very bad at keeping her own.

Miss Richland. But, to add to their deceit, the young

gentleman, it seems, pretends to make me serious proposals. My guardian and he are to be here presently, to open the affair in form. You know I am to lose half my fortune if I refuse him.

Garnet. Yet, what can you do? For being, as you are, in love with Mr. Honeywood, madam ——

Miss Richland. How! idiot, what do you mean? In love with Mr. Honeywood! Is this to provoke me?

Garnet. That is, madam, in friendship with him: I meant nothing more than friendship, as I hope to be married — nothing more.

Miss Richland. Well, no more of this. As to my guardian and his son, they shall find me prepared to receive them: I'm resolved to accept their proposal with seeming pleasure, to mortify them by compliance, and so throw the refusal at last upon them.

Garnet. Delicious! and that will secure your whole fortune to yourself. Well, who could have thought so innocent a face could cover so much 'cuteness!

Miss Richland. Why, girl, I only oppose my prudence to their cunning, and practise a lesson they have taught me against themselves.

Garnet. Then you're likely not long to want employment, for here they come, and in close conference.

Enter Croaker and Leontine.

Leontine. Excuse me, sir, if I seem to hesitate upon the point of putting to the lady so important a question.

Croaker. Lord! good sir, moderate your fears; you're so plaguy shy, that one would think you had changed sexes. I tell you we must have the half or the whole.

Come, let me see with what spirit you begin: Well, why do n't you? Eh! What? Well then, I must, it seems — Miss Richland, my dear, I believe you guess at our business; an affair which my son here comes to open, that nearly concerns your happiness.

Miss Richland. Sir, I should be ungrateful not to be pleased with any thing that comes recommended by you.

Croaker. How, boy, could you desire a finer opening? Why do n't you begin, I say? [*To Leontine.*

Leontine. 'Tis true, madam — my father, madam — has some intentions — hem — of explaining an affair, — which — himself can best explain, madam.

Croaker. Yes, my dear; it comes entirely from my son; it 's all a request of his own, madam. And I will permit him to make the best of it.

Leontine. The whole affair is only this, madam: my father has a proposal to make, which he insists none but himself shall deliver.

Croaker. My mind misgives me, the fellow will never be brought on. (*Aside.*) In short, madam, you see before you one that loves you — one whose whole happiness is all in you.

Miss Richland. I never had any doubts of your regard, sir; and I hope you can have none of my duty.

Croaker. That 's not the thing, my little sweeting — My love! no, no, another guess lover than I: there he stands, madam; his very looks declare the force of his passion — Call up a look, you dog! (*Aside.*) But then, had you seen him, as I have, weeping, speaking soliloquies and blank verse, sometimes melancholy, and sometimes absent ——

Miss Richland. I fear, sir, he 's absent now; or such a declaration would have come most properly from himself.

Croaker. Himself! Madam, he would die before he could make such a confession; and if he had not a channel for his passion through me, it would ere now have drowned his understanding.

Miss Richland. I must grant, sir, there are attractions in modest diffidence above the force of words. A silent address is the genuine eloquence of sincerity.

Croaker. Madam, he has forgot to speak any other language; silence is become his mother-tongue.

Miss Richland. And it must be confessed, sir, it speaks very powerfully in his favor. And yet I shall be thought too forward in making such a confession; shan't I, Mr. Leontine?

Leontine. Confusion! my reserve will undo me. But, if modesty attracts her, impudence may disgust her. I'll try. *(Aside.)* Do n't imagine from my silence, madam, that I want a due sense of the honor and happiness intended me. My father, madam, tells me your humble servant is not totally indifferent to you — he admires you: I adore you; and when we come together, upon my soul, I believe we shall be the happiest couple in all St. James's.

Miss Richland. If I could flatter myself you thought as you speak, sir ——

Leontine. Doubt my sincerity, madam? By your dear self I swear. Ask the brave if they desire glory? ask cowards if they covet safety——

Croaker. Well, well, no more questions about it.

Leontine. Ask the sick if they long for health? ask misers if they love money? ask ——

Croaker. Ask a fool if he can talk nonsense? What's come over the boy? What signifies asking, when there's not a soul to give you an answer? If you would ask to the purpose, ask this lady's consent to make you happy.

Miss Richland. Why, indeed, sir, his uncommon ardor almost compels me — forces me to comply. And yet I'm afraid he 'll despise a conquest gained with too much ease; won't you, Mr. Leontine?

Leontine. Confusion! *(Aside.)* Oh, by no means, madam, by no means. And yet, madam, you talked of force. There is nothing I would avoid so much as compulsion in a thing of this kind. No, madam, I will still be generous, and leave you at liberty to refuse.

Croaker. But I tell you, sir, the lady is not at liberty. It 's a match. You see she says nothing. Silence gives consent.

Leontine. But, sir, she talked of force. Consider, sir, the cruelty of constraining her inclinations.

Croaker. But I say there 's no cruelty. Do n't you know, blockhead, that girls have always a round-about way of saying yes before company? So get you both gone together into the next room, and hang him that interrupts the tender explanations. Get you gone, I say; I 'll not hear a word.

Leontine. But, sir, I must beg leave to insist ——

Croaker. Get off, you puppy, or I 'll beg leave to insist upon knocking you down. Stupid whelp! But I do n't wonder: the boy takes entirely after his mother.

[*Exeunt Miss Richland and Leontine.*

Enter Mrs. Croaker.

Mrs. Croaker. Mr. Croaker, I bring you something, my dear, that I believe will make you smile.

Croaker. I 'll hold you a guinea of that, my dear.

Mrs. Croaker. A letter; and as I knew the hand, I ventured to open it.

Croaker. And how can you expect your breaking open my letters should give me pleasure?

Mrs. Croaker. Pooh! it 's from your sister at Lyons, and contains good news: read it.

Croaker. What a Frenchified cover is here! That sister of mine has some good qualities; but I could never teach her to fold a letter.

Mrs. Croaker. Fold a fiddlestick! Read what it contains.

Croaker (reading).

'DEAR NICK, — An English gentleman, of large fortune, has for some time made private, though honorable, proposals to your daughter Olivia. They love each other tenderly, and I find she has consented, without letting any of the family know, to crown his addresses. As such good offers do n't come every day, your own good sense, his large fortune, and family considerations, will induce you to forgive her. Yours ever,

RACHAEL CROAKER.'

My daughter Olivia privately contracted to a man of large fortune! This is good news indeed. My heart never foretold me of this. And yet, how slily the little baggage has carried it since she came home; not a word on 't to the old ones for the world. Yet I thought I saw something she wanted to conceal.

Mrs. Croaker. Well, if they have concealed their amour, they shan't conceal their wedding; that shall be public, I'm resolved.

Croaker. I tell thee, woman, the wedding is the most foolish part of the ceremony. I can never get this woman to think of the most serious part of the nuptial engagement.

Mrs. Croaker. What! would you have me think of their funeral? But come, tell me, my dear, don't you owe more to me than you care to confess? — Would you have ever been known to Mr. Lofty, who has undertaken Miss Richland's claim at the Treasury, but for me? Who was it first made him an acquaintance at Lady Shabbaroon's rout. Who got him to promise us his interest? Is not he a back-stair favorite — one that can do what he pleases with those that do what they please? Is not he an acquaintance that all your groaning and lamentations could never have got us.

Croaker. He is a man of importance, I grant you. And yet what amazes me is, that, while he is giving away places to all the world, he can't get one for himself.

Mrs. Croaker. That perhaps, may be owing to his nicety. Great men are not easily satisfied.

Enter French Servant.

Servant. An expresse from Monsieur Lofty. He vil be vait upon your honors instammant. He be only giving four five instruction, read two tree memorial, call upon von ambassadeur. He vil be vid you in one tree minutes.

Mrs. Croaker. You see now, my dear. What an extensive department! Well, friend, let your master know that we are extremely honored by this honor. Was there anything ever in a higher style of breeding? All messages among the great are now done by express.

[*Exit French servant.*

Croaker. To be sure, no man does little things with more solemnity, or claims more respect than he. But he 's in the right on't. In our bad world, respect is given where respect is claimed.

Mrs. Croaker. Never mind the world, my dear; you were never in a pleasanter place in your life. Let us now think of receiving him with proper respect, (*a loud rapping at the door,*) and there he is, by the thundering rap.

Croaker. Ay, verily, there he is! as close upon the heels of his own express, as an endorsement upon the back of a bill. Well, I'll leave you to receive him, whilst I go to chide my little Olivia for intending to steal a marriage without mine or her aunt's consent. I must seem to be angry, or she too may begin to despise my authority.

[*Exit.*

Enter Lofty, speaking to his Servant.

Lofty. And if the Venetian ambassador, or that teasing creature, the Marquis should call, I'm not at home. Damme, I'll be pack-horse to none of them. — My dear madam, I have just snatched a moment — And if the ex presses to his Grace be ready, let them be sent off; they 're of importance. — Madam, I ask ten thousand pardons.

Mrs. Croaker. Sir, this honor ——

Lofty. And, Dubardieu! if the person calls about the commission, let him know that it is made out. As for Lord Cumbercourt's stale request, it can keep cold: you understand me. — Madam, I ask ten thousand pardons.

Mrs. Croaker. Sir, this honor ——

Lofty. And Dubardieu! if the man comes from the Cornish borough, you must do him; you must do him, I say — Madam, I ask ten thousand pardons. — And if the Russian ambassador calls; but he will scarce call to-day, I believe. — And now, madam, I have just got time to express my happiness in having the honor of being permitted to profess myself your most obedient, humble servant.

Mrs. Croaker. Sir, the happiness and honor are all mine; and yet, I'm only robbing the public while I detain you.

Lofty. Sink the public, madam, when the fair are to be attended. Ah, could all my hours be so charmingly devoted! Sincerely, don't you pity us poor creatures in affairs? Thus it is eternally; solicited for places here, teased for pensions there, and courted everywhere. I know you pity me. Yes, I see you do.

Mrs. Croaker. Excuse me, sir, 'Toils of empires pleasures are,' as Waller says.

Lofty. Waller — Waller; is he of the House?

Mrs. Croaker. The modern poet of that name, sir.

Lofty. Oh, a modern! We men of business despise the moderns! and as for the ancients, we have no time to read them. Poetry is a pretty thing enough for our wives and daughters; but not for us. Why now, here I stand that know nothing of books. I say, madam, I know nothing of books; and yet, I believe, upon a land-carriage fishery, a stamp act, or a jaghire, I can talk my two hours without feeling the want of them.

Mrs. Croaker. The world is no stranger to Mr. Lofty's eminence in every capacity.

Lofty. I vow to gad, madam, you make me blush. I'm nothing, nothing, nothing in the world; a mere obscure gentleman. To be sure, indeed, one or two of the present ministers are pleased to represent me as a formidable man. I know they are pleased to bespatter me at all their little, dirty levees. Yet, upon my soul, I wonder what they see in me to treat me so! Measures, not men, have always been my mark; and I vow, by all that 's honorable, my resentment has never done the men, as mere men, any manner of harm — that is, as mere men.

Mrs. Croaker. What importance, and yet what modesty!

Lofty. Oh, if you talk of modesty, madam, there, I own, I'm accessible to praise: modesty is my foible: it was so the Duke of Brentford used to say of me. 'I love Jack Lofty,' he used to say, 'no man has a finer knowledge of things; quite a man of information; and when he speaks upon his legs, by the Lord, he's prodigious — he scouts them; and yet all men have their faults; too much modesty is his,' says his Grace.

Mrs. Croaker. And yet, I dare say, you don't want assurance when you come to solicit for your friends.

Lofty. Oh, there, indeed, I'm in bronze. Apropos! I have just been mentioning Miss Richland's case to a certain personage; we must name no names. When I ask, I'm not to be put off, madam. No, no, I take my friend by the button. A fine girl, sir; great justice in her case. A friend of mine. Borough interest. Business must be done, Mr. Secretary. I say, Mr. Secretary, her business must be done, sir. That's my way, madam.

Mrs. Croaker. Bless me! you said all this to the Secretary of State, did you?

Lofty. I did not say the Secretary, did I? Well, curse it, since you have found me out, I will not deny it, — it was to the Secretary.

Mrs. Croaker. This was going to the fountain-head at once, not applying to the understrappers, as Mr. Honeywood would have had us.

Lofty. Honeywood! he! he! He was indeed a fine solicitor. I suppose you have heard what has just happened to him?

Mrs. Croaker. Poor, dear man! no accident, I hope?

Lofty. Undone, madam, that 's all. His creditors have taken him into custody — a prisoner in his own house.

Mrs. Croaker. A prisoner in his own house! How? At this very time? I'm quite unhappy for him.

Lofty. Why, so am I. The man, to be sure, was immensely good-natured. But then, I could never find that he had anything in him.

Mrs. Croaker. His manner, to be sure, was excessive harmless; some, indeed, thought it a little dull. For my part, I always concealed my opinion.

Lofty. It can't be concealed, madam; the man was dull — dull as the last new comedy! a poor, impracticable creature! I tried once or twice to know if he was fit for business; but he had scarce talents to be groom-porter to an orange-barrow.

Mrs. Croaker. How differently does Miss Richland think of him! For, I believe, with all his faults, she loves him.

Lofty. Loves him! does she? You should cure her of that by all means. Let me see; what if she were sent to him this instant, in his present doleful situation? My life for it, that works her cure. Distress is a perfect antidote to love. Suppose we join her in the next room? Miss Richland is a fine girl, has a fine fortune, and must not be thrown away. Upon my honor, madam, I have a regard for Miss Richland; and, rather than she should be thrown away I should think it no indignity to marry her myself. [*Exeunt.*

Enter Olivia and Leontine.

Leontine. And yet, trust me, Olivia, I had every reason to expect Miss Richland's refusal, as I did everything in my power to deserve it. Her indelicacy surprises me.

Olivia. Sure, Leontine, there 's nothing so indelicate in being sensible of your merit. If so, I fear I shall be the most guilty thing alive.

Leontine. But you mistake, my dear. The same attention I used to advance my merit with you, I practised to lessen it with her. What more could I do?

Olivia. Let us now rather consider what is to be done. We have both dissembled too long. I have always been ashamed — I am now quite weary of it. Sure, I could never have undergone so much for any other but you.

Leontine. And you shall find my gratitude equal to your kindest compliance. Though our friends should totally forsake us, Olivia, we can draw upon content for the deficiencies of fortune.

Olivia. Then why should we defer our scheme of humble happiness, when it is now in our power? I may be the favorite of your father, it is true; but can it ever be thought, that his present kindness to a supposed child, will continue to a known deciever?

Leontine. I have many reasons to believe it will. As his attachments are but few, they are lasting. His own marriage was a private one, as ours may be. Besides, I have sounded him already at a distance, and find all his answers exactly to our wish. Nay, by an expression or two that dropped from him, I am induced to think he knows of this affair.

Olivia. Indeed! But that would be a happiness too great too be expected.

Leontine. However it be, I'm certain you have power over him; and am persuaded, if you informed him of our situation, that he would be disposed to pardon it.

Olivia. You had equal expectations, Leontine, from your last scheme with Miss Richland, which you find has succeeded most wretchedly.

Leontine. And that 's the best reason for trying another.

Olivia. If it must be so, I submit.

Leontine. As we could wish, he comes this way. Now, my dearest Olivia, be resolute. I'll just retire within hearing, to come in at a proper time, either to share your danger, or confirm your victory. [*Exit.*

Enter Croaker.

Croaker. Yes, I must forgive her; and yet not too easily, neither. It will be proper to keep up the decorums of resentment a little, if it be only to impress her with an idea of my authority.

Olivia. How I tremble to approach him! — Might I presume, sir — if I interrupt you ——

Croaker. No, child, where I have an affection, it is not a little thing can interrupt me. Affection gets over little things.

Olivia. Sir, you 're too kind. I 'm sensible how ill I deserve this partiality; yet, Heaven knows, there is nothing I would not do to gain it.

Croaker. And you have but too well succeeded, you little hussy, you. With those endearing ways of yours, on my conscience, I could be brought to forgive any thing, unless it were a very great offence indeed.

Olivia. But mine is such an offence — When you know my guilt — Yes, you shall know it, though I feel the greatest pain in the confession.

Croaker. Why, then, if it be so very great a pain, you may spare yourself the trouble; for I know every syllable of the matter before you begin.

Olivia. Indeed! then I 'm undone.

Croaker. Ay, miss, you wanted to steal a match, without letting me know it, did you? But I 'm not worth being consulted, I suppose, when there 's to be a marriage in my own family. No, I 'm to have no hand in the disposal of my own children. No, I 'm nobody. I 'm to be a mere article of family lumber; a piece of cracked china, to be stuck up in a corner.

Olivia. Dear sir, nothing but the dread of your authority could induce us to conceal it from you.

Croaker. No, no, my consequence is no more; I 'm as little minded as a dead Russian in winter, just stuck up with a pipe in its mouth till there comes a thaw — It goes to my heart to vex her. [*Aside.*

Olivia. I was prepared, sir, for your anger, and despaired of pardon, even while I presumed to ask it. But your severity shall never abate my affection, as my punishment is but justice.

Croaker. And yet you should not despair, neither, Livy. We ought to hope all for the best.

Olivia. And do you permit me to hope, sir? Can I ever expect to be forgiven? But hope has too long deceived me.

Croaker. Why then, child, it shan't deceive you now, for I forgive you this very moment; I forgive you all! and now you are indeed my daughter.

Olivia. Oh transport! this kindness overpowers me.

Croaker. I was always against severity to our children. We have been young and giddy ourselves, and we can 't expect boys and girls to be old before their time.

Olivia. What generosity! But can you forget the many falsehoods, the dissimulation ——

Croaker. You did indeed dissemble, you urchin you; but where 's the girl that won't dissemble for a husband? My wife and I had never been married, if we had not dissembled a little beforehand.

Olivia. It shall be my future care never to put such generosity to a second trial. And as for the partner of my offence and folly, from his native honor, and the just sense he has of his duty, I can answer for him that ——

Enter Leontine.

Leontine. Permit him thus to answer for himself. *(Kneeling.)* Thus, sir, let me speak my gratitude for this unmerited forgiveness. Yes, sir, this even exceeds all your former tenderness: I now can boast the most indulgent of fathers. The life he gave, compared to this, was but a trifling blessing.

Croaker. And, good sir, who sent for you, with that fine tragedy face, and flourishing manner? I do n't know what we have to do with your gratitude upon this occasion.

Leontine. How, sir! is it possible to be silent, when so much obliged? Would you refuse me the pleasure of being grateful? of adding my thanks to my Olivia's? of sharing in the transports that you have thus occasioned?

Croaker. Lord, sir, we can be happy enough without your coming in to make up the party. I do n't know what 's the matter with the boy all this day; he has got into such a rhodomontade manner all this morning!

Leontine. But, sir, I that have so large a part in the benefit, is it not my duty to show my joy? Is the being admitted to your favor so slight an obligation? Is the happiness of marrying Olivia so small a blessing?

Croaker. Marrying Olivia! marrying Olivia! marrying his own sister! Sure the boy is out of his senses. His own sister!

Leontine. My sister!

Olivia. Sister! how have I been mistaken! [*Aside.*

Leontine. Some cursed mistake in all this I find. [*Aside.*

Croaker. What does the booby mean? or has he any meaning? Eh, what do you mean, you blockhead, you?

Leontine. Mean, sir? — why, sir — only when my sister is to be married, that I have the pleasure of marrying her, sir, — that is, of giving her away, sir, — I have made a point of it.

Croaker. Oh, is that all? Give her away. You have made a point of it? Then you had as good make a point of first giving away yourself, as I 'm going to prepare the writings between you and Miss Richland this very minute. What a fuss is here about nothing! Why what 's the matter now? I thought I had made you at least as happy as you could wish.

Olivia. Oh, yes, sir; very happy.

Croaker. Do you foresee any thing, child? You look as if you did. I think if any thing was to be foreseen, I have as sharp a look-out as another; and yet I foresee nothing. [*Exit.*

Leontine and Olivia.

Olivia. What can it mean?

Leontine. He knows something, and yet, for my life, I can 't tell what.

Olivia. It can 't be the connection between us, I 'm pretty certain.

Leontine. Whatever it be, my dearest, I 'm resolved to put it out of fortune's power to repeat our mortification. I 'll haste and prepare for our journey to Scotland, this very evening. My friend Honeywood has promised me his advice and assistance. I 'll go to him and repose our distresses on his friendly bosom; and I know so much of his honest heart, that if he can't relieve our uneasiness, he will at least share them. [*Exeunt.*

ACT THIRD.

Scene — YOUNG HONEYWOOD'S HOUSE.

Bailiff, Honeywood, Follower.

Bailiff. Lookye, sir, I have arrested as good men as you in my time — no disparagement of you neither — men that would go forty guineas on a game of cribbage. I challenge the town to show a man in more genteeler practice than myself.

Honeywood. Without all question, Mr. —— I forget your name, sir?

Bailiff. How can you forget what you never knew? he! he! he!

Honeywood. May I beg leave to ask your name?

Bailiff. Yes, you may.

Honeywood. Then, pray sir, what is your name?

Bailiff. That I did n't promise to tell you.—He! he! he!— A joke breaks no bones, as we say among us that practise the law.

Honeywood. You may have reason for keeping it a secret, perhaps?

Bailiff. The law does nothing without reason. I 'm ashamed to tell my name to no man, sir. If you can show cause, as why, upon a special capus, that I should prove my name — But, come, Timothy Twitch is my name. And, now you know my name, what have you to say to that?

Honeywood. Nothing in the world, good Mr. Twitch, but that I have a favor to ask, that 's all.

Bailiff. Ay, favors are more easily asked than granted, as we say among us that practise the law. I have taken an oath against granting favors. Would you have me perjure myself?

Honeywood. But my request will come recommended in so strong a manner, as, I believe, you 'll have no scruple *(pulling out his purse)*. The thing is only this: I believe I shall be able to discharge this trifle in two or three days at farthest; but as I would not have the affair known for the world, I have thoughts of keeping you, and your good friend here, about me, till the debt is discharged; for which I shall be properly grateful.

Bailiff. Oh! that 's another maxum, and altogether within my oath. For certain, if an honest man is to get any thing by a thing, there 's no reason why all things should not be done in civility.

Honeywood. Doubtless, all trades must live, Mr. Twitch; and yours is a necessary one.

[*Gives him money.*

Bailiff. Oh! your honor; I hope your honor takes nothing amiss as I does, as I does nothing but my duty in so doing. I 'm sure no man can say I ever give a gentleman, that was a gentleman, ill usage. If I saw that a gentleman was a gentleman, I have taken money not to see him for ten weeks together.

Honeywood. Tenderness is a virtue, Mr. Twitch.

Bailiff. Ay, sir, it 's a perfect treasure. I love to see a gentleman with a tender heart. I do n't know, but I think I have a tender heart myself. If all that I have lost by my heart was put together, it would make a — but no matter for that.

Honeywood. Do n't account it lost, Mr. Twitch. The ingratitude of the world can never deprive us of the conscious happiness of having acted with humanity ourselves.

Bailiff. Humanity, sir, is a jewel. It 's better than gold. I love humanity. People may say, that we in our way have no humanity; but I 'll show you my humanity this moment. There 's my follower here, little Flanigan, with a wife and four children — a guinea or two would be more to him, than twice as much to another. Now, as I can 't show him any humanity myself, I must beg leave you 'll do it for me.

Honeywood. I assure you, Mr. Twitch, yours is a most powerful recommendation.

[*Giving money to the follower.*

Bailiff. Sir, you 're a gentleman. I see you know what to do with your money. But, to business; we are to be with you here as your friends, I suppose. But set in case company comes. Little Flanigan here, to be sure, has a good face — a very good face; but then, he is a little seedy, as we say among us that practise the law, — not well in clothes. Smoke the pocket-holes.

Honeywood. Well, that shall be remedied without delay.

Enter Servant.

Servant. Sir, Miss Richland is below.

Honeywood. How unlucky! Detain her a moment. We must improve my good friend little Mr. Flanigan's appearance first. Here, let Mr. Flanigan have a suit of my clothes — quick — the brown and silver — Do you hear?

Servant. That your honor gave away to the begging gentleman that makes verses, because it was as good as new.

Honeywood. The white and gold then.

Servant. That, your honor, I made bold to sell, because it was good for nothing.

Honeywood. Well, the first that comes to hand then — the blue and gold. I believe Mr. Flanigan would look best in blue. [*Exit Flanigan.*

Bailiff. Rabbit me, but little Flanigan will look well in any thing. Ah, if your honor knew that bit of flesh as well as I do, you 'd be perfectly in love with him. There 's not a prettier scout in the four counties after a shy-cock than he: scents like a hound — sticks like a weasel. He was master of the ceremonies to the black Queen of Morocco, when I took him to follow me. (*Re-enter Flanigan.*) Heh! ecod, I thinks he looks so well, that I do n't care if I have a suit from the same place for myself.

Honeywood. Well, well, I hear the lady coming. Dear Mr. Twitch, I beg you 'll give your friend directions not to speak. As for yourself, I know you will say nothing without being directed.

Bailiff. Never you fear me; I 'll show the lady I

have something to say for myself as well as another. One man has one way of talking, and another man has another, that 's all the difference between them.

Enter Miss Richland and Garnet.

Miss Richland. You 'll be surprised, sir, with this visit. But you know I 'm yet to thank you for choosing my little library.

Honeywood. Thanks, madam, are unnecessary; as it was I that was obliged by your commands. Chairs here. Two of my very good friends, Mr. Twitch and Mr. Flanigan. Pray, gentlemen, sit without ceremony.

Miss Richland. Who can these odd-looking men be? I fear it is as I was informed. It must be so. [*Aside.*

Bailiff. (*After a pause.*) Pretty weather; very pretty weather for the time of the year, madam.

Follower. Very good circuit weather in the country.

Honeywood. You officers are generally favorites among the ladies. My friends, madam, have been upon very disagreeable duty, I assure you. The fair should, in some measure, recompense the toils of the brave.

Miss Richland. Our officers do indeed deserve every favor. The gentlemen are in the marine service, I presume, sir?

Honeywood. Why, madam, they do — occasionally serve in the Fleet, madam. A dangerous service!

Miss Richland. I 'm told so. And I own it has often surprised me, that while we have had so many instances of bravery there, we have had so few of wit at home to praise it.

Honeywood. I grant, madam, that our poets have not

written as our sailors have fought; but they have done all they could, and Hawke or Amherst could do no more.

Miss Richland. I 'm quite displeased when I see a fine subject spoiled by a dull writer.

Honeywood. We should not be so severe against dull writers, madam. It is ten to one but the dullest writer exceeds the most rigid French critic who presumes to despise him.

Follower. Damn the French, the parle vous, and all that belongs to them!

Miss Richland. Sir!

Honeywood. Ha, ha, ha! honest Mr. Flanigan. A true English officer, madam; he 's not contented with beating the French, but he will scold them too.

Miss Richland. Yet, Mr. Honeywood, this does not convince me but that severity in criticism is necessary. It was our first adopting the severity of French taste, that has brought them in turn to taste us.

Bailiff. Taste us! By the Lord, madam, they devour us. Give Mounseers but a taste, and I 'll be damn'd but they come in for a bellyfull.

Miss Richland. Very extraordinary this!

Follower. But very true. What makes the bread rising? the parle vous that devour us. What makes the mutton fivepence a pound? the parle vous that eat it up. What makes the beer threepence-halfpenny a pot?——

Honeywood. Ah! the vulgar rogues; all will be out. *(Aside.)* Right, gentlemen, very right, upon my word, and quite to the purpose. They draw a parallel, madam, between the mental taste and that of our senses. We are injured as much by the French severity in the one, as by French rapacity in the other. That 's their meaning.

Miss Richland. Though I do n't see the force of the parallel, yet I 'll own, that we should sometimes pardon books, as we do our friends, that have now and then agreeable absurdities to recommend them.

Bailiff. That 's all my eye. The King only can pardon, as the law says: for, set in case ——

Honeywood. I 'm quite of your opinion, sir. I see the whole drift of your argument. Yes, certainly, our presuming to pardon any work, is arrogating a power that belongs to another. If all have power to condemn, what writer can be free?

Bailiff. By his habus corpus. His habus corpus can set him free at any time: for, set in case ——

Honeywood. I 'm obliged to you, sir, for the hint. If, madam, as my friend observes, our laws are so careful of a gentleman's person, sure we ought to be equally careful of his dearer part, his fame.

Follower. Ay, but if so be a man 's nabb'd, you know ——

Honeywood. Mr. Flanigan, if you spoke for ever, you could not improve the last observation. For my own part, I think it conclusive.

Bailiff. As for the matter of that, mayhap ——

Honeywood. Nay, sir, give me leave, in this instance, to be positive. For where is the necessity of censuring works without genius, which must shortly sink of themselves? what is it, but aiming an unnecessary blow against a victim already under the hands of justice?

Bailiff. Justice! Oh, by the elevens! if you talk about justice, I think I am at home there: for, in a course of law ——

Honeywood. My dear Mr. Twitch, I discern what you 'd be at, perfectly; and I believe the lady must be sensible of the art with which it is introduced. I suppose you perceive the meaning, madam, of his course of law.

Miss Richland. I protest, sir, I do not. I perceive only that you answer one gentleman before he has finished, and the other before he has well begun.

Bailiff. Madam, you are a gentlewoman, and I will make the matter out. This here question is about severity, and justice, and pardon, and the like of they. Now, to explain the thing ——

Honeywood. Oh! curse your explanations! [*Aside.*

Enter Servant.

Servant. Mr. Leontine, sir, below, desires to speak with you upon earnest business.

Honeywood. That 's lucky. (*Aside.*) Dear madam, you 'll excuse me and my good friends here, for a few minutes. There are books, madam, to amuse you. Come, gentlemen, you know I make no ceremony with such friends. After you, sir. Excuse me. Well, if I must. But I know your natural politeness.

Bailiff. Before and behind, you know.

Follower. Ay, ay, before and behind, before and behind. [*Exeunt Honeywood, Bailiff, and Follower.*

Miss Richland. What can all this mean, Garnet?

Garnet. Mean, madam! why, what should it mean, but what Mr. Lofty sent you here to see? These people he calls officers, are officers sure enough: sheriff's officers — bailiffs, madam.

Miss Richland. Ay, it is certainly so. Well, though

his perplexities are far from giving me pleasure, yet I own there is something very ridiculous in them, and a just punishment for his dissimulation.

Garnet. And so they are: but I wonder, madam, that the lawyer you just employed to pay his debts and set him free, has not done it by this time. He ought at least to have been here before now. But lawyers are always more ready to get a man into troubles than out of them.

Enter Sir William.

Sir William. For Miss Richland to undertake setting him free, I own, was quite unexpected. It has totally unhinged my schemes to reclaim him. Yet it gives me pleasure to find, that among a number of worthless friendships, he has made one acquisition of real value; for there must be some softer passion on her side, that prompts this generosity. Ha! here before me? I 'll endeavor to sound her affections. Madam, as I am the person that have had some demands upon the gentleman of this house, I hope you 'll excuse me, if, before I enlarged him, I wanted to see yourself.

Miss Richland. The precaution was very unnecessary, sir. I suppose your wants were only such as my agent had power to satisfy.

Sir William. Partly, madam. But I was also willing you should be fully apprized of the character of the gentleman you intended to serve.

Miss Richland. It must come, sir, with a very ill grace from you. To censure it, after what you have done, would look like malice; and to speak favorably of a character you have oppressed, would be impeaching your own. And sure, his tenderness, his humanity, his universal friendship, may atone for many faults.

Sir William. That friendship, madam, which is exerted in too wide a sphere, becomes totally useless. Our bounty, like a drop of water, disappears when diffused too widely. They who pretend most to this universal benevolence, are either deceivers or dupes, — men who desire to cover their private ill-nature by a pretended regard for all, or men who, reasoning themselves into false feelings, are more earnest in pursuit of splendid, than of useful, virtues.

Miss Richland. I am surprised, sir, to hear one, who has probably been a gainer by the folly of others, so severe in his censure of it.

Sir William. Whatever I have gained by folly, madam, you see I am willing to prevent your losing by it.

Miss Richland. Your cares for me, sir, are unnecessary; I always suspect those services which are denied where they are wanted, and offered, perhaps, in hopes of a refusal. No, sir, my directions have been given, and I insist upon their being complied with.

Sir William. Thou amiable woman! I can no longer contain the expressions of my gratitude — my pleasure. You see before you one who has been equally careful of his interest; one who has for some time been a concealed spectator of his follies, and only punished in hopes to reclaim them, — his uncle!

Miss Richland. Sir William Honeywood! You amaze me. How shall I conceal my confusion? I fear, sir, you 'll think I have been too forward in my services. I confess I ——

Sir William. Do n't make any apologies, madam. I only find myself unable to repay the obligation. And yet, I have been trying my interest of late to serve you. Having learned, madam, that you had some demands upon Government, I have, though unasked, been your solicitor there.

Miss Richland. Sir, I'm infinitely obliged to your intentions. But my guardian has employed another gentleman, who assures him of success.

Sir William. Who, the important little man that visits here? Trust me, madam, he's quite contemptible among men in power, and utterly unable to serve you. Mr. Lofty's promises are much better known to people of fashion than his person, I assure you.

Miss Richland. How have we been deceived! As sure as can be, here he comes.

Sir William. Does he? Remember I'm to continue unknown. My return to England has not as yet been made public. With what impudence he enters!

Enter Lofty.

Lofty. Let the chariot — let my chariot drive off; I'll visit to his Grace's in a chair. Miss Richland here before me! Punctual, as usual, to the calls of humanity. I'm very sorry, madam, things of this kind should happen, especially to a man I have shown every where, and carried amongst us as a particular acquaintance.

Miss Richland. I find, sir, you have the art of making the misfortunes of others your own.

Lofty. My dear madam, what can a private man like

me do? One man can't do every thing; and then, I do so much in this way every day. Let me see — something considerable might be done for him by subscription; it could not fail if I carried the list. I'll undertake to set down a brace of dukes, two dozen lords, and half the Lower House, at my own peril.

Sir William. And, after all, it's more than probable, sir, he might reject the offer of such powerful patronage.

Lofty. Then, madam, what can we do? You know I never make promises. In truth, I once or twice tried to do something with him in the way of business; but as I often told his uncle, Sir William Honeywood, the man was utterly impracticable.

Sir William. His uncle! then that gentleman, I suppose, is a particular friend of yours.

Lofty. Meaning me, sir? — Yes; madam, as I often said, My dear Sir William, you are sensible I would do any thing, as far as my poor interest goes, to serve your family: but what can be done? there's no procuring first-rate places for ninth rate-abilities.

Miss Richland. I have heard of Sir William Honeywood; he's abroad in employment: he confided in your judgment, I suppose?

Lofty. Why, yes, madam, I believe Sir William had some reason to confide in my judgment — one little reason, perhaps.

Miss Richland. Pray, sir, what was it?

Lofty. Why, madam — but let it go no farther — it was I procured him his place.

Sir William. Did you, sir?

Lofty. Either you or I, sir?

Miss Richland. This, Mr. Lofty, was very kind indeed.

Lofty. I did love him, to be sure; he had some amusing qualities; no man was fitter to be a toast-master to a club, or had a better head.

Miss Richland. A better head?

Lofty. Ay, at a bottle. To be sure he was as dull as a choice spirit; but hang it, he was grateful, very grateful; and gratitude hides a multitude of faults.

Sir William. He might have reason, perhaps. His place is pretty considerable, I 'm told.

Lofty. A trifle, a mere trifle among us men of business. The truth is, he wanted dignity to fill up a greater.

Sir William. Dignity of person, do you mean, sir? I 'm told he 's much about my size and figure, sir?

Lofty. Ay, tall enough for a marching regiment; but then he wanted a something — a consequence of form — a kind of a — I believe the lady perceives my meaning.

Miss Richland. Oh, perfectly! you courtiers can do any thing, I see.

Lofty. My dear madam, all this is but a mere exchange; we do greater things for one another every day. Why, as thus, now: Let me suppose you the First Lord of the Treasury; you have an employment in you that I want — I have a place in me that you want; do me here, do you there: interest of both sides, few words, flat, done and done, and it 's over.

Sir William. A thought strikes me. *(Aside.)* Now you mention Sir William Honeywood, madam, and as he seems, sir, an acquaintance of yours, you 'll be glad to hear he is arrived from Italy: I had it from a friend who knows him as well as he does me, and you may depend on my information.

Lofty. *(Aside.)* The devil he is! If I had known that, we should not have been quite so well acquainted.

Sir William. He is certainly returned; and as this gentleman is a friend of yours, he can be of signal service to us, by introducing me to him: there are some papers relative to your affairs that require despatch, and his inspection.

Miss Richland. This gentleman, Mr. Lofty, is a person employed in my affairs — I know you 'll serve us.

Lofty. My dear madam, I live but to serve you. Sir William shall even wait upon him, if you think proper to command it.

Sir William. That would be quite unnecessary.

Lofty. Well, we must introduce you then. Call upon me — let me see — ay, in two days.

Sir William. Now, or the opportunity will be lost for ever.

Lofty. Well, if it must be now, now let it be; but damn it, that 's unfortunate: My Lord Grig's cursed Pensacola business comes on this very hour, and I 'm engaged to attend — another time ——

Sir William. A short letter to Sir William will do.

Lofty. You shall have it; yet, in my opinion, a letter is a very bad way of going to work; face to face, that 's my way.

Sir William. The letter, sir, will do quite as well.

Lofty. Zounds! sir, do you pretend to direct me? direct me in the business of office? Do you know me, sir? who am I?

Miss Richland. Dear Mr. Lofty, this request is not so much his as mine; if my commands — but you despise my power.

Lofty. Delicate creature! — your commands could even control a debate at midnight: to a power so constitutional, I am all obedience and tranquillity. He shall have a letter: where is my secretary? Dubardieu. And yet, I protest, I do n't like this way of doing business. I think if I first spoke to Sir William — but you will have it so. [*Exit with Miss Richland.*

Sir William. (Alone.) Ha! ha! ha! This too is one of my nephew's hopeful associates. O vanity! thou constant deceiver, how do all thy efforts to exalt serve but to sink us! Thy false colorings, like those employed to heighten beauty, only seem to mend that bloom which they contribute to destroy. I 'm not displeased at this interview; exposing this fellow's impudence to the contempt it deserves, may be of use to my design; at least, if he can reflect, it will be of use to himself.

Enter Jarvis.

How now, Jarvis, where 's your master, my nephew?

Jarvis. At his wit's end, I believe: he 's scarce gotten out of one scrape, but he 's running his head into another.

Sir William. How so?

Jarvis. The house has but just been cleared of the bailiffs, and now he's again engaging, tooth and nail, in assisting old Croaker's son to patch up a clandestine match with the young lady that passes in the house for his sister.

Sir William. Ever busy to serve others.

Jarvis. Ay, anybody but himself. The young couple,

it seems, are just setting out for Scotland; and he supplies them with money for the journey.

Sir William. Money! how is he able to supply others, who has scarce any for himself?

Jarvis. Why, there it is: he has no money, that's true; but then, as he never said *No* to any request in his life, he has given them a bill, drawn by a friend of his upon a merchant in the city, which I am to get changed; for you must know that I am to go with them to Scotland myself.

Sir William. How?

Jarvis. It seems the young gentleman is obliged to take a different road from his mistress, as he is to call upon an uncle of his that lives out of the way, in order to prepare a place for their reception when they return; so they have borrowed me from my master, as the properest person to attend the young lady down.

Sir William. To the land of matrimony! A pleasant journey, Jarvis.

Jarvis. Ay, but I'm only to have all the fatigues on 't.

Sir William. Well, it may be shorter, and less fatiguing, than you imagine. I know but too much of the young lady's family and connections, whom I have seen abroad. I have also discovered that Miss Richland is not indifferent to my thoughtless nephew; and will endeavor, though I fear in vain, to establish that connection. But come, the letter I wait for must be almost finished; I'll let you farther into my intentions in the next room.

[*Exeunt.*

ACT FOURTH.

Scene — CROAKER'S HOUSE.

Enter Lofty.

Lofty. Well, sure the devil's in me of late, for running my head into such defiles, as nothing but a genius like my own could draw me from. I was formerly contented to husband out my places and pensions with some degree of frugality; but curse it, of late I have given away the whole Court Register in less time than they could print the title-page; yet, hang it, why scruple a lie or two to come at a fine girl, when I every day tell a thousand for nothing? Ha! Honeywood here before me. Could Miss Richland have set him at liberty?

Enter Honeywood.

Mr. Honeywood, I'm glad to see you abroad again. I find my concurrence was not necessary in your unfortunate affairs. I had put things in a train to do your business; but it is not for me to say what I intended doing.

Honeywood. It was unfortunate, indeed, sir. But what adds to my uneasiness is, that while you seem to be acquainted with my misfortune, I myself continue still a stranger to my benefactor.

Lofty. How! not know the friend that served you?

Honeywood. Can 't guess at the person.

Lofty. Inquire.

Honeywood. I have; but all I can learn is, that he chooses to remain concealed, and that all inquiry must be fruitless.

Lofty. Must be fruitless?

Honeywood. Absolutely fruitless.

Lofty. Sure of that?

Honeywood. Very sure.

Lofty. Then I 'll be damn'd if you shall ever know it from me.

Honeywood. How, sir?

Lofty. I suppose now, Mr. Honeywood, you think my rent-roll very considerable, and that I have vast sums of money to throw away; I know you do. The world, to be sure, says such things of me.

Honeywood. The world, by what I learn, is no stranger to your generosity. But where does this tend?

Lofty. To nothing — nothing in the world. The town, to be sure, when it makes such a thing as me the subject of conversation, has asserted, that I never yet patronized a man of merit.

Honeywood. I have heard instances to the contrary, even from yourself.

Lofty. Yes, Honeywood; and there are instances to the contrary, that you shall never hear from myself.

Honeywood. Ha! dear sir, permit me to ask you but one question.

Lofty. Sir, ask me no questions; I say, sir, ask me no questions; I 'll be damn'd if I answer them.

Honeywood. I will ask no farther. My friend! my benefactor! it is, it must be here, that I am indebted for freedom — for honor. Yes, thou worthiest of men, from the beginning I suspected it, but was afraid to return thanks; which, if undeserved, might seem reproaches.

Lofty. I protest I do not understand all this, Mr. Honeywood: you treat me very cavalierly. I do assure you, sir — Blood, sir, can 't a man be permitted to enjoy the luxury of his own feelings, without all this parade?

Honeywood. Nay, do not attempt to conceal an action that adds to your honor. Your looks, your air, your manner, all confess it.

Lofty. Confess it, sir! torture itself, sir, shall never bring me to confess it. Mr. Honeywood, I have admitted you upon terms of friendship. Don't let us fall out; make me happy, and let this be buried in oblivion. You know I hate ostentation; you know I do. Come, come, Honeywood, you know I always loved to be a friend, and not a patron. I beg this may make no kind of distance between us. Come, come, you and I must be more familiar — indeed we must.

Honeywood. Heavens! Can I ever repay such friendship? Is there any way? Thou best of men, can I ever return the obligation?

Lofty. A bagatelle, a mere bagatelle! But I see your heart is laboring to be grateful. You shall be grateful. It would be cruel to disappoint you.

Honeywood. How? teach me the manner. Is there any way?

Lofty. From this moment you 're mine. Yes, my friend, you shall know it — I 'm in love.

Honeywood. And can I assist you.

Lofty. Nobody so well.

Honeywood. In what manner? I 'm all impatience.

Lofty. You shall make love for me.

Honeywood. And to whom shall I speak in your favor?

Lofty. To a lady with whom you have a great interest, I assure you — Miss Richland.

Honeywood. Miss Richland!

Lofty. Yes, Miss Richland. She has struck the blow up to the hilt in my bosom, by Jupiter.

Honeywood. Heavens! was ever any thing more unfortunate? It is too much to be endured.

Lofty. Unfortunate, indeed! And yet I can endure it, till you have opened the affair to her for me. Between ourselves, I think she likes me. I 'm not apt to boast, but I think she does.

Honeywood. Indeed! But do you know the person you apply to?

Lofty. Yes, I know you are her friend and mine: that 's enough. To you, therefore, I commit the success of my passion. I 'll say no more, let friendship do the rest. I have only to add, that if at any time my little interest can be of service — but, hang it, I 'll make no promises: you know my interest is yours at any time. No apologies my friend, I 'll not be answered; it shall be so. [*Exit.*

Honeywood. Open, generous, unsuspecting man! He little thinks that I love her too; and with such an ardent passion! But then it was ever but a vain and hopeless one: my torment, my persecution! What shall I do? Love, friendship; a hopeless passion, a deserving friend! Love that has been my tormenter; a friend, that has p haps distressed himself to serve me. It shall be so. Yes, I will discard the fondling hope from my bosom, and exert all my influence in his favor. And yet to see her in the possession of another!—Insupportable! But then to betray a generous, trusting friend!—Worse, worse! Yes, I'm resolved. Let me but be the instrument of their happiness, and then quit a country, where I must for ever despair of finding my own. [*Exit.*

Enter Olivia and Garnet, who carries a milliner's box.

Olivia. Dear me, I wish this journey were over. No news of Jarvis yet? I believe the old peevish creature delays purely to vex me.

Garnet. Why, to be sure, madam, I did hear him say, a little snubbing before marriage would teach you to bear it the better afterwards.

Olivia. To be gone a full hour, though he had only to get a bill changed in the city! How provoking!

Garnet. I'll lay my life, Mr. Leontine, that had twice as much to do, is setting off by this time from his inn: and here you are left behind.

Olivia. Well, let us be prepared for his coming, however. Are you sure you have omitted nothing, Garnet?

Garnet. Not a stick, madam; all's here. Yet I wish you could take the white and silver to be married in. It's the worst luck in the world in any thing but white. I knew one Bett Stubbs of our town, that was married in red; and as sure as eggs is eggs, the bridegroom and she had a miff before morning.

Olivia. No matter, I'm all impatience till we are out of the house.

Garnet. Bless me, madam, I had almost forgot the wedding ring! The sweet little thing. I do n't think it would go on my little finger. And what if I put in a gentleman's night-cap, in case of necessity, madam?—But here 's Jarvis.

Enter Jarvis.

Olivia. O Jarvis, are you come at last! We have been ready this half hour. Now let 's be going. Let us fly!

Jarvis. Ay, to Jericho; for we shall have no going to Scotland this bout, I fancy.

Olivia. How! what 's the matter?

Jarvis. Money, money is the matter, madam. We have got no money. What the plague do you send me of your fool's errand for? My master's bill upon the city is not worth a rush. Here it is; Mrs. Garnet may pin up her hair with it.

Olivia. Undone! How could Honeywood serve us so? What shall we do? Can 't we go without it?

Jarvis. Go to Scotland without money! To Scotland without money! Lord! how some people understand geography! We might as well set sail for Patagonia upon a cork-jacket.

Olivia. Such a disappointment! What a base, insincere man was your master, to serve us in this manner! Is this his good-nature?

Jarvis. Nay, do n't talk ill of my master, madam; I won't bear to hear any body talk ill of him but myself.

Garnet. Bless us! now I think on 't, madam, you need not be under any uneasiness: I saw Mr. Leontine receive forty guineas from his father just before he set out, and he can 't yet have left the inn. A short letter will reach him there.

Olivia. Well remembered, Garnet; I 'll write immediately. How 's this? Bless me, my hand trembles so, I can 't write a word. Do you write, Garnet; and, upon second thought, it will be better from you.

Garnet. Truly, madam, I write and indite but poorly. I never was cute at my learning. But I 'll do what I can to please you. Let me see. All out of my own head, I suppose?

Olivia. Whatever you please.

Garnet. (*Writing.*) 'Muster Croaker' — Twenty guineas, madam?

Olivia. Ay, twenty will do.

Garnet. 'At the bar of the Talbot till called for. — Expedition — Will be blown up — All of a flame — Quick despatch — Cupid, the little god of love.' — I conclude it, madam, with Cupid: I love to see a love letter end like poetry.

Olivia. Well, well, what you please, any thing. But how shall we send it? I can trust none of the servants of this family.

Garnet. Odso, madam, Mr. Honeywood's butler is in the next room: he's a dear, sweet man; he 'll do any thing for me.

Jarvis. He! the dog, he 'll certainly commit some blunder. He 's drunk and sober ten times a-day.

Olivia. No matter. Fly, Garnet: any body we can trust will do. [*Exit Garnet.*] Well, Jarvis, now we can have nothing more to interrupt us; you may take up the things, and carry them on to the inn. Have you no hands, Jarvis?

Jarvis. Soft and fair, young lady. You that are going to be married think things can never be done too fast; but we, that are old, and know what we are about, must elope methodically, madam.

Olivia. Well, sure, if my indiscretions were to be done over again——

Jarvis. My life for it, you would do them ten times over——

Olivia. Why will you talk so? If you knew how unhappy they make me——

Jarvis. Very unhappy, no doubt: I was once just as unhappy when I was going to be married myself. I'll tell you a story about that——

Olivia. A story! when I am all impatience to be away. Was there ever such a dilatory creature!

Jarvis. Well, madam, if we must march, why we will march, that's all. Though, odds-bobs, we have still forgot one thing we should never travel without—a case of good razors, and a box of shaving powder. But no matter, I believe we shall be pretty well shaved by the way. [*Going.*

Enter Garnet.

Garnet. Undone, undone, madam. Ah, Mr. Jarvis, you said right enough. As sure as death, Mr. Honeywood's rogue of a drunken butler dropped the letter before he went ten yards from the door. There's old Croaker has just picked it up, and is this moment reading it to himself in the hall.

Olivia. Unfortunate! we shall be discovered.

Garnet. No, madam; do n't be uneasy, he can make neither head nor tail of it. To be sure, he looks as if he was broke loose from Bedlam, about it, but he can 't find what it means for all that. O lud, he is coming this way all in the horrors.

Olivia. Then let us leave the house this instant for fear he should ask farther questions. In the mean time, Garnet, do you write and send off just such another.

[*Exeunt.*

Enter Croaker.

Croaker. Death and destruction! Are all the horrors of air, fire, and water, to be levelled only at me? Am I only to be singled out for gunpowder plots, combustibles, and conflagrations? Here it is — An incendiary letter dropped at my door. 'To Muster Croaker, these with speed.' Ay, ay, plain enough the direction: all in the genuine incendiary spelling, and as cramp as the devil. 'With speed.' Oh, confound your speed! But let me read it once more. (*Reads.*) 'Muster Croaker, as sone as yowe see this, leve twenty gunnes at the bar of the Talboot tell caled for, or yowe and yower experetion will be al blown up.' Ah, but too plain! Blood and gunpowder in every line of it. Blown up! murderous dog! All blown up! Heavens! what have I and my poor family done, to be all blown up? (*Reads.*) 'Our pockets are low, and money we must have.' Ay, there 's the reason; they 'll blow us up, because they have got low pockets. (*Reads.*) 'It is but a short time you have to consider; for if this takes wind, the house will quickly be all of a flame.' Inhuman monsters! blow us up, and then burn us! The earthquake at Lisbon was but a bonfire to it. *(Reads.)* 'Make quick despatch, and so no more at present. But may Cupid, the little god of love, go with you wherever you go.' The little god of love! Cupid, the little god of love, go with me! — Go you to the devil, you and your little Cupid together. I'm so frightened, I scarce know whether I sit, stand, or go. Perhaps this moment I'm treading on lighted matches, blazing brimstone, and barrels of gunpowder. They are preparing to blow me up into the clouds. Murder! We shall be all burnt in our beds; we shall be all burnt in our beds!

Enter Miss Richland.

Miss Richland. Lord, sir, what's the matter?

Croaker. Murder's the matter. We shall be all blown up in our beds before morning.

Miss Richland. I hope not, sir.

Croaker. What signifies what you hope, madam, when I have a certificate of it here in my hand? Will nothing alarm my family? Sleeping and eating — sleeping and eating is the only work from morning till night in my house. My insensible crew could sleep though rocked by an earthquake, and fry beef-steaks at a volcano.

Miss Richland. But, sir, you have alarmed them so often already; we have nothing but earthquakes, famines, plagues, and mad dogs from year's end to year's end. You remember, sir, it is not above a month ago, you assured us of a conspiracy among the bakers to poison us in our bread; and so kept the whole family a week upon potatoes.

Croaker. And potatoes were too good for them. But why do I stand talking here with a girl, when I should be facing the enemy without! Here, John, Nicodemus, search the house. Look into the cellars, to see if there be any combustibles below; and above, in the apartments, that no matches be thrown in at the windows. Let all the fires be put out, and let the engine be drawn out in the yard, to play upon the house in case of necessity. [*Exit.*

Miss Richland. (*Alone.*) What can he mean by all this? Yet why should I inquire, when he alarms us in this manner almost every day. But Honeywood has desired an interview with me in private. What can he mean? or rather, what means this palpitation at his approach? It is the first time he ever showed anything in his conduct that seemed particular. Sure, he cannot mean to — but he 's here.

Enter Honeywood.

Honeywood. I presumed to solicit this interview, madam, before I left town, to be permitted ——

Miss Richland. Indeed! leaving town, sir?

Honeywood. Yes, madam, perhaps the kingdom. I have presumed, I say, to desire the favor of this interview in order to disclose something which our long friendship prompts. And yet my fears ——

Miss Richland. His fears! what are his fears to mine! (*Aside.*) We have, indeed, been long acquainted, sir; very long. If I remember, our first meeting was at the French ambassador's. Do you recollect how you were pleased to rally me upon my complexion there?

Honeywood. Perfectly, madam; I presumed to reprove you for painting; but your warmer blushes soon convinced the company that the coloring was all from nature.

Miss Richland. And yet you only meant it in your good-natured way, to make me pay a compliment to myself. In the same manner, you danced that night with the most awkward woman in company, because you saw nobody else would take her out.

Honeywood. Yes; and was rewarded the next night by dancing with the finest woman in company, whom everybody wished to take out.

Miss Richland. Well, sir, if you thought so then, I fear your judgment has since corrected the errors of a first impression. We generally show to most advantage at first. Our sex are like poor tradesmen, that put all their best goods to be seen at the windows.

Honeywood. The first impression, madam, did indeed decieve me. I expected to find a woman with all the faults of conscious, flattered beauty: I expected to find her vain and insolent. But every day has since taught me, that it is possible to possess sense without pride, and beauty without affectation.

Miss Richland. This, sir, is a style very unusual with Mr. Honeywood; and I should be glad to know why he thus attempts to increase that vanity, which his own lessons have taught me to despise.

Honeywood. I ask pardon, madam. Yet, from our long friendship, I presumed I might have some right to offer, without offence, what you may refuse without offending.

Miss Richland. Sir! I beg you 'd reflect: though I

fear I shall scarce have any power to refuse a request of yours, yet you may be precipitate: consider, sir.

Honeywood. I own my rashness; but as I plead the cause of friendship, of one who loves — don't be alarmed, madam — who loves you with the most ardent passion, whose whole happiness is placed in you ——

Miss Richland. I fear, sir, I shall never find whom you mean, by this description of him.

Honeywood. Ah, madam, it but too plainly points him out! though he should be too humble himself to urge his pretensions, or you too modest to understand them.

Miss Richland. Well, it would be affectation any longer to pretend ignorance; and I will own, sir, I have long been prejudiced in his favor. It was but natural to wish to make his heart mine, as he seemed himself ignorant of its value.

Honeywood. I see she always loved him. *(Aside)* I find, madam, you 're already sensible of his worth, his passion. How happy is my friend to be the favorite of one with such sense to distinguish merit, and such beauty to reward it!

Miss Richland. Your friend, sir! what friend?

Honeywood. My best friend — my friend Mr. Lofty, madam.

Miss Richland. He, sir?

Honeywood. Yes, he, madam. He is, indeed, what your warmest wishes might have formed him; and to his other qualities he adds that of the most passionate regard for you.

Miss Richland. Amazement! — No more of this, I beg you, sir.

Honeywood. I see your confusion, madam, and know how to interpret it. And, since I so plainly read the language of your heart, shall I make by friend happy, by communicating your sentiments?

Miss Richland. By no means.

Honeywood. Excuse me, I must; I know you desire it.

Miss Richland. Mr. Honeywood, let me tell you, that you wrong my sentiments and yourself. When I first applied to your friendship, I expected advice and assistance; but now, sir, I see that it is in vain to expect happiness from him who has been so bad an economist of his own; and that I must disclaim his friendship who ceases to be a friend to himself. [*Exit.*

Honeywood. How is this? she has confessed she loved him, and yet she seemed to part in displeasure. Can I have done anything to reproach myself with? No! I believe not: yet, after all, these things should not be done by a third person: I should have spared her confusion. My friendship carried me a little too far.

Enter Croaker, with the letter in his hand, and Mrs. Croaker.

Mrs. Croaker. Ha! ha! ha! And so, my dear, it 's your supreme wish that I should be quite wretched upon this occasion? Ha! ha!

Croaker. (*Mimicking.*) Ha! ha! ha! And so, my dear, it 's your supreme pleasure to give me no better consolation?

Mrs. Croaker. Positively, my dear; what is this incendiary stuff and trumpery to me? Our house may travel through the air, like the house of Loretto, for aught I care, If I 'm to be miserable in it.

Croaker. Would to heaven it were converted into a house of correction for your benefit. Have we not everything to alarm us? Perhaps this very moment the tragedy is beginning.

Mrs. Croaker. Then let us reserve our distress till the rising of the curtain, or give them the money they want, and have done with them.

Croaker. Give them my money! — and pray, what right have they to my money?

Mrs. Croaker. And pray, what right, then, have you to my good-humor?

Croaker. And so your good-humor advises me to part with my money? Why, then, to tell your good-humor a piece of my mind, I 'd sooner part with my wife. Here is Mr. Honeywood; see what he 'll say to it. My dear Honeywood, look at this incendiary letter dropped at my door. It will freeze you with terror; and yet lovey can read it — can read it, and laugh.

Mrs. Croaker. Yes, and so will Mr. Honeywood.

Croaker. If he does, I 'll suffer to be hanged the next minute in the rogue's place, that 's all.

Mrs. Croaker. Speak, Mr. Honeywood; is there any thing more foolish than my husband's fright upon this occasion?

Honeywood. It would not become me to decide, madam; but, doubtless, the greatness of his terrors now will but invite them to renew their villany another time.

Mrs. Croaker. I told you, he'd be of my opinion.

Croaker. How, sir! Do you maintain that I should

lie down under such an injury, and show, neither by my fears nor complaints, that I have something of the spirit of a man in me?

Honeywood. Pardon me, sir. You ought to make the loudest complaints, if you desire redress. The surest way to have redress is to be earnest in the pursuit of it.

Croaker. Ay, whose opinion is he of now?

Mrs. Croaker. But do n't you think that laughing off our fears is the best way?

Honeywood. What is the best, madam, few can say; but I 'll maintain it to be a very wise way.

Croaker. But we 're talking of the best. Surely the best way is to face the enemy in the field, and not wait till he plunders us in our very bed-chamber.

Honeywood. Why, sir, as to the best, that — that s a very wise way too.

Mrs. Croaker. But can any thing be more absurd, than to double our distresses by our apprehensions, and put it in the power of every low fellow, that can scrawl ten words of wretched spelling, to torment us?

Honeywood. Without doubt, nothing more absurd.

Croaker. How! would it not be more absurd to despise the rattle till we are bit by the snake?

Honeywood. Without doubt, perfectly absurd.

Croaker. Then you are of my opinion.

Honeywood. Entirely.

Mrs. Croaker. And you reject mine?

Honeywood. Heavens forbid, madam! No, sure no reasoning can be more just than yours. We ought certainly to despise malice, if we cannot oppose it, and not make the incendiary's pen as fatal to our repose as the highwayman's pistol.

Mrs. Croaker. Oh, then you think I 'm quite right?

Honeywood. Perfectly right.

Croaker. A plague of plagues, we can't be both right. I ought to be sorry, or I ought to be glad. My hat must be on my head, or my hat must be off.

Mrs. Croaker. Certainly, in two opposite opinions, if one be perfectly reasonable, the other can 't be perfectly right.

Honeywood. And why may not both be right, madam? Mr. Croaker in earnestly seeking redress, and you in waiting the event in good-humor? Pray, let me see the letter again. I have it. This letter requires twenty guineas to be left at the bar of the Talbot Inn. If it be indeed an incendiary letter, what if you and I, sir, go there; and when the writer comes to be paid his expected booty, seize him?

Croaker. My dear friend, it 's the very thing — the very thing. While I walk by the door, you shall plant yourself in ambush near the bar; burst out upon the miscreant like a masked battery; extort a confession at once, and so hang him up by surprise.

Honeywood. Yes, but I would not choose to exercise too much severity. It is my maxim, sir, that crimes generally punish themselves.

Croaker. Well, but we may upbraid him a little, I suppose. *(Ironically.)*

Honeywood. Ay, but not punish him too rigidly.

Croaker. Well, well, leave that to my own benevolence.

Honeywood. Well, I do; but remember that universal benevolence is the first law of nature.

[*Exeunt Honeywood and Mrs. Croaker.*

Croaker. Yes; and my universal benevolence will hang the dog, if he had as many necks as a hydra.

ACT FIFTH.

Scene — AN INN.

Enter Olivia and Jarvis.

Olivia. Well, we have got safe to the inn, however. Now, if the post-chaise were ready ——

Jarvis. The horses are just finishing their oats; and, as they are not going to be married, they choose to take their own time.

Olivia. You are for ever giving wrong motives to my impatience.

Jarvis. Be as impatient as you will, the horses must take their own time; besides, you do n't consider we have got no answer from our fellow-traveller yet. If we hear nothing from Mr. Leontine, we have only one way left us.

Olivia. What way?

Jarvis. The way home again.

Olivia. Not so. I have made a resolution to go, and nothing shall induce me to break it.

Jarvis. Ay; resolutions are well kept, when they jump with inclination. However, I 'll go hasten things without. And I 'll call, too, at the bar to see if any thing

should be left for us there. • Do n't be in such a plaguy hurry, madam, and we shall go the faster, I promise you.
[*Exit Jarvis.*

Enter Landlady.

Landlady. What! Solomon, why do n't you move? Pipes and tobacco for the Lamb there. Will nobody answer? To the Dolphin; quick. The Angel has been outrageous this half hour. Did your ladyship call, madam?

Olivia. No, madam.

Landlady. I find as you are for Scotland, madam — but that 's no business of mine; married, or not married, I ask no questions. To be sure, we had a sweet little couple set off from this two days ago for the same place. The gentleman, for a tailor, was, to be sure, as fine a spoken tailor as ever blew froth from a full pot. And the young lady so bashful, it was near half an hour before we could get her to finish a pint of raspberry between us.

Olivia. But this gentleman and I are not going to be married, I assure you.

Landlady. May be not. That 's no business of mine: for certain Scotch marriages seldom turn out well. There was, of my own knowledge, Miss Macfag, that married her father's footman. Alack-a-day, she and her husband soon parted, and now keep separate cellars in Hedge-lane.

Olivia. *(Aside.)* A very pretty picture of what lies before me!

Enter Leontine.

Leontine. My dear Olivia, my anxiety, till you were

out of danger, was too great to be resisted. I could not help coming to see you set out, though it exposes us to a discovery.

Olivia. May everything you do prove as fortunate. Indeed, Leontine, we have been most cruelly disappointed. Mr. Honeywood's bill upon the city has, it seems, been protested, and we have been utterly at a loss how to proceed.

Leontine. How! an offer of his own too! Sure he could not mean to deceive us?

Olivia. Depend upon his sincerity; he only mistook the desire for the power of serving us. But let us think no more of it. I believe the post-chaise is ready by this.

Landlady. Not quite yet; and begging your ladyship's pardon, I do n't think your ladyship quite ready for the post-chaise. The north road is a cold place, madam. I have a drop in the house of as pretty raspberry as ever was tipt over tongue. Just a thimblefull to keep the wind off your stomach. To be sure, the last couple we had here, they said it was a perfect nosegay. Ecod, I sent them both away as good-natured — Up went the blinds, round went the wheels, and Drive away, post-boy! was the word.

Enter Croaker.

Croaker. Well, while my friend Honeywood is upon the post of danger at the bar, it must be my business to have an eye about me here. I think I know an incendiary's look; for wherever the devil makes a purchase, he never fails to set his mark. Ha! who have we here? My son and daughter! What can they be doing here?

Landlady. I tell you, madam, it will do you good; I think I know by this time what 's good for the north road. It 's a raw night, madam.——Sir —

Leontine. Not a drop more, good madam. I should now take it as a greater favor, if you hasten the horses, for I am afraid to be seen myself.

Landlady. That shall be done. Wha, Solomon! are you all dead there? Wha, Solomon, I say!

[*Exit, bawling.*

Olivia. Well, I dread lest an expedition begun in fear, should end in repentance. Every moment we stay increases our danger, and adds to my apprehensions.

Leontine. There 's no danger, trust me, my dear; there can be none. If Honeywood has acted with honor, and kept my father, as he promised, in employment till we are out of danger, nothing can interrupt our journey.

Olivia. I have no doubt of Mr. Honeywood's sincerity, and even his desire to serve us. My fears are from your father's suspicions. A mind so disposed to be alarmed without a cause, will be but too ready when there 's a reason.

Leontine. Why, let him, when we are out of his power. But believe me, Olivia, you have no great reason to dread his resentment. His repining temper, as it does no manner of injury to himself, so will it never do harm to others. He only frets to keep himself employed, and scolds for his private amusement.

Olivia. I do n't know that; but I 'm sure, on some occasions, it makes him look most shockingly.

Croaker discovering himself.

Croaker. How does he look now? — How does he look now?

Olivia. Ah!

Leontine. Undone!

Croaker. How do I look now? Sir, I am your very humble servant. Madam, I am yours! What! you are going off, are you? Then, first, if you please, take a word or two from me with you before you go. Tell me first where you are going; and when you have told me that, perhaps I shall know as little as I did before.

Leontine. If that be so, our answer might but increase your displeasure, without adding to your information.

Croaker. I want no information from you, puppy; and you too, good madam, what answer have you got? Eh! *(A cry without, Stop him.)* I think I heard a noise. My friend Honeywood without — has he seized the incendiary? Ah, no, for now I hear no more on 't.

Leontine. Honeywood without! Then, sir, it was Mr. Honeywood that directed you hither?

Croaker. No, sir, it was not Mr. Honeywood conducted me hither.

Leontine. Is it possible?

Croaker. Possible! why he 's in the house now, sir; more anxious about me than my own son, sir.

Leontine. Then, sir, he 's a villain.

Croaker. How, sirrah! a villain, because he takes most care of your father? I 'll not bear it. I tell you I 'll not bear it. Honeywood is a friend to the family, and I 'll have him treated as such.

Leontine. I shall study to repay his friendship as it deserves.

Croaker. Ah, rogue, if you knew how earnestly he entered into my griefs, and pointed out the means to detect them, you would love him as I do. *(A cry without, Stop him.)* Fire and fury! they have seized the incendiary: they have the villain, the incendiary in view. Stop him! stop an incendiary! a murderer! stop him! [*Exit.*

Olivia. Oh, my terrors! What can this tumult mean?

Leontine. Some new mark, I suppose, of Mr. Honeywood's sincerity. But we shall have satisfaction: he shall give me instant satisfaction.

Olivia. It must not be, my Leontine, if you value my esteem or my happiness. Whatever be our fate, let us not add guilt to our misfortunes: consider that our innocence will shortly be all that we have left us. You must forgive him.

Leontine. Forgive him! Has he not in every instance betrayed us? Forced me to borrow money from him, which appears a mere trick to delay us; promised to keep my father engaged till we were out of danger, and here brought him to the very scene of our escape?

Olivia. Do n't be precipitate. We may yet be mistaken.

Enter Post-boy, dragging in Jarvis; Honeywood entering soon after.

Postboy. Ay, master, we have him fast enough. Here is the incendiary dog. I 'm entitled to the reward; I 'll take my oath I saw him ask for the money at the bar, and then run for it.

Honeywood. Come, bring him along. Let us see him. Let him learn to blush for his crimes. *(Discovering his mistake.)* Death! what 's here? Jarvis, Leontine, Olivia! What can all this mean?

Jarvis. Why, I 'll tell you what it means: that I was an old fool, and that you are my master — that 's all.

Honeywood. Confusion!

Leontine. Yes, sir, I find you have kept your word with me. After such baseness, I wonder how you can venture to see the man you have injured!

Honeywood. My dear Leontine, by my life, my honor——

Leontine. Peace, peace, for shame; and do not continue to aggravate baseness by hypocrisy. I know you, sir, I know you.

Honeywood. Why, won't you hear me? By all that's just, I knew not——

Leontine. Hear you, sir! to what purpose? I now see through all your low arts; your ever complying with every opinion; your never refusing any request; your friendship 's as common as a prostitute's favors, and as fallacious; all these, sir, have long been contemptible to the world, and are now perfectly so to me.

Honeywood. Ha! contemptible to the world! that reaches me. [*Aside.*

Leontine. All the seeming sincerity of your professions, I now find were only allurements to betray; and all your seeming regret for their consequences, only calculated to cover the cowardice of your heart. Draw, villain!

Enter Croaker, out of breath.

Croaker. Where is the villain? Where is the incendiary? *(Seizing the Postboy.)* Hold him fast, the dog; he has the gallows in his face. Come, you dog, confess; confess all, and hang yourself.

Postboy. Zounds! master, what do you throttle me for?

Croaker. *(Beating him.)* Dog, do you resist? do you resist?

Postboy. Zounds! master, I'm not he; there's the man that we thought was the rogue, and turns out to be one of the company.

Croaker. How!

Honeywood. Mr. Croaker, we have all been under a strange mistake here; I find there is nobody guilty; it was all an error — entirely an error of our own.

Croaker. And I say, sir, that you're in error; for there's guilt and double guilt, a plot, a damned jesuitcial, pestilential plot, and I must have proof of it.

Honeywood. Do but hear me.

Croaker. What! you intend to bring 'em off, I suppose? I'll hear nothing.

Honeywood. Madam, you seem at least calm enough to hear reason.

Olivia. Excuse me.

Honeywood. Good Jarvis, let me then explain it to you.

Jarvis. What signifies explanations when the thing is done?

Honeywood. Will nobody hear me? Was there ever such a set, so blinded by passion and prejudice? *(To the Postboy.)* My good friend, I believe you 'll be surprised when I assure you ——

Postboy. Sure me nothing — I 'm sure of nothing but a good beating.

Croaker. Come then you, madam, if you ever hope for any favor or forgiveness, tell me sincerely all you know of this affair.

Olivia. Unhappily, sir, I 'm but too much the cause of your suspicions: You see before you, sir, one that, with false pretences, has stept into your family to betray it; not your daughter ——

Croaker. Not my daughter!

Olivia. Not your daughter — but a mean deceiver — who — support me, I cannot ——

Honeywood. Help, she 's going; give her air.

Croaker. Ay, ay, take the young woman to the air; I would not hurt a hair of her head, whose ever daughter she may be — not so bad as that neither.

[*Exeunt all but Croaker.*

Yes, yes, all 's out; I now see the whole affair: my son is either married, or going to be so, to this lady, whom he imposed upon me as his sister. Ay, certainly so; and yet I do n't find it afflicts me so much as one might think. There 's the advantage of fretting away our misfortunes beforehand, — we never feel them when they come.

Enter Miss Richland and Sir William.

Sir William. But how do you know, madam, that my nephew intends setting off from this place?

Miss Richland. My maid assured me he was come to this inn, and my own knowledge of his intending to leave the kingdom, suggested the rest. But what do I see? my guardian here before us! Who, my dear sir, could have expected meeting you here? To what accident do we owe this pleasure?

Croaker. To a fool, I believe.

Miss Richland. But to what purpose did you come?

Croaker. To play the fool.

Miss Richland. But with whom?

Croaker. With greater fools than myself.

Miss Richland. Explain.

Croaker. Why, Mr. Honeywood brought me here, to do nothing now I am here; and my son is going to be married to I do n't know who, that is here: so now you are as wise as I am.

Miss Richland. Married! to whom, sir?

Croaker. To Olivia, my daughter, as I took her to be; but who the devil she is, or whose daughter she is, I know no more than the man in the moon.

Sir William. Then, sir, I can inform you; and, though a stranger, yet you shall find me a friend to your family It will be enough, at present, to assure you, that both in point of birth and fortune, the young lady is at least your son's equal. Being left by her father, Sir James Woodville ——

Croaker. Sir James Woodville! What! of the West?

Sir William. Being left by him, I say, to the care of a mercenary wretch, whose only aim was to secure her fortune to himself, she was sent to France, under pretence of education; and there every art was tried to fix her for life in a convent, contrary to her inclinations. Of this I was informed upon my arrival at Paris; and, as I had been once her father's friend, I did all in my power to frustrate her guardian's base intentions. I had even meditated to rescue her from his authority, when your son stept in with more pleasing violence, gave her liberty, and you a daughter.

Croaker. But I intend to have a daughter of my own choosing, sir. A young lady, sir, whose fortune, by my interest with those that have interest, will be double what my son has a right to expect. Do you know Mr. Lofty, sir?

Sir William. Yes, sir: and know that you are deceived in him. But step this way, and I'll convince you.

[*Croaker and Sir William seem to confer.*

Enter Honeywood.

Honeywood. Obstinate man, still to persist in his outrage! Insulted by him, despised by all, I now begin to grow contemptible even to myself. How have I sunk, by too great an assiduity to please! How have I overtaxed all my abilities, lest the approbation of a single fool should escape me! But all is now over: I have survived my reputation, my fortune, my friendships, and nothing remains henceforward for me but solitude and repentance.

Miss Richland. Is it true, Mr. Honeywood, that you

are setting off, without taking leave of your friends? The report is, that you are quitting England: Can it be?

Honeywood. Yes, madam; and though I am so unhappy as to have fallen under your displeasure, yet, thank Heaven! I leave you to happiness — to one who loves you, and deserves your love — to one who has power to procure you affluence, and generosity to improve your enjoyment of it.

Miss Richland. And are you sure, sir, that the gentleman you mean is what you describe him?

Honeywood. I have the best assurances of it — his serving me. He does indeed deserve the highest happiness, and that is in your power to confer. As for me, weak and wavering as I have been, obliged by all, and incapable of serving any, what happiness can I find but in solitude? what hope, but in being forgotten?

Miss Richland. A thousand: to live among friends that esteem you, whose happiness it will be to be permitted to oblige you.

Honeywood. No, madam, my resolution is fixed. Inferiority among strangers is easy; but among those that once were equals, insupportable. Nay, to show you how far my resolution can go, I can now speak with calmness of my former follies, my vanity, my dissipation, my weakness. I will even confess, that, among the number of my other presumptions, I had the insolence to think of loving you. Yes, madam, while I was pleading the passion of another, my heart was tortured with its own. But it is over; it was unworthy our friendship, and let it be forgotten.

Miss Richland. You amaze me!

Honeywood. But you'll forgive it, I know you will: since the confession should not have come from me even now, but to convince you of the sincerity of my intention of — never mentioning it more. [*Going.*

Miss Richland. Stay, sir, one moment — Ha! he here ——

Enter Lofty.

Lofty. Is the coast clear? None but friends? I have followed you here with a trifling piece of intelligence; but it goes no farther; things are not yet ripe for a discovery. I have spirits working at a certain board; your affair at the Treasury will be done in less than — a thousand years. Mum!

Miss Richland. Sooner, sir, I should hope.

Lofty. Why, yes, I believe it may, if it falls into proper hands, that know where to push and where to parry; that know how the land lies — eh, Honeywood?

Miss Richland. It has fallen into yours.

Lofty. Well, to keep you no longer in suspense, your thing is done. It is done, I say — that's all. I have just had assurances from Lord Neverout, that the claim has been examined, and found admissible. *Quietus* is the word, madam.

Honeywood. But how? his lordship has been at Newmarket these ten days.

Lofty. Indeed! then Sir Gilbert Goose must have been most damnably mistaken. I had it of him.

Miss Richland. He! why, Sir Gilbert and his family have been in the country this month.

Lofty. This month! it must certainly be so — Sir

Gilbert's letter did come to me from Newmarket, so that he must have met his lordship there; and so it came about. I have his letter about me; I'll read it to you. *(Taking out a large bundle.)* That's from Paoli of Corsica, that from the Marquis of Squilachi. Have you a mind to see a letter from Count Poniatowski, now King of Poland? Honest Pon — *(Searching.)* Oh, sir, what, are you here too? I'll tell you what, honest friend, if you have not absolutely delivered my letter to Sir William Honeywood, you may return it. The thing will do without him.

Sir William. Sir, I have delivered it; and must inform you, it was received with the most mortifying contempt.

Croaker. Contempt! Mr. Lofty, what can that mean?

Lofty. Let him go on, let him go on, I say. You'll find it come to something presently.

Sir William. Yes, sir; I believe you'll be amazed, if, after waiting some time in the antechamber — after being surveyed with insolent curiosity by the passing servants, I was at last assured, that Sir William Honeywood knew no such person, and I must certainly have been imposed upon.

Lofty. Good! let me die; very good. Ha! ha! ha!

Croaker. Now, for my life, I can't find out half the goodness of it.

Lofty. You can't? Ha! ha!

Croaker. No, for the soul of me: I think it was as confounded a bad answer as ever was sent from one private gentleman to another.

Lofty. And so you can't find out the force of the

message? Why, I was in the house at that very time Ha! ha! it was I that sent that very answer to my own letter. Ha! ha!

Croaker. Indeed! How? why?

Lofty. In one word, things between Sir William and me must be behind the curtain. A party has many eyes. He sides with Lord Buzzard, I side with Sir Gilbert Goose. So that unriddles the mystery.

Croaker. And so it does, indeed; and all my suspicions are over.

Lofty. Your suspicions! what, then, you have been suspecting, you have been suspecting, have you! Mr. Croaker, you and I were friends — we are friends no longer. Never talk to me. It 's over; I say, it 's over.

Croaker. As I hope for your favor, I did not mean to offend. It escaped me. Do n't be discomposed.

Lofty. Zounds! sir, but I am discomposed, and will be discomposed. To be treated thus! Who am I? Was it for this I have been dreaded both by ins and outs? Have I been libelled in the Gazetteer, and praised in the St James's; have I been chaired at Wildman's, and a speaker at Merchant Tailors' Hall; have I had my hand to addresses, and my head in the print-shops, — and talk to me of suspects?

Croaker. My dear sir, be pacified. What can you have but asking pardon?

Lofty. Sir, I will not be pacified — Suspects! Who am I? To be used thus! Have I paid court to men in favor to serve my friends, the lords of the Treasury, Sir William Honeywood, and the rest of the gang, and talk to me of suspects! Who am I, I say, who am I?

Sir William. Since you are so pressing for an answer, I'll tell you who you are:—A gentleman as well acquainted with politics as with men in power; as well acquainted with persons of fashion as with modesty; with lords of the Treasury as with truth; and, with all, as you are with Sir William Honeywood. I am Sir William Honeywood. *(Discovering his ensigns of the Bath.)*

Croaker. Sir William Honeywood!

Honeywood. Astonishment! my uncle! *(Aside.)*

Lofty. So then, my confounded genius has been all this time only leading me up to the garret, in order to fling me out of the window.

Croaker. What, Mr. Importance, and are these your works? Suspect you! You, who have been dreaded by the ins and outs; you, who have had your hand to addresses, and your head stuck up in print-shops? If you were served right, you should have your head stuck up in the pillory.

Lofty. Ay, stick it where you will; for by the Lord, it cuts but a very poor figure where it sticks at present.

Sir William. Well, Mr. Croaker, I hope you now see how incapable this gentleman is of serving you, and how little Miss Richland has to expect from his influence.

Croaker. Ay, sir, too well I see it; and I can't but say I have had some boding of it these ten days. So I'm resolved, since my son has placed his affections on a lady of moderate fortune, to be satisfied with his choice, and not run the hazard of another Mr. Lofty in helping him to a better.

Sir William. I approve your resolution; and here

they come, to receive a confirmation of your pardon and consent.

Enter Mrs. Croaker, Jarvis, Leontine, and Olivia.

Mrs. Croaker. Where's my husband? Come, come, lovey, you must forgive them. Jarvis here has been to tell me the whole affair; and I say, you must forgive them. Our own was a stolen match, you know, my dear; and we never had any reason to repent of it.

Croaker. I wish we could both say so. However, this gentleman, Sir William Honeywood, has been beforehand with you in obtaining their pardon. So, if the two poor fools have a mind to marry, I think we can tack them together without crossing the Tweed for it.

[*Joining their hands.*

Leontine. How blest and unexpected! What, what can we say to such goodness? But our future obedience shall be the best reply. And as for this gentleman, to whom we owe ——

Sir William. Excuse me, sir, if I interrupt your thanks, as I have here an interest that calls me. (*Turning to Honeywood.*) Yes, sir, you are surprised to see me; and I own that a desire of correcting your follies led me hither. I saw with indignation the errors of a mind that only sought applause from others; that easiness of disposition which, though inclined to the right, had not courage to condemn the wrong. I saw with regret those splendid errors, that still took name from some neighboring duty; your charity, that was but injustice; your benevolence, that was but weakness; and your friendship but credulity. I saw with regret, great talents and extensive learning only employed to add sprightliness to error, and increase your perplexities. I saw your mind with a thousand natural charms; but the greatness of its beauty served only to heighten my pity for its prostitution.

Honeywood. Cease to upbraid me, sir: I have for some time but to strongly felt the justice of your reproaches. But there is one way still left me. Yes, sir, I have determined this very hour to quit for ever a place where I have made myself the voluntary slave of all, and to seek among strangers that fortitude which may give strength to the mind, and marshal all its dissipated virtues. Yet, ere I depart, permit me to solicit favor for this gentleman, who, notwithstanding what has happened, has laid me under the most signal obligations. Mr. Lofty ——

Lofty. Mr. Honeywood, I 'm resolved upon a reformation as well as you. I now begin to find that the man who first invented the art of speaking truth was a much cunninger fellow than I thought him. And to prove that I design to speak truth for the future, I must now assure you, that you owe your late enlargement to another; as, upon my soul, I had no hand in the matter. So now, if any of the company has a mind for preferment, he may take my place; I 'm determined to resign. [*Exit.*

Honeywood. How have I been deceived!

Sir William. No, sir, you have been obliged to a kinder, fairer friend, for that favor, — to Miss Richland. Would she complete our joy, and make the man she has honored by her friendship happy in her love, I should then forget all, and be as blest as the welfare of my dearest kinsman can make me.

Miss Richland. After what is past, it would be but affectation to pretend to indifference. Yes, I will own an attachment, which I find was more than friendship. And if my entreaties cannot alter his resolution to quit the country, I will even try if my hand has not power to detain him. [*Giving her hand.*

Honeywood. Heavens! how can I have deserved all this? How express my happiness — my gratitude? A moment like this overpays an age of apprehension.

Croaker. Well, now I see content in every face; but Heaven send we be all better this day three months!

Sir William. Henceforth, nephew, learn to respect yourself. He who seeks only for applause from without, has all his happiness in another's keeping.

Honeywood. Yes, sir, I now too plainly perceive my errors: my vanity, in attempting to please all by fearing to offend any; my meanness, in approving folly lest fools should disapprove. Henceforth, therefore, it shall be my study to reserve my pity for real distress; my friendship for real merit; and my love for her who first taught me what it is to be happy. [*Exeunt omnes*

EPILOGUE.*

SPOKEN BY MRS. BULKLEY.

As puffing quacks some caitiff wretch procure
To swear the pill or drop has wrought a cure;
Thus, on the stage, our play-wrights still depend
For epilogues and prologues on some friend,
Who knows each art of coaxing up the town,
And makes full many a bitter pill go down.
Conscious of this, our bard has gone about,
And teased each rhyming friend to help him out:
An epilogue! things can 't go on without it!
It could not fail, would you but set about it:
'Young man,' cries one (a bard laid up in clover),
'Alas! young man, my writing days are over!
Let boys play tricks, and kick the straw, not I;
Your brother-doctor there, perhaps, may try.'
'What I, dear sir?' the Doctor interposes,
'What, plant my thistle, sir, among his roses!
No, no, I 've other contests to maintain;
To-night I head our troops at Warwick-Lane.
Go, ask your manager.'—'Who, me? Your pardon;
Those things are not our forte at Covent Garden.'

* The author, in expectation of an Epilogue from a friend at Oxford, deferred writing one himself till the very last hour. What is here offered, owes all its success to the graceful manner of the actress who spoke it.

Our author's friends, thus placed at happy distance
Give him good words indeed, but no assistance.
As some unhappy wight, at some new play,
At the pit-door stands elbowing a way,
While oft, with many a smile, and many a shrug,
He eyes the centre, where his friends sit snug;
His simpering friends, with pleasure in their eyes,
Sinks as he sinks, and as he rises rise:
He nods, they nod; he cringes, they grimace;
But not a soul will budge to give him place.
Since, then, unhelp'd, our bard must now conform
'To 'bide the pelting of this pitiless storm,'
Blame where you must, be candid where you can,
And be each critic the *Good-Natured Man.*

SHE STOOPS TO CONQUER;

OR,

THE MISTAKES OF A NIGHT.

A COMEDY.

She Stoops to Conquer was represented for the first time, March 15, 1773. It was very successful, and became a stock play. Goldsmith originally entitled it, *The Old House a New Inn.*

DEDICATION.

TO SAMUEL JOHNSON, LL. D.

DEAR SIR — By inscribing this slight performance to you, I do not mean so much to compliment you as myself. It may do me some honor to inform the public, that I have lived many years in intimacy with you. It may serve the interests of mankind also to inform them that the greatest wit may be found in a character, without impairing the most unaffected piety.

I have, particularly, reason to thank you for your partiality to this performance. The undertaking a comedy, not merely sentimental, was very dangerous; and Mr. Colman, who saw this piece in its various stages, always thought it so. However, I ventured to trust it to the public; and, though it was necessarily delayed till late in the season, I have every reason to be grateful.

I am, dear Sir,
Your most sincere friend and admirer,
OLIVER GOLDSMITH.

DRAMATIS PERSONÆ.

MEN,

Sir Charles Marlow.
Young Marlow (his son.)
Hardcastle.
Hastings.
Tony Lumpkin.
Diggory.

WOMEN.

Mrs. Hardcastle.
Miss Hardcastle
Miss Neville.
Maid.

Landlord, Servants, etc.

SHE STOOPS TO CONQUER;

OR,

THE MISTAKES OF A NIGHT.

PROLOGUE.

BY DAVID GARRICK, ESQ.

Enter Mr. Woodward, dressed in black, and holding a handkerchief to his eyes.

EXCUSE me, sirs, I pray — I can 't yet speak —
I 'm crying now — and have been all the week.
''Tis not alone this mourning suit,' good masters:
'I 've that within,' for which there are no plasters!
Pray, would you know the reason why I 'm crying?
The Comic Muse, long sick, is now a-dying!
And if she goes, my tears will never stop;
For, as a player, I can 't squeeze out one drop;
I am undone, that 's all — shall lose my bread —
I 'd rather — but that 's nothing — lose my head.
When the sweet maid is laid upon the bier,
Shuter and I shall be chief mourners here.
To her a mawkish drab of spurious breed,
Who deals in sentimentals, will succeed.
Poor Ned and I are dead to all intents;
We can as soon speak Greek as sentiments:
Both nervous grown, to keep our spirits up,

We now and then take down a hearty cup.
What shall we do? If Comedy forsake us,
They 'll turn us out, and no one else will take us.
But why can 't I be moral? Let me try:
My heart thus pressing — fix'd my face and eye —
With a sententious look that nothing means
(Faces are blocks in sentimental scenes),
Thus I begin, 'All is not gold that glitters,
Pleasures seem sweet, but prove a glass of bitters.
When ign'rance enters, folly is at hand:
Learning is better far than house or land.
Let not your virtue trip: who trips may stumble,
And virtue is not virtue if she tumble.'
I give it up — morals won't do for me;
To make you laugh, I must play tragedy.
One hope remains, — hearing the maid was ill,
A Doctor comes this night to show his skill;
To cheer her heart, and give your muscles motion,
He, in Five Draughts prepared, presents a potion,
A kind of magic charm; for, be assured,
If you will swallow it, the maid is cured:
But desperate the Doctor's and her case is,
If you reject the dose and make wry faces.
This truth he boasts, will boast it while he lives,
No pois'nous drugs are mixed in what he gives.
Should he succeed, you 'll give him his degree;
If not, within he will receive no fee.
The college, you, must his pretensions back,
Pronounce him Regular, or dub him Quack.

ACT FIRST.

Scene 1 — A CHAMBER IN AN OLD-FASHIONED HOUSE.

Enter Mrs. Hardcastle and Mr. Hardcastle.

Mrs. Hardcastle. I vow, Mr. Hardcastle, you 're very particular. Is there a creature in the whole country but ourselves, that does not take a trip to town now and then, to rub off the rust a little? There 's the two Miss Hoggs, and our neighbor Mrs. Grigsby, go to take a month's polishing every winter.

Hardcastle. Ay, and bring back vanity and affectation to last them the whole year. I wonder why London cannot keep its own fools at home. In my time, the follies of the town crept slowly among us, but now they travel faster than a stage coach. Its fopperies come down not only as inside passengers, but in the very basket.

Mrs. Hardcastle. Aye, your times were fine times indeed: you have been telling us of them for many a long year. Here we live in an old rumbling mansion, that looks for all the world like an inn, but that we never see company. Our best visitors are old Mrs. Oddfish, the curate's wife, and little Cripplegate, the lame dancing-master; and all our entertainment your old stories of Prince Eugene and the Duke of Marlborough. I hate such old-fashioned trumpery.

Hardcastle. And I love it. I love every thing that 's old: old friends, old times, old manners, old books, old wine; and, I believe, Dorothy, *(taking her hand,)* you 'll own, I 've been pretty fond of an old wife.

Mrs. Hardcastle. Lord, Mr. Hardcastle, you're for ever at your Dorothys, and your old wives. You may be a Darby, but I 'll be no Joan, I promise you. I 'm not so old as you 'd make me, by more than one good year. Add twenty to twenty and make money of that.

Hardcastle. Let me see; twenty added to twenty makes just fifty and seven.

Mrs. Hardcastle. It 's false, Mr. Hardcastle; I was but twenty when I was brought to-bed of Tony, that I had by Mr. Lumpkin, my first husband; and he 's not come to years of discretion yet.

Hardcastle. Nor ever will, I dare answer for him. Ay, you have taught him finely!

Mrs. Hardcastle. No matter. Tony Lumpkin has a good fortune. My son is not to live by his learning. I do n't think a boy wants much learning to spend fifteen hundred a-year.

Hardcastle. Learning, quotha! a mere composition of tricks and mischief.

Mrs. Hardcastle. Humor, my dear, nothing but humor. Come, Mr. Hardcastle, you must allow the boy a little humor.

Hardcastle. I 'd sooner allow him a horse-pond. If burning the footman's shoes, frightening the maids, and worrying the kittens, be humor, he has it. It was but yesterday he fastened my wig to the back of my chair, and when I went to make a bow, I popt my bald head in Mrs. Frizzle's face.

Mrs. Hardcastle. And am I to blame? The poor boy was always too sickly to do any good. A school would be his death. When he comes to be a little stronger, who knows what a year or two's Latin may do for him?

Hardcastle. Latin for him! A cat and fiddle. No, no; the alehouse and the stable are the only schools he'll ever go to.

Mrs. Hardcastle. Well, we must not snub the poor boy now, for I believe we shan't have him long among us. Any body that looks in his face may see he's consumptive.

Hardcastle. Ay, if growing too fat be one of the symptoms.

Mrs. Hardcastle. He coughs sometimes.

Hardcastle. Yes, when his liquor goes the wrong way.

Mrs. Hardcastle. I'm actually afraid of his lungs.

Hardcastle. And truly so am I; for he sometimes whoops like a speaking trumpet — *(Tony hallooing behind the scenes.)* — Oh, there he goes — a very consumptive figure, truly!

Enter Tony, crossing the Stage.

Mrs. Hardcastle. Tony, where are you going, my charmer? Won't you give papa and I a little of your company, lovey?

Tony. I'm in haste, mother; I cannot stay.

Mrs. Hardcastle. You shan't venture out this raw evening, my dear; you look most shockingly.

Tony. I can't stay, I tell you. The Three Pigeons expects me down every moment. There's some fun going forward.

Hardcastle. Ay, the alehouse, the old place; I thought so.

Mrs. Hardcastle. A low, paltry set of fellows.

Tony. Not so low neither. There's Dick Muggins, the exciseman, Jack Slang, the horse-doctor, little Aminadab, that grinds the music-box, and Tom Twist, that spins the pewter platter.

Mrs. Hardcastle. Pray, my dear, disappoint them for one night at least.

Tony. As for disappointing them, I should not so much mind; but I can 't abide to disappoint myself.

Mrs. Hardcastle. *(Detaining him.)* You shan't go.

Tony. I will, I tell you.

Mrs. Hardcastle. I say you shan't.

Tony. We 'll see which is the strongest, you or I.

[*Exit, hauling her out.*

Hardcastle. *(Alone.)* Ay, there goes a pair that only spoil each other. But is not the whole age in combination to drive sense and discretion out of doors? There 's my pretty darling, Kate! the fashions of the times have almost infected her too. By living a year or two in town, she is as fond of gauze and French frippery as the best of them.

Enter Mrs. Hardcastle.

Hardcastle. Blessings on my pretty innocence! drest out as usual, my Kate. Goodness! what a quantity of superfluous silk hast thou got about thee, girl! I could never teach the fools of this age, that the indigent world could be clothed out of the trimmings of the vain.

Miss Hardcastle. You know our agreement, sir. You allow me the morning to receive and pay visits, and to dress in my own manner; and in the evening I put on my housewife's dress to please you.

Hardcastle. Well, remember I insist on the terms of our agreement; and, by the by, I believe I shall have occasion to try your obedience this very evening.

Miss Hardcastle. I protest, sir, I do n't comprehend your meaning.

Hardcastle. Then, to be plain with you, Kate, I expect the young gentleman I have chosen to be your husband from town this very day. I have his father's letter, in which he informs me his son is set out, and that he intends to follow him shortly after.

Miss Hardcastle. Indeed! I wish I had known something of this before. Bless me, how shall I behave. It 's a thousand to one I shan't like him; our meeting will be so formal, and so like a thing of business, that I shall find no room for friendship or esteem.

Hardcastle. Depend upon it, child, I never will control your choice; but Mr. Marlow, whom I have pitched upon, is the son of my old friend, Sir Charles Marlow, of whom you have heard me talk so often. The young gentleman has been bred a scholar, and is designed for an employment in the service of his country. I am told he's a man of an excellent understanding.

Miss Hardcastle. Is he?

Hardcastle. Very generous.

Miss Hardcastle. I believe I shall like him.

Hardcastle. Young and brave.

Miss Hardcastle. I 'm sure I shall like him.

Hardcastle. And very handsome.

Miss Hardcastle. My dear papa, say no more, *(kissing his hand)* he 's mine — I 'll have him.

Hardcastle. And, to crown all, Kate, he 's one of the

the most bashful and reserved young fellows in all the world.

Miss Hardcastle. Eh! you have frozen me to death again. That word reserved has undone all the rest of his accomplishments. A reserved lover, it is said, always makes a suspicious husband.

Hardcastle. On the contrary, modesty seldom resides in a breast that is not enriched with nobler virtues. It was the very feature in his character that first struck me.

Miss Hardcastle. He must have more striking features to catch me, I promise you. However, if he be so young, so handsome, and so every thing as you mention, I believe he 'll do still. I think I 'll have him.

Hardcastle. Ay, Kate, but there is still an obstacle. It 's more than an even wager he may not have you.

Miss Hardcastle. My dear papa, why will you mortify one so? Well, if he refuses, instead of breaking my heart at his indifference, I 'll only break my glass for its flattery, set my cap to some newer fashion, and look out for some less difficult admirer.

Hardcastle. Bravely resolved! In the mean time, I 'll go prepare the servants for his reception: as we seldom see company, they want as much training as a company of recruits the first day's muster. [*Exit.*

Miss Hardcastle. (*Alone.*) Lud, this news of papa's puts me all in a flutter. Young, handsome; these he put last, but I put them foremost. Sensible, good-natured; I like all that. But then, reserved and sheepish; that 's much against him. Yet can 't he be cured of his timidity, by being taught to be proud of his wife? Yes; and can't

I — But I vow I 'm disposing of the husband, before I have secured the lover.

Enter Miss Neville.

Miss Hardcastle. I 'm glad you 're come, Neville, my dear. Tell me, Constance, how do I look this evening? Is there anything whimsical about me? Is it one of my well-looking days, child? am I in face to day?

Miss Neville. Perfectly, my dear. Yet now I look again — bless me! — sure no accident has happened among the canary birds or the gold fishes? Has your brother or the cat been meddling? or has the last novel been too moving?

Miss Hardcastle. No; nothing of all this. I have been threatened — I can scarce get it out — I have been threatened with a lover.

Miss Neville. And his name ——

Miss Hardcastle. Is Marlow.

Miss Neville. Indeed!

Miss Hardcastle. The son of Sir Charles Marlow.

Miss Neville. As I live, the most intimate friend of Mr. Hastings, my admirer. They are never asunder. I believe you must have seen him when we lived in town.

Miss Hardcastle. Never.

Miss Neville. He 's a very singular character, I assure you. Among women of reputation and virtue, he is the modestest man alive; but his acquaintance give him a very different character among creatures of another stamp — you understand me.

Miss Hardcastle. An odd character, indeed. I shall never be able to manage him. What shall I do! Pshaw!

think no more of him, but trust to occurrences for success. But how goes on your own affair, my dear? has my mother been courting you for my brother Tony, as usual?

Miss Neville. I have just come from one of our agreeable *tete-a-tetes.* She has been saying a hundred tender things, and setting off her pretty monster as the very pink of perfection.

Miss Hardcastle. And her partiality is such, that she actually thinks him so. A fortune like yours is no small temptation. Besides, as she has the sole management of it, I 'm not surprised to see her unwilling to let it go out of the family.

Miss Neville. A fortune like mine, which chiefly consists in jewels, is no such mighty temptation. But, at any rate, if my dear Hastings be but constant, I make no doubt to be too hard for her at last. However, I let her suppose that I am in love with her son; and she never once dreams that my affections are fixed upon another.

Miss Hardcastle. My good brother holds out stoutly. I could almost love him for hating you so.

Miss Neville. It is a good-natured creature at bottom, and I 'm sure would wish to see me married to any body but himself. But my aunt's bell rings for our afternoon's walk round the improvements. Allons! Courage is necessary, as our affairs are critical.

Miss Hardcastle. Would it were bed-time, and all were well. [*Exeunt.*

Scene II. — AN ALEHOUSE ROOM.

Several shabby fellows with punch and tobacco; Tony at the head of the table, a little higher than the rest, a mallet in his hand.

Omnes. Hurrea! hurrea! hurrea! bravo!

First Fellow. Now, gentlemen, silence for a song. The Squire is going to knock himself down for a song.

Omnes. Ay, a song, a song!

Tony. Then I 'll sing you, gentlemen, a song I made upon this alehouse, The Three Pigeons.

SONG.

Let schoolmasters puzzle their brain,
  With grammar, and nonsense, and learning;
Good liquor, I stoutly maintain,
  Gives *genus* a better discerning.
Let them brag of their heathenish gods,
  Their Lethes, their Styxes, and Stygians,
Their *quis*, and their *quæs*, and their *quods*,
  They 're all but a parcel of pigeons.
          Toroddle, toroddle, toroll.

When methodist preachers come down,
  A-preaching that drinking is sinful,
I 'll wager the rascals a crown,
  They always preach best with a skinful.
But when you come down with your pence,
  For a slice of their scurvy religion,
I 'll leave it to all men of sense,
  But you, my good friend, are the pigeon.
          Toroddle, toroddle, toroll.

Then come, put the jorum about,
  And let us be merry and clever,
Our hearts and our liquors are stout,
  Here 's the Three Jolly Pigeons for ever

Let some cry up woodcock or hare,
  Your bustards, your ducks, and your widgeons;
But of all the birds in the air,
  Here 's health to the Three Jolly Pigeons.
                Toroddle, toroddle, toroll.

Omnes. Bravo, bravo!

First Fellow. The Squire has got some spunk in him.

Second Fellow. I loves to hear him sing, bekeays he never gives us nothing that 's low.

Third Fellow. Oh, damn any thing that 's low, I cannot bear it.

Fourth Fellow. The genteel thing is the genteel thing at any time: if so be that a gentleman bees in a concatenation accordingly.

Third Fellow. I like the maxum of it, Master Muggins. What though I am obligated to dance a bear, a man may be a gentleman for all that. May this be my poison, if my bear ever dances but to the very genteelest of tunes; 'Water Parted,' or 'The minuet in Ariadne.'

Second Fellow. What a pity it is the Squire is not come to his own. It would be well for all the publicans within ten miles round of him.

Tony. Ecod, and so it would, Master Slang. I 'd then show what it was to keep choice of company.

Second Fellow. Oh, he takes after his own father for that. To be sure, old Squire Lumpkin was the finest gentleman I ever set my eyes on. For winding the straight horn, or beating a thicket for a hare or a wench, he never had his fellow. It was a saying in the place, that he kept the best horses, dogs, and girls, in the whole county.

Tony. Ecod, and when I 'm of age, I 'll be no bastard, I promise you. I have been thinking of Bet Bouncer and the miller's gray mare to begin with. But come, my boys, drink about and be merry, for you pay no reckoning. Well, Stingo, what 's the matter?

Enter Landlord.

Landlord. There be two gentlemen in a post-chaise at the door. They have lost their way upon the forest; and they are talking something about Mr. Hardcastle.

Tony. As sure as can be, one of them must be the gentleman that 's coming down to court my sister. Do they seem to be Londoners?

Landlord. I believe they may. They look woundily like Frenchmen.

Tony. Then desire them to step this way, and I 'll set them right in a twinkling. [*Exit Landlord.* Gentlemen, as they may n't be good enough company for you, step down for a moment, and I 'll be with you in the squeezing of a lemon. [*Exeunt mob.*

Tony. (*Alone.*) Father-in-law has been calling me whelp and hound this half year. Now, if I pleased, I could be so revenged upon the old grumbletonian. But then I 'm afraid — afraid of what? I shall soon be worth fifteen hundred a year, and let him frighten me out of that if he can.

Enter Landlord, conducting Marlow and Hastings.

Marlow. What a tedious uncomfortable day have we had of it! We were told it was but forty miles across the country, and we have come above threescore.

Hastings. And all, Marlow, from that unaccountable reserve of yours, that would not let us inquire more frequently on the way.

Marlow. I own, Hastings, I am unwilling to lay myself under an obligation to every one I meet; and often stand the chance of an unmannerly answer.

Hastings. At present, however, we are not likely to receive any answer.

Tony. No offence, gentlemen. But I 'm told you have been inquiring for one Mr. Hardcastle, in these parts. Do you know what part of the country you are in?

Hastings. Not in the least, sir, but should thank you for information.

Tony. Nor the way you came?

Hastings. No, sir; but if you can inform us ——

Tony. Why, gentlemen, if you know neither the road you are going, nor where you are, nor the road you came, the first thing I have to inform you is, that — you have lost your way.

Marlow. We wanted no ghost to tell us that.

Tony. Pray, gentlemen, may I be so bold as to ask the place from whence you came?

Marlow. That 's not necessary towards directing us where we are to go.

Tony. No offence; but question for question is all fair, you know. Pray, gentlemen, is not this same Hardcastle a cross-grained, old-fashioned, whimsical fellow, with an ugly face: a daughter, and a pretty son?

Hastings. We have not seen the gentleman; but he has the family you mention.

Tony. The daughter, a tall, trapesing, trolloping, talkative maypole; the son, a pretty, well-bred, agreeable youth, that every body is fond of?

Marlow. Our information differs in this. The daughter is said to be well-bred, and beautiful; the son an awkward booby, reared up and spoiled at his mother's apron-string.

Tony. He-he-hem! — Then, gentlemen, all I have to tell you is, that you won't reach Mr. Hardcastle's house this night, I believe.

Hastings. Unfortunate!

Tony. It 's a damned long, dark, boggy, dirty, dangerous way. Stingo, tell the gentlemen the way to Mr. Hardcastle's *(winking upon the Landlord)*. Mr. Hardcastle's, of Quagmire Marsh — you understand me?

Landlord. Master Hardcastle's! Lock-a-daisy, my masters, you 're come a deadly deal wrong! When you came to the bottom of the hill, you should have crossed down Squash Lane.

Marlow. Cross down Squash Lane?

Landlord. Then you were to keep straight forward, till you came to four roads.

Marlow. Come to where four roads meet?

Tony. Ay; but you must be sure to take only one of them.

Marlow. O sir, you 're facetious.

Tony. Then keeping to the right, you are to go sideways, till you come upon Crack-skull common: there you must look sharp for the track of the wheel, and go forward till you come to farmer Murrain's barn. Coming to the farmer's barn, you are to turn to the right, and then to the left, and then to the right about again, till you find out the old mill ——

Marlow. Zounds, man! we could as soon find out the longitude.

Hastings. What 's to be done, Marlow?

Marlow. This house promises but a poor reception; though perhaps the landlord can accommodate us.

Landlord. Alack, master, we have but one spare bed in the whole house.

Tony. And to my knowledge, that 's taken up by three lodgers already. *(After a pause in which the rest seem disconcerted)* I have hit it: do n't you think, Stingo, our landlady could accommodate the gentlemen by the fire-side, with — three chairs and a bolster?

Hastings. I hate sleeping by the fire-side.

Marlow. And I detest your three chairs and a bolster.

Tony. You do, do you? — then, let me see, — what if you go on a mile farther, to the Buck's Head; the old Buck's Head on the hill, one of the best inns in the whole country.

Hastings. O ho! so we have escaped an adventure for this night, however.

Landlord. *(Apart to Tony.)* Sure, you ben't sending them to your father's as an inn, be you?

Tony. Mum, you fool you. Let them find that out. *(To them.)* You have only to keep on straight forward, till you come to a large old house by the road side. You 'll see a pair of large horns over the door. That 's the sign. Drive up the yard, and call stoutly about you.

Hastings. Sir, we are obliged to you. The servants can 't miss the way?

Tony. No, no: but I tell you though the landlord is rich, and going to leave off business; so he wants to be thought a gentleman, saving your presence, he! he! he! He'll be for giving you his company; and, ecod, if you mind him, he'll persuade you that his mother was an alderman, and his aunt a justice of peace.

Landlord. A troublesome old blade, to be sure; but as keeps as good wines and beds as any in the whole country.

Marlow. Well, if he supplies us with these, we shall want no further connection. We are to turn to the right, did you say?

Tony. No, no, straight forward; I'll just step myself, and show you a piece of the way. *(To the Landlord.)* Mum!

Landlord. Ah, bless your heart, for a sweet, pleasant —— damned mischievous son of a whore. [*Exeunt.*

ACT SECOND.

Scene I.—AN OLD-FASHIONED HOUSE.

Enter Hardcastle, followed by three or four awkward Servants.

Hardcastle. Well, I hope you are perfect in the table exercise I have been teaching you these three days. You all know your posts and your places, and can show that you have been used to good company, without ever stirring from home.

Omnes. Ay, ay.

Hardcastle. When company comes, you are not to pop out and stare, and then run in again, like frighted rabbits in a warren.

Omnes. No, no.

Hardcastle. You, Diggory, whom I have taken from the barn, are to make a show at the side table; and you, Roger, whom I have advanced from the plough, are to place yourself behind my chair. But you 're not to stand so, with your hands in your pockets. Take your hands from your pockets, Roger — and from your head, you blockhead you. See how Diggory carries his hands. They 're little too stiff, indeed, but that's no great matter.

Diggory. Ay, mind how I hold them. I learned to hold my hands this way, when I was upon drill for the malitia. And so being upon drill —

Hardcastle. You must not be so talkative, Diggory You must be all attention to the guests; you must hear us talk, and not think of talking; you must see us drink, and not think of drinking; you must see us eat, and not think of eating.

Diggory. By the laws, your worship, that 's parfectly unpossible. Whenever Diggory sees yeating going forward, ecod, he 's always wishing for a mouthful himself.

Hardcastle. Blockhead! is not a bellyful in the kitchen as good as a bellyful in the parlor? Stay your stomach with that reflection.

Diggory. Ecod, I thank your worship, I'll make a shift to stay my stomach with a slice of cold beef in the pantry.

Hardcastle. Diggory, you are too talkative. Then, if

I happen to say a good thing, or tell a good story, at table, you must not all burst out a-laughing, as if you made part of the company.

Diggory. Then, ecod, your worship must not tell the story of the Ould Grouse in the gun-room ; I can 't help laughing at that — he! he! he! — for the soul of me. We have laughed at that these twenty years — ha! ha! ha!

Hardcastle. Ha! ha! ha! The story is a good one. Well, honest Diggory, you may laugh at that; but still remember to be attentive. Suppose one of the company should call for a glass of wine, how will you behave? A glass of wine, sir, if you please, *(To Diggory)* — Eh, why do n't you move?

Diggory. Ecod, your worship, I never have courage, till I see the eatables and drinkables brought upo' the table, and then I 'm as bauld as a lion.

Hardcastle. What, will nobody move?

First Servant. I 'm not to leave this pleace.

Second Servant. I 'm sure it 's no pleace of mine.

Third Servant. Nor mine, for sartain.

Diggory. Wauns, and I 'm sure it canna be mine.

Hardcastle. You numskulls! and so while, like your betters, you are quarrelling for places, the guests must be starved. O you dunces! I find I must begin all over again —— But do n't I hear a coach drive into the yard? To your posts, you blockheads. I 'll go in the mean time, and give my old friend's son a hearty welcome at the gate. [*Exit Hardcastle.*

Diggory. By the elevens, my place is quite gone out of my head.

Roger. I know that my place is to be every where.

First Servant. Where the devil is mine?

Second Servant. My pleace is to be no where at all; and so Ize go about my business.

[*Exeunt Servants, running about, as if frightened, several ways.*

Enter Servant, with candles, showing in Marlow and Hastings.

Servant. Welcome, gentlemen, very welcome! This way.

Hastings. After the disappointments of the day, welcome once more, Charles, to the comforts of a clean room and a good fire. Upon my word, a very well-looking house: antique, but creditable.

Marlow. The usual fate of a large mansion. Having first ruined the master by good house-keeping, it at last comes to levy contributions as an inn.

Hastings. As you say, we passengers are to be taxed to pay all these fineries. I have often seen a good side-board, or a marble chimney-piece, though not actually put in the bill, inflame a reckoning confoundedly.

Marlow. Travellers, George, must pay in all places; the only difference is, that in good inns you pay dearly for luxuries, in bad inns you are fleeced and starved.

Hastings. You have lived pretty much among them. In truth I have been often surprised, that you who have seen so much of the world, with your natural good sense, and your many opportunities, could never yet acquire a requisite share of assurance.

Marlow. The Englishman's malady. But tell me,

George, where could I have learned that assurance you talk of? My life has been chiefly spent in a college or an inn, in seclusion from that lovely part of the creation that chiefly teach men confidence. I do n't know that I was ever familiarly acquainted with a single modest woman, except my mother. — But among females of another class, you know ——

Hastings. Ay, among them you are impudent enough, of all conscience.

Marlow. They are of us, you know.

Hastings. But in the company of women of reputation I never saw such an idiot — such a trembler; you look for all the world as if you wanted an opportunity of stealing out of the room.

Marlow. Why, man, that 's because I do want to steal out of the room. Faith, I have often formed a resolution to break the ice, and rattle away at any rate. But I do n't know how, a single glance from a pair of fine eyes has totally overset my resolution. An impudent fellow may counterfeit modesty, but I 'll be hanged if a modest man can ever counterfeit impudence.

Hastings. If you could but say half the fine things to them, that I have heard you lavish upon the bar-maid of an inn, or even a college bed-maker ——

Marlow. Why, George, I can 't say fine things to them — they freeze, they petrify me. They may talk of a comet, or a burning mountain, or some such bagatelle; but to me, a modest woman, drest out in all her finery, is the most tremendous object of the whole creation.

Hastings. Ha! ha! ha! At this rate, man, how can you ever expect to marry?

Marlow. Never; unless, as among kings and princes, my bride were to be courted by proxy. If, indeed, like an Eastern bridegroom, one were to be introduced to a wife he never saw before, it might be endured. But to go through all the terrors of a formal courtship, together with the episode of aunts, grandmothers, and cousins, and at last to blurt out the broad staring question of 'Madam, will you marry me?' No, no, that 't a strain much above me, I assure you.

Hastings. I pity you. But how do you intend behaving to the lady you are come down to visit at the request of your father?

Marlow. As I behave to all other ladies: bow very low; answer yes, or no, to all her demands. But for the rest, I do n't think I shall venture to look in her face till I see my father's again.

Hastings. I 'm surprised that one who is so warm a friend, can be so cool a lover.

Marlow. To be explicit, my dear Hastings, my chief inducement down was to be instrumental in forwarding your happiness, not my own. Miss Neville loves you, the family do n't know you; as my friend, you are sure of a reception, and let honor do the rest.

Hastings. My dear Marlow! — But I 'll suppress the emotion. Were I a wretch, meanly seeking to carry off a fortune, you should be the last man in the world I would apply to for assistance. But Miss Neville's person is all I ask, and that is mine, both from her deceased father's consent, and her own inclination.

Marlow. Happy man! You have talents and art to captivate any woman. I 'm doomed to adore the sex, and yet to converse with the only part of it I despise. This stammer in my address, and this awkward unprepossessing visage of mine, can never permit me to soar above the reach of a milliner's 'prentice, or one of the Duchesses of Drury-lane. Pshaw! this fellow here to interrupt us.

Enter Hardcastle.

Hardcastle. Gentlemen, once more you are heartily welcome. Which is Mr. Marlow? Sir, you are heartily welcome. It 's not my way, you see, to receive my friends with my back to the fire. I like to give them a hearty reception in the old style at my gate. I like to see their horses and trunks taken care of.

Marlow. *(Aside.)* He has got our names from the servants already. *(To him.)* We approve your caution and hospitality, sir. *(To Hastings.)* I have been thinking, George, of changing our travelling dresses in the morning. I am grown confoundedly ashamed of mine.

Hardcastle. I beg, Mr. Marlow, you 'll use no ceremony in this house.

Hastings. I fancy, Charles, you 're right: the first blow is half the battle. I intend opening the campaign with the white and gold.

Hardcastle. Mr. Marlow — Mr. Hastings — gentlemen — pray be under no restraint in this house. This is Liberty-hall, gentlemen. You may do just as you please here.

Marlow. Yet, George, if we open the campaign too fiercely at first, we may want ammunition before it is over. I think to reserve the embroidery to secure a retreat.

Hardcastle. Your talking of a retreat, Mr. Marlow, puts me in mind of the Duke of Marlborough, when we went to besiege Denain. He first summoned the garrison ——

Marlow. Do n't you think the *ventre d'or* waistcoat will do with the plain brown?

Hardcastle. He first summoned the garrison, which might consist of about five thousand men ——

Hastings. I think not: brown and yellow mix but very poorly.

Hardcastle. I say, gentlemen, as I was telling you, he summoned the garrison, which might consist of about five thousand men ——

Marlow. The girls like finery.

Hardcastle. Which might consist of about five thousand men, well appointed with stores, ammunition, and other implements of war. Now, says the Duke of Marlborough to George Brooks, that stood next to him — You must have heard of George Brooks — 'I 'll pawn my dukedom,' says he, 'but I take that garrison without spilling a drop of blood.' So ——

Marlow. What, my good friend, if you gave us a glass of punch in the mean time; it would help us to carry on the siege with vigor.

Hardcastle. Punch, sir! *(Aside.)* This is the most unaccountable kind of modesty I ever met with.

Marlow. Yes, sir, punch. A glass of warm punch, after our journey, will be comfortable. This is Liberty-hall, you know.

Enter Roger with a cup.

Hardcastle. Here 's a cup, sir.

Marlow. *(Aside.)* So this fellow, in his Liberty-hall, will only let us have just what he pleases.

Hardcastle. *(Taking the cup.)* I hope you 'll find it to your mind. I have prepared it with my own hands, and I believe you 'll own the ingredients are tolerable. Will you be so good as to pledge me, sir? Here, Mr. Marlow, here is to our better acquaintance. *(Drinks.)*

Marlow. *(Aside.)* A very impudent fellow this; but he 's a character, and I 'll humor him a little. Sir, my service to you. *(Drinks.)*

Hastings. *(Aside.)* I see this fellow wants to give us his company, and forgets that he 's an innkeeper, before he has learned to be a gentleman.

Marlow. From the excellence of your cup, my old friend, I suppose you have a good deal of business in this part of the country. Warm work, now and then, at elections, I suppose.

Hardcastle. No, sir, I have long given that work over. Since our betters have hit upon the expedient of electing each other, there is no business 'for us that sell ale.'

Hastings. So, then, you have no turn for politics, I find.

Hardcastle. Not in the least. There was a time, indeed, I fretted myself about the mistakes of government, like other people; but, finding myself every day grow more angry, and the government growing no better, I left it to mend itself. Since that, I no more trouble my head about Hyder Ally, or Ally Cawn, than about Ally Croaker. Sir, my service to you.

Hastings. So that with eating above stairs and drinking below, with receiving your friends within and amusing them without, you lead a good, pleasant, bustling life of it.

Hardcastle. I do stir about a great deal, that 's certain. Half the differences of the parish are adjusted in this very parlor.

Marlow. *(After drinking.)* And you have an argument in your cup, old gentleman, better than any in Westminster-hall.

Hardcastle. Ay, young gentleman, that, and a little philosophy.

Marlow. *(Aside.)* Well, this is the first time I ever heard of an inkeeper's philosophy.

Hastings. So, then, like an experienced general, you attack them on every quarter. If you find their reason manageable, you attack it with your philosophy; if you find they have no reason, you attack them with this. Here 's your health, my philosopher. *(Drinks.)*

Hardcastle. Good, very good, thank you; ha! ha! ha! Your generalship puts me in mind of Prince Eugene, when he fought the Turks at the battle of Belgrade. You shall hear.

Marlow. Instead of the battle of Belgrade, I believe it 's almost time to talk about supper. What has your philosophy got in the house for supper?

Hardcastle. For supper, sir! *(Aside.)* Was ever such a request to a man in his own house!

Marlow. Yes, sir, supper, sir; I begin to feel an appetite. I shall make devilish work to-night in the larder, I promise you.

Hardcastle. *(Aside.)* Such a brazen dog sure never my eyes beheld. *(To him.)* Why, really, sir, as for supper.

I can 't well tell. My Dorothy and the cook-maid settle these things between them. I leave these kind of things entirely to them.

Marlow. You do, do you?

Hardcastle. Entirely. By the by, I believe they are in actual consultation upon what 's for supper this moment in the kitchen.

Marlow. Then I beg they 'll admit me as one of their privy-council. It 's a way I have got. When I travel I always choose to regulate my own supper. Let the cook be called. No offence, I hope, sir.

Hardcastle. O no, sir, none in the least; yet I do n't know how, our Bridget, the cook-maid, is not very communicative upon these occasions. Should we send for her, she might scold us all out of the house.

Hastings. Let 's see your list of the larder, then. I ask it as a favor. I always match my appetite to my bill of fare.

Marlow. *(To Hardcastle, who looks at them with surprise.)* Sir, he 's very right, and it 's my way too.

Hardcastle. Sir, you have a right to command here. Here, Roger, bring us the bill of fare for to-night's supper: I believe it 's drawn out.— Your manner, Mr. Hastings, puts me in mind of my uncle, Colonel Wallop. It was a saying of his, that no man was sure of his supper till he had eaten it.

Enter Roger.

Hastings. *(Aside.)* All upon the high rope! His uncle a colonel! we shall soon hear of his mother being a justice of the peace. But let 's hear the bill of fare.

Marlow. *(Perusing.)* What 's here? For the first

course; for the second course; for the dessert. The devil, sir, do you think we have brought down the whole Joiners' Company, or the Corporation of Bedford, to eat up such a supper? Two or three little things, clean and comfortable, will do.

Hastings. But let 's hear it.

Marlow. (*Reading.*) 'For the first course,—at the top, a pig, and pruin-sauce.'

Hastings. Damn your pig, I say.

Marlow. And damn your pruin-sauce, say I.

Hardcastle. And yet, gentlemen, to men that are hungry, pig with pruin-sauce is very good eating.

Marlow. 'At the bottom a calf's tongue and brains.'

Hastings. Let your brains be knocked out, my good sir, I do n't like them.

Marlow. Or you may clap them on a plate by themselves.

Hardcastle. (*Aside.*) Their impudence confounds me. (*To them.*) Gentlemen, you are my guests, make what alterations you please. Is there any thing else you wish to retrench, or alter, gentlemen?

Marlow. 'Item: A pork pie, a boiled rabbit and sausages, a Florentine, a shaking pudding, and a dish of tiff—taff—taffety cream!'

Hastings. Confound your made dishes; I shall be as much at a loss in this house as at a green and yellow dinner at the French ambassador's table. I 'm for plain eating.

Hardcastle. I 'm sorry, gentlemen, that I have nothing you like; but if there be any thing you have a particular fancy to——

Marlow. Why, really sir, your bill of fare is so exquisite, that any one part of it is full as good as another. Send us what you please. So much for supper. And now to see that our beds are aired, and properly taken care of.

Hardcastle. I entreat you 'll leave all that to me. You shall not stir a step.

Marlow. Leave that to you! I protest, sir, you must excuse me: I always look to these things myself.

Hardcastle. I must insist, sir, you 'll make yourself easy on that head.

Marlow. You see I 'm resolved on it. *(Aside.)* A very troublesome fellow this, as ever I met with.

Hardcastle. Well, sir, I 'm resolved at least to attend you. *(Aside.)* This may be modern modesty, but I never saw any thing look so like old-fashioned impudence.

[*Exeunt Marlow and Hardcastle.*

Hastings. (Alone.) So I find this fellow's civilities begin to grow troublesome. But who can be angry at those assiduities which are meant to please him? Ha! what do I see? Miss Neville, by all that 's happy!

Enter Miss Neville.

Miss Neville. My dear Hastings! To what unexpected good fortune — to what accident, am I to ascribe this happy meeting?

Hastings. Rather let me ask the same question, as I could never have hoped to meet my dearest Constance at an inn.

Miss Neville. An inn! sure you mistake: my aunt, my guardian, lives here. What could induce you to think this house an inn?

Hastings. My friend, Mr. Marlow, with whom I came down, and I, have been sent here as to an inn, I assure you. A young fellow whom we accidentally met at a house hard by, directed us hither.

Miss Neville. Certainly it must be one of my hopeful cousin's tricks, of whom you have heard me talk so often; ha! ha! ha!

Hastings. He whom your aunt intends for you? he of whom I have such just apprehensions?

Miss Neville. You have nothing to fear from him, I assure you. You'd adore him if you knew how heartily he despises me. My aunt knows it too, and has undertaken to court me for him, and actually begins to think she has made a conquest.

Hastings. Thou dear dissembler! You must know, my Constance, I have just seized this happy opportunity of my friend's visit here to get admittance into the family. The horses that carried us down are now fatigued with their journey, but they 'll soon be refreshed; and, then, if my dearest girl will trust in her faithful Hastings, we shall soon be landed in France, where even among slaves the laws of marriage are respected.

Miss Neville. I have often told you, that though ready to obey you, I yet should leave my little fortune behind with reluctance. The greatest part of it was left me by my uncle, the India director, and chiefly consists in jewels. I have been for some time persuading my aunt to let me wear them. I fancy I 'm very near succeeding. The instant they are put into my possession, you shall find me ready to make them and myself yours.

Hastings. Perish the baubles! Your person is all I

desire. In the mean time, my friend Marlow must not be let into his mistake. I know the strange reserve of his temper is such, that if abruptly informed of it, he would instantly quit the house before our plan was ripe for execution.

Miss Neville. But how shall we keep him in the deception? — Miss Hardcastle is just returned from walking — What if we still continue to deceive him? — This, this way —— [*They confer.*

Enter Marlow.

Marlow. The assiduities of these good people tease me beyond bearing. My host seems to think it ill manners to leave me alone, and so he claps not only himself, but his old-fashioned wife on my back. They talk of coming to sup with us too; and then, I suppose, we are to run the gauntlet through all the rest of the family. What have we got here?

Hastings. My dear Charles! Let me congratulate you — The most fortunate accident! — Who do you think is just alighted?

Marlow. Cannot guess.

Hastings. Our mistresses, boy, Miss Hardcastle and Miss Neville. Give me leave to introduce Miss Constance Neville to your acquaintance. Happening to dine in the neighborhood, they called on their return to take fresh horses here. Miss Hardcastle has just stept into the next room, and will be back in an instant. Was n't it lucky? eh!

Marlow. (*Aside.*) I have been mortified enough of

all conscience, and here comes something to complete my embarrassment.

Hastings. Well, but was n't it the most fortunate thing in the world?

Marlow. Oh, yes. Very fortunate — a most joyful encounter. But our dresses, George, you know, are in disorder — What if we should postpone the happiness till to-morrow? — To-morrow at her own house — It will be every bit as convenient — and rather more respectful — To-morrow let it be. [*Offering to go.*

Hastings. By no means, sir. Your ceremony will displease her. The disorder of your dress will show the ardor of your impatience. Besides, she knows you are in the house, and will permit you to see her.

Marlow. Oh, the devil! How shall I support it? — Hem! hem! Hastings, you must not go. You are to assist me, you know. I shall be confoundedly ridiculous. Yet hang it! I 'll take courage. Hem!

Hastings. Pshaw, man! it 's but the first plunge, and all 's over. She 's but a woman, you know.

Marlow. And of all women, she that I dread most to encounter.

Enter Miss Hardcastle, as returned from walking.

Hastings. (*Introducing them.*) Miss Hardcastle, Mr. Marlow, I 'm proud of bringing two persons of such merit together, that only want to know, to esteem each other.

Miss Hardcastle. (*Aside.*) Now for meeting my modest gentleman with a demure face, and quite in his own manner. (*After a pause, in which he appears very uneasy *and disconcerted.)* I'm glad of your safe arrival, sir. I'm told you had some accidents by the way.

Marlow. Only a few, madam. Yes, we had some. Yes, madam, a good many accidents, but should be sorry — madam — or rather glad of any accidents — that are so agreeably concluded. Hem!

Hastings. *(To him.)* You never spoke better in your whole life. Keep it up, and I'll insure you the victory.

Miss Hardcastle. I'm afraid you flatter, sir. You that have seen so much of the finest company, can find little entertainment in an obscure corner of the country.

Marlow. *(Gathering courage.)* I have lived, indeed, in the world, madam; but I have kept very little company. I have been but an observer upon life, madam, while others were enjoying it.

Miss Neville. But that, I am told, is the way to enjoy it at last.

Hastings. *(To him.)* Cicero never spoke better. Once more, and you are confirmed in assurance for ever.

Marlow. *(To him.)* Hem! stand by me then, and when I'm down, throw in a word or two to set me up again.

Miss Hardcastle. An observer, like you, upon life, were, I fear, disagreeably employed, since you must have had much more to censure than to approve.

Marlow. Pardon me, madam. I was always willing to be amused. The folly of most people is rather an object of mirth than uneasiness.

Hastings. *(To him.)* Bravo, bravo. Never spoke so well in your whole life. Well, Miss Hardcastle, I see that you and Mr. Marlow are going to be very good company. I believe our being here will but embarrass the interview.

Marlow. Not in the least, Mr. Hastings. We like your company of all things. *(To him.)* Zounds! George, sure you won't go? how can you leave us?

Hastings. Our presence will but spoil conversation, so we 'll retire to the next room. *(To him.)* You do n't consider, man, that we are to manage a little tête-à-tête of our own. [*Exeunt.*

Miss Hardcastle. (*After a pause.*) But you have not been wholly an observer, I presume, sir: the ladies, I should hope, have employed some part of your addresses.

Marlow. (*Relapsing into timidity.*) Pardon me, madam, I — I — I — as yet have studied — only — to — deserve them.

Miss Hardcastle. And that, some say, is the very worst way to obtain them.

Marlow. Perhaps so, madam. But I love to converse only with the more grave and sensible part of the sex — But I 'm afraid I grow tiresome.

Miss Hardcastle. Not at all, sir; there is nothing I like so much as grave conversation myself; I could hear it for ever. Indeed I have often been surprised how a man of sentiment could ever admire those light, airy pleasures, where nothing reaches the heart.

Marlow. It 's —— a disease —— of the mind, madam. In the variety of tastes there must be some who, wanting a relish —— for —— um — u — um —

Miss Hardcastle. I understand you, sir. There must be some who, wanting a relish for refined pleasures, pretend to despise what they are incapable of tasting.

Marlow. My meaning, madam, but infinitely better expressed. And I can 't help observing —— a ——

Miss Hardcastle. (*Aside.*) Who could ever suppose this fellow impudent upon some occasions! (*To him.*) You were going to observe, sir ——

Marlow. I was observing, madam — I protest, madam, I forget what I was going to observe.

Miss Hardcastle. (*Aside.*) I vow and so do I. (*To him.*) You were observing, sir, that in this age of hypocrisy — something about hypocrisy, sir.

Marlow. Yes, madam. In this age of hypocrisy, there are few who, upon strict inquiry, do not — a — a ——

Miss Hardcastle. I understand you perfectly, sir.

Marlow. (*Aside.*) Egad! and that 's more than I do myself.

Miss Hardcastle. You mean that, in this hypocritical age, there are a few that do not condemn in public what they practise in private, and think they pay every debt to virtue when they praise it.

Marlow. True, madam; those who have most virtue in their mouths, have least of it in their bosoms. But I 'm sure I tire you, madam.

Miss Hardcastle. Not in the least, sir; there 's something so agreeable and spirited in your manner, such life and force — Pray, sir, go on.

Marlow. Yes, madam, I was saying —— that there are some occasions — when a total want of courage, madam, destroys all the —— and puts us —— upon — a — a — a ——

Miss Hardcastle. I agree with you entirely: a want

of courage upon some occasions, assumes the appearance of ignorance, and betrays us when we most want to excel. I beg you 'll proceed.

Marlow. Yes, madam. Morally speaking, madam — but I see Miss Neville expecting us in the next room. I would not intrude for the world.

Miss Hardcastle. I protest, sir, I never was more agreeably entertained in all my life. Pray go on.

Marlow. Yes, madam, I was —— But she beckons us to join her. Madam, shall I do myself the honor to attend you?

Miss Hardcastle. Well, then, I 'll follow.

Marlow. *(Aside.)* This pretty smooth dialogue has done for me. [*Exit.*

Miss Hardcastle. *(Alone.)* Ha! ha! ha! Was there ever such a sober, sentimental interview? I 'm certain he scarce looked in my face the whole time. Yet the fellow, but for his unaccountable bashfulness, is pretty well too. He has good sense, but then so buried in his fears, that it fatigues one more than ignorance. If I could teach him a little confidence, it would be doing somebody that I know of a piece of service. But who is that somebody? That, faith, is a question I can scarce answer. [*Exit.*

Enter Tony and Miss Neville, followed by Mrs. Hardcastle and Hastings.

Tony. What do you follow me for, cousin Con? I wonder you 're not ashamed to be so very engaging.

Miss Neville. I hope, cousin, one may speak to one's own relations, and not be to blame.

Tony. Ay, but I know what sort of a relation you want to make me though; but it won't do. I tell you, cousin Con, it won't do; so I beg you 'll keep your distance — I want no nearer relationship.

[*She follows, coquetting him to the back scene.*

Mrs. Hardcastle. Well, I vow, Mr. Hastings, you are very entertaining. There 's nothing in the world I love to talk of so much as London, and the fashions; though I was never there myself.

Hastings. Never there! You amaze me! From your air and manner, I concluded you had been bred all your life either at Ranelagh, St. James's, or Tower Wharf.

Mrs. Hardcastle. Oh, sir, you 're only pleased to say so. We country persons can have no manner at all. I 'm in love with the town, and that serves to raise me above some of our neighboring rustics; but who can have a manner, that has never seen the Pantheon, the Grotto Gardens, the Borough, and such places, where the nobility chiefly resort? All I can do is to enjoy London at second-hand. I take care to know every tête-à-tête from the Scandalous Magazine, and have all the fashions, as they come out, in a letter from the two Miss Rickets of Crooked Lane. Pray, how do you like this head, Mr. Hastings?

Hastings. Extremely elegant and degagée, upon my word, madam. Your friseur is a Frenchman, I suppose?

Mrs. Hardcastle. I protest, I dressed it myself from a print in the Ladies Memorandum-book for the last year.

Hastings. Indeed! Such a head in a side-box at the

play-house, would draw as many gazers as my Lady Mayoress at a city ball.

Mrs. Hardcastle. I vow, since inoculation began, there is no such thing to be seen as a plain woman; so one must dress a little particular, or one may escape in the crowd.

Hastings. But that can never be your case, madam, in any dress. (*Bowing.*)

Mrs. Hardcastle. Yet what signifies my dressing, when I have such a piece of antiquity by my side as Mr. Hardcastle? all I can say will never argue down a single button from his clothes. I have often wanted him to throw off his great flaxen wig, and where he was bald, to plaster it over, like my Lord Pately, with powder.

Hastings. You are right, madam; for, as among the ladies there are none ugly, so among the men there are none old.

Mrs. Hardcastle. But what do you think his answer was? Why, with his usual Gothic vivacity, he said I only wanted him to throw off his wig to convert it into a *tête* for my own wearing.

Hastings. Intolerable! At your age you may wear what you please, and it must become you.

Mrs. Hardcastle. Pray, Mr. Hastings, what do you take to be the most fashionable age about town?

Hastings. Some time ago, forty was all the mode; but I 'm told the ladies intend to bring up fifty for the ensuing winter.

Mrs. Hardcastle. Seriously? Then I shall be too young for the fashion.

Hastings. No lady begins now to put on jewels till

she 's past forty. For instance, miss there, in a polite circle, would be considered as a child — a mere maker of samplers.

Mrs. Hardcastle. And yet, my niece thinks herself as much a woman, and is as fond of jewels, as the oldest of us all.

Hastings. Your niece, is she? And that young gentleman — a brother of yours, I should presume?

Mrs. Hardcastle. My son, sir. They are contracted to each other. Observe their little sports. They fall in and out ten times a-day, as if they were man and wife already. (*To them.*) Well, Tony, child, what soft things are you saying to your cousin Constance this evening?

Tony. I have been saying no soft things; but that it 's very hard to be followed about so. Ecod! I 've not a place in the house now that 's left to myself, but the stable.

Mrs. Hardcastle. Never mind him, Con, my dear: he's in another story behind your back.

Miss Neville. There 's something generous in my cousin's manner. He falls out before faces, to be forgiven in private.

Tony. That 's a damned confounded — crack.

Mrs. Hardcastle. Ah! he 's a sly one. Do n't you think they 're like each other about the mouth, Mr. Hastings? The Blenkinsop mouth to a T. They 're of a size, too. Back to back, my pretties, that Mr. Hastings may see you. Come, Tony.

Tony. You had as good not make me, I tell you.

(*Measuring.*)

Miss Neville. O lud! he has almost cracked my head.

Mrs. Hardcastle. Oh, the monster! for shame, Tony. You a man, and behave so!

Tony. If I'm a man, let me have my fortin. Ecod! I'll not be made a fool of no longer.

Mrs. Hardcastle. Is this, ungrateful boy, all that I'm to get for the pains I have taken in your education? I that have rocked you in your cradle, and fed that pretty mouth with a spoon? Did not I work that waistcoat to make you genteel? Did not I prescribe for you every day, and weep while the receipt was operating?

Tony. Ecod! you had reason to weep, for you have been dosing me ever since I was born. I have gone through every receipt in the Complete Housewife ten times over; and you have thoughts of coursing me through Quincey next spring. But, ecod! I tell you, I'll not be made a fool of no longer.

Mrs. Hardcastle. Wasn't it all for your good, viper? Wasn't it all for your good?

Tony. I wish you'd let me and my good alone, then. Snubbing this way when I'm in spirits! If I'm to have any good, let it come of itself; not to keep dinging it, dinging it into one so.

Mrs. Hardcastle. That's false; I never see you when you're in spirits. No, Tony, you then go to the alehouse or kennel. I'm never to be delighted with your agreeable wild notes, unfeeling monster!

Tony. Ecod! mamma, your own notes are the wildest of the two.

Mrs. Hardcastle. Was ever the like? But I see he wants to break my heart; I see he does.

Hastings. Dear madam, permit me to lecture the

young gentleman a little. I 'm certain I can persuade him to his duty.

Mrs. Hardcastle. Well, I must retire. Come, Constance, my love. You see, Mr. Hastings, the wretchedness of my situation: was ever poor woman so plagued with a dear, sweet, pretty, provoking, undutiful boy!

[*Exeunt Mrs. Hardcastle and Miss Neville.*

Tony. (*Singing.*)

There was a young man riding by,
And fain would have his will.
Rang do didlo dee.

Do n't mind her. Let her cry. It 's the comfort of her heart. I have seen her and sister cry over a book for an hour together; and they said they liked the book the better the more it made them cry.

Hastings. Then you 're no friend to the ladies, I find, my pretty young gentleman?

Tony. That 's as I find 'um.

Hastings. Not to her of your mother's choosing, I dare answer? And yet she appears to me a pretty, well-tempered girl.

Tony. That 's because you do n't know her as well as I. Ecod! I know every inch about her; and there's not a more bitter cantanckerous toad in all Christendom.

Hastings. (*Aside.*) Pretty encouragement for a lover!

Tony. I have seen her since the height of that. She has as many tricks as a hare in a thicket, or a colt the first day's breaking.

Hastings. To me she appears sensible and silent.

Tony. Ay, before company. But when she 's with her playmates, she 's as loud as a hog in a gate.

Hastings. But there is a meek modesty about her that charms me.

Tony. Yes, but curb her never so little, she kicks up, and you 're flung in a ditch.

Hastings. Well, but you must allow her a little beauty. Yes, you must allow her some beauty.

Tony. Bandbox! She 's all a made-up thing, mun. Ah! could you but see Bet Bouncer of these parts, you might then talk of beauty. Ecod! she has two eyes as black as sloes, and cheeks as broad and red as a pulpit cushion. She 'd make two of she.

Hastings. Well, what say you to a friend that would take this bitter bargain off your hands?

Tony. Anan!

Hastings. Would you thank him that would take Miss Neville, and leave you to happiness and your dear Betsey?

Tony. Ay; but where is there such a friend — for who would take her?

Hastings. I am he. If you but assist me, I'll engage to whip her off to France, and you shall never hear more of her.

Tony. Assist you! Ecod I will to the last drop of my blood. I 'll clap a pair of horses to your chaise that shall trundle you off in a twinkling, and may be get you a part of her fortin besides, in jewels, that you little dream of.

Hastings. My dear Squire, this looks like a lad of spirit.

Tony. Come along, then, and you shall see more of my spirit before you have done with me. (*Singing.*)

We are the boys
That fears no noise,
Where the thundering cannons roar.

[*Exeunt.*

ACT THIRD.

Enter Hardcastle.

Hardcastle. WHAT could my old friend Sir Charles mean by recommending his son as the modestest young man in town? To me he appears the most impudent piece of brass that ever spoke with a tongue. He has taken possession of the easy chair by the fire-side already. He took off his boots in the parlor, and desired me to see them taken care of. I'm desirous to know how his impudence affects my daughter. She will certainly be shocked at it.

Enter Miss Hardcastle, plainly dressed.

Hardcastle. Well, my Kate, I see you have changed your dress, as I bid you; and yet, I believe, there was no great occasion.

Miss Hardcastle. I find such a pleasure, sir, in obeying your commands, that I take care to observe them without ever debating their propriety.

Hardcastle. And yet, Kate, I sometimes give you

some cause, particularly when I recommended my modest gentleman to you as a lover to-day.

Miss Hardcastle. You taught me to expect something extraordinary, and I find the original exceeds the description.

Hardcastle. I was never so surprised in my life! He has quite confounded all my faculties.

Miss Hardcastle. I never saw any thing like it; and a man of the world, too!

Hardcastle. Ay, he learned it all abroad — what a fool was I, to think a young man could learn modesty by travelling. He might as soon learn wit at a masquerade.

Miss Hardcastle. It seems all natural to him.

Hardcastle. A good deal assisted by bad company and a French dancing-master.

Miss Hardcastle. Sure you mistake, papa. A French dancing-master could never have taught him that timid look — that awkward address — that bashful manner.

Hardcastle. Whose look? whose manner, child?

Miss Hardcastle. Mr. Marlow's: his *mauvaise hmte,* his timidity, struck me at the first sight.

Hardcastle. Then your first sight deceived you: for I think him one of the most brazen first sights that ever astonished my senses.

Miss Hardcastle. Sure, sir, you rally! I never saw any one so modest.

Hardcastle. And can you be serious? I never saw such a bouncing, swaggering puppy since I was born. Bully Dawson was but a fool to him.

Miss Hardcastle. Surprising! He met me with a re

spectful bow, a stammering voice, and a look fixed on the ground.

Hardcastle. He met me with a loud voice, a lordly air, and a familiarity that made my blood freeze again.

Miss Hardcastle. He treated me with diffidence and respect; censured the manners of the age; admired the prudence of girls that never laughed, tired me with apologies for being tiresome, then left the room with a bow, and 'Madam, I would not for the world detain you.'

Hardcastle. He spoke to me as if he knew me all his life before, asked twenty questions, and never waited for an answer, interrupted my best remarks with some silly pun, and when I was in my best story of the Duke of Marlborough and Prince Eugene, he asked if I had not a good hand at making punch. Yes, Kate, he asked your father if he was a maker of punch.

Miss Hardcastle. One of us must certainly be mistaken.

Hardcastle. If he be what he has shown himself, I'm determined he shall never have my consent.

Miss Hardcastle. And if he be the sullen thing I take him, he shall never have mine.

Hardcastle. In one thing, then, we are agreed — to reject him.

Miss Hardcastle. Yes — but upon conditions. For if you should find him less impudent, and I more presuming; if you find him more respectful, and I more importunate — I do n't know — the fellow is well enough for a man — certainly we do n't meet many such at a horse-race in the country.

Hardcastle. If we should find him so —— But that 's

impossible. The first appearance has done my business. I 'm seldom deceived in that.

Miss Hardcastle. And yet there may be many good qualities under that first appearance.

Hardcastle. Ay, when a girl finds a fellow's outside to her taste, she then sets about guessing the rest of his furniture. With her a smooth face stands for good sense, and a genteel figure for every virtue.

Miss Hardcastle. I hope, sir, a conversation begun with a compliment to my good sense, won't end with a sneer at my understanding!

Hardcastle. Pardon me, Kate. But if young Mr. Brazen can find the art of reconciling contradictions, he may please us both, perhaps.

Miss Hardcastle. And as one of us must be mistaken, what if we go to make farther discoveries?

Hardcastle. Agreed. But depend on 't, I 'm in the right.

Miss Hardcastle. And, depend on 't, I 'm not much in the wrong. [*Exeunt.*

Enter Tony, running in with a casket.

Tony. Ecod! I have got them. Here they are. My cousin Con's necklaces, bobs and all. My mother shan't cheat the poor souls out of their fortin neither. O my genus, is that you?

Enter Hastings.

Hastings. My dear friend, how have you managed with your mother? I hope you have amused her with pretending love for your cousin, and that you are willing to be reconciled at last? Our horses will be refreshed in a short time, and we shall soon be ready to set off.

Tony. And here 's something to bear your charges by the way —*(giving the casket)*— your sweetheart's jewels. Keep them; and hang those, I say, that would rob you of one of them.

Hastings. But how have you procured them from your mother?

Tony. Ask me no questions, and I 'll tell you no fibs. I procured them by the rule of thumb. If I had not a key to every draw in my mother's bureau, how could I go to the alehouse so often as I do? An honest man may rob himself of his own at any time.

Hastings. Thousands do it every day. But, to be plain with you, Miss Neville is endeavoring to procure them from her aunt this very instant. If she succeeds, it will be the most delicate way, at least, of obtaining them.

Tony. Well, keep them, till you know how it will be. But I know how it will be well enough,— she 'd as soon part with the only sound tooth in her head.

Hastings. But I dread the effects of her resentment, when she finds she has lost them.

Tony. Never you mind her resentment; leave me to manage that. I do n't value her resentment the bounce of a cracker. Zounds! here they are. Morrice! Prance!

[*Exit Hastings.*

Tony, Mrs. Hardcastle, and Miss Neville.

Mrs. Hardcastle. Indeed, Constance, you amaze me.

Such a girl as you want jewels! It will be time enough for jewels, my dear, twenty years hence, when your beauty begins to want repairs.

Miss Neville. But what will repair beauty at forty, will certainly improve it at twenty, madam.

Mrs. Hardcastle. Yours, my dear, can admit of none. That natural blush is beyond a thousand ornaments. Besides, child, jewels are quite out at present. Don't you see half the ladies of our acquaintance, my Lady Killdaylight, and Mrs. Crump, and the rest of them, carry their jewels to town, and bring nothing but paste and marcasites back?

Miss Neville. But who knows, madam, but somebody that shall be nameless would like me best with all my little finery about me?

Mrs. Hardcastle. Consult your glass, my dear, and then see if, with such a pair of eyes, you want any better sparklers. What do you think, Tony, my dear? Does your cousin Con want any jewels in your eyes to set off her beauty?

Tony. That 's as hereafter may be.

Miss Neville. My dear aunt, if you knew how it would oblige me.

Mrs. Hardcastle. A parcel of old-fashioned rose and table-cut things. They would make you look like the court of King Solomon at a puppet-show. Besides, I believe I can 't readily come at them. They may be missing for aught I know to the contrary.

Tony. *(Apart to Mrs. Hardcastle.)* Then why don't you tell her so at once, as she 's so longing for them? Tell her they 're lost. It 's the only way to quiet her. Say they 're lost, and call me to bear witness.

Mrs. Hardcastle. (Apart to Tony.) You know, my dear, I 'm only keeping them for you. So if I say they are gone, you 'll bear me witness, will you? He! he! he!

Tony. Never fear me. Ecod! I 'll say I saw them taken out with my own eyes.

Miss Neville. I desire them but for a day, madam — just to be permitted to show them as relics, and then they may be locked up again.

Mrs. Hardcastle. To be plain with you, my dear Constance, if I could find them you should have them. They are missing, I assure you. Lost, for aught I know; but we must have patience, wherever they are.

Miss Neville. I 'll not believe it; this is but a shallow pretence to deny me. I know they are too valuable to be so slightly kept, and as you are to answer for the loss —

Mrs. Hardcastle. Do n't be alarmed, Constance. If they be lost, I must restore an equivalent. But my son knows they are missing, and not to be found.

Tony. That I can bear witness to. They are missing, and not to be found; I 'll take my oath on 't.

Mrs. Hardcastle. You must learn resignation, my dear; for though we lose our fortune, yet we should not lose our patience. See me, how calm I am.

Miss Neville. Ay, people are generally calm at the misfortunes of others.

Mrs. Hardcastle. Now, I wonder a girl of your good sense should waste a thought upon such trumpery. We shall soon find them; and in the mean time you shall make use of my garnets till your jewels be found.

Miss Neville. I detest garnets.

Mrs. Hardcastle. The most becoming things in the world to set off a clear complexion. You have often seen how well they look upon me. You shall have them. [*Exit.*

Miss Neville. I dislike them of all things. You shan't stir. Was ever any thing so provoking, to mislay my own jewels, and force me to wear her trumpery?

Tony. Do n't be a fool. If she gives you the garnets, take what you can get. The jewels are your own already. I have stolen them out of her bureau, and she does not know it. Fly to your spark; he 'll tell you more of the matter. Leave me to manage her.

Miss Neville. My dear cousin!

Tony. Vanish. She's here, and has missed them already. [*Exit Miss Neville.*] Zounds! how she fidgets and spits about like a catharine wheel!

Enter Mrs. Hardcastle.

Mrs. Hardcastle. Confusion! thieves! robbers! we are cheated, plundered, broke open, undone.

Tony. What 's the matter, what 's the matter, mamma? I hope nothing has happened to any of the good family?

Mrs. Hardcastle. We are robbed. My bureau has been broken open, the jewels taken out, and I 'm undone.

Tony. Oh! is that all? Ha! ha! ha! By the laws, I never saw it better acted in my life. Ecod, I thought you was ruined in earnest, ha! ha! ha!

Mrs. Hardcastle. Why, boy, I am ruined in earnest. My bureau has been broken open, and all taken away.

Tony. Stick to that, ha! ha! ha! stick to that. I'll bear witness, you know! call me to bear witness.

Mrs. Hardcastle. I tell you, Tony, by all that's precious, the jewels are gone, and I shall be ruined for ever.

Tony. Sure I know they are gone, and I am to say so.

Mrs. Hardcastle. My dearest Tony, but hear me. They're gone, I say.

Tony. By the laws, mamma, you make me for to laugh, ha! ha! I know who took them well enough, ha! ha! ha!

Mrs. Hardcastle. Was there ever such a blockhead, that can't tell the difference between jest and earnest! I tell you I'm not in jest, booby.

Tony. That's right, that's right; you must be in a bitter passion, and then nobody will suspect either of us. I'll bear witness that they are gone.

Mrs. Hardcastle. Was there ever such a cross-grained brute, that won't hear me! Can you bear witness that you're no better than a fool? Was ever poor woman so beset with fools on one hand, and thieves on the other!

Tony. I can bear witness to that.

Mrs. Hardcastle. Bear witness again, you blockhead, you, and I'll turn you out of the room directly. My poor niece, what will become of her? Do you laugh, you unfeeling brute, as if you enjoyed my distress?

Tony. I can bear witness to that.

Mrs. Hardcastle. Do you insult me, monster? I'll teach you to vex your mother, I will!

Tony. I can bear witness to that. *(He runs off, she follows him.)*

Enter Miss Hardcastle and Maid.

Miss Hardcastle. What an unaccountable creature is that brother of mine, to send them to the house as an inn; ha! ha! I do n't wonder at his impudence.

Maid. But what is more, madam, the young gentleman, as you passed by in your present dress, asked me if you were the bar-maid. He mistook you for the bar-maid, madam!

Miss Hardcastle. Did he? Then, as I live, I 'm resolved to keep up the delusion. Tell me, Pimple, how do you like my present dress? Do n't you think I look something like Cherry in the Beaux' Stratagem?

Maid. It 's the dress, madam, that every lady wears in the country, but when she visits or receives company.

Miss Hardcastle. And are you sure he does not remember my face or person?

Maid. Certain of it.

Miss Hardcastle. I vow I thought so; for though we spoke for some time together, yet his fears were such that he never once looked up during the interview. Indeed, if he had, my bonnet would have kept him from seeing me.

Maid. But what do you hope from keeping him in his mistake?

Miss Hardcastle. In the first place, I shall be seen, and that is no small advantage to a girl who brings her face to market. Then I shall perhaps make an acquaintance, and that 's no small victory gained over one who never addresses any but the wildest of her sex. But my chief aim is to take my gentleman off his guard, and, like an invisible champion of romance, examine the giant's force before I offer to combat.

Maid. But are you sure you can act your part, and disguise your voice so that he may mistake that, as he has already mistaken your person?

Miss Hardcastle. Never fear me. I think I have got the true bar cant — Did your honor call? — Attend the Lion there. — Pipes and tobacco for the Angel. — The Lamb has been outrageous this half hour.

Maid. It will do, madam. But he 's here.

[*Exit Maid.*

Enter Marlow.

Marlow. What a bawling in every part of the house! I have scarce a moment's repose. If I go to the best room, there I find my host and his story; if I fly to the gallery, there we have my hostess with her courtesy down to the ground. I have at last got a moment to myself, and now for recollection. [*Walks and muses.*

Miss Hardcastle. Did you call, sir? Did your honor call?

Marlow. (*Musing.*) As for Miss Hardcastle, she 's too grave and sentimental for me.

Miss Hardcastle. Did your honor call?

[*She still places herself before him, he turning away.*

Marlow. No, child. (*Musing.*) Besides, from the glimpse I had of her, I think she squints.

Miss Hardcastle. I 'm sure, sir, I heard the bell ring.

Marlow. No, no. (*Musing.*) I have pleased my

father, however, by coming down, and I'll to-morrow please myself by returning. *(Taking out his tablets and perusing.)*

Miss Hardcastle. Perhaps the other gentleman called, sir?

Marlow. I tell you no.

Miss Hardcastle. I should be glad to know, sir: we have such a parcel of servants.

Marlow. No, no, I tell you. *(Looks full in her face)* Yes, child, I think I did call. I wanted — I wanted — I vow, child, you are vastly handsome.

Miss Hardcastle. O la, sir, you'll make one ashamed.

Marlow. Never saw a more sprightly, malicious eye. Yes, yes, my dear, I did call. Have you got any of your — a — what d'ye call it, in the house?

Miss Hardcastle. No, sir, we have been out of that these ten days.

Marlow. One may call in this house, I find, to very little purpose. Suppose I should call for a taste, just by way of trial, of the nectar of your lips, perhaps I might be disappointed in that too.

Miss Hardcastle. Nectar! nectar! That's a liquor there's no call for in these parts. French, I suppose. We keep no French wines here, sir.

Marlow. Of true English growth, I assure you.

Miss Hardcastle. Then it's odd I should not know it. We brew all sorts of wines in this house, and I have lived here these eighteen years.

Marlow. Eighteen years! Why, one would think, child, you kept the bar before you were born. How old are you?

Miss Hardcastle. Oh, sir, I must not tell my age. They say women and music should never be dated.

Marlow. To guess at this distance, you can't be much above forty. *(Approaching)* Yet nearer, I do n't think so much. *(Approaching)* By coming close to some women, they look younger still; but when we come very close indeed — *(Attempting to kiss her.)*

Miss Hardcastle. Pray, sir, keep your distance. One would think you wanted to know one's age as they do horses, by mark of mouth.

Marlow. I protest, child, you use me extremely ill. If you keep me at this distance, how is it possible you and I can ever be acquainted?

Miss Hardcastle. And who wants to be acquainted with you? I want no such acquaintance, not I. I 'm sure you did not treat Miss Hardcastle, that was here a while ago, in this obstropalous manner. I 'll warrant me, before her you looked dashed, and kept bowing to the ground, and talked, for all the world, as if you were before a justice of the peace.

Marlow. *(Aside)* Egad, she has hit it, sure enough! *(To her)* In awe of her, child? Ha! ha! ha! A mere awkward, squinting thing! No, no. I find you do n't know me. I laughed and rallied her a little; but I was unwilling to be too severe. No, I could not be too severe. curse me!

Miss Hardcastle. Oh, then, sir, you are a favorite, I find, among the ladies?

Marlow. Yes, my dear, a great favorite. And yet, hang me, I do n't see what they find in me to follow. At the ladies' club in town I 'm called their agreeable Rattle.

Rattle, child, is not my real name, but one I 'm known by. My name is Solomons; Mr. Solomons, my dear, at your service. *(Offering to salute her.)*

Miss Hardcastle. Hold, sir, you are introducing me to your club, not to yourself. And you 're so great a favorite there, you say?

Marlow. Yes, my dear. There 's Mrs. Mantrap, Lady Betty Blackleg, the Countess of Sligo, Mrs. Langhorns, old Miss Biddy Buckskin, and your humble servant, keep up the spirit of the place.

Miss Hardcastle. Then it 's a very merry place, I suppose?

Marlow. Yes, as merry as cards, suppers, wine, and old women can make us.

Miss Hardcastle. And their agreeable Rattle, ha! ha! ha!

Marlow. (Aside) Egad! I do n't quite like this chit. She looks knowing, methinks. You laugh, child?

Miss Hardcastle. I can't but laugh to think what time they all have for minding their work, or their family.

Marlow. (Aside) All 's well; she don't laugh at me. *(To her)* Do you ever work, child?

Miss Hardcastle. Aye, sure. There 's not a screen or a quilt in the whole house but what can bear witness to that.

Marlow. Odso! then you must show me your embroidery. I embroider and draw patterns myself a little. If you want a judge of your work, you must apply to me. *(Seizing her hand.)*

Miss Hardcastle. Ay, but the colors do n't look well by candle-light. You shall see all in the morning. *(Struggling.)*

Marlow. And why not now, my angel? Such beauty fires beyond the power of resistance. Pshaw! the father here! My old luck: I never nicked seven that I did not throw ames ace three times following.*

[*Exit Marlow.*

Enter Hardcastle, who stands in surprise.

Hardcastle. So, madam. So I find this is your modest lover. This is your humble admirer, that kept his eyes fixed on the ground, and only adored at humble distance. Kate, Kate, art thou not ashamed to deceive your father so?

Miss Hardcastle. Never trust me, dear papa, but he 's still the modest man I first took him for; you 'll be convinced of it as well as I.

Hardcastle. By the hand of my body, I believe his impudence is infectious! Did n't I see him seize your hand? Did n't I see him hawl you about like a milk-maid? And now you talk of his respect and his modesty, forsooth!

Miss Hardcastle. But if I shortly convince you of his modesty, that he has only the faults that will pass off with time, and the virtues that will improve with age, I hope you 'll forgive him.

Hardcastle. The girl would actually make one run mad! I tell you I 'll not be convinced. I am convinced. He has scarcely been three hours in the house, and he

* Ames ace, or ambs ace, is two aces thrown at the same time on two dice. As seven is the main, to throw ames ace thrice running, when the player nicks, that is, hazards his money on seven, is singularly bad luck.

has already encroached on all my prerogatives. You may like his impudence, and call it modesty; but my son-in-law, madam, must have very different qualifications.

Miss Hardcastle. Sir, I ask but this night to convince you.

Hardcastle. You shall not have half the time, for I have thoughts of turning him out this very hour.

Miss Hardcastle. Give me that hour, then, and I hope to satisfy you.

Hardcastle. Well, an hour let it be then. But I'll have no trifling with your father. All fair and open, do you mind me.

Miss Hardcastle. I hope, sir, you have ever found that I considered your commands as my pride; for your kindness is such, that my duty as yet has been inclination.

[*Exeunt.*

ACT FOURTH.

Enter Hastings and Miss Neville.

Hastings. You surprise me: Sir Charles Marlow expected here this night! Where have you had your information?

Miss Neville. You may depend upon it. I just saw his letter to Mr. Hardcastle, in which he tells him he intends setting out in a few hours after his son.

Hastings. Then, my Constance, all must be completed before he arrives. He knows me; and should he find me here, would discover my name, and, perhaps, my designs, to the rest of the family.

Miss Neville. The jewels, I hope, are safe?

Hastings. Yes, yes. I have sent them to Marlow, who keeps the keys of our baggage. In the mean time, I 'll go to prepare matters for our elopement. I have had the Squire's promise of a fresh pair of horses; and if I should not see him again, will write him further directions. [*Exit.*

Miss Neville. Well, success attend you! In the mean time, I 'll go amuse my aunt with the old pretence of a violent passion for my cousin. [*Exit.*

Enter Marlow, followed by a Servant.

Marlow. I wonder what Hastings could mean by sending me so valuable a thing as a casket to keep for him, when he knows the only place I have is the seat of a post-coach at an inn-door. Have you deposited the casket with the landlady, as I ordered you? Have you put it into her own hands?

Servant. Yes, your honor.

Marlow. She said she 'd keep it safe, did she?

Servant. Yes; she said she 'd keep it safe enough. She asked me how I came by it; and she said she had a great mind to make me give an account of myself. [*Exit Servant.*

Marlow. Ha! ha! ha! They 're safe, however. What an unaccountable set of beings have we got amongst! This little bar-maid, though, runs in my mind most strangely, and drives out the absurdities of all the rest of the family. She 's mine, she must be mine, or I 'm greatly mistaken.

Enter Hastings.

Hastings. Bless me! I quite forgot to tell her that I intended to prepare at the bottom of the garden. Marlow here, and in spirits too!

Marlow. Give me joy, George! Crown me, shadow me with laurels: Well, George, after all, we modest fellows don't want for success among the women.

Hastings. Some women, you mean. But what success has your honor's modesty been crowned with now, that it grows so insolent upon us?

Marlow. Did n't you see the tempting, brisk, lovely, little thing, that runs about the house with a bunch of keys to its girdle?

Hastings. Well, and what then?

Marlow. She 's mine, you rogue you. Such fire, such motion, such eyes, such lips — but, egad! she would not let me kiss them though.

Hastings. But are you so sure, so very sure of her?

Marlow. Why, man, she talked of showing me her work above stairs, and I am to approve the pattern.

Hastings. But how can you, Charles, go about to rob a woman of her honor?

Marlow. Pshaw! pshaw! We all know the honor of the bar-maid of an inn. I do n't intend to rob her, take my word for it; there's nothing in this house I sha n't honestly pay for.

Hastings. I believe the girl has virtue.

Marlow. And if she has, I should be the last man in the world that would attempt to corrupt it.

Hastings. You have taken care, I hope, of the casket I sent you to lock up? It's in safety?

Marlow. Yes, yes; it's safe enough. I have taken care of it. But how could you think the seat of a post-coach at an inn-door a place of safety? Ah! numscull! I have taken better precautions for you than you did for yourself — I have —

Hastings. What?

Marlow. I have sent it to the landlady to keep for you.

Hastings. To the landlady!

Marlow. The landlady.

Hastings. You did?

Marlow. I did. She's to be answerable for its forth-coming, you know.

Hastings. Yes, she'll bring it forth with a witness.

Marlow. Was n't I right? I believe you'll allow that I acted prudently upon this occasion.

Hastings. (*Aside.*) He must not see my uneasiness.

Marlow. You seem a little disconcerted though, me-thinks. Sure nothing has happened?

Hastings. No, nothing. Never was in better spirits in all my life. And so you left it with the landlady, who, no doubt, very readily undertook the charge.

Marlow. Rather too readily; for she not only kept the casket, but, through her great precaution, was going to keep the messenger too. Ha! ha! ha!

Hastings. He! he! he! They're safe, however.

Marlow. As a guinea in a miser's purse.

Hastings. *(Aside.)* So now all hopes of fortune are at an end, and we must set off without it. *(To him)* Well, Charles, I 'll leave you to your meditations on the pretty bar-maid, and, he! he! he! may you be as successful for yourself as you have been for me!

[*Exit.*

Marlow. Thank ye, George: I ask no more. — Ha! ha! ha!

Enter Hardcastle.

Hardcastle. I no longer know my own house. It 's turned all topsy-turvy. His servants have got drunk already. I 'll bear it no longer; and yet, from my respect for his father, I 'll be calm. *(To him)* Mr. Marlow, your servant. I 'm your very humble servant. *(Bowing low.)*

Marlow. Sir, your humble servant. *(Aside.)* What is to be the wonder now?

Hardcastle. I believe, sir, you must be sensible, sir, that no man alive ought to be more welcome than your father's son, sir. I hope you think so?

Marlow. I do from my soul, sir. I don't want much entreaty. I generally make my father's son welcome wherever he goes.

Hardcastle. I believe you do, from my soul, sir. But though I say nothing to your own conduct, that of your servants is insufferable. Their manner of drinking is setting a very bad example in this house, I assure you.

Marlow. I protest, my very good sir, that is no fault of mine. If they do n't drink as they ought, they are to blame. I ordered them not to spare the cellar. I did, I assure you. *(To the side-scene)* Here, let one of my servants come up. *(To him)* My positive directions were, that as I did not drink myself, they should make up for my deficiencies below.

Hardcastle. Then they had your orders for what they do? I'm satisfied!

Marlow. They had, I assure you. You shall hear it from one of themselves.

Enter Servant, drunk.

Marlow. You, Jeremy! Come forward, sirrah! What were my orders? Were you not told to drink freely, and call for what you thought fit, for the good of the house?

Hardcastle. *(Aside.)* I begin to lose my patience.

Jeremy. Please your honor, liberty and Fleet-street forever! Though I'm but a servant, I'm as good as another man. I'll drink for no man before supper, sir, damme! Good liquor will sit upon a good supper, but a good supper will not sit upon —— hiccup —— upon my conscience, sir. [*Exit.*

Marlow. You see my old friend, the fellow is as drunk as he can possibly be. I do n't know what you 'd have more, unless you 'd have the poor devil soused in a beer-barrel.

Hardcastle. Zounds, he 'll drive me distracted, if I contain myself any longer! Mr. Marlow: sir, I have submitted to your insolence for more than four hours, and I see no likelihood of its coming to an end. I 'm now resolved to be master here, sir, and I desire that you and your drunken pack may leave my house directly.

Marlow. Leave your house! — Sure, you jest, my good friend? What! when I am doing what I can to please you.

Hardcastle. I tell you, sir, you do n't please; so I desire you will leave my house.

Marlow. Sure you cannot be serious? at this time o' night, and such a night? You only mean to banter me.

Hardcastle. I tell you, sir, I 'm serious! and now that my passions are roused, I say this house is mine, and I command you to leave it directly.

Marlow. Ha! ha! ha! A puddle in a storm. I shan't stir a step, I assure you. (*In a serious tone.*) This your house, fellow! It 's my house. This is my house. Mine while I choose to stay. What right have you to bid me leave this house, sir? I never met with such impudence, curse me; never in my whole life before.

Hardcastle. Nor I, confound me if ever I did! To come to my house, to call for what he likes, to turn me out of my own chair, to insult the family, to order his servants to get drunk, and then to tell me, "This house is mine, sir!" By all that 's impudent, it makes me laugh. Ha! ha! ha! Pray, sir, (*bantering*) as you take the house, what think you of taking the rest of the furniture? There 's a pair of silver candle-sticks, and there 's a fire-screen, and here's a pair of brazen-nosed bellows; perhaps you may take a fancy to them?

Marlow. Bring me your bill, sir; bring me your bill and let 's make no more words about it.

Hardcastle. There are a set of prints, too. What think you of the Rake's Progress for your own apartment?

Marlow. Bring me your bill, I say, and I'll leave you and your infernal house directly.

Hardcastle. Then there's a mahogany table that you may see your face in.

Marlow. My bill, I say.

Hardcastle. I had forgot the great chair for your own particular slumbers, after a hearty meal.

Marlow. Zounds! bring me my bill, I say, and let's hear no more on 't.

Hardcastle. Young man, young man, from your father's letter to me, I was taught to expect a well-bred, modest man as a visitor here, but now I find him no better than a coxcomb and a bully! but he will be down here presently, and shall hear more of it. [*Exit.*

Marlow. How 's this! Sure I have not mistaken the house. Everything looks like an inn; the servants cry coming; the attendance is awkward; the bar-maid, too, to attend us. But she 's here, and will further inform me. Whither so fast, child? A word with you.

Enter Miss Hardcastle.

Miss Hardcastle. Let it be short, then. I'm in a hurry. *(Aside)* I believe he begins to find out his mistake. But it 's too soon quite to undeceive him.

Marlow. Pray, child, answer me one question. What are you, and what may your business in this house be?

Miss Hardcastle. A relation of the family, sir.

Marlow. What, a poor relation?

Miss Hardcastle. Yes, sir, a poor relation, appointed to keep the keys, and to see that the guests want nothing in my power to give them.

Marlow. That is, you act as the bar-maid of this inn

Miss Hardcastle. Inn! O la —— what brought that into your head? One of the best families in the county keep an inn! — Ha! ha! ha! old Mr. Hardcastle's house an inn!

Marlow. Mr. Hardcastle's house! Is this Mr. Hardcastle's house, child?

Miss Hardcastle. Ay, sure. Whose else should it be?

Marlow. So then, all 's out, and I have been damnably imposed upon. Oh, confound my stupid head, I shall be laughed at over the whole town! I shall be stuck up in caricature in all the print-shops. The Dullissimo-Maccaroni. To mistake this house of all others for an inn, and my father's old friend for an inn-keeper! What a swaggering puppy must he take me for! What a silly puppy do I find myself! There, again, may I be hanged, my dear, but I mistook you for the bar-maid.

Miss Hardcastle. Dear me! dear me! I'm sure there 's nothing in my behavior to put me upon a level with one of that stamp.

Marlow. Nothing, my dear, nothing. But I was in for a list of blunders, and could not help making you a subscriber. My stupidity saw everything the wrong way. I mistook your assiduity for assurance, and your simplicty for allurement. But it's over — this house I no more show my face in.

Miss Hardcastle. I hope, sir, I have done nothing to disoblige you. I'm sure I should be sorry to affront any gentleman who has been so polite, and said so many civil things to me. I'm sure I should be sorry *(pretending to cry)* if he left the family on my account. I'm sure I should be sorry people said anything amiss, since I have no fortune but my character.

Marlow. *(Aside)* By Heaven! she weeps. This is the first mark of tenderness I ever had from a modest woman, and it touches me. *(To her.)* Excuse me, my lovely girl; you are the only part of the family I leave with reluctance. But, to be plain with you, the difference of our birth, fortune, and education, make an honorable connection impossible; and I can never harbor a thought of seducing simplicity that trusted in my honor, of bringing ruin upon one whose only fault was being too lovely.

Miss Hardcastle. *(Aside.)* Generous man! I now begin to admire him. *(To him.)* But I am sure my family is as good as Miss Hardcastle's; and though I 'm poor, that 's no great misfortune to a contented mind; and until this moment, I never thought that it was bad to want fortune.

Marlow. And why now, my pretty simplicity?

Miss Hardcastle. Because it puts me at a distance from one, that if I had a thousand pounds, I would give it all to.

Marlow. *(Aside.)* This simplicity bewitches me so, that if I stay, I 'm undone. I must make one bold effort and leave her. *(To her.)* Your partiality in my favor my dear, touches me most sensibly; and were I to live for myself alone, I could easily fix my choice. But I owe too much to the opinion of the world, too much to the authority of a father; so that — I can speak it — it affects me — Farewell. [*Exit.*

Miss Hardcastle. I never knew half his merit till now. He shall not go if I have power or art to detain him. I'll still preserve the character in which I *stooped to conquer*, but will undeceive my papa, who, perhaps, may laugh him out of his resolution. [*Exit.*

Enter Tony and Miss Neville.

Tony. Ay, you may steal for yourselves the next time. I have done my duty. She has got the jewels again, that 's a sure thing; but she believes it was all a mistake of the servants.

Miss Neville. But, my dear cousin, sure you won't forsake us in this distress? If she in the least suspects that I am going off, I shall certainly be locked up, or sent to my aunt Pedigree's, which is ten times worse.

Tony. To be sure, aunts of all kinds are damned bad things. But what can I do? I have got you a pair of horses that will fly like Whistle Jacket; and I 'm sure you can't say but I have courted you nicely before her face. Here she comes; we must court a bit or two more, for fear she should suspect us.

[*They retire, and seem to fondle.*

Enter Mrs. Hardcastle.

Mrs. Hardcastle. Well, I was greatly fluttered, to be sure, but my son tells me it was all a mistake of the servants. I shan't be easy, however, till they are fairly married, and then let her keep her own fortune. But what do I see? fondling together, as I 'm alive. I never saw Tony so sprightly before. Ah! have I caught you, my pretty doves? What, billing, exchanging glances and broken murmurs? Ah!

Tony. As for murmurs, mother, we grumble a littl

now and then, to be sure; but there 's no love lost between us.

Mrs. Hardcastle. A mere sprinkling, Tony, upon the flame, only to make it burn brighter.

Miss Neville. Cousin Tony promises us to give us more of his company at home. Indeed, he shant leave us any more. It won't leave us, cousin Tony, will it?

Tony. Oh, it's a pretty creature. No, I 'd sooner leave my horse in a pound, than leave you when you smile upon one so. Your laugh makes you so becoming.

Miss Neville. Agreeable cousin! Who can help admiring that natural humor, that pleasant, broad, red, thoughtless, *(patting his cheek,)* — ah! it's a bold face!

Mrs. Hardcastle. Pretty innocence!

Tony. I'm sure I always loved cousin Con's hazel eyes, and her pretty long fingers, that she twists this way and that over haspicholls, like a parcel of bobbins.

Mrs. Hardcastle. Ah! he would charm the bird from the tree. I was never so happy before. My boy takes after his father, poor Mr. Lumpkin, exactly. The jewels, my dear Con, shall be yours incontinently. You shall have them. Is n't he a sweet boy, my dear? You shall be married to-morrow, and we 'll put off the rest of his education, like Dr. Drowsy's sermons, to a fitter opportunity.

Enter Diggory.

Diggory. Where 's the Squire? I have got a letter for your worship.

Tony. Give it to my mamma. She reads all my letters first.

Diggory. I had orders to deliver it into your own hands.

Tony. Who does it come from?

Diggory. Your worship mun ask that o' the letter itself.

Tony. I could wish to know though. (*Turning the letter, and gazing on it.*)

Miss Neville. (*Aside*) Undone! undone! A letter to him from Hastings: I know the hand. If my aunt sees it, we are ruined forever. I'll keep her employed a little, if I can. (*To Mrs. Hardcastle*) But I have not told you, madam, of my cousin's smart answer just now to Mr. Marlow. We so laughed — You must know, madam — This way a little, for he must not hear us. (*They confer.*)

Tony. (*Still gazing*) A damned cramp piece of penmanship, as ever I saw in my life. I can read your print-hand very well; but here there are such handles, and shanks, and dashes, that one can scarce tell the head from the tail. "To Anthony Lumpkin, Esquire." It's very odd, I can read the outside of my letters, where my own name is, well enough. But when I come to open it, it's all —— buzz. That's hard — very hard; for the inside of the letter is always the cream of the correspondence.

Mrs. Hardcastle. Ha! ha! ha! Very well, very well. And so my son was too hard for the philosopher?

Miss Neville. Yes, madam; but you must bear the

rest, madam. A little more this way, or he may hear us. You 'll hear how he puzzled him again.

Mrs. Hardcastle. He seems strangely puzzled now himself, methinks.

Tony. (*Still gazing*) A damned up-and-down hand, as if it was disguised in liquor. (*Reading*) "Dear Sir," — Ay, that's that. Then there 's an M, and a T, and an S, but whether the next be an izzard or an R, confound me I cannot tell!

Mrs. Hardcastle. What's that, my dear; can I give you any assistance?

Miss Neville. Pray, aunt, let me read it. Nobody reads a cramp hand better than I. (*Twitching the letter from him*) Do you know who it is from?

Tony. Can't tell, except from Dick Ginger, the feeder.

Miss Neville. Ay, so it is: (*pretending to read*) Dear Squire, hoping that you're in health, as I am at this present. The gentlemen of the Shake Bag Club has cut the gentlemen of the Goose Green quite out of feather. The odds —— um —— odd battle — um — long — fighting — um — here, here, it 's all about cocks and fighting; it 's of no consequence — here, put it up, put it up. *Thrusting the crumpled letter upon him.)*

Tony. But I tell you, miss, it 's of all the consequence in the world. I would not lose the rest of it for a guinea. Here, mother, do you make it out. Of no consequence!

[*Giving Mrs. Hardcastle the letter.*

Mrs. Hardcastle. How 's this! (*Reads.*) "Dear Squire, I 'm now waiting for Miss Neville, with a postchaise and pair, at the bottom of the garden, but I find my horses yet unable to perform the journey. I expect you 'll assist us with a pair of fresh horses, as you promised. Despatch is necessary as the hag" — ay, the hag — "your mother will otherwise suspect us. Yours, Hastings." Grant me, patience: I shall run distracted! My rage chokes me!

Miss Neville. I hope, madam, you'll suspend your resentment for a few moments, and not impute to me any impertinence, or sinister design, that belongs to another.

Mrs. Hardcastle. (*Courtesying very low*) Fine spoken madam, you are most miraculously polite and engaging, and quite the very pink of courtesy and circumspection, madam. (*Changing her tone*) And you, you great ill-fashioned oaf, with scarce sense enough to keep your mouth shut, — were you, too, joined against me? But I'll defeat all your plots in a moment. As for you, madam, since you have got a pair of fresh horses ready, it would be cruel to disappoint them. So, if you please, instead of running away with your spark, prepare this very moment, to run off with me. Your old aunt Pedigree will keep you secure, I'll warrant me. You too, sir, may mount your horse, and guard us upon the way. — Here, Thomas, Roger, Diggory! — I'll show you, that I wish you better than you do yourselves. [*Exit.*

Miss Neville. So, now I'm completely ruined.

Tony. Ay, that's a sure thing.

Miss Neville. What better could be expected, from being connected with such a stupid fool, and after all the nods and signs I made him?

Tony. By the laws, miss, it was your own cleverness, and not my stupidity, that did your business! You were so nice and so busy with your Shake Bags and Goose

Greens, that I thought you could never be making believe.

Enter Hastings.

Hastings. So, sir, I find by my servant, that you have shown my letter, and betrayed us. Was this well done, young gentleman?

Tony. Here's another. Ask miss, there, who betrayed you. Ecod! it was her doing, not mine.

Enter Marlow.

Marlow. So, I have been finely used here among you. Rendered contemptible, driven into ill-manners, despised, insulted, laughed at.

Tony. Here's another. We shall have all Bedlam broke loose presently.

Miss Neville. And there, sir, is the gentleman to whom we all owe every obligation.

Marlow. What can I say to him? a mere boy, an idiot, whose ignorance and age are a protection.

Hastings. A poor contemptible booby, that would but disgrace correction.

Miss Neville. Yet with cunning and malice enough to make himself merry with all our embarrassments.

Hastings. An insensible cub.

Marlow. Replete with tricks and mischief.

Tony. Baw! damme, but I'll fight you both, one after the other —— with baskets.

Marlow. As for him, he's below resentment. But your conduct, Mr. Hastings, requires an explanation. You knew of my mistakes, yet would not undeceive me.

Hastings. Tortured as I am with my own disappoint ments, is this a time for explanations? It is not friendly, Mr. Marlow.

Marlow. But, sir ——

Miss Neville. Mr. Marlow, we never kept on your mistake, till it was too late to undeceive you. Be pacified.

Enter Servant.

Servant. My mistress desires you'll get ready immediately, madam. The horses are putting-to. Your hat and things are in the next room. We are to go thirty miles before morning.

[*Exit Servant.*

Miss Neville. Well, well, I'll come presently.

Marlow. (*To Hastings.*) Was it well done, sir, to assist in rendering me ridiculous? — To hang me out for the scorn of all my acquaintance? Depend upon it, sir I shall expect an explanation.

Hastings. Was it well done, sir, if you're upon that subject, to deliver what I entrusted to yourself, to the care of another, sir?

Miss Neville. Mr. Hastings! Mr. Marlow! Why will you increase my distress by this groundless dispute? I implore — I entreat you ——

Enter Servant.

Servant. Your cloak, madam. My mistress is impatient. [*Exit Servant.*

Miss Neville. I come. Pray, be pacified. If I leave you thus, I shall die with apprehension.

Enter Servant.

Servant. Your fan, muff, and gloves, madam. The horses are waiting. [*Exit Servant.*

Miss Neville. Oh, Mr. Marlow, if you knew what a scene of constraint and ill-nature lies before me, I am sure it would convert your resentment into pity!

Marlow. I 'm so distracted with a variety of passions, that I do n't know what I do. Forgive me, madam. George, forgive me. You know my hasty temper, and should not exasperate it.

Hastings. The torture of my situation is my only excuse.

Miss Neville. Well, my dear Hastings, if you have that esteem for me that I think — that I am sure you have, your constancy for three years will but increase the happiness of our future connection. If ——

Mrs. Hardcastle. (*Within.*) Miss Neville! Constance, why, Constance, I say!

Miss Neville. I 'm coming! Well, constancy, remember, constancy is the word. [*Exit.*

Hastings. My heart! how can I support this? To be so near happiness, and such happiness!

Marlow. (*To Tony.*) You see now, young gentleman, the effects of your folly. What might be amusement to you, is here disappointment, and even distress.

Tony. (*From a reverie.*) Ecod, I have hit it: it 's here! Your hands. Yours, and yours, my poor Sulky. My boots there, ho! — Meet me, two hours hence, at the bottom of the garden; and if you do n't find Tony Lumpkin a more good-natured fellow than you thought for, I 'll give you leave to take my best horse, and Bet Bouncer into the bargain. Come along. My boots, ho! [*Exeunt.*

ACT FIFTH.

Enter Hastings and Servant.

Hastings. You saw the old lady and Miss Neville drive off, you say?

Servant. Yes, your honor. They went off in a post-coach, and the young Squire went on horseback. They 're thirty miles off by this time.

Hastings. Then all my hopes are over!

Servant. Yes, sir. Old Sir Charles is arrived. He and the old gentleman of the house have been laughing at Mr. Marlow's mistake this half hour. They are coming this way. [*Exit.*

Hastings. Then I must not be seen. So now to my fruitless appointment at the bottom of the garden. This is about the time. [*Exit.*

Enter Sir Charles Marlow and Hardcastle.

Hardcastle. Ha! ha! ha! The peremptory tone in which he sent forth his sublime commands!

Sir Charles. And the reserve with which I suppose he treated all your advances.

Hardcastle. And yet he might have seen something in me above a common innkeeper, too.

Sir Charles. Yes, Dick, but he mistook you for an uncommon innkeeper; ha! ha! ha!

Hardcastle. Well, I 'm in too good spirits to think of anything but joy. Yes, my dear friend, this union of our families will make our personal friendships hereditary, and though my daughter's fortune is but small ——

Sir Charles. Why, Dick, will you talk of fortune to me? My son is possessed of more than a competence already, and can want nothing but a good and virtuous girl to share his happiness and increase it. If they like each other, as you say they do ——

Hardcastle. If, man! I tell you they do like each other. My daughter as good as told me so.

Sir Charles. But girls are apt to flatter themselves, you know.

Hardcastle. I saw him grasp her hand in the warmest manner, myself; and here he comes to put you out of your *ifs*, I warrant him.

Enter Marlow.

Marlow. I come, sir, once more, to ask pardon for my strange conduct. I can scarce reflect on my insolence without confusion.

Hardcastle. Tut, boy, a trifle. You take it too gravely. An hour or two's laughing with my daughter, will set all to rights again. She 'll never like you the worse for it.

Marlow. Sir, I shall be always proud of her approbation.

Hardcastle. Approbation is but a cold word, Mr. Marlow; if I am not deceived, you have something more than approbation thereabouts. You take me!

Marlow. Really, sir, I 've not that happiness.

Hardcastle. Come, boy, I 'm an old fellow, and know what 's what as well as you that are younger. I know what has past between you; but mum.

Marlow. Sure, sir, nothing has past between us, but the most profound respect on my side, and the most distant reserve on hers. You don't think, sir, that my impudence has been past upon all the rest of the family!

Hardcastle. Impudence! No, I don't say that — not quite impudence — though girls like to be played with, and rumpled a little too, sometimes. But she has told no tales, I assure you.

Marlow. I never gave her the slightest cause.

Hardcastle. Well, well, I like modesty in its place well enough; but this is over-acting, young gentleman. You may be open. Your father and I will like you the better for it.

Marlow. May I die, sir, if I ever ——

Hardcastle. I tell you, she don't dislike you; and as I am sure you like her ——

Marlow. Dear sir, I protest, sir ——

Hardcastle. I see no reason why you should not be joined as fast as the parson can tie you.

Marlow. But hear me, sir ——

Hardcastle. Your father approves the match, I admire it; every moment's delay will be doing mischief, so ——

Marlow. But why don't you hear me? By all that 's just and true, I never gave Miss Hardcastle the slightest mark of my attachment, or even the most distant hint to suspect me of affection. We had but one interview, and that was formal, modest, and uninteresting.

Hardcastle. (*Aside.*) This fellow's formal, modest impudence is beyond bearing.

Sir Charles. And you never grasped her hand, or made any protestations?

Marlow. As Heaven is my witness, I came down in obedience to your commands; I saw the lady without emotion, and parted without reluctance. I hope you 'll exact no farther proofs of my duty, nor prevent me from leaving a house in which I suffer so many mortifications.

[*Exit.*

Sir Charles. I'm astonished at the air of sincerity with which he parted.

Hardcastle. And I 'm astonished at the deliberate intrepidity of his assurance.

Sir Charles. I dare pledge my life and honor upon his truth.

Hardcastle. Here comes my daughter, and I would stake my happiness upon her veracity.

Enter Miss Hardcastle.

Hardcastle. Kate, come hither, child. Answer us sincerely, and without reserve: has Mr. Marlow made you any professions of love and affection?

Miss Hardcastle. The question is very abrupt, sir! But since you require unreserved sincerity — I think he has.

Hardcastle. (*To Sir Charles*) You see.

Sir Charles. And pray, madam, have you and my son had more than one interview?

Miss Hardcastle. Yes, sir, several.

Hardcastle. (*To Sir Charles*) You see.

Sir Charles. But did he profess any attachment?

Miss Hardcastle. A lasting one.

Sir Charles. Did he talk of love?

Miss Hardcastle. Much, sir.

Sir Charles. Amazing! And all this formally?

Miss Hardcastle. Formally.

Hardcastle. Now, my friend, I hope you are satisfied.

Sir Charles. And how did he behave, madam?

Miss Hardcastle. As most professed admirers do! said some civil things of my face; talked much of his want of merit, and the greatness of mine; mentioned his heart, gave a short tragedy speech, and ended with pretended rapture.

Sir Charles. Now I 'm perfectly convinced, indeed. I know his conversation among women to be modest and submissive. This forward, canting, ranting manner by no means describes him, and, I am confident, he never sat for the picture.

Miss Hardcastle. Then what, sir, if I should convince you to your face of my sincerity? If you and my papa, in about half an hour, will place yourselves behind that screen, you shall hear him declare his passion to me in person.

Sir Charles. Agreed. And if I find him what you describe, all my happiness in him must have an end.
[*Exit.*

Miss Hardcastle. And if you do n't find him what I describe, I fear my happiness must never have a beginning.

SCENE CHANGES TO THE BACK OF THE GARDEN.

Enter Hastings.

Hastings. What an idiot am I to wait here for a fellow who probably takes a delight in mortifying me. He never intended to be punctual, and I'll wait no longer. What do I see? It is he! and perhaps with news of my Constance.

Enter Tony, booted and spattered.

Hastings. My honest Squire! I now find you a man of your word. This looks like friendship.

Tony. Ay, I'm your friend, and the best friend you have in the world, if you knew but all. This riding by night, by the by, is cursedly tiresome. It has shook me worse than the basket of a stage-coach.

Hastings. But how? where did you leave your fellow-travellers? Are they in safety? Are they housed?

Tony. Five-and-twenty miles in two hours and a half is no such bad driving. The poor beasts have smoked for it: rabbit me! but I'd rather ride forty miles after a fox, than ten with such varmint.

Hastings. Well, but where have you left the ladies? I die with impatience.

Tony. Left them! Why, where should I leave them but where I found them?

Hastings. This is a riddle.

Tony. Riddle me this, then. What's that goes round the house, and round the house, and never touches the house?

Hastings. I 'm still astray.

Tony. Why, that 's it, mun. I have led them astray. By jingo, there 's not a pond or a slough within five miles of the place but they can tell the taste of.

Hastings. Ha! ha! ha! I understand: you took them in a round while they supposed themselves going forward, and so you have at last brought them home again.

Tony. You shall hear. I first took them down Feather-bed Lane, where we stuck fast in the mud. I then rattled them crack over the stones of Up-and-down Hill. I then introduced them to the gibbet on Heavy-tree Heath; and from that, with a circumbendibus, I fairly lodged them in the horse-pond at the bottom of the garden.

Hastings. But no accident, I hope?

Tony. No, no: only mother is confoundedly frightened. She thinks herself forty miles off. She 's sick of the journey; and the cattle can scarce crawl. So, if your own horses be ready, you may whip off with cousin, and I 'll be bound that no soul here can budge a foot to follow you.

Hastings. My dear friend, how can I be grateful?

Tony. Ay, now it 's dear friend; noble Squire! Just now, it was all idiot, cub, and run me through the guts. Damn your way of fighting, I say. After we take a knock in this part of the country, we kiss and be friends. But if you had run me through the guts, then I should be dead, and you might go kiss the hangman.

Hastings. The rebuke is just. But I must hasten to relieve Miss Neville: if you keep the old lady employed, I promise to take care of the young one. [*Exit Hastings.*

Tony. Never fear me. Here she comes; vanish! She's got from the pond, and draggled up to the waist like a mermaid.

Enter Mrs. Hardcastle.

Mrs. Hardcastle. Oh, Tony, I'm killed. Shook! Battered to death! I shall never survive it. That last jolt, that laid us against the quickset-hedge, has done my business.

Tony. Alack, mamma! it was all your own fault. You would be for running away by night, without knowing one inch of the way.

Mrs. Hardcastle. I wish we were at home again. I never met so many accidents in so short a journey. Drenched in the mud, overturned in a ditch, stuck fast in a slough, jolted to a jelly, and at last to lose our way! Whereabouts do you think we are, Tony?

Tony. By my guess, we should be upon Crack-skull Common, about forty miles from home.

Mrs. Hardcastle. O lud! O lud! The most notorious spot in all the country. We only want a robbery to make a complete night on 't.

Tony. Do n't be afraid, mamma; do n't be afraid. Two of the five that kept here are hanged, and the other three may not find us. Do n't be afraid. — Is that a man that's galloping behind us. No, it 's only a tree. — Do n't be afraid.

Mrs. Hardcastle. The fright will certainly kill me.

Tony. Do you see anything like a black hat moving behind the thicket?

Mrs. Hardcastle. Oh, death!

Tony. No; it's only a cow. Don't be afraid, mamma; don't be afraid.

Mrs. Hardcastle. As I'm alive, Tony, I see a man coming towards us. Ah! I am sure on't. If he perceives us, we are undone.

Tony. (*Aside.*) Father-in-law, by all that's unlucky, come to take one of his night walks. (*To her.*) Ah! it's a highwayman, with pistols as long as my arm. A damn'd ill-looking fellow!

Mrs. Hardcastle. Good Heaven, defend us! He approaches.

Tony. Do you hide yourself in that thicket, and leave me to manage him. If there be any danger, I'll cough and cry hem. When I cough, be sure to keep close.

[*Mrs. Hardcastle hides behind a tree in the back scene.*

Enter Hardcastle.

Hardcastle. I 'm mistaken, or I heard voices of people in want of help. Oh, Tony, is that you? I did not expect you so soon back. Are your mother and her charge in safety?

Tony. Very safe, sir, at my aunt Pedigree's. Hem.

Mrs. Hardcastle. (*From behind*) Ah, death! I find there 's danger.

Hardcastle. Forty miles in three hours; sure that 's too much, my youngster.

Tony. Stout horses and willing minds make short journeys, as they say. Hem.

Mrs. Hardcastle. (*From behind*) Sure, he 'll do the dear boy no harm.

Hardcastle. But I heard a voice here; I should be glad to know from whence it came.

Tony. It was I, sir, talking to myself, sir. I was saying that forty miles in four hours was very good going. Hem. As to be sure it was. Hem. I have got a sort of cold by being out in the air. We 'll go in, if you please. Hem.

Hardcastle. But if you talked to yourself, you did not answer yourself. I 'm certain I heard two voices, and am resolved *(raising his voice)* to find the other out.

Mrs. Hardcastle. *(From behind)* Oh! he 's coming to find me out. Oh!

Tony. What need you go, sir, if I tell you? Hem. I 'll lay down my life for the truth — hem — I 'll tell you all, sir. [*Detaining him.*

Hardcastle. I tell you I will not be detained. I insist on seeing. It 's in vain to expect I 'll believe you.

Mrs. Hardcastle. *(Running forward from behind)* O lud! he 'll murder my poor boy, my darling! Here, good gentleman, whet your rage upon me. Take my money, my life, but spare that young gentleman; spare my child if you have any mercy.

Hardcastle. My wife, as I 'm a Christian. From whence can she have come? or what does she mean?

Mrs. Hardcastle. *(Kneeling)* Take compassion on us, good Mr. Highwayman. Take our money, our watches, all we have, but spare our lives. We will never bring you to justice; indeed we won't, good Mr. Highwayman.

Hardcastle. I believe the woman 's out of her senses. What, Dorothy, don't you know me?

Mrs. Hardcastle. Mr. Hardcastle, as I 'm alive! My

fears blinded me. But who, my dear, could have expected to meet you here, in this frightful place, so far from home? What has brought you to follow us?

Hardcastle. Sure, Dorothy, you have not lost your wits? So far from home, when you are within forty yards of your own door! *(To him)* This is one of your old tricks, you graceless rogue, you. *(To her)* Don't you know the gate and the mulberry tree? and don't you remember the horse-pond, my dear?

Mrs. Hardcastle. Yes, I shall remember the horse-pond as long as I live; I have caught my death in it. *(To Tony)* And is it to you, you graceless varlet, I owe all this? I 'll teach you to abuse your mother — I will.

Tony. Ecod, mother, all the parish says you have spoiled me, and so you may take the fruits on't.

Mrs. Hardcastle. I 'll spoil you, I will.

[*Follows him off the stage.*

Hardcastle. There 's morality, however, in his reply.

[*Exit.*

Enter Hastings and Miss Neville.

Hastings. My dear Constance, why will you deliberate thus? If we delay a moment, all is lost forever Pluck up a little resolution, and we shall soon be out of the reach of her malignity.

Miss Neville. I find it impossible. My spirits are so sunk with the agitations I have suffered, that I am unable to face any new danger. Two or three years' patience will at last crown us with happiness.

Hastings. Such a tedious delay is worse than inconstancy. Let us fly, my charmer! Let us date our happiness from this very moment. Perish fortune! Love and content will increase what we possess beyond a monarch's revenue. Let me prevail!

Miss Neville. No, Mr. Hastings, no. Prudence once more comes to my relief, and I will obey its dictates. In the moment of passion, fortune may be despised, but it ever produces a lasting repentance. I 'm resolved to apply to Mr. Hardcastle's compassion and justice for redress.

Hastings. But though he had the will, he has not the power, to relieve you.

Miss Neville. But he has influence, and upon that I am resolved to rely.

Hastings. I have no hopes. But, since you persist, I must reluctantly obey you. [*Exeunt.*

SCENE CHANGES.

Enter Sir Charles Marlow and Miss Hardcastle.

Sir Charles. What a situation am I in! If what you say appears, I shall then find a guilty son. If what he says be true, I shall then lose one that, of all others, I most wished for a daughter.

Miss Hardcastle. I am proud of your approbation; and to show I merit it, if you place yourselves as I directed, you shall hear his explicit declaration. But he comes.

Sir Charles. I 'll to your father, and keep him to the appointment. [*Exit Sir Charles.*

Enter Marlow.

Marlow. Though prepared for setting out, I come once more to take leave; nor did I, till this moment, know the pain I feel in the separation.

Miss Hardcastle. (*In her own natural manner*) I believe these sufferings cannot be very great, sir, which you can so easily remove. A day or two longer, perhaps, might lessen your uneasiness, by showing the little value of what you now think proper to regret.

Marlow. (*Aside*) This girl every moment improves upon me. (*To her*) It must not be, madam; I have already trifled too long with my heart. My very pride begins to submit to my passion. The disparity of education and fortune, the anger of a parent, and the contempt of my equals, begin to lose their weight; and nothing can restore me to myself but this painful effort of resolution.

Miss Hardcastle. Then go, sir; I 'll urge nothing more to detain you. Though my family be as good as hers you came down to visit, and my education, I hope, not inferior, what are these advantages without equal affluence? I must remain contented with the slight approbation of imputed merit; I must have only the mockery of your addresses, while all your serious aims are fixed on fortune.

Enter Hardcastle and Sir Charles Marlow, from behind.

Sir Charles. Here, behind this screen.

Hardcastle. Ay, ay; make no noise. I 'll engage my Kate covers him with confusion at last.

Marlow. By Heavens! madam, fortune was ever my smallest consideration. Your beauty at first caught my eye; for who could see that without emotion? But every moment that I converse with you, steals in some new grace, heightens the picture, and gives it stronger expression. What at first seemed rustic plainness, now appears refined simplicity. What seemed forward assurance, now strikes me as the result of courageous innocence and conscious virtue.

Sir Charles. What can it mean? He amazes me!

Hardcastle. I told you how it would be. Hush!

Marlow. I am now determined to stay, madam, and I have too good an opinion of my father's discernment, when he sees you, to doubt his approbation.

Miss Hardcastle. No, Mr. Marlow, I will not, cannot detain you. Do you think I could suffer a connection in which there is the smallest room for repentance? Do you think I would take the mean advantage of a transient passion to load you with confusion? Do you think I could ever relish that happiness which was acquired by lessening yours?

Marlow. By all that's good, I can have no happiness but what's in your power to grant me! Nor shall I ever feel repentance but in not having seen your merits before. I will stay even contrary to your wishes; and though you should persist to shun me, I will make my respectful assiduities atone for the levity of my past conduct.

Miss Hardcastle. Sir, I must entreat you 'll desist. As our acquaintance began, so let it end, in indifference. I might have given an hour or two to levity; but seriously, Mr. Marlow, do you think I could ever submit to a connection where I must appear mercenary, and you imprudent? Do you think I could ever catch at the confident addresses of a secure admirer.

Marlow. (*Kneeling.*) Does this look like security? Does this look like confidence? No, madam, every moment that shows me your merit, only serves to increase my diffidence and confusion. Here let me continue ——

Sir Charles. I can hold it no longer. Charles, Charles, how hast thou deceived me! Is this your indifference, your uninteresting conversation?

Hardcastle. Your cold contempt; your formal interview! What have you to say now?

Marlow. That I 'm all amazement! What can it mean?

Hardcastle. It means that you can say and unsay things at pleasure: that you can address a lady in private, and deny it in public: that you have one story for us, and another for my daughter.

Marlow. Daughter! — This lady your daughter?

Hardcastle. Yes, sir, my only daughter — my Kate; whose else should she be?

Marlow. Oh, the devil!

Miss Hardcastle. Yes, sir, that very identical tall, squinting lady you were pleased to take me for (*courtesying;*) she that you addressed as the mild, modest, sentimental man of gravity, and the bold, forward, agreeable Rattle of the ladies' club. Ha! ha! ha!

Marlow. Zounds, there 's no bearing this; it 's worse than death!

Miss Hardcastle. In which of your characters, sir, will you give us leave to address you? As the faltering gentleman, which looks on the ground, that speaks just to be heard, and hates hypocrisy; or the loud, confident creature, that keeps it up with Mrs. Mantrap, and old Miss Biddy Buckskin, till three in the morning! — Ha! ha! ha!

Marlow. Oh, curse on my noisy head! I never attempted to be impudent yet that I was not taken down! I must be gone.

Hardcastle. By the hand of my body, but you shall not. I see it was all a mistake, and I am rejoiced to find it. You shall not stir, I tell you. I know she 'll forgive you. Won't you forgive him, Kate? We 'll all forgive you. Take courage, man.

[*They retire, she tormenting him to the back scene.*

Enter Mrs. Hardcastle and Tony.

Mrs. Hardcastle. So, so, they 're gone off. Let them go, I care not.

Hardcastle. Who gone?

Mrs. Hardcastle. My dutiful niece and her gentleman, Mr. Hastings, from town. He who came down with our modest visitor here.

Sir Charles. Who, my honest George Hastings? As worthy a fellow as lives, and the girl could not have made a more prudent choice.

Hardcastle. Then, by the hand of my body, I 'm proud of the connection.

Mrs. Hardcastle. Well, if he has taken away the lady, he has not taken her fortune: that remains in this family to console us for her loss.

Hardcastle. Sure, Dorothy, you would not be so mercenary?

Mrs. Hardcastle. Ay, that 's my affair, not yours.

Hardcastle. But you know if your son, when of age, refuses to marry his cousin, her whole fortune is then at her own disposal.

Mrs. Hardcastle. Ay, but he 's not of age, and she has not thought proper to wait for his refusal.

Enter Hastings and Miss Neville.

Mrs. Hardcastle. (*Aside*) What, returned so soon! I begin not to like it.

Hastings. (*To Hardcastle*) For my late attempt to fly off with your niece, let my present confusion be my punishment. We are now come back, to appeal from your justice to your humanity. By her father's consent I first paid her my addresses, and our passions were first founded in duty.

Miss Neville. Since his death, I have been obliged to stoop to dissimulation to avoid oppression. In an hour of levity, I was ready even to give up my fortune to secure my choice: But I am now recovered from the delusion, and hope, from your tenderness, what is denied me from a nearer connection.

Mrs. Hardcastle. Pshaw, pshaw; this is all but the whining end of a modern novel.

Hardcastle. Be it what it will, I 'm glad they 're come back to reclaim their due. Come hither, Tony, boy. Do you refuse this lady's hand, whom I now offer you?

Tony. What signifies my refusing? You know I can't refuse her till I 'm of age, father.

Hardcastle. While I thought concealing your age, boy, was likely to conduce to your improvement, I concurred with your mother's desire to keep it secret. But since I find she turns it to a wrong use, I must now declare you have been of age these three months.

Tony. Of age! Am I of age, father?

Hardcastle. Above three months.

Tony. Then you'll see the first use I'll make of my liberty. *(Taking Miss Neville's hand)* Witness all men by these presents, that I, Anthony Lumpkin, esquire, of BLANK place, refuse you, Constantia Neville, spinster, of no place at all, for my true and lawful wife. So Constance Neville may marry whom she pleases, and Tony Lumpkin is his own man again.

Sir Charles. O brave Squire!

Hastings. My worthy friend!

Mrs. Hardcastle. My undutiful offspring!

Marlow. Joy, my dear George, I give you joy sincerely! And, could I prevail upon my little tyrant here to be less arbitrary, I should be the happiest man alive, if you would return me the favor.

Hastings. *(To Miss Hardcastle)* Come, madam, you are now driven to the very last scene of all your contrivances. I know you like him, I'm sure he loves you, and you must and shall have him.

Hardcastle. *(Joining their hands)* And I say so too. And, Mr. Marlow, if she makes as good a wife as she has a daughter, I don't believe you'll ever repent your bargain. So now to supper. To-morrow we shall gather all the poor of the parish about us, and the mistakes of the night shall be crowned with a merry morning. So, boy, take her; and as you have been mistaken in the mistress, my wish is, that you may never be mistaken in the wife. [*Exeunt Omnes.*

EPILOGUE.

BY DR. GOLDSMITH.

SPOKEN BY MRS. BULKLEY IN THE CHARACTER OF MISS HARDCASTLE.

WELL, having stoop'd to conquer with success,
And gain'd a husband without aid from dress,
Still, as a bar-maid, I could wish it too,
As I have conquer'd him to conquer you:
And let me say, for all your resolution,
That pretty bar-maids have done execution.
Our life is all a play, composed to please;
'We have our exits and our entrances.'
The first act shows the simple country maid,
Harmless and young, of everything afraid;
Blushes when hired, and, with unmeaning action,
'I hopes as how to give you satisfaction.'
Her second act displays a livelier scene,—
Th' unblushing bar-maid of a country inn,
Who whisks about the house, at market caters,
Talks loud, coquets the guests, and scolds the waiters.
Next the scene shifts to town, and there she soars,
The chop-house toast of ogling *connoisseurs:*
On squires and cits she there displays her arts,
And on the gridiron broils her lovers' hearts;
And, as she smiles, her triumphs to complete,
E'en common-councilmen forget to eat.

The fourth act shews her wedded to the squire,
And madam now begins to hold it higher;
Pretends to taste, at opera cries *caro*,
And quits her Nancy Dawson for Che Faro:
Doats upon dancing, and, in all her pride,
Swims round the room, the Heinel of Cheapside;
Ogles and leers, with artificial skill,
Till, having lost in age the power to kill,
She sits all night at cards, and ogles at spadille.
Such, through our lives, th' eventful history!
The fifth and last act still remains for me:
The bar-maid now for your protection prays,
Turns female Barrister, and pleads for Bays.

EPILOGUE,*

TO BE SPOKEN IN THE CHARACTER OF TONY LUMPKIN,

BY J. CRADOCK, ESQ.

Well, now all's ended, and my comrades gone,
Pray what becomes of mother's nonly son?
A hopeful blade! — in town I'll fix my station,
And try to make a bluster in the nation:
As for my cousin Neville, I renounce her —
Off, in a crack, I'll carry big Bet Bouncer.
  Why should not I in the great world appear?
I soon shall have a thousand pounds a year!
No matter what a man may here inherit,
In London — gad, they 've some regard to spirit:
I see the horses prancing up the streets,
And big Bet Bouncer bobs to all she meets;
Then hoiks to jigs and pastimes every night —
Not to the plays — they say it an't polite:
To Sadler's Wells, perhaps, or operas go,
And once, by chance, to the roratorio.
Thus, here and there, forever up and down;
We'll set the fashions, too, to half the town;
And then at auctions — money ne'er regard —
Buy pictures, like the great, ten pounds a-yard:
Zounds! we shall make these London gentry say,
We know what's damn'd genteel as well as they!

* This came too late to be spoken.

ESSAYS.

INTRODUCTION.

There is not, perhaps, a more whimsical figure in nature, than a man of real modesty who assumes an air of impudence; who, while his heart beats with anxiety, studies ease and affects good-humor. In this situation, however, every unexperienced writer, as I am, finds himself. Impressed with terrors of the tribunal before which he is going to appear, his natural humor turns to pert ness, and for real wit he is obliged to substitute vivacity.

For my part, as I was never distinguished for address, and have often even blundered in making my bow. I am at a loss whether to be merry or sad on this solemn occasion. Should I modestly decline all merit, it is too probable the hasty reader may take me at my word. If, on the other hand, like laborers in the magazine trade, I humbly presume to promise an epitome of all the good things that were ever said or written, those readers I most desire to please may forsake me.

My bookseller, in this dilemma, perceiving my embarrassment, instantly offered his assistance and advice. "You must know, sir," says he, "that the republic of letters is at present divided into several classes. One writer excels at a plan or a title-page; another works away at the body of the book; and a third is a dab at an index. Thus a magazine is not the result of any single man's industry, but goes through as many hands as a new pin, before it is fit for the public. I fancy, sir," continues he, "I can provide an eminent hand, and upon moderate terms, to draw up a promising plan to smooth up our readers a little ; and pay them, as Colonel Chartres paid his seraglio, at the rate of three-halfpence in hand, and three shillings more in promises."

He was proceeding in his advice, which, however, I thought proper to decline, by assuring him, that as I intended to pursue no fixed method, so it was impossible to form any regular plan; determined never to be tedious in order to be logical; wherever pleasure presented, I was resolved to follow.

It will be improper, therefore, to pall the reader's curiosity by lessening his surprise, or anticipate any pleasure I am to procure him, by saying what shall come next. Happy, could any effort of mine but repress one criminal pleasure, or but for a moment fill up an interval of anxiety? How gladly would I lead mankind from the vain prospects of life, to prospects of innocence and ease, where every breeze breathes health, and every sound is but the echo of tranquillity!

But whatever may be the merit of his intentions, every writer is now convinced that he must be chiefly indebted to good fortune for finding readers willing to allow him any degree of reputation. It has been remarked, that almost every character which has excited either attention or pity, has owed part of its success to merit, and part to a happy concurrence of circumstances in its favor. Had Caesar or Cromwell exchanged countries, the one might have been a serjeant, and the other an exciseman. So it is with wit, which generally succeeds more from being happily addressed, than from its native poignancy. A jest calculated to spread at a gaming-table, may be received with perfect indifference should it happen to drop in a mackerel-boat. We have all seen dunces triumph in some companies, where men of real humor were disregarded, by a general combination in favor of stupidity. To drive the observation as far as it will go, should the labors of a writer, who designs his performances for readers of a more refined appetite, fall into the hands of a devourer of compilations, what can he expect but contempt and confusion? If his merits are to be determined by judges who estimate the value of a book from its bulk, or its frontispiece, every rival must acquire an easy superiority, who with persuasive eloquence promises four extraordinary pages of letter-press, or three beautiful prints, curiously colored from Nature.

Thus, then, though I cannot promise as much entertainment, or as much elegance, as others have done, yet the reader may be assured he shall have as much of both as I can. He shall, at least, find me alive while I study his entertainment; for I solemnly assure him, I was never yet possessed of the secret of writing and sleeping.

During the course of this paper, therefore, all the wit and learning I have, are heartily at his service; which if, after so candid a confession, he should, notwithstanding, still find intolerably dull, or low, or sad stuff, this I protest is more than I know; I have a clear conscience, and am entirely out of the secret.

Yet I would not have him, upon the perusal of a single paper, pronounce me incorrigible; he may try a second, which, as there is a studied difference in subject and style, may be more suited to his taste; if this also fails, I must refer him to a third, or even a fourth, in case of extremity; if he should still continue refractory, and find me dull to the last, I must inform him, with Bayes in the Rehearsal, that I think him a very odd kind of fellow, and desire no more of his acquaintance; but still, if my readers impute the general tenor of my subject to me as a fault, I must beg leave to tell them a story.

A traveller, in his way to Italy, found himself in a country where the inhabitants had each a large excrescence depending from the chin; a deformity which, as it was endemic, and the people little used to strangers, it had been the custom, time immemorial, to look upon as the greatest beauty. Ladies grew toasts from the size of their chins, and no men were beaux whose faces were not broadest at the bottom. It was Sunday; a country-church was at hand, and our traveller was willing to perform the duties of the day. Upon his first appearance at the church-door, the eyes of all were fixed on the stranger; but what was their amazement, when they found that he actually wanted that emblem of beauty, a pursed chin! Stifled bursts of laughter, winks, and whispers, circulated from visage to visage; the prismatic figure of the stranger's face, was a fund of infinite gaiety Our traveller could no longer patiently continue an object of deformity to point at. "Good folks," said he, "I perceive that I am a very ridiculous figure here, but I assure you I am reckoned no way deformed at home."

LOVE AND FRIENDSHIP; OR THE STORY OF ALCANDER AND SEPTIMIUS.

Taken from a Byzantine Historian.

ATHENS, even long after the decline of the Roman empire, still continued the seat of learning, politeness, and wisdom. Theodoric, the Ostrogoth, repaired the schools which barbarity was suffering to fall into decay, and continued those pensions to men of learning, which avaricious governors had monopolized.

In this city, and about this period, Alcander and Septimius were fellow-students together; the one, the most subtle reasoner of all the Lyceum; the other, the most eloquent speaker in the Academic grove. Mutual admiration soon begot a friendship. Their fortunes were nearly equal, and they were natives of the two most celebrated cities in the world; for Alcander was of Athens, Septimius came from Rome.

In this state of harmony they lived for some time together, when Alcander, after passing the first part of his youth in the indolence of philosophy, thought at length of entering into the busy world; and as a step previous to this, placed his affections on Hypatia, a lady of exquisite beauty. The day of their intended nuptials was fixed; the previous ceremonies were performed; and nothing now remained but her being conducted in triumph to the apartment of the intended bridegroom.

Alcander's exultation in his own happiness, or being unable to enjoy any satisfaction without making his friend Septimius a partner, prevailed upon him to introduce

Hypatia to his fellow-student; which he did, with all the gaiety of a man who found himself equally happy in friendship and love. But this was an interview fatal to the future peace of both; for Septimius no sooner saw her but he was smitten with an involuntary passion; and though he used every effort to suppress desires at once so imprudent and unjust, the emotions of his mind in a short time became so strong, that they brought on a fever, which the physicians judged incurable.

During this illness Alcander watched him with all the anxiety of fondness, and brought his mistress to join in those amiable offices of friendship. The sagacity of the physicians, by these means, soon discovered that the cause of their patient's disorder was love; and Alcander, being apprized of their discovery, at length extorted a confession from the reluctant dying lover.

It would but delay the narrative to describe the conflict between love and friendship in the breast of Alcander on this occasion; it is enough to say that the Athenians were at that time arrived at such refinement in morals, that every virtue was carried to excess: in short, forgetful of his own felicity, he gave up his intended bride, in all her charms, to the young Roman. They were married privately by his connivance, and this unlooked-for change of fortune wrought as unexpected a change in the constitution of the now happy Septimius. In a few days he was perfectly recovered, and set out with his fair partner for Rome. Here, by an exertion of those talents which he was so eminently possessed of, Septimius, in a few years, arrived at the highest dignities of the state, and was constituted the city judge, or praetor.

In the mean time Alcander not only felt the pain of being separated from his friend and his mistress, but a prosecution was commenced against him by the relations of Hypatia, for having basely given up his bride, as was suggested for money. His innocence of the crime laid to his charge, and even his eloquence in his own defence, were not able to withstand the influence of a powerful party. He was cast, and condemned to pay an enormous fine. However, being unable to raise so large a sum at the time appointed, his possessions were confiscated, he himself was stripped of the habit of freedom, exposed as a slave in the market-place, and sold to the highest bidder.

A merchant of Thrace becoming his purchaser, Alcander, with some other companions of distress, was carried into that region of desolation and sterility. His stated employment was to follow the herds of an imperious master, and his success in hunting was all that was allowed him to supply his precarious subsistence. Every morning awaked him to a renewal of famine or toil, and every change of season served but to aggravate his unsheltered distress. After some years of bondage, however, an opportunity of escaping offered; he embraced it with ardor; so that travelling by night, and lodging in caverns by day, to shorten a long story, he at last arrived in Rome. The same day on which Alcander arrived, Septimius sat administering justice in the forum, whither our wanderer came, expecting to be instantly known, and publicly acknowledged by his former friend. Here he stood the whole day amongst the crowd, watching the eyes of the judge, and expecting to be taken notice of;

but he was so much altered by a long succession of hardships, that he continued unnoticed amongst the rest; and in the evening, when he was going up to the prætor's chair, he was brutally repulsed by the attending lictors. The attention of the poor is generally driven from one ungrateful object to another; for night coming on, he now found himself under the necessity of seeking a place to lie in, and yet knew not where to apply. All emaciated, and in rags, as he was, none of the citizens would harbor so much wretchedness; and sleeping in the streets might be attended with interruption or danger; in short, he was obliged to take up his lodgings in one of the tombs without the city, the usual retreat of guilt, poverty, and despair. In this mansion of horror, laying his head upon an inverted urn, he forgot his miseries for a while in sleep, and found on his flinty couch more ease than beds of down can supply to the guilty.

As he continued here about midnight two robbers came to make this their retreat, but happening to disagree about the division of their plunder, one of them stabbed the other to the heart, and left him weltering in blood at the entrance. In these circumstances he was found next morning dead at the mouth of the vault. This naturally inducing a farther inquiry, an alarm was spread; the cave was examined; and Alcander being found, was immediately apprehended, and accused of robbery and murder. The circumstances against him were strong, and the wretchedness of his appearance confirmed suspicion. Misfortune and he were now so long acquainted, that he at last became regardless of life. He detested a world where he had found only ingratitude, falsehood, and cruelty; he was determined to make no defence; and thus, lowering with resolution, he was dragged bound with cords before the tribunal of Septimius. As the proofs were positive against him, and he offered nothing in his own vindication, the judge was proceeding to doom him to a most cruel and ignominious death, when the attention of the multitude was soon diverted by another object. The robber, who had been really guilty, was apprehended selling his plunder, and, struck with a panic, had confessed his crime. He was brought bound to the same tribunal, and acquitted every other person of any partnership in his guilt. Alcander's innocence therefore appeared; but the sullen rashness of his conduct remained a wonder to the surrounding multitude; but their astonishment was still farther increased when they saw their judge start from his tribunal to embrace the supposed criminal. Septimius recollected his friend and former benefactor, and hung upon his neck with tears of pity and joy. Need the sequel be related? — Alcander was acquitted, shared the friendship and honors of the principal citizens of Rome, lived afterwards in happiness and ease, and left it to be engraved on his tomb, that no circumstances are so desperate which Prodence may not relieve.

ON HAPPINESS OF TEMPER.

When I reflect on the unambitious retirement in which I passed the early part of my life in the country, I cannot avoid feeling some pain in thinking that those happy days are never to return. In that retreat all nature seemed capable of affording pleasure; I then made no refinements on happiness, but could be pleased with the most awkward efforts of rustic mirth, thought cross-purposes the highest stretch of human wit, and questions and commands the most rational way of spending the evening. Happy could so charming an illusion continue! I find that age and knowledge only contribute to sour our dispositions. My present enjoyments may be more refined, but they are infinitely less pleasing. The pleasure the best actor gives, can no way compare to that I have received from a country wag who imitated a quaker's sermon. The music of the finest singer is dissonance to what I felt when our old dairy-maid sung me into tears with Johnny Armstrong's Last Good Night, or the Cruelty of Barbara Allen.

Writers of every age have endeavored to show that pleasure is in us, and not in the objects offered for our amusement. If the soul be happily disposed, everything becomes capable of affording entertainment, and distress will almost want a name. Every occurrence passes in review like the figures of a procession: some may be awkward, others ill-dressed; but none but a fool is for this enraged with the master of the ceremonies.

I remember to have once seen a slave in a fortification in Flanders, who appeared no way touched with his situation. He was maimed, deformed, and chained; obliged to toil from the appearance of day till night-fall; and condemned to this for life: yet, with all these circumstances of apparent wretchedness, he sung, would have danced but that he wanted a leg, and appeared the mer riest, happiest man of all the garrison. What a practical philosopher was here! a happy constitution supplied philosophy; and though seemingly destitute of wisdom, he was really wise. No reading or study had contributed to disenchant the fairy-land around him. Every thing furnished him with an opportunity of mirth; and, though some thought him, from his insensibility, a fool, he was such an idiot as philosophers should wish to imitate; for all philosophy is only forcing the trade of happiness, when nature seems to deny the means.

They who, like our slave, can place themselves on that side of the world in which every thing appears in a pleasing light, will find something in every occurrence to excite their good-humor. The most calamitous events, either to themselves or others, can bring no new affliction; the whole world is to them a theatre, on which comedies only are acted. All the bustle of heroism, or the rants of ambition, serve only to heighten the absurdity of the scene, and make the humor more poignant. They feel, in short, as little anguish at their own distress, or the complaints of others, as the undertaker, though dressed in black, feels sorrow at a funeral.

Of all the men I ever read of, the famous cardinal de Retz possessed this happiness of temper in the highest degree. As he was a man of gallantry, and despised all that wore the pedantic appearance of philosophy, wherever pleasure was to be sold, he was generally foremost to raise the auction. Being a universal admirer of the fair sex, when he found one lady cruel, he generally fell in love with another, from whom he expected a more favorable reception. If she too rejected his addresses, he never thought of retiring into deserts, or pining in hopeless distress: he persuaded himself, that instead of loving the lady, he only fancied that he had loved her, and so all was well again. When Fortune wore her angriest look, and he at last fell into the power of his most deadly enemy, Cardinal Mazarine (being confined a close prisoner in the castle of Valenciennes), he never attempted to support his distress by wisdom or philosophy, for he pretended to neither. He only laughed at himself and his persecutor, and seemed infinitely pleased at his new situation. In this mansion of distress, though secluded from his friends, though denied all the amusements, and even the coveniences of life, he still retained his good-humor, laughed at all the little spite of his enemies, and carried the jest so far as to be revenged by writing the life of his jailer.

All that the wisdom of the proud can teach is to be stubborn or sullen under misfortunes. The cardinal's example will instruct us to be merry in circumstances ot the highest affliction. It matters not whether our good-humor be construed by others into insensibility, or even idiotism; it is happiness to ourselves, and none but a fool would measure his satisfaction by what the world thinks of it; for my own part, I never pass by one of our prisons for debt, that I do not envy that felicity which is still going forward among those people, who forget the cares of the world by being shut out from its silly ambition.

The happiest silly fellow I ever knew, was of the number of those good-natured creatures that are said to do no harm to any but themselves. Whenever he fell into misery, he usually called it seeing life. If his head was broke by a chairman, or his pocket picked by a sharper, he comforted himself by imitating the Hibernian dialect of the one, or the more fashionable cant of the other. Nothing came amiss to him. His inattention to money-matters had incensed his father to such a degree, that all the intercession of friends in his favor was fruitless. The old gentleman was on his death-bed. The whole family, and Dick among the number, gathered around him. "I leave my second son, Andrew," said the expiring miser, "my whole estate, and desire him to be frugal." Andrew, in a sorrowful tone, as is usual on these occasions, prayed Heaven to prolong his life and health to enjoy it himself. "I recommend Simon, my third son, to the care of his elder brother, and leave him beside four thousand pounds." — "Ah! father," cried Simon, in great affliction to be sure, "may Heaven give you life and health to enjoy it yourself!" At last, turning to poor Dick, "As for you, you have always been a sad dog; you'll never come to good; you'll never be rich; I'll leave you a shilling to buy a halter." — "Ah! father," cries Dick, without any emotion, "may Heaven give you life and health to enjoy it yourself!" This was all the trouble the loss of fortune gave this thoughtless, imprudent creature. However, the tenderness of an uncle recompensed the neglect of a father; and my friend is now not only excessively good-humored, but competently rich.

Yes, let the world cry out at a bankrupt who appears at a ball, at an author who laughs at the public which pronounces him a dunce, at a general who smiles at the approach of the vulgar, or the lady who keeps her good-humor in spite of scandal; but such is the wisest behavior that any of us can possibly assume. It is certainly a better way to oppose calamity by dissipation, than to take up the arms of reason or resolution to oppose it; by the first method, we forget our miseries; by the last, we only conceal them from others: by struggling with misfortunes, we are sure to receive some wounds in the conflict; but a sure method to come off victorious, is by running away.

DESCRIPTION OF VARIOUS CLUBS.

I REMEMBER to have read in some philosopher (I believe in Tom Brown's works), that, let a man's character, sentiments, or complexion, be what they will, he can find company in London to match them. If he be splenetic, he may every day meet companions on the seats in St. James's Park, with whose groans he may mix his own, and pathetically talk of the weather. If he be passionate, he may vent his rage among the old orators at Slaughter's coffee-house, and damn the nation because it keeps him from starving. If he be phlegmatic, he may sit in silence at the Humdrum club in Ivy-lane; and, if actually mad, he may find very good company in Moorfields, either at Bedlam or the Foundry, ready to cultivate a nearer acquaintance.

But, although such as have a knowledge of the town may easily class themselves with tempers congenial to their own, a countryman who comes to live in London finds nothing more difficult. With regard to myself, none ever tried with more assiduity, or came off with such indifferent success. I spent a whole season in the search, during which time my name has been enrolled in societies, lodges, convocations, and meetings, without number. To some I was introduced by a friend, to others invited by an advertisement; to these I introduced my self, and to those I changed my name to gain admittance. In short, no coquette was ever more solicitous to match her ribands to her complexion, than I to suit my club to my temper; for I was too obstinate to bring my temper to conform to it.

The first club I entered, upon coming to town, was that of the Choice Spirits. The name was entirely suited to my taste; I was a lover of mirth, good-humor, and even sometimes of fun, from my childhood.

As no other passport was requisite but the payment of two shillings at the door, I introduced myself without farther ceremony to the members, who were already as sembled, and had, for some time, begun upon business. The grand, with a mallet in his hand, presided at the head of the table. I could not avoid, upon my entrance, making use of all my skill in physiognomy, in order to discover that superiority of genius in men who had taken a title so superior to the rest of mankind. I expected to see the lines of every face marked with strong thinking; but, though I had some skill in this science, I could for my life discover nothing but a pert simper, fat or profound stupidity.

My speculations were soon interrupted by the grand who had knocked down Mr. Spriggins for a song. I was, upon this, whispered by one of the company who sat next me, that I should now see something touched off to a nicety, for Mr. Spriggins was going to give us Mad Tom in all its glory. Mr. Spriggins endeavored to excuse himself; for, as he was to act a madman and a king, it was impossible to go through the part properly without a crown and chains. His excuses were overruled by a great majority, and with much vociferation. The president ordered up the jack-chain; and, instead of a crown, our performer covered his brows with an inverted jordan. After he had rattled his chain, and shook his head, to the great delight of the whole company, he began his song. As I have heard few young fellows offer to sing in company that did not expose themselves, it was no great disappointment to me to find Mr. Spriggins among the number; however, not to seem an odd fish, I rose from my seat in rapture, cried out, "Bravo! encore!" and slapped the table as loud as any of the rest.

The gentleman who sat next me seemed highly pleased with my taste, and the ardor of my approbation; and whispering told me I had suffered an immense loss; for, had I come a few minutes sooner, I might have heard Geeho Dobbin sung in a tiptop manner, by the pimpled-nose spirit at the president's right elbow: but he was evaporated before I came.

As I was expressing my uneasiness at this disappointment, I found the attention of the company employed upon a fat figure, who, with a voice more rough than the Staffordshire giant's, was giving us the "Softly sweet, in Lydian measure," of Alexander's Feast. After a short pause of admiration, to this succeeded a Welsh dialogue, with the humors of Teague and Taffy; after that came on Old Jackson, with a story between every stanza: next was sung the Dust-Cart, and then Solomon's Song. The glass began now to circulate pretty freely; those who were silent when sober, would now be heard in their turn; every man had his song, and he saw no reason why he should not be heard as well as any of the rest: one begged to be heard while he gave Death and the Lady in high taste; another sung to a plate which he kept trundling on the edges; nothing was now heard but singing; voice rose above voice, and the whole became one universal shout, when the landlord came to acquaint the company that the reckoning was drunk out. Rabelais calls the moments in which a reckoning is mentioned, the most melancholy of our lives: never was so much noise so quickly quelled, as by this short but pathetic oration of our landlord. "Drunk out!" was echoed in a tone of discontent round the table: "drunk out already! that was very odd! that so much punch could be drunk out already! impossible!" The landlord, however, seeming resolved not to retreat from his first assurances, the company was dissolved, and a president chosen for the night ensuing.

A friend of mine, to whom I was complaining sometime after of the entertainment I have been describing, proposed to bring me to the club that he frequented; which he fancied, would suit the gravity of my temper exactly. "We have at the Muzzy club," says he, "no riotous mirth nor awkward ribaldry; no confusion or bawling; all is conducted with wisdom and decency: besides, some of our members are worth forty thousand pounds; men of prudence and foresight every one of them: these are the proper acquaintance, and to such I will to-night introduce you." I was charmed at the proposal; to be acquainted with men worth forty thousand pounds, and to talk wisdom the whole night, were offers that threw me into rapture.

At seven o'clock, I was accordingly introduced by my friend; not indeed to the company, for, though I made my best bow, they seemed insensible of my approach; but to the table at which they were sitting. Upon my entering the room, I could not avoid feeling a secret veneration from the solemnity of the scene before me; the members kept a profound silence, each with a pipe in his mouth and a pewter pot in his hand, and with faces that might easily be construed into absolute wisdom. Happy society! thought I to myself, where the members think before they speak, deliver nothing rashly, but convey their thoughts to each other pregnant with meaning, and matured by reflection.

In this pleasing speculation I continued a full half hour, expecting each moment that somebody would begin to open his mouth; every time the pipe was laid down, I expected it was to speak; but it was only to spit. At length, resolving to break the charm myself, and overcome their extreme diffidence, for to this I imputed their silence, I rubbed my hands, and looking as wise as possible, observed that the nights began to grow a little coolish at this time of the year. This, as it was directed to none of the company in particular, none thought himself obliged to answer; wherefore I continued still to rub my hands and look wise. My next effort was addressed to a gentlemen who sat next me; to whom I observed, that the beer was extremely good; my neighbor made no reply, but by a large puff of tobacco smoke.

I now began to be uneasy in this dumb society, till one of them a little relieved me by observing, that bread had not risen these three weeks. "Ah!" says another, still keeping the pipe in his mouth, "that puts me in mind of a pleasant story about that — hem — very well; you must know — but, before I begin — sir, my service to you — where was I?"

My next club goes by the name of the Harmonical Society; probably from that love of order and friendship which every person commends in institutions of this nature. The landlord was himself founder. The money spent is fourpence each; and they sometimes whip for a double reckoning. To this club few recommendations are requisite except the introductory fourpence, and my landlord's good word, which, as he gains by it, he never refuses.

We all here talked and behaved as every body else usually does on his club-night; we discussed the topic of the day, drank each other's healths, snuffed the candles with our fingers, and filled our pipes from the same plate of tobacco. The company saluted each other in the common manner. Mr. Bellows-mender hoped Mr. Currycomb-maker had not caught cold going home the last club-night; and he returned the compliment by hoping that young Master Bellows-mender had got well again of the chin-cough. Doctor Twist told us a story of a parliament man with whom he was intimately acquainted; while the bug-man, at the same time, was telling a better story of a noble lord with whom he could do anything. A gentleman in a black wig and leather breeches, at the other end of the table, was engaged in a long narrative of the ghost in Cock-lane: he had read it in the papers of the day, and was telling it to some that sat next him, who could not read. Near him Mr. Dibbins was disputing on the old subject of religion with a Jew pedlar, over the table, while the president vainly knocked down Mr. Leathersides for a song. Besides the combination of these voices, which I could hear all together, and which formed an upper part to the concert, there were several others playing under parts by themselves, and endeavoring to fasten on some luckless neighbor's ear, who was himself bent upon the same design against some other.

We have often heard of the speech of a corporation, and this induced me to transcribe a speech of this club, taken in short hand, word for word, as it was spoken by every member of the company. It may be necessary to observe, that the man who told of the ghost had the loudest voice and the longest story to tell, so that his continuing narrative filled every chasm in the conversation.

"So, sir, d'ye perceive me, the ghost giving three loud raps at the bed-post" — "Says my lord to me, My dear Smokeum, you know there is no man upon the face of the yearth for whom I have so high" — "A damnable false heretical opinion of all sound doctrine and good learning; for I'll tell it aloud, and spare not, that" — "Silence for a song; Mr. Leathersides for a song" — As I was walking upon the highway, I met a young damsel" — "Then what brings you here? says the parson to the ghost" — "Sanconiathon, Manetho, and Berosus" — "The whole way from Islington turnpike to Dog-house bar" — "Dam"— "As for Abel Drugger, sir, he 's damn'd low in it; my prentice boy has more of the gentleman than he" — "For murder will out one time or another; and none but a ghost, you know, gentlemen, can"— "Damme if I do n't; for my friend, whom you know, gentlemen, and who is a parliament man, a man of consequence, a dear honest creature, to be sure; we were laughing last night at" — "Death and damnation upon all his posterity by simply barely tasting"— "Sour grapes, as the fox said once when he could not reach them; and I'll, I'll tell you a story about that, that will make you burst your sides with laughing. A fox once" — "Will nobody listen to the song?" — "As I was a walking upon the highway, I met a young damsel both buxom and gay" — "No ghost, gentlemen, can be murdered; nor did I ever hear but of one ghost killed in all my life, and that was stabbed in the belly with a" — "My blood and soul if I do n't" — "Mr. Bellows-mender; I have the honor of drinking your very good health' — "Blast me if I do" —"Dam" — "Blood" — "Bugs" — "Fire" — "Whiz" — "Blid" — "Tit" — "Rat" —"Trip"—The rest all riot, nonsense, and rapid confusion.

Were I to be angry at men for being fools, I could here find ample room for declamation; but, alas! I have been a fool myself; and why should I be angry with them for being something so natural to every child of humanity?

Fatigued with this society, I was introduced, the following night, to a club of fashion. On taking my place, I found the conversation sufficiently easy, and tolerably good-natured; for my lord and Sir Paul were not yet arrived. I now thought myself completely fitted, and resolving to seek no farther, determined to take up my residence here for the winter: while my temper began to open insensibly to the cheerfulness I saw diffused on every face in the room: but the delusion soon vanished, when the waiter came to apprize us that his lordship and Sir Paul were just arrived.

From this moment all our felicity was at an end; our new guests bustled into the room, and took their seats at the head of the table. Adieu now all confidence; every creature strove who should most recommend himself to our members of distinction. Each seemed quite regardless of pleasing any but our new guests; and what before wore the appearance of friendship, was now turned into rivalry.

Yet I could not observe that, amidst all this flattery and obsequious attention, our great men took any notice of the rest of the company. Their whole discourse was addressed to each other. Sir Paul told his lordship a long story of Moravia the Jew; and his lordship gave Sir Paul a very long account of his new method of managing silkworms; he led him, and consequently the rest of the company, through all the stages of feeding, sunning, and hatching; with an episode on mulberry-trees, a digression upon grass-seeds, and a long parenthesis about his new postilion. In this manner we travelled on, wishing every story to be the last; but all in vain:—

"Hills over hills, and Alps on alps arose."

The last club in which I was enrolled a member, was a society of moral philosophers, as they called themselves, who assembled twice a week, in order to show the absurdity of the present mode of religion, and establish a new one in its stead.

I found the members very warmly disputing when I arrived; not indeed about religion or ethics, but about who had neglected to lay down his preliminary sixpence upon entering the room. The president swore that he had laid his own down, and so swore all the company.

During this contest, I had an opportunity of observing the laws, and also the members, of the society. The president, who had been, as I was told, lately a bankrupt, was a tall, pale figure, with a long black wig; the next to him was dressed in a large white wig, and a black cravat; a third, by the brownness of his complexion seemed a native of Jamaica; and a fourth, by his hue, appeared to be a blacksmith. But their rules will give the most just idea of their learning and principles.

"I. We, being a laudable society of moral philosophers, intend to dispute twice a week about religion and priestcraft; leaving behind us old wives' tales, and following good learning and sound sense; and if so be, that any other persons has a mind to be of the society, they shall be entitled so to do, upon paying the sum of three shillings, to be spent by the company in punch.

"II. That no member get drunk before nine of the clock, upon pain of forfeiting three-pence, to be spent by the company in punch.

"III. That as members are sometimes apt to go away

without paying, every person shall pay sixpence upon his entering the room; and all disputes shall be settled by a majority; and all fines shall be paid in punch.

"IV. That sixpence shall be every night given to the president, in order to buy books of learning for the good of the society; the president has already put himself to a good deal of expense in buying books for the club; particularly the works of Tully, Socrates, Cicero, which he will soon read to the society.

"V. All them who brings a new argument against religion, and who, being a philosopher, and a man of learning, as the rest of us is, shall be admitted to the freedom of the society, upon paying sixpence only, to be spent in punch.

"VI. Whenever we are to have an extraordinary meeting, it shall be advertised by some outlandish name in the newspapers.

"Saunders Mac Wild, President.
Anthony Blewit, Vice President,
his † mark.
William Turpin, Secretary."

ON THE POLICY OF CONCEALING OUR WANTS, OR POVERTY.

It is usually said by grammarians, that the use of language is to express our wants and desires; but men who know the world, hold, and I think with some show of reason, that he who best knows how to keep his necessities private, is the most likely person to have them redressed; and that the true use of speech is not so much to express our wants as to conceal them.

When we reflect on the manner in which mankind generally confer their favors, there appears something so attractive in riches, that the large heap generally collects from the smaller; and the poor find as much pleasure in increasing the enormous mass of the rich, as the miser, who owns it, sees happiness in its increase. Nor is there anything in this repugnant to the laws of humanity. Seneca himself allows, that, in conferring benefits, the present should always be suited to the dignity of the receiver. Thus the rich receive large presents, and are thanked for accepting them. Men of middling stations are obliged to be content with presents something less; while the beggar, who may be truly said to want indeed, is well paid if a farthing rewards his warmest solicitations.

Every man who has seen the world, and has had his ups and downs in life, as the expression is, must have frequently experienced the truth of this doctrine; and must know, that to have much, or to seem to have it, is the only way to have more. Ovid finely compares a man of broken fortune to a falling column; the lower it sinks, the greater weight is it obliged to sustain. Thus, when a man's circumstances are such that he has no occasion to borrow, he finds numbers willing to lend him; but should his wants be such, that he sues for a trifle, it is two to one whether he may be trusted with the smallest sum. A certain young fellow, whom I knew, whenever he had occasion to ask his friend for a guinea, used to prelude his request as if he wanted two hundred; and talked so familiarly of large sums, that none could ever think he wanted a small one. The same gentleman, whenever he wanted credit for a suit of clothes, always made the proposal in a laced coat; for he found, by experience, that if he appeared shabby on these occasions, his tailor had taken an oath against trusting, or, what was every whit as bad, his foreman was out of the way, and would not be at home for some time.

There can be no inducement to reveal our wants, except to find pity, and by this means relief; but before a poor man opens his mind in such circumstances, he should first consider whether he is contented to lose the esteem of the person he solicits, and whether he is willing to give up friendship to excite compassion. Pity and friendship are passions incompatible with each other; and it is impossible that both can reside in any breast, for the smallest space, without impairing each other. Friendship is made up of esteem and pleasure; pity is composed of sorrow and contempt: the mind may, for some time, fluctuate between them, but it can never entertain both at once.

In fact, pity, though it may often relieve, is but, at best, a short-lived passion, and seldom affords distress more than transitory assistance; with some it scarce lasts from the first impulse till the hand can be put into the pocket; with others it may continue for twice that space; and on some of extraordinary sensibility, I have seen it operate for half an hour together; but still, last as it may, it generally produces but beggarly effects, and where, from this motive, we give five farthings, from others we give pounds: whatever be our feelings from the first impulse of distress, when the same distress solicits a second time, we then feel with diminished sensibility; and, like the repetition of an echo, every stroke becomes weaker; till, at last, our sensations lose all mixture of sorrow, and degenerate into downright contempt.

These speculations bring to my mind the fate of a very good-natured fellow who is now no more. He was bred in a counting-house, and his father dying just as he was out of his time, left him a handsome fortune, and many friends to advise with. The restraint in which my friend had been brought up, had thrown a gloom upon his temper, which some regarded as prudence; and, from such considerations, he had every day repeated offers of friendship. Such as had money, were ready to offer him their assistance that way; and they who had daughters, frequently, in the warmth of affection, advised him to marry. My friend, however, was in good circumstances; he wanted neither their money, friends, nor a wife; and therefore modestly declined their proposals.

Some errors, however, in the management of his affairs, and several losses in trade, soon brought him to a different way of thinking; and he at last considered, that it was his best way to let his friends know that their offers were at length acceptable. His first address was to a scrivener, who had formerly made him frequent offers of money and friendship, at a time when, perhaps, he knew those offers would have been refused. As a man, therefore, confident of not being refused, he requested the use of a hundred guineas for a few days, as he just then had occasion for money. "And pray, sir," replied the scrivener, "do you want all this money?" — "Want it, sir!" says the other; "if I did not want it I should not have asked it." — "I am sorry for that," says the friend, "for those who want money when they borrow, will always want money when they should come to pay. To say the truth, sir, money is money now; and I believe it is all sunk in the bottom of the sea, for my part; he that has got a little, is a fool if he does not keep what he has got."

Not quite disconcerted by this refusal, our adventurer was resolved to try another, who he knew was the very best friend he had in the world. The gentleman whom he now addressed, received his proposal with all the affability that could be expected from generous friendship. "Let me see, you want a hundred guineas: and pray, dear Jack, would not fifty answer?" — "If you have but fifty to spare, sir, I must be contented." — "Fifty to spare! I do not say that, for I believe I have but twenty about me." — "Then I must borrow the other thirty from some other friend." — "And pray," replied the friend, "would it not be the best way to borrow the whole money from that other friend, and then one note will serve for all, you know? You know, my dear sir, that you need make no ceremony with me at any time; you know, I'm your friend; and when you choose a bit of dinner or so — You, Tom, see the gentleman down. You won't forget to dine with us now and then. Your very humble servant."

Distressed, but not discouraged, at this treatment, he was at last resolved to find that assistance from love, which he could not have from friendship. A young lady, a distant relation by the mother's side, had a fortune in her own hands; and, as she had already made all the advances that her sex's modesty would permit, he made his proposal with confidence. He soon, however, perceived that no bankrupt ever found the fair one kind. She had lately fallen deeply in love with another, who had more money, and the whole neighborhood thought it would be a match.

Every day now began to strip my poor friend of his former finery; his clothes flew, piece by piece, to the pawnbroker's, and he seemed at length equipped in the genuine livery of misfortune. But still he thought himself secure from actual necessity; the numberless invitations he had received to dine, even after his losses, were yet unanswered; he was therefore now resolved to accept of a dinner, because he wanted one; and in this manner he actually lived among his friends a whole week without being openly affronted. The last place I saw him in was at a reverend divine's. He had, as he fancied, just nicked the time of dinner, for he came in as the cloth was laying. He took a chair, without being desired, and talked for some time without being attended to. He assured the company, that nothing procured so good an appetite as a walk in the Park, where he had been that morning. He went on, and praised the figure of the damask tablecloth; talked of a feast where he had been the day before, but that the venison was over-done. But all this procured him no invitation: finding, therefore, the gentleman of the house insensible to all his fetches, he thought proper, at last to retire, and mend his appetite by a second walk in the Park.

You then, O ye beggars of my acquaintance, whether in rags or lace, whether in Kent street or the Mall, whether at the Smyrna or St. Giles's, might I be permitted to advise as a friend, never seem to want the favor which you solicit. Apply to every passion but human pity for redress: you may find permanent relief from vanity, from self-interest, or from avarice, but from compassion never. The very eloquence of a poor man is disgusting; and that mouth which is opened even by wisdom, is seldom expected to close without the horrors of a petition.

To ward off the gripe of poverty, you must pretend to be a stranger to her, and she will at least use you with ceremony. If you be caught dining upon a half-penny porringer of peas-soup and potatoes, praise the wholesomeness of your frugal repast. You may observe that Dr. Cheyne has prescribed peas-broth for the gravel; hint that you are not one of those who are always making a deity of your belly. If, again, you are obliged to wear a flimsy stuff in the midst of winter, be the first to remark, that stuffs are very much worn at Paris; or, if there be found any irreparable defects in any part of your equipage, which cannot be concealed by all the arts of sitting cross-legged, coaxing, or darning, say, that neither you nor Sir Samson Gideon were ever very fond of dress. If you be a philosopher, hint that Plato or Seneca are the tailors you choose to employ; assure the company that man ought to be content with a bare covering, since what now is so much his pride, was formerly his shame. In short, however caught, never give out; but ascribe to the frugality of your disposition what others might be apt to attribute to the narrowness of your circumstances. To be poor, and to seem poor, is a certain method never to rise; pride in the great is hateful; in the wise it is ridiculous; but beggarly pride is a rational vanity, which I have been taught to applaud and excuse.

ON GENEROSITY AND JUSTICE.

Lysippus is a man whose greatness of soul the whole world admires. His generosity is such, that it prevents a demand, and saves the receiver the confusion of a request. His liberality also does not oblige more by its greatness, than by his inimitable grace in giving. Sometimes he even distributes his bounties to strangers, and has been known to do good offices to those who professed themselves his enemies. All the world are unanimous in the praise of his generosity: there is only one sort of people who complain of his conduct. Lysippus does not pay his debts.

It is no difficult matter to account for a conduct so seemingly incompatible with itself. There is greatness in being generous, and there is only simple justice in satisfying creditors. Generosity is the part of a soul raised above the vulgar. There is in it something of what we admire in heroes, and praise with a degree of rapture. Justice, on the contrary, is a mechanic virtue, only fit for tradesmen, and what is practised by every broker in Change-alley.

In paying his debts a man barely does his duty, and it is an action attended with no sort of glory. Should Lysippus satisfy his creditors, who would be at the pains of telling it to the world? Generosity is a virtue of a very different complexion. It is raised above duty, and from its elevation attracts the attention and the praises of us little mortals below.

In this manner do men generally reason upon justice and generosity. The first is despised, though a virtue essential to the good of society, and the other attracts our esteem, which too frequently proceeds from an impetuosity of temper, rather directed by vanity than reason. Lysippus is told that his banker asks a debt of forty pounds, and that a distressed acquaintance petitions for the same sum. He gives it without hesitating to the latter, for he demands as a favor what the former requires as a debt.

Mankind in general are not sufficiently acquainted with the import of the word justice: it is commonly believed to consist only in a performance of those duties to which the laws of society can oblige us. This I allow is sometimes the import of the word, and in this sense justice is distinguished from equity; but there is a justice still more extensive, and which can be shown to embrace all the virtues united.

Justice may be defined, that virtue which impels us to give to every person what is his due. In this extended sense of the word, it comprehends the practice of every virtue which reason prescribes, or society should expect. Our duty to our Maker, to each other, and to ourselves, are fully answered, if we give them what we owe them. Thus justice, properly speaking, is the only virtue; and all the rest have their origin in it.

The qualities of candor, fortitude, charity, and generosity, for instance, are not in their own nature virtues;

and if ever they deserve the title, it is owing only to justice, which impels and directs them. Without such a moderator, candor might become indiscretion, fortitude obstinacy, charity imprudence, and generosity mistaken profusion.

A disinterested action, if it be not conducted by justice, is, at best, indifferent in its nature, and not unfrequently even turns to vice. The expenses of society, of presents, of entertainments, and the other helps to cheerfulness, are actions merely indifferent, when not repugnant to a better method of disposing of our superfluities; but they become vicious when they obstruct or exhaust our abilities from a more virtuous disposition of our circumstances.

True generosity is a duty as indispensably necessary as those imposed upon us by law. It is a rule imposed on us by reason, which should be the sovereign law of a rational being. But this generosity does not consist in obeying every impulse of humanity, in following blind passion for our guide, and impairing our circumstances by present benefactions, so as to render us incapable of future ones.

Misers are generally characterized as men without honor, or without humanity, who live only to accumulate, and to this passion sacrifice every other happiness. They have been described as madmen, who, in the midst of abundance, banish every pleasure, and make, from imaginary wants, real necessities. But few, very few, correspond to this exaggerated picture; and, perhaps, there is not one in whom all these circumstances are found united. Instead of this, we find the sober and the industrious branded by the vain and the idle with this odious appellation; men who, by frugality and labor, raise themselves above their equals, and contribute their share of industry to the common stock.

Whatever the vain or the ignorant may say, well were it for society, had we more of these characters amongst us. In general these close men are found at last the true benefactors of society. With an avaricious man we seldom lose in our dealings, but too frequently in our commerce with prodigality.

A French priest, whose name was Godinot, went for a long time by the name of the Griper. He refused to relieve the most apparent wretchedness, and by a skilful management of his vineyard, had the good fortune to acquire immense sums of money. The inhabitants of Rheims, who were his fellow-citizens, detested him; and the populace, who seldom love a miser, wherever he went, followed him with shouts of contempt. He still, however, continued his former simplicity of life, his amazing and unremitted frugality. He had long perceived the wants of the poor in the city, particularly in having no water but what they were obliged to buy at an advanced price; wherefore, that whole fortune which he had been amassing, he laid out in an aqueduct, by which he did the poor more useful and lasting service, than if he had distributed his whole income in charity every day at his door.

Among men long conversant with books, we too frequently find those misplaced virtues, of which I have been now complaining. We find the studious animated with a strong passion for the great virtues, as they are mistakingly called, and utterly forgetful of the ordinary ones. The declamations of philosophy are generally rather exhausted on those supererogatory duties, than on such as are indispensably necessary. A man, therefore, who has taken his ideas of mankind from study alone, generally comes into the world with a heart melting at every fictitious distress. Thus he is induced, by misplaced liberality, to put himself into the indigent circumstances of the person he relieves.

I shall conclude this paper with the advice of one of the ancients, to a young man whom he saw giving away all his substance to pretended distress. 'It is possible, that the person you relieve may be an honest man; and I know that you, who relieve him, are such. You see then, by your generosity, that you rob a man who is certainly deserving, to bestow it on one who may possibly be a rogue; and, while you are unjust in rewarding uncertain merit, you are doubly guilty by stripping yourself."

ON THE EDUCATION OF YOUTH.

As few subjects are more interesting to society, so few have been more frequently written upon, than the education of youth. Yet it is a little surprising that it has been treated almost by all in a declamatory manner. They have insisted largely on the advantages that result from it, both to individuals and to society; and have expatiated in the praise of what none have ever been so hardy as to call in question.

Instead of giving us fine but empty harangues upon this subject, instead of indulging each his particular and whimsical systems, it had been much better if the writers on this subject had treated it in a more scientific manner, repressed all the sallies of imagination, and given us the result of their observations with didactic simplicity. Upon this subject, the smallest errors are of the most dangerous consequence, and the author should venture the imputation of stupidity upon a topic, where his slightest deviations may tend to injure the rising generation. However, such are the whimsical and erroneous productions written upon this subject. Their authors have studied to be uncommon, not to be just; and at present, we want a treatise upon education, not to tell us anything new, but to explode the errors which have been introduced by the admirers of novelty. It is in this manner books become numerous; a desire of novelty produces a book, and other books are required to destroy the former.

I shall, therefore, throw out a few thoughts upon this subject, which, though known, have not been attended to by others; and shall dismiss all attempts to please, while I study only instruction.

The manner in which our youth of London are at present educated, is, some in free-schools in the city, but the far greater number in boarding-schools about town. The parent justly consults the health of his child and finds an education in the country tends to promote this, much more than a continuance in town. Thus far he is right; if there were a possibility of having even our free-schools kept a little out of town, it would certainly conduce to the health and vigor of, perhaps, the mind as well as the body. It may be thought whimsical, but it is truth; I have found by experience, that they, who have spent all their lives in cities, contract not only an effeminacy of habit, but even of thinking.

But when I have said that the boarding-schools are preferable to free-schools, as being in the country, this is certainly the only advantage I can allow them: otherwise it is impossible to conceive the ignorance of those who take upon them the important trust of education. Is any man unfit for any of the professions, he finds his last resource in setting up a school. Do any become bankrupts in trade, they still set up a boarding-school, and drive a trade this way, when all others fail; nay, I have been told of butchers and barbers, who have turned schoolmasters; and, more surprising still, made fortunes in their new profession.

Could we think ourselves in a country of civilized people, could it be conceived that we have any regard for posterity, when such are permitted to take the charge of the morals, genius, and health, of those dear little pledges, who may one day be the guardians of the liberties of Europe; and who may serve as the honor and bulwark of their aged parents? The care of our children, is it below the state? Is it fit to indulge the caprice of the ignorant with the disposal of their children in this particular? For the state to take the charge of all its children, as in Persia or Sparta, might at present be inconvenient; but surely, with great ease, it might cast an eye to their instructors. Of all professions in society, I do not know a more useful, or a more honorable one, than a schoolmaster; at the same time that I do not see any more generally despised, or whose talents are so ill rewarded.

Were the salaries of schoolmasters to be augmented from a diminution of useless sinecures, how might it turn to the advantage of this people! a people whom, without flattery, I may, in other respects, term the wisest and greatest upon earth. But while I would reward the deserving, I would dismiss those utterly unqualified for their employment; in short, I would make the business of a schoolmaster every way more respectable by increasing their salaries, and admitting only men of proper abilities.

It is true we have schoolmasters appointed, and they have some small salaries; but where at present there is only one schoolmaster appointed, there should at least be two; and wherever the salary is at present twenty pounds, it should be a hundred. Do we give immoderate benefices to those who instruct ourselves, and shall we deny even subsistence to those who instruct our children? Every member of society should be paid in proportion as he is necessary; and I will be bold enough to say, that schoolmasters in a state are more necessary than clergymen, as children stand in more need of instruction than their parents.

But instead of this, as I have already observed, we send them to board in the country, to the most ignorant set of men that can be imagined. But, lest the ignorance of the master be not sufficient, the child is generally consigned to the usher. This is commonly some poor needy animal, little superior to a footman either in learning or spirit, invited to his place by an advertisement, and kept there merely from his being of a complying disposition, and making the children fond of him. 'You give your-child to be educated to a slave,' says a philosopher to a rich man; 'instead of one slave you will then have two.'

It were well, however, if parents upon fixing their children in one of these houses, would examine the abilities of the usher, as well as the master; for whatever they are told to the contrary, the usher is generally the person most employed in their education. If, then, a gentleman, upon putting his son to one of these houses, sees the usher disregarded by the master, he may depend upon it, that he is equally disregarded by the boys; the truth is, in spite of all their endeavors to please, they are generally the laughing-stock of the school. Every trick is played upon the usher: the oddity of his manners, his dress, or his language, are a fund of eternal ridicule; the master himself, now and then, cannot avoid joining in the laugh; and the poor wretch, eternally resenting this ill-usage, seems to live in a state of war with all the family. This is a very proper person, is it not, to give children a relish for learning? They must esteem learning very much, when they see its professors used with such little ceremony! If the usher be despised, the father may be assured that his child will never be properly instructed.

But let me suppose that there are some schools without these inconveniences, where the masters and ushers are men of learning, reputation, and assiduity. If there are to be found such, they cannot be prized in a state sufficiently. A boy will learn more true wisdom in a public school in a year, than by private education in five. It is not from masters, but from their equals, youth learn a knowledge of the world; the little tricks they play each other, the punishment that frequently attends the commission, is a just picture of the great world; and all the ways of men are practised in a public school in miniature. It is true, a child is early made acquainted with some vices in a school; but it is better to know these when a boy, than be first taught them when a man; for their novelty then may have irresistible charms.

In a public education, boys early learn temperance; and if the parents and friends would give them less money upon their usual visits, it would be much to their advantage; since it may justly be said, that a great part of their disorders arise from surfeit, 'plus occidit gula quam gladius.' And now I am come to the article of health, it may not be amiss to observe, that Mr. Locke and some others have advised that children should be inured to cold, to fatigue, and hardship, from their youth; but Mr. Locke was but an indifferent physician. Habit, I grant, has great influence over our constitutions; but we have not precise ideas upon this subject.

We know that among savages, and even among our peasants, there are found children born with such constitutions, that they cross rivers by swimming, endure cold, thirst, hunger, and want of sleep, to a surprising degree; that when they happen to fall sick, they are cured without the help of medicine, by nature alone. Such examples are adduced to persuade us to imitate their manner of education, and accustom ourselves betimes to support the same fatigues. But had these gentlemen considered first how many lives are lost in this ascetic practice; had they considered, that those savages and peasants are generally not so long lived as they who have led a more indolent life; that the more laborious the life is, the less populous is the country; had they considered, that what physicians call the 'stamina vitæ,' by fatigue and labor become rigid, and thus anticipate old age; that the number who survive those rude trials, bears no proportion to those who die in the experiment; had these things been properly considered, they would not have thus extolled an education begun in fatigue and hardships. Peter the Great, willing to inure the children of his seamen to a life of hardship, ordered that they should only drink sea-water; but they unfortunately all died under the trial.

But while I would exclude all unnecessary labors, yet still I would recommend temperance in the highest degree. No luxurious dishes with high seasoning, nothing given children to force an appetite; as little sugared or salted provisions as possible, though ever so pleasing; but milk, morning and night, should be their constant food. This diet would make them more healthy than any of those slops that are usually cooked by the mistress of a boarding-school; besides, it corrects any consumptive habits, not unfrequently found amongst the children of city parents.

As boys should be educated with temperance, so the first greatest lesson that should be taught them is to admire frugality. It is by the exercise of this virtue alone, they can ever expect to be useful members of society. It is true, lectures continually repeated upon this subject, may make some boys, when they grow up, run into an extreme, and become misers; but it were well had we more misers than we have amongst us. I know few characters more useful in society; for a man's having a larger or smaller share of money lying useless by him, no way injures the commonwealth; since, should every miser now exhaust his stores, this might make gold more plenty, but it would not increase the commodities or pleasures of life; they would still remain as they are at present: it matters not, therefore, whether men are misers or not, if they be only frugal, laborious, and fill the station they have chosen. If they deny themselves the necessaries of life, society is no way injured by their folly.

Instead, therefore, of romances, which praise young men of spirit, who go through a variety of adventures, and at last conclude a life of dissipation, folly and extravagance, in riches and matrimony, there should be some men of wit employed to compose books that might equally interest the passions of our youth, where such a one might be praised for having resisted allurements when young, and how he, at last, became lord mayor; how he was married to a lady of great sense, fortune, and beauty: to be as explicit as possible, the old story of Whittington, were his cat left out, might be more serviceable to the tender mind, than either Tom Jones, Joseph Andrews, or a hundred others, where frugality is the only good quality the hero is not possessed of. Were our schoolmasters, if any of them have sense enough to draw up such a work, thus employed, it would be much more serviceable to their pupils, than all the grammars and dictionaries they may publish these ten years.

Children should early be instructed in the arts from which they may afterwards draw the greatest advantages. When the wonders of nature are never exposed to our view, we have no great desire to become acquainted with those parts of learning which pretend to account for the phenomena. One of the ancients complains, that as soon as young men have left school, and are obliged to converse with the world, they fancy themselves transported into a new region. "Ut, cum in forum venerint, existiment se in alium terrarum orbem delatos." We should early, therefore, instruct them in the experiments, if I may so express it, of knowledge, and leave to maturer age the accounting for the causes. But, instead of that, when boys begin natural philosophy in colleges, they have not the least curiosity for those parts of the science which are proposed for their instruction; they have never before seen the phenomena, and consequently have no curiosity to learn the reasons. Might natural philosophy, therefore, be made their pastime in school, by this means it would in college become their amusement.

In several of the machines now in use, there would be ample field both for instruction and amusement; the different sorts of the phosphorus, the artificial pyrites, magnetism, electricity, the experiments upon the rarefaction and weight of the air, and those upon elastic bodies, might employ their idle hours; and none should be called from play to see such experiments but such as thought proper. At first, then, it would be sufficient if the instruments, and the effects of their combination, were only shown; the causes would be deferred to a maturer age, or to those times when natural curiosity prompts us to discover the wonders of nature. Man is placed in this world as a spectator; when he is tired of wondering at all the novelties about him, and not till then, does he desire to be made acquainted with the causes that create those wonders.

What I have observed with regard to natural philosophy, I would extend to every other science whatsoever. We should teach them as many of the facts as were possible, and defer the causes until they seemed of themselves desirous of knowing them. A mind thus leaving school, stored with all the simple experiences of science, would be the fittest in the world for the college-course; and, though such a youth might not appear so bright or so talkative, as those who had learned the real principles and causes of some of the sciences, yet he would make a wiser man, and would retain a more lasting passion for letters, than he who was early burdened with the disagreeable institution of effect and cause.

In history, such stories alone should be laid before them as might catch the imagination; instead of this, they are too frequently obliged to toil through the four empires, as they are called, where their memories are burdened by a number of disgusting names, that destroy all their future relish for our best historians, who may be termed the truest teachers of wisdom.

Every species of flattery should be carefully avoided; a boy who happens to say a sprightly thing is generally applauded so much, that he sometimes continues a coxcomb all his life after. He is reputed a wit at fourteen, and becomes a blockhead at twenty. Nurses, footmen, and such, should therefore be driven away as much as possible. I was even going to add, that the mother herself should stifle her pleasure or her vanity, when little master happens to say a good or a smart thing. Those modest, lubberly boys, who seem to want spirit, generally go through their business with more ease to themselves, and more satisfaction to their instructors.

There has, of late, a gentleman appeared, who thinks the study of rhetoric essential to a perfect education. That bold male eloquence, which often, without pleasing, convinces, is generally destroyed by such institutions. Convincing eloquence is infinitely more serviceable to its possessor, than the most florid harangue, or the most pathetic tones, that can be imagined ; and the man who is thoroughly convinced himself, who understands his subject, and the language he speaks in, will be more apt to silence opposition, than he who studies the force of his periods, and fills our ears with sounds, while our minds are destitute of conviction.

It was reckoned the fault of the orators at the decline of the Roman empire, when they had been long instructed by rhetoricians, that their periods were so harmonious, as that they could be sung as well as spoken. What a ridiculous figure must one of these gentlemen cut, thus measuring syllables, and weighing words, when he should plead the cause of his client! Two architects were once candidates for the building a certain temple at Athens; the first harangued the crowd very learnedly upon the different orders of architecture, and showed them in what manner the temple should be built; the other, who got up after him, only observed, that what his brother had spoken, he could do; and thus he at once gained his cause.

To teach men to be orators, is little less than to teach them to be poets; and for my part, I should have too great a regard for my child, to wish him a manor only in a bookseller's shop.

Another passion which the present age is apt to run into, is to make children learn all things; the languages, the sciences, music, the exercises, and painting. Thus the child soon becomes a talker in all, but a master in none. He thus acquires a superficial fondness for everything, and only shows his ignorance when he attempts to exhibit his skill.

As I deliver my thoughts, without method, or connection, so the reader must not be surprised to find me once more addressing schoolmasters on the present method of teaching the learned languages, which is commonly by literal translations. I would ask such, if they were to travel a journey, whether those parts of the road in which they found the greatest difficulties, would not be the most strongly remembered? Boys who, if I may continue the allusion, gallop through one of the ancients with the assistance of a translation, can have but a very slight acquaintance either with the author or his language. It is by the exercise of the mind alone that a language is learned; but a literal translation on the opposite page, leaves no exercise for the memory at all. The boy will not be at the fatigue of remembering, when his doubts are at once satisfied by a glance of the eye: whereas, were every word to be sought from a dictionary, the learner would attempt to remember them, to save himself the trouble of looking out for them for the future.

To continue in the same pedantic strain, of all the various grammars now taught in the schools about town, I would recommend only the old common one. I have forgot whether Lily's, or an emendation of him. The others may be improvements; but such improvements seem to me only mere grammatical niceties, no way influencing the learner; but perhaps loading him with subtilties, which at a proper age, he must be at some pains to forget.

Whatever pains a master may take to make the learning of the languages agreeable to his pupil, he may depend upon it, it will be at first extremely unpleasant. The rudiments of every language, therefore, must be given as a task, not as an amusement. Attempting to deceive children into instruction of this kind, is only deceiving ourselves; and I know no passion capable of conquering a child's natural laziness but fear. Solomon has said it before me; nor is there any more certain, though perhaps more disagreeable truth, than the proverb in verse, too well known to repeat on the present occasion. It is very probable that parents are told of some masters who never use the rod, and consequently are thought the properest instructors for their children; but, though tenderness is a requisite quality in an instructor, yet there is too often the truest tenderness in well-timed correction.

Some have justly observed, that all passions should be banished on this terrible occasion; but I know not how, there is a frailty attending human nature that few masters are able to keep their temper whilst they correct. I knew a good-natured man, who was sensible of his own weakness in this respect, and consequently had recoure to the following expedient to prevent his passions from being engaged, yet at the same time administer justice with impartiality. Whenever any of his pupils committed a fault, he summoned a jury of his peers, I mean of the boys of his own or the next classes to him: his accusers stood forth; he had liberty of pleading in his own defence, and one or two more had the liberty of pleading against him; when found guilty by the pannel, he was consigned to the footman, who attended in the house, and had previous orders to punish, but with lenity. By this means the master took off the odium of punishment from himself; and the footman, between whom and the boys there could not be even the slightest intimacy, was placed in such a light as to be shunned by every boy in the school.

ON THE VERSATILITY OF POPULAR FAVOR.

An alehouse-keeper, near Islington, who had long lived at the sign of the French King, upon the commencement of the last war with France, pulled down his old sign, and put up that of the Queen of Hungary. Under the influence of her red face and golden sceptre, he continued to sell ale, till she was no longer the favorite of his customers; he changed her, therefore, some time ago, for the King of Prussia; who may probably be changed in turn, for the next great man that shall be set up for vulgar admiration.

Our publican, in this, imitates the great exactly; who deal out their figures, one after the other, to the gazing crowd. When we have sufficiently wondered at one, that is taken in, and another exhibited in its room, which seldom holds its station long; for the mob are ever pleased with variety.

I must own, I have such an indifferent opinion of the vulgar, that I am ever led to suspect that merit which raises their shout; at least, I am certain to find those great, and sometimes good men, who find satisfaction in such acclamations, made worse by it; and history has too frequently taught me, that the head which has grown this day giddy with the roar of the million, has the very next been fixed upon a pole.

As Alexander VI. was entering a little town in the neighborhood of Rome, which had been just evacuated by the enemy, he perceived the townsmen busy in the market place in pulling down from a gibbet a figure which had been designed to represent himself. There were also some knocking down a neighboring statue of one of the Orsini family, with whom he was at war, in order to put Alexander's effigy in its place. It is possible a man who knew less of the world would have condemned the adulation of those barefaced flatterers; but Alexander seemed pleased at their zeal, and turning to Borgia, his son, said with a smile, "Vides, mi fili, quam leve discrimen patibulum inter et statuam:—You see, my son, the small difference between a gibbet and a statue." If the great could be taught any lesson, this might serve to teach them upon how weak a foundation their glory stands, which is built upon popular applause; for as such praise what seems like merit, they as quickly condemn what has only the appearance of guilt.

Popular glory is a perfect coquette; her lovers must toil, feel every inquietude, indulge every caprice; and, perhaps, at last, be jilted into the bargain. True glory, on the other hand, resembles a woman of sense: her admirers must play no tricks; they feel no great anxiety, for they are sure, in the end, of being rewarded in proportion to their merit. When Swift used to appear in public, he generally had the mob shouting in his train. "Pox take these fools," he would say; "how much joy might all this bawling give my lord mayor!"

We have seen those virtues which have, while living, retired from the public eye, generally transmitted to posterity as the truest objects of admiration and praise. Perhaps the character of the late Duke of Marlborough may one day be set up, even above that of his more talked-of predecessor; since an assemblage of all the mild and amiable virtues are far superior to those vulgarly called the great ones. I must be pardoned for this short tribute to the memory of a man, who, while living, would as much detest to receive any thing that wore the appearance of flattery, as I should to offer it.

I know not how to turn so trite a subject out of the beaten road of common-place, except by illustrating it rather by the assistance of my memory than judgment; and, instead of making reflections, by telling a story.

A Chinese who had long studied the works of Confucius, who knew the characters of fourteen thousand words, and could read a great part of every book that came in his way, once took it into his head to travel into Europe, and observe the customs of a people whom he thought not very much inferior, even to his own countrymen, in the arts of refining upon every pleasure. Upon his arrival at Amsterdam, his passion for letters naturally led him into a bookseller's shop; and, as he could speak a little Dutch, he civilly asked the bookseller for the works of the immortal Xixofou. The bookseller assured him he had never heard the book mentioned before. "What! have you never heard of that immortal poet?" returned the other, much surprised; "that light of the eyes, that favorite of kings, that rose of perfection! I suppose you know nothing of the immortal Fipsihihi, second cousin to the moon?" "Nothing at all, indeed, sir," returned the other. "Alas!" cries our traveller, "to what purpose, then, has one of these fasted to death, and the other offered himself up as a sacrifice to the Tartar enemy, to gain a renown which has never travelled beyond the precincts of China?"

There is scarce a village in Europe, and not one university, that is not thus furnished with its little great men. The head of a petty corporation, who opposes the designs of a prince, who would tyranically force his subjects to save their best clothes for Sundays; the puny pedant who finds one undiscovered property in the polype, or describes an unheeded process in the skeleton of a mole, and whose mind, like his microscope, perceives nature only in detail; the rhymer who makes smooth verses, and paints to our imagination, when he should only speak to our hearts: all equally fancy themselves walking forward to immortality, and desire the crowd behind them to look on. The crowd takes them at their word. Patriot, philosopher, and poet, are shouted in their train.—"Where was there ever so much merit seen? No times so important as our own; ages, yet unborn, shall gaze with wonder and applause!" To such music, the important pigmy moves forward, bustling and swelling, and aptly compared to a puddle in a storm.

I have lived to see generals who once had crowds hallooing after them wherever they went, who were bepraised by newspapers and magazines, those echoes of the voice of the vulgar, and yet they have long sunk into merited obscurity, with scarce even an epitaph left to flatter. A few years ago the herring fishery employed all Grub-street; it was the topic in every coffee-house, and the burden of every ballad. We were to drag up oceans of gold from the bottom of the sea; we were to supply all Europe with herrings upon our own terms. At present we hear no more of all this. We have fished up very little gold, that I can learn; nor do we furnish the world with herrings, as was expected. Let us wait but a few years longer, and we shall find all our expectations a herring-fishery.

SPECIMEN OF A MAGAZINE IN MINIATURE.

We essayists, who are allowed but one subject at a time, are by no means so fortunate as the writers of magazines, who write upon several. If a magaziner be dull upon the Spanish war, he soon has us up again with the ghost in Cock-lane; if the reader begins to doze upon that, he is quickly roused by an eastern tale; tales prepare us for poetry, and poetry for the meteorological history of the weather. It is the life and soul of a magazine, never to be long dull upon one subject; and the reader, like the sailor's horse, has at least the comfortable refreshment of having the spur often changed.

As I see no reason why they should carry off all the rewards of genius, I have some thoughts, for the future, of making this essay a magazine in miniature: I shall hop from subject to subject, and if properly encouraged, I intend in time to adorn my feuille-volant with pictures. But to begin, in the usual form, with

A modest Address to the Public.

The public has been so often imposed upon by the unperforming promises of others, that it is with the utmost modesty we assure them of our inviolable design of giving the very best collection that ever astonished society. The public we honor and regard, and therefore to instruct and entertain them is our highest ambition, with labors calculated as well to the head as the heart. If four extraordinary pages of letter-press be any recommendation of our wit, we may at least boast the honor of vindicating our own abilities. To say more in favor of the Infernal Magazine, would be unworthy the public; to say less, would be injurious to ourselves. As we have no interested motives for this undertaking, being a society of gentlemen of distinction, we disdain to eat or write like hirelings; we are all gentlemen, resolved to sell our sixpenny magazine merely for our own amusement.

Be careful to ask for the Infernal Magazine.

DEDICATION.

TO THAT MOST INGENIOUS OF ALL PATRONS, THE TRIPOLINE AMBASSADOR.

May it please your Excellency,

As your taste in the fine arts is universally allowed and admired, permit the authors of the Infernal Magazine to lay the following sheets humbly at your excellency's toe; and should our labors ever have the happiness of one day adorning the courts of Fez, we doubt not that the influence wherewith we are honored, shall be ever retained with the most warm ardor by,

May it please your Excellency,

Your most devoted humble servants,

The Authors of the Infernal Magazine.

A SPEECH,

SPOKEN BY THE INDIGENT PHILOSOPHER, TO PERSUADE HIS CLUB AT CATEATON NOT TO DECLARE WAR AGAINST SPAIN.

My honest friends and brother politicians, I perceive that the intended war with Spain makes many of you uneasy. Yesterday, as we were told, the stocks rose, and you were glad; to-day they fall, and you are again miserable. But, my dear friends, what is the rising or falling of the stocks to us, who have no money? Let Nathan Ben Funk, the Dutch Jew, be glad or sorry for this; but my good Mr. Bellows-mender, what is all this to you or me? You must mend broken bellows, and I write bad prose, as long as we live, whether we like a Spanish war or not. Believe me, my honest friends, whatever you may talk of liberty and your own reason, both that liberty and reason are conditionally resigned by every poor man in every society; and as we were born to work, so others are born to watch over us while we are working. In the name of common sense then, my good friends, let the great keep watch over us, and let us mind our business, and perhaps we may at last get money ourselves, and set beggars at work in our turn. I have a Latin sentence that is worth its weight in gold, and which I shall beg leave to translate for your instruction. An author, called Lily's Grammar, finely observes, that "Æs in presenti perfectum format:" that is, "Ready money makes a perfect man." Let us then get ready money, and let them that will, spend theirs by going to war with Spain.

RULES FOR BEHAVIOR.

DRAWN UP BY THE INDIGENT PHILOSOPHER.

If you be a rich man, you may enter the room with three loud hems, march deliberately up to the chimney, and turn your back to the fire. If you be a poor man, I would advise you to shrink into the room as fast as you can, and place yourself, as usual, upon the corner of a chair, in a remote corner.

When you are desired to sing in company, I would advise you to refuse; for it is a thousand to one but that you torment us with affectation or a bad voice.

If you be young, and live with an old man, I would advise you not to like gravy. I was disinherited myself for liking gravy.

Do not laugh much in public: the spectators that are not as merry as you, will hate you, either because they envy your happiness, or fancy themselves the subject of your mirth.

RULES FOR RAISING THE DEVIL.

Translated from the Latin of Danæus de Sortiariis, a writer contemporary with Calvin, and one of the Reformers of our Church.

The person who desires to raise the devil, is to sacrifice a dog, a cat, and a hen, all of his own property, to Beelzebub. He is to swear an eternal obedience, and then to receive a mark in some unseen place, either under the eye-lid, or in the roof of the mouth, inflicted by the devil himself. Upon this he has power given him over three spirits; one for earth, another for air, and a third for the sea. Upon certain times the devil holds an assembly of magicians, in which each is to give an account of what evil he has done, and what he wishes to do. At this assembly he appears in the shape of an old man, or often like a goat with large horns. They, upon this occasion, renew their vows of obedience; and then form a grand dance in honor of their false deity. The deity instructs them in every method of injuring mankind, in gathering poisons, and of riding upon occasion through the air. He shows them the whole method, upon examination, of giving evasive answers; his spirits have power to assume the form of angels of light, and there is but one method of detecting them, viz. to ask them in proper form, what method is the most certain to propagate the faith over all the world? To this they are not permitted by the superior Power to make a false reply, nor are they willing to give the true one; wherefore they continue silent, and are thus detected.

BEAU TIBBS: A CHARACTER.

Though naturally pensive, yet I am fond of gay company, and take every opportunity of thus dismissing the mind from duty. From this motive I am often found in the centre of a crowd; and wherever pleasure is to be sold, am always a purchaser. In those places, without being remarked by any, I join in whatever goes forward, work my passions into a similitude of frivolous earnestness, shout as they shout, and condemn as they happen to disapprove. A mind thus sunk for a while below its natural standard, is qualified for stronger flights, as those first retire who would spring forward with greater vigor.

Attracted by the serenity of the evening, a friend and I lately went to gaze upon the company in one of the public walks near the city. Here we sauntered together for some time, either praising the beauty of such as were handsome, or the dresses of such as had nothing else to recommend them. We had gone thus deliberately forward for some time, when my friend, stopping on a sudden, caught me by the elbow, and led me out of the public walk. I could perceive by the quickness of his pace, and by his frequently looking behind, that he was attempting to avoid somebody who followed: we now turned to the right, then to the left: as we went forward, he still went faster, but in vain; the person whom he attempted to escape, hunted us through every doubling, and gained upon us each moment; so that at last we fairly stood still, resolving to face what we could not avoid.

Our pursuer soon came up, and joined us with all the familiarity of an old acquaintance. "My dear Charles," cries he, shaking my friend's hand, "where have you been hiding this half a century? Positively, I had fancied you had gone down to cultivate matrimony and your estate in the country." During the reply, I had an opportunity of surveying the appearance of our new companion. His hat was pinched up with peculiar smartness: his looks were pale, thin, and sharp; round his neck he wore a broad black riband, and in his bosom a buckle studded with glass; his coat was trimmed with tarnished twist; he wore by his side a sword with a black hilt: and his stockings of silk, though newly washed, were grown yellow by long service. I was so much engaged with the peculiarity of his dress, that I attended only to the latter part of my friend's reply; in which he complimented Mr. Tibbs on the taste of his clothes and the bloom in his countenance. "Psha, psha, Charles," cries the figure, "no more of that if you love me: you know I hate flattery, on my soul I do; and yet, to be sure, an intimacy with the great will improve one's appearance, and a course of venison will fatten; and yet, faith, I despise the great as much as you do: but there are a great many damned honest fellows among them, and we must not quarrel with one half because the other wants breeding. If they were all such as my Lord Mudler, one of the most good-natured creatures that ever squeezed a lemon, I should myself be among the number of their admirers. I was yesterday to dine at the Duchess of Piccadilly's. My Lord was there. Ned, says he to me, Ned, says he, I will hold gold to silver I can tell where you were poaching last night. Poaching! my lord, says I; faith you have missed already; for I staid at home and let the girls poach for me. That is my way: I take a fine woman as some animals do their prey; stand still, and swoop, they fall into my mouth."

"Ah, Tibbs, thou art a happy fellow," cried my companion, with looks of infinite pity. "I hope your fortune is as much improved as your understanding in such company." "Improved!" replied the other, "you shall know — but let it go no farther, — a great secret — five hundred a year to begin with. — My lord's word of honor for it — His lordship took me in his own chariot yesterday, and we had a tête-à-tête dinner in the country, where we talked of nothing else." "I fancy you forgot, sir," cried I, "you told us but this moment of your dining yesterday in town?" "Did I say so?" replied he, coolly. "To be sure, if I said so, it was so. — Dined in town: egad, now I remember, I did dine in town; but I dined in the country too; for you must know, my boys, I eat two dinners. By the by, I am grown as nice as the devil in my eating. I will tell you a pleasant affair about that: we were a select party of us to dine at Lady Grogram's, an affected piece, but let it go no farther; a secret: Well, says I, I will hold a thousand guineas, and say Done first, that — But, dear Charles, you are an honest creature; lend me half-a-crown for a minute or two, or so, just till — But hark'ee, ask me for it the next time we meet, or it may be twenty to one but I forget to pay you."

When he left us, our conversation naturally turned upon so extraordinary a character. "His very dress," cries my friend, is not less extraordinary than his conduct. If you meet him this day, you find him in rags; if the next, in embroidery. With those persons of distinction, of whom he talks so familiarly, he has scarce a coffee-house acquaintance. However, both for the interest of society, and, perhaps, for his own, Heaven has made him poor; and while all the world perceives his wants, he fancies them concealed from every eye. An agreeable companion, because he understands flattery: and all must be pleased with the first part of his conversation, though all are sure of its ending with a demand on their purse. While his youth countenances the levity of his conduct, he may thus earn a precarious subsistence; but, when age comes on, the gravity of which is incompatible with buffoonery, then will he find himself forsaken by all; condemned in the decline of life to hang upon some rich family whom he once despised, there to undergo all the ingenuity of studied contempt; to be employed only as a spy upon the servants, or a bugbear to fright children into duty."

BEAU TIBBS — CONTINUED.

There are some acquaintances whom it is no easy matter to shake off. My little beau yesterday overtook me again in one of the public walks, and slapping me on the shoulder, saluted me with an air of the most perfect familiarity. His dress was the same as usual, except that he had more powder in his hair, wore a dirtier shirt, and had on a pair of Temple spectacles, and his hat under his arm.

As I knew him to be a harmless, amusing little thing, I could not return his smiles with any degree of severity; so we walked forward on terms of the utmost intimacy, and in a few minutes discussed all the usual topics preliminary to particular conversation.

The oddities that marked his character, however, soon began to appear; he bowed to several well-dressed persons, who, by their manner of returning the compliment, appeared perfect strangers. At intervals he drew out a pocket-book, seeming to take memorandums before all the company with much importance and assiduity. In this manner he led me through the length of the whole Mall, fretting at his absurdities, and fancying myself laughed at as well as him by every spectator.

When we were got to the end of our procession, "Blast me," cries he, with an air of vivacity, "I never saw the Park so thin in my life before; there's no company at all to-day. Not a single face to be seen." "No company," interrupted I, peevishly, "no company where there is such a crowd! Why, man, there is too much. What are the thousands that have been laughing at us but company?" "Lord, my dear," returned he with the utmost good-humor, "you seem immensely chagrined; but, blast me, when the world laughs at me, I laugh at the world, and so we are even. My Lord Trip, Bill Squash, the Creolian, and I, sometimes make a party at being ridiculous; and so we say and do a thousand things for the joke's sake. But I see you are grave; and if you are for a fine grave sentimental companion, you shall dine with my wife to-day; I must insist on 't; I 'll introduce you to Mrs. Tibbs, a lady of as elegant qualifications as any in nature; she was bred, but that 's between ourselves, under the inspection of the countess of Shoreditch. A charming body of voice! But no more of that — she shall give us a song. You shall see my little girl, too, Carolina Wilhelmina Amelia Tibbs, a sweet pretty creature; I design her for my Lord Drumstick's eldest son; but that 's in friendship, let it go no farther; she 's but six years old, and yet she walks a minuet, and plays on the guitar, immensely, already. I intend she shall be as perfect as possible in every accomplishment. In the first place, I 'll make her a scholar; I 'll teach her Greek myself, and I intend to learn that language purposely to instruct her, but let that be a secret."

Thus saying, without waiting for a reply, he took me by the arm and hauled me along. We passed through many dark alleys, and winding ways; for, from some motives to me unknown, he seemed to have a particular aversion to every frequented street; at last, however, we got to the door of a dismal-looking house in the outlets of the town, where he informed me he chose to reside for the benefit of the air.

We entered the lower door, which seemed ever to lie most hospitably open; and I began to ascend an old and creaking staircase; when, as he mounted to show me the way, he demanded, whether I delighted in prospects; to which answering in the affirmative, "Then," said he, "I shall show you one of the most charming out of my windows; we shall see the ships sailing, and the whole country for twenty miles round, tip top, quite high. My Lord Swamp would give ten thousand guineas for such a one; but as I sometimes pleasantly tell him, I always love to keep my prospects at home, that my friends may come to see me the oftener."

By this time we were arrived as high as the stairs would permit us to ascend, till we came to what he was facetiously pleased to call the first floor down the chimney; and, knocking at the door, a voice with a Scotch accent from within demanded, "Wha 's there?" My conductor answered that it was he. But this not satisfying the querist, the voice again repeated the demand; to which he answered louder than before; and now the door was opened by an old maid-servant with cautious reluctance.

When we were got in, he welcomed me to his house with great ceremony, and turning to the old woman, asked where her lady was. "Good troth," replied she, in the northern dialect, "she 's washing your twa shirts at the next door, because they have taken an oath against lending out the tub any longer." "My two shirts!" cries he, in a tone that faltered with confusion, "what does the idiot mean?"—"I ken what I mean well enough," replied the other; "she 's washing your twa shirts at the next door, because——" "Fire and fury, no more of thy stupid explanations," he cried. "Go and inform her we have got company. Were that Scotch hag," continued he, turning to me, "to be forever in my family, she would never learn politeness, nor forget that absurd, poisonous accent of hers, or testify the smallest specimen of breeding or high life; and yet it is very surprising, too, as I had her from a parliament man, a friend of mine, from the Highlands, one of the politest men in the world; but that 's a secret."

We waited some time for Mrs. Tibbs' arrival, during which interval I had a full opportunity of surveying the chamber and all its furniture; which consisted of four chairs with old wrought bottoms, that he assured me were his wife's embroidery; a square table that had been once japanned; a cradle in one corner, a lumber-cabinet in the other; a broken shepherdess, and a mandarine without a head, were stuck over the chimney; and round the walls several paltry unframed pictures, which he observed were all of his own drawing. "What do you think, sir, of that head in the corner, done in the manner of Grisoni? There 's the true keeping in it; it 's my own face; and, though there happens to be no likeness, a countess offered me a hundred for its fellow: I refused her, for, hang it, that would be mechanical, you know."

The wife at last made her appearance; at once a slattern and coquette; much emaciated, but still carrying the remains of beauty. She made twenty apologies for being seen in such an odious dishabille, but hoped to be excused, as she had stayed out all night at Vauxhall Gardens with the countess, who was excessively fond of the horns, "And, indeed, my dear," added she, turning to her husband, "his lordship drank your health in a bumper." "Poor Jack!" cries he, "a dear good-natured creature, I know he loves me; but I hope, my dear, you have given orders for dinner; you need make no great preparations neither, there are but three of us; something elegant, and little will do; a turbot, an ortolan, or a ——" "Or what do you think, my dear," interrupts the wife, "of a nice pretty bit of ox-cheek, piping hot, and dressed with a little of my own sauce?" "The very thing," replies he; it will eat best with some smart bottled beer; but be sure to let 's have the sauce his Grace was so fond of. I hate your immense loads of meat; that is country all over; extreme disgusting to those who are in the least acquainted with high life."

By this time my curiosity began to abate, and my appetite to increase; the company of fools may at first make us smile, but at last never fails of rendering us melancholy. I therefore pretended to recollect a prior engagement, and after having shown my respects to the house, by giving the old servant a piece of money at the door, I took my leave; Mr. Tibbs assuring me, that dinner, if I stayed, would be ready at least in less than two hours.

ON THE IRRESOLUTION OF YOUTH.

As it has been observed that few are better qualified to give others advice, than those who have taken the least of it themselves; so in this respect I find myself perfectly authorized to offer mine; and must take leave to throw together a few observations upon that part of a young man's conduct, on his entering into life, as it is called.

The most usual way among young men who have no resolution of their own, is first to ask one friend's advice, and follow it for some time; than to ask advice of another, and turn to that; so of a third, still unsteady, always changing. However, every change of this nature is for the worse; people may tell you of your being unfit for some peculiar occupations in life; but heed them not whatever employment you follow with perseverance and assiduity, will be found fit for you; it will be your support in youth, and comfort in age. In learning the useful part of every profession, very moderate abilities will suffice: great abilities are generally obnoxious to the possessors. Life has been compared to a race; but the allusion still improves by observing, that the most swift are ever the most apt to stray from the course.

To know one profession only, is enough for one man to know; and this, whatever the professors may tell you to the contrary, is soon learned. Be contented, therefore, with one good employment; for if you understand two at a time, people will give you business in neither.

A conjurer and a tailor once happened to converse together. "Alas!" cries the tailor, "what an unhappy poor creature am I! If people take it into their heads to live without clothes, I am undone; I have no other trade to have recourse to." "Indeed, friend, I pity you sincerely," replies the conjurer; "but, thank Heaven, things are not quite so bad with me: for, if one trick should fail, I have a hundred tricks more for them yet. However, if at any time you are reduced to beggary, apply to me, and I will relieve you." A famine overspread the land; the tailor made a shift to live, because his customers could not be without clothes; but the poor conjurer, with all his hundred tricks, could find none that had money to throw away: it was in vain that he promised to eat fire, or to vomit pins; no single creature would relieve him, till he was at last obliged to beg from the very tailor whose calling he had formerly despised.

There are no obstructions more fatal to fortune than pride and resentment. If you must resent injuries at all, at least suppress your indignation till you become rich, and then show away. The resentment of a poor man is like the efforts of a harmless insect to sting; it may get him crushed, but cannot defend him. Who values that anger which is consumed only in empty menaces?

Once upon a time a goose fed its young by a pond-side; and a goose, in such circumstances, is always extremely proud, and excessively punctilious. If any other animal, without the least design to offend, happened to pass that way, the goose was immediately at it. The pond, she said, was hers, and she would maintain her right in it, and support her honor, while she had a bill to hiss, or a wing to flutter. In this manner she drove away ducks, pigs, and chickens; nay, even the insidious cat was seen to scamper. A lounging mastiff, however, happened to pass by, and thought it no harm if he should lap a little of the water, as he was thirsty. The guardian goose flew at him like a fury, pecked at him with her beak, and slapped him with her feathers. The dog grew angry, and had twenty times a mind to give her a sly snap; but suppressing his indignation, because his master was nigh, "A pox take thee," cries he, "for a fool; sure, those who have neither strength nor weapons to fight, at least should be civil." So saying, he went forward to the pond, quenched his thirst, in spite of the goose, and followed his master.

Another obstruction to the fortune of youth is, that

while they are willing to take offence from none, they are also equally desirous of giving nobody offence. From hence they endeavor to please all, comply with every request, and attempt to suit themselves to every company; have no will of their own, but, like wax, catch every contiguous impression. By thus attempting to give universal satisfaction, they at last find themselves miserably disappointed: to bring the generality of admirers on our side, it is sufficient to attempt pleasing a very few.

A painter of eminence was once resolved to finish a piece which should please the whole world. When, therefore he had drawn a picture, in which his utmost skill was exhausted, it was exposed in the public market-place, with directions at the bottom for every spectator to mark with a brush, that lay by, every limb and feature which seemed erroneous. The spectators came, and in the general applauded; but each, willing to show his talent at criticism, stigmatized whatever he thought proper. At evening, when the painter came, he was mortified to find the picture one universal blot, not a single stroke that had not the marks of disapprobation. Not satisfied with this trial, the next day he was resolved to try them in a different manner: and exposing his picture as before, desired that every spectator would mark those beauties he approved or admired. The people complied, and the artist returning, found his picture covered with the marks of beauty; every stroke that had been yesterday condemned, now received the character of approbation. "Well," cries the painter, "I now find that the best way to please all the world, is to attempt pleasing one half of it."

ON MAD DOGS.

INDULGENT nature seems to have exempted this island from many of those epidemic evils which are so fatal in other parts of the world. A want of rain for a few days beyond the expected season, in some parts of the globe, spreads famine, desolation, and terror, over the whole country; but, in this fortunate island of Britain, the inhabitant courts health in every breeze, and the husbandman ever sows in joyful expectation.

But though the nation be exempt from real evils, it is not more happy on this account than others. The people are afflicted, it is true, with neither famine nor pestilence; but then there is a disorder peculiar to the country, which every season makes strange ravages among them; it spreads with pestilential rapidity, and infects almost every rank of people; what is still more strange, the natives have no name for this peculiar malady, though well known to foreign physicians by the appellation of Epidemic Terror.

A season is never known to pass in which the people are not visited by this cruel calamity in one shape or another, seemingly different, though ever the same; one year it issues from a baker's shop in the shape of a sixpenny loaf, the next it takes the appearance of a comet with a fiery tail, the third it threatens like a flat bottomed boat, and the fourth it carries consternation in the bite of a mad dog. The people, when once infected, lose their relish for happiness, saunter about with looks of despondence, ask after the calamities of the day, and receive no comfort but in heightening each other's distress. It is insignificant how remote or near, how weak or powerful, the object of terror may be, when once they resolve to fright and be frighted; the merest trifles sow consternation and dismay; each proportions his fears, not to the object, but to the dread he discovers in the countenance of others; for, when once the fermentation is begun, it goes on of itself, though the original cause be discontinued which at first set it in motion.

A dread of mad dogs is the epidemic terror which now prevails, and the whole nation is at present actually groaning under the malignity of its influence. The people sally from their houses with that circumspection which is prudent in such as expect a mad dog at every turning. The physician publishes his prescription, the beadle prepares his halter, and a few of unusual bravery arm themselves with boots and buff gloves, in order to face the enemy, if he should offer to attack them. In short, the whole people stand bravely upon their defence, and seem, by their present spirit, to show a resolution of being tamely bit by mad dogs no longer.

Their manner of knowing whether a dog be mad or no, somewhat resembles the ancient gothic custom of trying witches. The old woman suspected was tied hand and foot, and thrown into the water. If she swam, then she was instantly carried off to be burnt for a witch; if she sunk, then indeed she was acquitted of the charge, but drowned in the experiment. In the same manner a crowd gather round a dog suspected of madness, and they begin by teasing the devoted animal on every side. If he attempts to stand on the defensive, and bite, then he is unanimously found guilty, for "a mad dog always snaps at everything." If, on the contrary, he strives to escape by running away, then he can expect no compassion, for "mad dogs always run straight forward before them."

It is pleasant enough for a neutral being like me, who have no share in those ideal calamities, to mark the stages of this national disease. The terror at first feebly enters with a disregarded story of a little dog that had gone through a neighboring village, which was thought to be mad by several who had seen him. The next account comes, that a mastiff ran through a certain town, and bit five geese, which immediately ran mad, foamed at the bill, and died in great agonies soon after. Then comes an affecting story of a little boy bit in the leg, and gone down to be dipped in the salt water. When the people have sufficiently shuddered at that, they are next congealed with a frightful account of a man who was said lately to have died from a bite he had received some years before. This relation only prepares the way for another, still more hideous; as how the master of a family, with seven small children, were all bit by a mad lap-dog; and how the poor father first perceived the infection by calling for a draught of water, where he saw the lap-dog swimming in the cup.

When epidemic terror is thus once excited, every morning comes loaded with some new disaster: as in stories of ghosts each loves to hear the account, though it only serves to make him uneasy; so here, each listens with eagerness, and adds to the tidings with new circumstances of peculiar horror. A lady for instance, in the country, of very weak nerves, has been frighted by the barking of a dog; and this, alas! too frequently happens. The story soon is improved, and spreads, that a mad dog had frighted a lady of distinction. These circumstances begin to grow terrible before they have reached the neighboring village; and there the report is, that a lady of quality was bit by a mad mastiff. This account every moment gathers new strength, and grows more dismal as it approaches the capital; and by the time it has arrived in town, the lady is described with wild eyes, foaming mouth, running mad upon all four, barking like a dog, biting her servants, and at last smothered between two beds by the advice of her doctors; while the mad mastiff is, in the mean time, ranging the whole country over, slavering at the mouth, and seeking whom he may devour.

My land-lady, a good-natured woman, but a little credulous, waked me some mornings ago before the usual hour, with horror and astonishment in her looks. She desired me, if I had any regard for my safety, to keep within; for a few days ago, so dismal an accident had happened, as to put all the world upon their guard. A mad dog down in the country, she assured me, had bit a farmer, who soon becoming mad, ran into his own yard and bit a fine brindled cow; the cow quickly became as mad as the man, began to foam at the mouth, and raising herself up, walked about on her hind legs, sometimes barking like a dog, and sometimes attempting to talk like the farmer. Upon examining the grounds of this story, I found my landlady had it from one neighbor, who had it from another neighbor, who heard it from very good authority.

Were most stories of this nature well examined, it

would be found that numbers of such as have been said to suffer are in no way injured; and that of those who have been actually bitten, not one in a hundred was bit by a mad dog. Such accounts, in general, therefore, only serve to make the people miserable by false terrors; and sometimes fright the patient into actual frenzy, by creating those very symptoms they pretended to deplore.

But even allowing three or four to die in a season of this terrible death (and four is probably too large a concession), yet still it is not considered how many are preserved in their health and in their property by this devoted animal's services. The midnight robber is kept at a distance; the insidious thief is often detected; the healthful chase repairs many a worn constitution; and the poor man finds in his dog a willing assistant, eager to lessen his toil, and content with the smallest retribution.

"A dog," says one of the English poets, "is an honest creature, and I am a friend to dogs." Of all the beasts that graze the lawn, or hunt the forest, a dog is the only animal, that leaving his fellows, attempts to cultivate the friendship of man: to man he looks, in all his necessities, with speaking eye for assistance; exerts for him all the little service in his power with cheerfulness and pleasure; for him bears famine and fatigue with patience and resignation; no injuries can abate his fidelity, no distress induce him to forsake his benefactor; studious to please, and fearing to offend, he is still an humble, steadfast dependant; and in him alone fawning is not flattery. How unkind then to torture this faithful creature, who has left the forest to claim the protection of man! How ungrateful a return to the trusty animal for all its services.

ON THE INCREASED LOVE OF LIFE WITH AGE.

Age, that lessens the enjoyment of life, increases our desire of living. Those dangers, which, in the vigor of youth, we had learned to despise, assume new terrors as we grow old. Our caution increasing as our years increase, fear becomes at last the prevailing passion of the mind, and the small remainder of life is taken up in useless efforts to keep off our end, or provide for a continued existence.

Strange contradiction in our nature, and to which even the wise are liable! If I should judge of that part of life which lies before me by that which I have already seen, the prospect is hideous. Experience tells me, that my past enjoyments have brought no real felicity; and sensation assures me, that those I have felt are stronger than those which are yet to come. Yet experience and sensation in vain persuade; hope, more powerful than either, dresses out the distant prospect in fancied beauty; some happiness, in long perspective, still beckons me to pursue; and, like a losing gamester, every new disappointment increases my ardor to continue the game.

Whence then is this increased love of life, which grows upon us with our years! Whence comes it, that we thus make greater efforts to preserve our existence, at a period when it becomes scarce worth the keeping! Is it that nature, attentive to the preservation of mankind, increases our wishes to live, while she lessens our enjoyments; and, as she robs the senses of every pleasure, equips imagination in the spoil? Life would be insupportable to an old man, who, loaded with infirmities, feared death no more than when in the vigor of manhood: the numberless calamities of decaying nature, and the consciousness of surviving every pleasure, would at once induce him, with his own hand, to terminate the scene of misery; but happily the contempt of death forsakes him at a time when it could only be prejudicial; and life acquires an imaginary value in proportion as its real value is no more.

Our attachment to every object around us increases, in general, from the length of our acquaintance with it. "I would not choose," says a French philosopher, "to see an old post pulled up with which I had been long acquainted." A mind long habituated to a certain set of objects, insensibly becomes fond of seeing them; visits them from habit, and parts from them with reluctance: from hence proceeds the avarice of the old in every kind of possession; they love the world and all that it produces; they love life and all its advantages; not because it gives them pleasure, but because they have known it long.

Chinvang the Chaste, ascending the throne of China, commanded that all who were unjustly detained in prison, during the preceding reigns, should be set free. Among the number who came to thank their deliverer on this occasion, there appeared a majestic old man, who, falling at the emperor's feet, addressed him as follows: "Great father of China, behold a wretch, now eighty-five years old, who was shut up in a dungeon at the age of twenty-two. I was imprisoned, though a stranger to crime, or without being even confronted by my accusers. I have now lived in solitude and darkness for more than sixty years, and am grown familiar with distress. As yet dazzled with the splendor of that sun to which you have restored me, I have been wandering the streets to find out some friend that would assist, or relieve, or remember me; but my friends, my family, and relations, are all dead, and I am forgotten. Permit me then, O Chinvang, to wear out the wretched remains of life in my former prison; the walls of my dungeon are to me more pleasing than the most splendid palace: I have not long to live, and shall be unhappy except I spend the rest of my days where my youth was passed, in that prison from whence you were pleased to release me."

The old man's passion for confinement is similar to that we all have for life. We are habituated to the prison; we look round with discontent, are displeased with the abode, and yet the length of our captivity only increases our fondness for the cell. The trees we have planted, the houses we have built, or the posterity we have begotten, all serve to bind us closer to the earth, and embitter our parting. Life sues the young like a new acquaintance; the companion, as yet unexhausted, is at once instructive and amusing; its company pleases; yet, for all this, it is but little regarded. To us, who are declined in years, life appears like an old friend; its jests have been anticipated in former conversation; it has no new story to make us smile, no new improvement with which to surprise; yet still we love it; destitute of every enjoyment, still we love it; husband the wasting treasure with increasing frugality, and feel all the poignancy of anguish in the fatal separation.

Sir Philip Mordaunt was young, beautiful, sincere, brave — an Englishman. He had a complete fortune of his own, and the love of the king his master, which was equivalent to riches. Life opened all her treasures before him, and promised a long succession of future happiness. He came, tasted of the entertainment, but was disgusted even at the beginning. He professed an aversion to living; was tired of walking round the same circle; had tried every enjoyment, and found them all grow weaker at every repetition. "If life be, in youth, so displeasing," cried he to himself, "what will it appear when age comes on? If it be at present indifferent, sure it will then be execrable." This thought imbittered every reflection; till, at last, with all the serenity of perverted reason, he ended the debate with a pistol! Had this self-deluded man been apprised, that existence grows more desirable to us the longer we exist, he would then have faced old age without shrinking; he would have boldly dared to live; and serve that society, by his future assiduity, which he basely injured by his desertion.

ON THE LADIES' PASSION FOR LEVELLING ALL DISTINCTION OF DRESS.

FOREIGNERS observe that there are no ladies in the world more beautiful, or more ill-dressed, than those of England. Our country-women have been compared to those pictures, where the face is the work of a Raphael, but the draperies thrown out by some empty pretender, destitute of taste, and entirely unacquainted with design.

If I were a poet, I might observe, on this occasion, that so much beauty, set off with all the advantages of dress, would be too powerful an antagonist for the opposite sex; and therefore it was wisely ordered that our ladies should want taste, lest their admirers should entirely want reason.

But to confess a truth, I do not find they have greater aversion to fine clothes than the women of any other country whatsoever. I cannot fancy that a shopkeeper's wife in Cheapside has a greater tenderness for the fortune of her husband, than a citizen's wife in Paris; or that miss in a boarding-school is more an economist in dress than mademoiselle in a nunnery.

Although Paris may be accounted the soil in which almost every fashion takes its rise, its influence is never so general there as with us. They study there the happy method of uniting grace and fashion, and never excuse a woman for being awkwardly dressed, by saying her clothes are in the mode. A French woman is a perfect architect in dress; she never, with Gothic ignorance, mixes the orders; she never tricks out a squabby Doric shape with Corinthian finery; or, to speak without metaphor, she conforms to general fashion only when it happens not to be repugnant to private beauty.

The English ladies, on the contrary, seem to have no other standard of grace but the run of the town. If fashion gives the word, every distinction of beauty, complexion, or stature, ceases. Sweeping trains, Prussian bonnets, and trollopees, as like each other as if cut from the same piece, level all to one standard. The Mall, the gardens, and playhouses, are filled with ladies in uniform; and their whole appearance shows as little variety of taste as if their clothes were bespoke by the colonel of a marching regiment, or fancied by the artist who dresses the three battalions of guards.

But not only the ladies of every shape and complexion, but of every age, too, are possessed of this unaccountable passion for levelling all distinction in dress. The lady of no quality travels first behind the lady of some quality; and a woman of sixty is as gaudy as her granddaughter. A friend of mine, a good-natured old man, amused me the other day with an account of his journey to the Mall. It seems, in his walk thither, he, for some time, followed a lady, who, as he thought, by her dress, was a girl of fifteen. It was airy, elegant, and youthful. My old friend had called up all his poetry on this occasion, and fancied twenty Cupids prepared for execution in every folding of her white negligee. He had prepared his imagination for an angel's face; but what was his mortification to find that the imaginary goddess was no other than his cousin Hannah, some years older than himself.

But to give it in his own words: "After the transports of our first salute," said he, "were over, I could not avoid running my eye over her whole appearance. Her gown was of cambric, cut short before, in order to discover a high-heeled shoe, which was buckled almost at the toe. Her cap consisted of a few bits of cambric, and flowers of painted paper stuck on one side of her head. Her bosom, that had felt no hand but the hand of time these twenty years, rose, suing to be pressed. I could, indeed, have wished her more than a handkerchief of Paris net to shade her beauties; for, as Tasso says of the rose-bud, 'Quanto si nostra men, tanto e piu bella." A female breast is generally thought the most beautiful as it is more sparingly discovered.

As my cousin had not put on all this finery for nothing she was at that time sallying out to the Park, where I had overtaken her. Perceiving, however, that I had on my best wig, she offered, if I would squire her there, to send home the footman. Though I trembled for our reception in public, yet I could not, with any civility, refuse; so, to be as gallant as possible, I took her hand in my arm, and thus we marched on together.

When we made our entry at the Park, two antiquated figures, so polite and so tender, soon attracted the eyes of the company. As we made our way among crowds who were out to show their finery as well as we, wherever we came, I perceived we brought good-humor with us. The polite could not forbear smiling, and the vulgar burst out into a horse-laugh, at our grotesque figures. Cousin Hannah, who was perfectly conscious of the rectitude of her own appearance, attributed all this mirth to the oddity of mine; while I as cordially placed the whole to her account. Thus, from being two of the best natured creatures alive, before we got half way up the Mall, we both began to grow peevish, and, like two mice on a string, endeavored to revenge the impertinence of others upon ourselves. 'I am amazed, cousin Jeffery," says miss, "that I can never get you to dress like a Christian. I knew we should have the eyes of the Park upon us, with your great wig so frizzled, and yet so beggarly, and your monstrous muff. I hate those odious muffs.' I could have patiently borne a criticism on all the rest of my equipage: but as I had always a peculiar veneration for my muff, I could not forbear being piqued a little; and, throwing my eyes with a spiteful air on her bosom, "I could heartily wish, madam," replied I, "that, for your sake, my muff was cut into a tippet."

As my cousin, by this time, was grown heartily ashamed of her gentleman-usher, and as I was never very fond of any kind of exhibition myself, it was mutually agreed to retire for a while to one of the seats, and, from that retreat, remark on others as freely as they had remarked on us.

When seated, we continued silent for some time, employed in very different speculations. I regarded the whole company, now passing in review before me, as drawn out merely for my amusement. For my entertainment the beauty had, all that morning been improving her charms: the beau had put on lace, and the young doctor a big wig, merely to please me. But quite different were the sentiments of cousin Hannah: she regarded every well-dressed woman as a victorious rival; hated every face that seemed dressed in good-humor, or wore the appearance of greater happiness than her own. I perceived her uneasiness, and attempted to lessen it, by observing that there was no company in the Park to-day. To this she readily assented; "And yet," says she, "it is full enough of scrubs of one kind or another." My smiling at this observation gave her spirits to pursue the bent of her inclination, and now she began to exhibit her skill in secret history, as she found me disposed to listen. "Observe," says she to me, "that old woman in tawdry silk, and dressed out beyond the fashion. That is Miss Biddy Evergreen. Miss Biddy, it seems, has money; and as she considers that money was never so scarce as it is now, she seems resolved to keep what she has to herself. She is ugly enough, you see; yet, I assure you, she has refused several offers, to my knowledge, within this twelvemonth. Let me see, three gentlemen from Ireland, who study the law, two waiting captains, her doctor, and a Scotch preacher who had liked to have carried her off. All her time is passed between sickness and finery. Thus she spends the whole week in a close chamber, with no other company but her monkey, her apothecary, and cat; and comes dressed out to the Park every Sunday, to show her airs, to get new lovers, to catch a new cold, and to make new work for the doctor.

"'There goes Mrs. Roundabout, I mean the fat lady in the lustring trollopee. Between you and I, she is but a cutler's wife. See how she's dressed, as fine as hands and pins can make her, while her two marriageble daughters, like bunters in stuff gowns, are now taking sixpenny-worth of tea at the White-conduit house. Odious puss, how she waddles along, with her train two yards behind her! She puts me in mind of my lord Bantam's Indian sheep, which are obliged to have their monstrous tails trundled along in a go-cart. For all her airs, it goes to her husband's heart to see four yards of good lustring wearing against the ground, like one of his knives on a grindstone. To speak my mind, cousin Jeffery, I never liked those tails; for suppose a young fellow should be rude, and the lady should offer to step back in the fright, instead of retiring, she treads upon her train, and falls fairly on her back; and then you know, cousin, — her clothes may be spoiled.

"'Ah! Miss Mazzard! I knew we should not miss

her in the Park; she in the monstrous Prussian bonnet. Miss, though so very fine, was bred a milliner; and might have had some custom if she had minded her business; but the girl was fond of finery, and, instead of dressing her customers, laid out all her goods in adorning herself. every new gown she put on impaired her credit; she still, however, went on, improving her appearance and lessening her little fortune, and is now, you see, become a belle and a bankrupt.'

"My cousin was proceeding in her remarks, which were interrupted by the approach of the very lady she had been so freely describing. Miss had perceived her at a distance, and approached to salute her. I found by the warmth of the two ladies' protestations, that they had been long intimate, esteemed friends and acquaintance. Both were so pleased at this happy rencounter, that they were resolved not to part for the day. So we all crossed the Park together, and I saw them into a hackney-coach at St. James's."

ASEM; AN EASTERN TALE:

OR THE WISDOM OF PROVIDENCE IN THE MORAL GOVERNMENT OF THE WORLD.

WHERE Tauris lifts his head above the storm, and presents nothing to the sight of the distant traveller but a prospect of nodding rocks, falling torrents, and all the variety of tremendous nature; on the bleak bosom of this frightful mountain, secluded from society, and detesting the ways of men, lived Asem, the man-hater.

Asem had spent his youth with men; had shared in their amusements; and had been taught to love his fellow-creatures with the most ardent affection; but, from the tenderness of his disposition, he exhausted all his fortune in relieving the wants of the distressed. The petitioner never sued in vain; the weary traveller never passed his door; he only desisted from doing good when he had no longer the power of relieving.

From a fortune thus spent in benevolence he expected a grateful return from those he had formerly relieved; and made his application with confidence of redress: the ungrateful world soon grew weary of his importunity; for pity is but a short-lived passion. He soon, therefore, began to view mankind in a very different light from that in which he had before beheld them: he perceived a thousand vices he had never before suspected to exist: wherever he turned, ingratitude, dissimulation, and treachery, contributed to increase his detestation of them. Resolved, therefore, to continue no longer in a world which he hated, and which repaid his detestation with contempt, he retired to this region of sterility, in order to brood over his resentment in solitude, and converse with the only honest heart he knew; namely, his own.

A cave was his only shelter from the inclemency of the weather; fruits, gathered with difficulty from the mountain's side, his only food; and his drink was fetched with danger and toil from the headlong torrent. In this manner he lived, sequestered from society, passing the hours in meditation, and sometimes exulting that that he was able to live independently of his fellow-creatures.

At the foot of the mountain an extensive lake displayed its glassy bosom, reflecting on its broad surface the impending horrors of the mountain. To this capacious mirror he would sometimes descend, and, reclining on its steep banks, cast an eager look on the smooth expanse that lay before him. "How beautiful," he often cried, "is nature! how lovely, even in her wildest scenes! How finely contrasted is the level plain that lies beneath me, with yon awful pile that hides its tremendous head in clouds! But the beauty of these scenes is no way comparable with their utility; from hence a hundred rivers are supplied, which distribute health and verdure to the various countries through which they flow. Every part of the universe is beautiful, just, and wise, but man: vile man is a solecism in nature, the only monster in the creation. Tempests and whirlwinds have their use; but vicious, ungrateful man is a blot in the fair page of universal beauty. Why was I born of that detested species, whose vices are almost a reproach to the wisdom of the Divine Creator? Were men entirely free from vice, all would be uniformity, harmony, and order. A world of moral rectitude should be the result of a perfectly moral agent. Why, why, then, O Alla! must I be thus confined in darkness, doubt, and despair?"

Just as he uttered the word despair, he was going to plunge into the lake beneath him, at once to satisfy his doubts, and put a period to his anxiety; when he perceived a most majestic being walking on the surface of the water, and approaching the bank on which he stood So unexpected an object at once checked his purpose; he stopped, contemplated, and fancied he saw something awful and divine in his aspect.

"Son of Adam," cried the genius, "stop thy rash purpose; the Father of the Faithful has seen thy justice, thy integrity, thy miseries; and hath sent me to afford and administer relief. Give me thine hand, and follow without trembling, wherever I shall lead; in me behold the genius of conviction, kept by the great prophet, to turn from their errors those who go astray, not from curiosity, but a rectitude of intention. Follow me, and be wise."

Asem immediately descended upon the lake, and his guide conducted him along the surface of the water; till, coming near the centre of the lake, they both began to sink; the waters closed over their heads; they descended several hundred fathoms, till Asem, just ready to give up his life as inevitably lost, found himself with his celestial guide in another world, at the bottom of the waters, where human foot had never trod before. His astonishment was beyond description, when he saw a sun like that he had left, a serene sky over his head, and blooming verdure under his feet.

"I plainly perceive your amazement," said the genius; "but suspend it for a while. This world was formed by Alla, at the request, and under the inspection of our great prophet; who once entertained the same doubts which filled your mind when I found you, and from the consequence of which you were so lately rescued. The rational inhabitants of this world are formed agreeable to your own ideas; they are absolutely without vice. In other respects it resembles your earth; but differs from it in being wholly inhabited by men who never do wrong. If you find this world more agreeable than that you so lately left, you have free permission to spend the remainder of your days in it; but permit me for some time, to attend you, that I may silence your doubts, and make you better acquainted with your company and your new habitation."

"A world without vice! Rational beings without immorality!" cried Asem, in a rapture; "I thank thee, O Alla, who hast at length heard my petitions: this, this indeed, will produce happiness, ecstasy, and ease. O for an immortality, to spend it among men who are incapable of ingratitude, injustice, fraud, violence, and a thousand other crimes that render society miserable!"

"Cease thine acclamations," replied the genius. "Look around thee; reflect on every object and action before us, and communicate to me the result of thine observations. Lead wherever you think proper, I shall be your attendant and instructor." Asem and his companion travelled on in silence for some time; the former being entirely lost in astonishment; but, at last, recovering his former serenity, he could not help observing that the face of the country bore a near resemblance to that he had left, except that this subterranean world still seemed to retain its primeval wildness.

"Here," cried Asem, "I perceive animals of prey, and others that seem only designed for their subsistence; it is the very same in the world over our heads. But had I been permitted to instruct our prophet, I would have removed this defect, and formed no voracious or destructive animals, which only prey on the other parts of the creation." — "Your tenderness for inferior animals, is, I find, remarkable," said the genius, smiling. "But, with regard to meaner creatures, this world exactly resembles the other; and, indeed, for obvious reasons: for the earth can support a more considerable number of animals, by their thus becoming food for each other, than if they had lived entirely on her vegetable productions. So that animals of different natures thus formed, instead of lessening their multitudes, subsist in the greatest number possible. But let us hasten on to the inhabited country before us, and see what that offers for instruction."

They soon gained the utmost verge of the forest, and entered the country inhabited by men without vice; and Asem anticipated in idea the rational delight he hoped to experience in such an innocent society. But they had scarce left the confines of the wood, when they beheld one of the inhabitants flying with hasty steps, and terror in his countenance, from an army of squirrels that closely pursued him. "Heavens!" cried Asem, "why does he fly? What can he fear from animals so contemptible?" He had scarce spoken, when he perceived two dogs pursuing another of the human species, who, with equal terror and haste, attempted to avoid them. "This," cried Asem to his guide, "is truly surprising; nor can I conceive the reason for so strange an action." "Every species of animals," replied the genius, "has of late grown very powerful in this country; for the inhabitants, at first, thinking it unjust to use either fraud or force in destroying them, they have insensibly increased, and now frequently ravage their harmless frontiers." "But they should have been destroyed," cried Asem; "you see the consequence of such neglect." "Where is then that tenderness you so lately expressed for subordinate animals?" replied the genius, smiling: "you seem to have forgot that branch of justice." "I must acknowledge my mistake," returned Asem; "I am now convinced that we must be guilty of tyranny and injustice to the brute creation, if we would enjoy the world ourselves. But let us no longer observe the duty of man to these irrational creatures, but survey their connections with one another."

As they walked farther up the country, the more he was surprised to see no vestiges of handsome houses, no cities, nor any mark of elegant design. His conductor, perceiving his surprise, observed that the inhabitants of this new world were perfectly content with their ancient simplicity; each had a house, which, though homely, was sufficient to lodge his little family; they were too good to build houses which could only increase their own pride, and the envy of the spectator; what they built was for convenience, and not for show. "At least, then," said Asem, "they have neither architects, painters, nor statuaries, in their society; but these are idle arts, and may be spared. However, before I spend much more time here, you shall have my thanks for introducing me into the society of some of their wisest men: there is scarce any pleasure to me equal to a refined conversation; there is nothing of which I am so much enamoured as wisdom." "Wisdom!" replied his instructor: "how ridiculous! We have no wisdom here, for we have no occasion for it; true wisdom is only a knowledge of our own duty, and the duty of others to us; but of what use is such wisdom here? Each intuitively performs what is right in himself, and expects the same from others. If by wisdom you should mean vain curiosity, and empty speculation, as such pleasures have their origin in vanity, luxury, or avarice, we are too good to pursue them." "All this may be right," says Asem; "but, methinks I observe a solitary disposition prevail among the people; each family keeps separately within their own precincts, without society, or without intercourse." "That, indeed, is true," replied the other; "here is no established society, nor should there be any: all societies are made either through fear or friendship; the people we are among are too good to fear each other; and there are no motives to private friendship, where all are equally meritorious." "Well, then," said the sceptic," as I am to spend my time here, if I am to have neither the polite arts, nor wisdom, nor friendship, in such a world, I should be glad, at least, of an easy companion, who may tell me his thoughts, and to whom I may communicate mine." "And to what purpose should either do this?" says the genius: "flattery or curiosity are vicious motives, and never allowed of here; and wisdom is out of the question.

Still, however," said Asem, "the inhabitants must be happy; each is contented with his own possessions, nor avariciously endeavors to heap up more than is necessary for his own subsistence; each has therefore leisure for pitying those that stand in need of his compassion." He had scarce spoken when his ears were assaulted with the lamentations of a wretch who sat by the way-side, and, in the most deplorable distress, seemed gently to murmur at his own misery. Asem immediately ran to his relief, and found him in the last stage of a consumption. "Strange," cried the son of Adam, "that men who are free from vice should thus suffer so much misery without relief!" "Be not surprised," said the wretch, who was dying; "would it not be the utmost injustice for beings, who have only just sufficient to support themselves, and are content with a bare subsistence, to take it from their own mouths to put it into mine? They never are possessed of a single meal more than is necessary; and what is barely necessary cannot be dispensed with." "They should have been supplied with more than is necessary," cried Asem; "and yet I contradict my own opinion but a moment before: all is doubt, perplexity, and confusion. Even the want of ingratitude is no virtue here, since they never receive a favor. They have, however, another excellence yet behind; the love of their country is still, I hope, one of their darling virtues." "Peace, Asem," replied the guardian, with a countenance not less severe than beautiful, "nor forfeit all thy pretensions to wisdom; the same selfish motives by which we prefer our own interest to that of others, induce us to regard our country preferable to that of another. Nothing less than universal benevolence is free from vice, and that you see is practised here." "Strange," cries the disappointed pilgrim, in an agony of distress; "what sort of a world am I now introduced to? There is scarce a single virtue, but that of temperance, which they practise; and in that they are no way superior to the brute creation. There is scarce an amusement which they enjoy; fortitude, liberality, friendship, wisdom, conversation, and love of country, are all virtues entirely unknown here; thus it seems, that to be unacquainted with vice is not to know virtue. Take me, O my genius, back to that very world which I have despised; a world which has Alla for its contriver, is much more wisely formed than that which has been projected by Mohammed. Ingratitude, contempt, and hatred, I can now suffer, for perhaps I have deserved them. When I arraigned the wisdom of Providence, I only showed my own ignorance; henceforth let me keep from vice myself, and pity it in others."

He had scarce ended, when the genius, assuming an air of terrible complacency, called all his thunders around him, and vanished in a whirlwind. Asem, astonished at the terror of the scene, looked for his imaginary world; when, casting his eyes around, he perceived himself in the very situation, and in the very place, where he first began to repine and despair; his right foot had been just advanced to take the fatal plunge, nor had it been yet withdrawn; so instantly did Providence strike the series of truths just imprinted on his soul. He now departed from the water-side in tranquillity, and, leaving his horrid mansion, travelled to Segestan, his native city; where he diligently applied himself to commerce, and put in practice that wisdom he had learned in solitude. The frugality of a few years soon produced opulence; the number of his domestics increased; his friends came to him from every part of the city, nor did he receive them with disdain; and a youth of misery was concluded with an old age of elegance, affluence, and ease.

ON THE ENGLISH CLERGY AND POPULAR PREACHERS.

It is allowed on all hands, that our English divines receive a more liberal education, and improve that education by frequent study, more than any others of this reverend profession in Europe. In general, also, it may be observed, that a greater degree of gentility is affixed to the character of a student in England than elsewhere; by which means our clergy have an opportunity of seeing better company while young, and of sooner wearing off those prejudices which they are apt to imbibe even in the best-regulated universities, and which may be justly termed the vulgar errors of the wise.

Yet, with all these advantages, it is very obvious, that the clergy are no where so little thought of, by the populace, as here; and, though our divines are foremost with respect to abilities, yet they are found last in the effects of their ministry; the vulgar, in general, appearing no way impressed with a sense of religious duty. I am not for whining at the depravity of the times, or for endeavoring to paint a prospect more gloomy than in nature; but certain it is, no person who has travelled will contradict me, when I aver, that the lower orders of mankind, in other countries, testify, on every occasion, the profoundest awe of religion; while in England they are scarcely awakened into a sense of its duties, even in circumstances of the greatest distress.

This dissolute and fearless conduct foreigners are apt to attribute to climate, and constitution; may not the vulgar being pretty much neglected in our exhortations from the pulpit, be a conspiring cause? Our divines seldom stoop to their mean capacities; and they who want instruction most, find least in our religious assemblies.

Whatever may become of the higher orders of mankind, who are generally possessed of collateral motives to virtue, the vulgar should be particularly regarded, whose behavior in civil life is totally hinged upon their hopes and fears. Those who constitute the basis of the great fabric of society, should be particularly regarded; for, in policy, as architecture, ruin is most fatal when it begins from the bottom.

Men of real sense and understanding prefer a prudent mediocrity to a precarious popularity, and, fearing to outdo their duty, leave it half done. Their discourses from the pulpit are generally dry, methodical, and unaffecting: delivered with the most insipid calmness; insomuch, that should the peaceful preacher lift his head over the cushion, which alone he seems to address, he might discover his audience, instead of being awakened to remorse, actually sleeping over his methodical and labored composition.

This method of preaching is, however, by some called an address to reason, and not to the passions; this is styled the making of converts from conviction; but such are indifferently acquainted with human nature, who are not sensible that men seldom reason about their debaucheries till they are committed. Reason is but a weak antagonist when headlong passion dictates; in all such cases we should arm one passion against another: it is with the human mind as in nature; from the mixture of two opposites, the result is most frequently neutral tranquillity. Those who attempt to reason us out of follies, begin at the wrong end, since the attempt naturally presupposes us capable of reason; but to be made capable of this, is one great point of the cure.

There are but few talents requisite to become a popular preacher; for the people are easily pleased, if they perceive any endeavors in the orator to please them; the meanest qualifications will work this effect, if the preacher sincerely sets about it. Perhaps little, indeed very little more is required, than sincerity and assurance; and a becoming sincerity is always certain of producing a becoming assurance. "Si vis me flere, dolendum est primum tibi ipsi," is so trite a quotation, that it almost demands an apology to repeat it; yet though all allow the justice of the remark, how few do we find put it in practice! Our orators, with the most faulty bashfulness, seem impressed rather with an awe of their audience, than with a just respect for the truths they are about to deliver: they, of all professions, seem the most bashful, who have the greatest right to glory in their commission.

The French preachers generally assume all that dignity which becomes men who are ambassadors from Christ; the English divines, like erroneous envoys, seem more solicitous not to offend the court to which they are sent, than to drive home the interests of their employer. The bishop of Massillon, in the first sermon he ever preached, found the whole audience, upon his getting into the pulpit, in a disposition no way favorable to his intentions; their nods, whispers, or drowsy behavior, showed him that there was no great profit to be expected from his sowing in a soil so improper; however, he soon changed the disposition of his audience by his manner of beginning. "If," says he, "a cause the most important that could be conceived, were to be tried at the bar before qualified judges; if this cause interested ourselves in particular; if the eyes of the whole kingdom were fixed upon the event; if the most eminent counsel were employed on both sides; and if we had heard from our infancy of this yet-undetermined trial, — would you not all sit with due attention, and warm expectation, to the pleadings on each side? Would not all your hopes and fears be hinged on the final decision? and yet, let me tell you, have this moment a cause of much greater importance before you; a cause where not one nation, but all the world, are spectators; tried not before a fallible tribunal, but the awful throne of Heaven; where not your temporal and transitory interests are the subject of debate, but your eternal happiness or misery; where the cause is still undetermined, but, perhaps, the very moment I am speaking may fix the irrevocable decree that shall last forever: and yet, notwithstanding all this, you can hardly sit with patience to hear the tidings of your own salvation; I plead the cause of Heaven, and yet I am scarcely attended to," etc.

The style, the abruptness of a beginning like this, in the closet would appear absurd; but in the pulpit it is attended with the most lasting impressions: that style which, in the closet, might justly be called flimsy, seems the true mode of eloquence here. I never read a fine composition under the title of a sermon, that I do not think the author has miscalled his piece; for the talents to be used in writing well entirely differ from those of speaking well. The qualifications for speaking, as has been already observed, are easily acquired; they are accomplishments which may be taken up by every candidate who will be at the pains of stooping. Impressed with a sense of the truths he is about to deliver, a preacher disregards the applause or the contempt of his audience, and he insensibly assumes a just and manly sincerity. With this talent alone we see what crowds are drawn around enthusiasts, even destitute of common sense; what numbers converted to Christianity. Folly may sometimes set an example for wisdom to practise; and our regular divines may borrow instruction from even Methodists, who go their circuits, and preach prizes among the populace. Even Whitefield may be placed as a model to some of our young divines; let them join to their own good sense his earnest manner of delivery.

It will be perhaps objected, that by confining the excellences of a preacher to proper assurance, earnestness, and openness of style, I make the qualifications too trifling for estimation; there will be something called oratory brought up on this occasion; action, attitude, grace, elocution, may be repeated as absolutely necessary to complete the character; but let us not be deceived; common sense is seldom swayed by fine tones, musical periods, just attitudes, or the display of a white handkerchief; oratorial behavior, except in very able hands indeed, generally sinks into awkward and paltry affectation.

It must be observed, however, that these rules are calculated only for him who would instruct the vulgar, who stand in most need of instruction; to address philosophers, and to obtain the character of a polite preacher among the polite — a much more useless, though more sought-for character — requires a different method of proceeding. All I shall observe on this head is, to entreat the polemic divine, in his controversy with the deist, to act rather offensively than to defend; to push home the grounds of his belief, and the impracticability of theirs, rather than to spend time in solving the objections of every opponent. "It is ten to one," says a late writer on the art of war, "but that the assailant who attacks the enemy in his trenches is always victorious."

Yet upon the whole, our clergy might employ themselves more to the benefit of society, by declining all controversy, than by exhibiting even the profoundest skill in polemic disputes; their contests with each other often turn on speculative trifles; and their disputes with the deist are almost at an end, since they can have no more than victory; and that they are already possessed of, as their antagonists have been driven into a confession of the necessity of revelation, or an open avowal of atheism. To continue the dispute longer would only endanger it; the sceptic is ever expert at puzzling a debate which he finds himself unable to continue, "and, like an Olympic boxer, generally fights best when undermost."

ON THE ADVANTAGES TO BE DERIVED FROM SENDING A JUDICIOUS TRAVELLER INTO ASIA.

I have frequently been amazed at the ignorance of almost all the European travellers, who have penetrated any considerable way eastward into Asia. They have all been influenced either by motives of commerce or piety, and their accounts are such as might reasonably be expected from men of a very narrow or very prejudiced education — the dictates of superstition, or the result of ignorance. Is it not surprising, that, of such a variety of adventurers, not one single philosopher should be found among the number? For, as to the travels of Gemelli, the learned are long agreed that the whole is but an imposture.

There is scarce any country, how rude or uncultivated soever, where the inhabitants are not possessed of some peculiar secrets, either in nature or art, which might be transplanted with success; thus, for instance, in Siberian Tartary, the natives extract a strong spirit from milk, which is a secret probably unknown to the chemists in Europe. In the most savage parts of India they are possessed of the secret of dying vegetable substances scarlet, and likewise that of refining lead into a metal, which, for hardness and color, is little inferior to silver; not one of which secrets but would, in Europe, make a man's fortune. The power of the Asiatics in producing winds, or bringing down rain, the Europeans are apt to treat as fabulous, because they have no instances of the like nature among themselves: but they would have treated the secrets of gunpowder, and the mariner's compass, in the same manner, had they been told the Chinese used such arts before the invention was common with themselves at home.

Of all the English philosophers, I most reverence Bacon, that great and hardy genius; he it is, who, undaunted by the seeming difficulties that oppose, prompts human curiosity to examine every part of nature; and even exhorts man to try whether he cannot subject the tempest, the thunder, and even earthquakes, to human control. Oh! had a man of his daring spirit, of his genius, penetration, and learning, travelled to those countries which have been visited only by the superstitious and mercenary, what might not mankind expect! How would he enlighten the regions to which he travelled! and what a variety of knowledge and useful improvement would he not bring back in exchange!

There is probably no country so barbarous, that would not disclose all it knew, if it received equivalent information; and I am apt to think, that a person who was ready to give more knowledge than he received, would be welcome wherever he came. All his care in travelling should only be, to suit his intellectual banquet to the people with whom he conversed; he should not attempt to teach the unlettered Tartar astronomy, nor yet instruct the polite Chinese in the arts of subsistence; he should endeavor to improve the barbarian in the secrets of living comfortably; and the inhabitants of a more refined country, in the speculative pleasures of science. How much more nobly would a philosopher, thus employed, spend his time, than by sitting at home, earnestly intent upon adding one star more to his catalogue, or one monster more to his collection; or still, if possible, more triflingly sedulous, in the incatenation of fleas, or the sculpture of cherry-stones.

I never consider this subject without being surprised that none of those societies so laudably established in England for the promotion of arts and learning, have ever thought of sending one of their members into the most eastern parts of Asia, to make what discoveries he was able. To be convinced of the utility of such an undertaking, let them but read the relations of their own travellers. It will there be found, that they are as often deceived themselves as they attempt to deceive others. The merchants tell us, perhaps, the price of different commodities, the methods of baling them up, and the properest manner for a European to preserve his health in the country. The missionary, on the other hand, informs us with what pleasure the country to which he was sent embraced Christianity, and the numbers he converted; what methods he took to keep Lent in a region where there were no fish, or the shifts he made to celebrate the rites of his religion, in places where there was neither bread nor wine; such accounts, with the usual appendage of marriages and funerals, inscriptions, rivers, and mountains, make up the whole of a European traveller's diary: but as to all the secrets of which the inhabitants are possessed, those are universally attributed to magic; and when the traveller can give no other account of the wonders he sees performed, he very contentedly ascribes them to the devil.

It was a usual observation of Boyle, the English chemist, that, if every artist would but discover what new observations occurred to him in the exercise of his trade, philosophy would thence gain innumerable improvements. It may be observed with still greater justice, that, if the useful knowledge of every country, howsoever barbarous, was gleaned by a judicious observer, the advantages would be inestimable. Are there not, even in Europe, many useful inventions known or practised but in one place? Their instrument, as an example, for cutting down corn in Germany, is much more handy and expeditious, in my opinion, than the sickle used in England. The cheap and expeditious manner of making vinegar, without previous fermentation, is known only in a part of France. If such discoveries therefore remain still to be known at home, what funds of knowledge might not be collected in countries yet unexplored, or only passed through by ignorant travellers in hasty caravans.

The caution with which foreigners are received in Asia, may be alleged as an objection to such a design. But how readily have several European merchants found admission into regions the most suspicious, under the character of sanjapins, or northern pilgrims? To such not even China itself denies access.

To send out a traveller properly qualified for these purposes, might be an object of national concern; it would, in some measure, repair the breaches made by ambition; and might show that there were still some who boasted a greater name than that of patriots, who professed themselves lovers of men.

The only difficulty would remain in choosing a proper person for so arduous an enterprise. He should be a man of philosophical turn; one apt to deduce consequences of general utility from particular occurrences; neither swollen with pride, nor hardened by prejudice; neither wedded to one particular system, nor instructed only in one particular science; neither wholly a botanist, nor quite an antiquarian, his mind should be tinctured with miscellaneous knowledge; and his manners humanized by an intercourse with men. He should be, in some measure, an enthusiast to the design: fond of travelling, from a rapid imagination, and an innate love of change: furnished with a body capable of sustaining every fatigue, and a heart not easily terrified at danger.

A REVERIE AT THE BOAR'S-HEAD TAVERN, IN EASTCHEAP.

THE improvements we make in mental acquirements only render us each day more sensible of the defects of our constitution: with this in view, therefore, let us often recur to the amusements of youth; endeavor to forget age and wisdom, and, as far as innocence goes, be as much a boy as the best of them.

Let idle declaimers mourn over the degeneracy of the age, but, in my opinion, every age is the same. This I am sure of, that man, in every season, is a poor, fretful being, with no other means to escape the calamities of the times, but by endeavoring to forget them; for, if he attempts to resist, he is certainly undone. If I feel poverty and pain, I am not so hardy as to quarrel with the executioner, even while under correction; I find myself no way disposed to make fine speeches, while I am making wry faces. In a word, let me drink when the fit is on, to make me insensible; and drink when it is over, for joy that I feel pain no longer.

The character of old Falstaff, even with all his faults, gives me more consolation than the most studied efforts of wisdom: I here behold an agreeable old fellow, forgetting age, and showing me the way to be young at sixty-five. Sure I am well able to be as merry, though not so comical, as he. Is it not in my power to have, though not so much wit, at least as much vivacity? Age, care, wisdom, reflection, begone!—I give you to the winds. Let's have t' other bottle: here's to the memory of Shakspeare, Falstaff, and all the merry men of Eastcheap.

Such were the reflections that naturally arose while I sat at the Boar's-head tavern, still kept at Eastcheap. Here, by a pleasant fire, in the very room where old Falstaff cracked his jokes, in the very chair which was sometimes honored by Prince Henry, and sometimes polluted by his immoral, merry companions, I sat and ruminated on the follies of youth; wished to be young again; but was resolved to make the best of life while it lasted, and now and then compared past and present times together. I considered myself as the only living representative of the old knight; and transported my imagination back to the times when the prince and he gave life to the revel, and made even debauchery not disgusting. The room also conspired to throw my reflection back into antiquity: the oak floor, the Gothic windows, and the ponderous chimney-piece, had long withstood the tooth of time: the watchmen had gone twelve: my companions had all stolen off, and none now remained with me but the landlord. From him I could have wished to know the history of a tavern that had such a long succession of customers; I could not help thinking that an account of this kind would be a pleasing contrast of the manners of different ages; but my landlord could give me no information. He continued to doze, and sot, and tell a tedious story, as most other landlords usually do; and, though he said nothing, yet was never silent; one good joke followed another good joke, and the best joke of all was generally begun towards the end of a bottle. I found at last, however, his wine and his conversation operate by degrees: he insensibly began to alter his appearance. His cravat seemed quilled into a ruff, and his breeches swelled into a fardingale. I now fancied him changing sexes; and, as my eyes began to close in slumber, I imagined my fat landlord actually converted into as fat a landlady. However, sleep made but few changes in my situation: the tavern, the apartment, and the table, continued as before; nothing suffered mutation but my host, who was fairly altered into a gentlewoman, whom I knew to be Dame Quickly, mistress of this tavern in the days of Sir John; and the liquor we were drinking, which seemed converted into sack and sugar.

"My dear Mrs. Quickly," cried I, (for I knew her perfectly well at first sight), "I am heartily glad to see you. How have you left Falstaff, Pistol, and the rest of our friends below stairs? Brave and hearty, I hope?" "In good sooth," replied she, "he did deserve to live for ever; but he maketh foul work on't where he hath flitted. Queen Proserpine and he have quarrelled, for his attempting a rape upon her divinity; and were it not that she still had bowels of compassion, it more than seems probable he might have now been sprawling in Tartarus."

I now found that spirits still preserve the frailties of the flesh; and that, according to the laws of criticism and dreaming, ghosts have been known to be guilty of even more than Platonic affection: wherefore, as I found her too much moved on such a topic to proceed, I was resolved to change the subject; and, desiring she would pledge me in a bumper, observed with a sigh, that our sack was nothing now to what it was in former days. "Ah, Mrs. Quickly, those were merry times when you drew sack for Prince Henry: men were twice as strong, and twice as wise, and much braver, and ten thousand times more charitable, than now. Those were the times! The battle of Agincourt was a victory indeed! Ever since that, we have only been degenerating; and I have lived to see the day when drinking is no longer fashionable. When men wear clean shirts, and women show their necks and arms, all are degenerated, Mrs. Quickly; and we shall probably, in another century, be frittered away into beaux or monkeys. Had you been on earth to see what I have seen, it would congeal all the blood in your body (your soul, I mean). Why, our very nobility now have the intolerable arrogance, in spite of what is every day remonstrated from the press; our very nobility, I say, have the assurance to frequent assemblies, and presume to be as merry as the vulgar. See, my very friends have scarce manhood enough to sit till eleven; and I only am left to make a night on't. Pr'ythee do me the favor to console me a little for their absence by the story of your own adventures, or the history of the tavern where we are now sitting. I fancy the narrative may have something singular."

"Observe this apartment," interrupted my companion, of neat device and excellent workmanship. In this room I have lived, child, woman, and ghost, more than three hundred years; I am ordered by Pluto to keep an annual register of every transaction that passeth here: and I have whilom compiled three hundred tomes, which eftsoons may be submitted to thy regards." "None of your whiloms nor eftsoons, Mrs. Quickly, if you please," I replied; "I know you can talk every whit as well as I can: for, as you have lived here so long, it is but natural to suppose you should learn the conversation of the company

Believe me, dame, at best, you have neither too much sense, nor too much language, to spare; so give me both as well as you can: but first, my service to you; old women should water their clay a little now and then; and now to your story."

"The story of my own adventures," replied the vision, "is but short and unsatisfactory; for, believe me, Mr. Rigmarole, believe me, a woman with a butt of sack at her elbow is never long-lived. Sir John's death afflicted me to such a degree, that I sincerely believe, to drown sorrow, I drank more liquor myself than I drew for my customers: my grief was sincere, and the sack was excellent. The prior of a neighboring convent (for our priors then had as much power as a Middlesex justice now), he, I say, it was who gave me license for keeping a disorderly house; upon condition that I should never make hard bargains with the clergy: that he should have a bottle of sack every morning, and the liberty of confessing which of my girls he thought proper in private every night. I had continued for several years to pay this tribute; and he, it must be confessed, continued as rigorously to exact it. I grew old insensibly; my customers continued, however, to compliment my looks while I was by, but I could hear them say I was wearing when my back was turned. The prior, however, still was constant, and so were half his convent; but one fatal morning he missed the usual beverage, for I had incautiously drunk over-night the last bottle myself. What will you have on't? The very next day Doll Tearsheet and I were sent to the house of correction, and accused of keeping a low bawdy-house. In short, we were so well purified there with stripes, mortification and penance, that we were afterward utterly unfit for worldly conversation: though sack would have killed me, had I stuck to it, yet I soon died for want of a drop of something comfortable, and fairly left my body to the care of the beadle.

"Such is my own history; but that of the tavern, where I have ever since been stationed, affords greater variety. In the history of this, which is one of the oldest in London, you may view the different manners, pleasures, and follies of men, at different periods. You will find mankind neither better nor worse now than formerly; the vices of an uncivilized people are generally more detestable, though not so frequent, as those in polite society. It is the same luxury which formerly stuffed your alderman with plum-porridge, and now crams him with turtle. It is the same low ambition that formerly induced a courtier to give up his religion to please his king, and now persuades him to give up his conscience to please his minister. It is the same vanity that formerly stained our ladies' cheeks and necks with woad, and now paints them with carmine. Your ancient Briton formerly powdered his hair with red earth, like brick-dust, in order to appear frightful; your modern Briton cuts his hair on the crown, and plasters it with hogs'-lard and flour; and this to make him look killing. It is the same vanity, the same folly, and the same vice, only appearing different, as viewed through the glass of fashion. In a word, all mankind are a ——"

"Sure the woman is dreaming," interrupted I—"None

of your reflections, Mrs. Quickly, if you love me; they only give me the spleen. Tell me your history at once. I love stories, but hate reasoning."

"If you please, then, sir," returned my companion, "I'll read you an abstract, which I made, of the three hundred volumes I mentioned just now:

"My body was no sooner laid in the dust, than the prior and several of his convent came to purify the tavern from the pollutions with which they said I had filled it. Masses were said in every room, relics were exposed upon every piece of furniture, and the whole house washed with a deluge of holy water. My habitation was soon converted into a monastery; instead of customers now applying for sack and sugar, my rooms were crowded with images, relics, saints, whores, and friars. Instead of being a scene of occasional debauchery, it was now filled with continued lewdness. The prior led the fashion, and the whole convent imitated his pious example. Matrons came hither to confess their sins, and to commit new. Virgins came hither who seldom went virgins away. Nor was this a convent peculiarly wicked; every convent at that period was equally fond of pleasure, and gave a boundless loose to appetite. The laws allowed it; each priest had a right to a favorite companion, and a power of discarding her as often as he pleased. The laity grumbled, quarrelled with their wives and daughters, hated their confessors, and maintained them in opulence and ease. These, these were happy times, Mr. Rigmarole: these were times of piety, bravery, and simplicity!"—"Not so very happy, neither, good madam; pretty much like the present: those that labor, starve; and those that do nothing wear fine clothes and live in luxury."

"In this manner the fathers lived, for some years, without molestation; they transgressed, confessed themselves to each other, and were forgiven. One evening, however, our prior keeping a lady of distinction somewhat too long at confession, her husband unexpectedly came upon them, and testified all the indignation which was natural upon such an occasion. The prior assured the gentleman that it was the devil who had put it into his heart; and the lady was very certain, that she was under the influence of magic, or she could never have behaved in so unfaithful a manner. The husband, however, was not to be put off by such evasions, but summoned both before the tribunal of justice. His proofs were flagrant, and he expected large damages. Such, indeed, he had a right to expect, were the tribunals of those days constituted in the same manner as they are now. The cause of the priest was to be tried before an assembly of priests; and a layman was to expect redress only from their impartiality and candor. What plea then do you think the prior made to obviate this accusation? He denied the fact, and challenged the plaintiff to try the merits of their cause by single combat. It was a little hard, you may be sure, upon the poor gentleman, not only to be made a cuckold, but to be obliged to fight a duel into the bargain; yet such was the justice of the times. The prior threw down his glove, and the injured husband was obliged to take it up, in token of his accepting the challenge. Upon this, the priest supplied his champion, for it was not lawful for the clergy to fight; and the defendant and plaintiff, according to custom, were put in prison; both ordered to fast and pray, every method being previously used to induce both to a confession of the truth. After a month's imprisonment, the hair of each was cut, their bodies anointed with oil, the field of battle appointed, and guarded by soldiers, while his majesty presided over the whole in person. Both the champions were sworn not to seek victory either by fraud or magic. They prayed and confessed upon their knees; and, after these ceremonies, the rest was left to the courage and conduct of the combatants. As the champion whom the prior had pitched upon, had fought six or eight times upon similar occasions, it was no way extraordinary to find him victorious in the present combat. In short, the husband was discomfited; he was taken from the field of battle, stripped to his shirt, and, after one of his legs was cut off, as justice ordained in such cases, he was hanged as a terror to future offenders. These, these were the times, Mr. Rigmarole! you see how much more just, and wise, and valiant, our ancestors were than we." "I rather fancy, madam, that the times then were pretty much like our own; where a multiplicity of laws give a judge as much power as a want of law; since he is ever sure to find among the number some to countenance his partiality."

"Our convent, victorious over their enemies, now gave a loose to every demonstration of joy. The lady became a nun, the prior was made a bishop, and three Wickliffites were burned in the illuminations and fireworks that were made on the present occasion. Our convent now began to enjoy a very high degree of reputation. There was not one in London that had the character of hating heretics so much as ours. Ladies of the first distinction chose from our convent their confessors; in short, it flourished, and might have flourished to this hour, but for a fatal accident, which terminated in its overthrow. The lady whom the prior had placed in a nunnery, and whom he continued to visit for some time with great punctuality, began at last to perceive that she was quite forsaken. Secluded from conversation, as usual, she now entertained the visions of a devotee; found herself strangely disturbed; but hesitated in determining, whether she was possessed by an angel or a demon. She was not long in suspense: for, upon vomiting a large quantity of crooked pins, and finding the palms of her hands turned outwards, she quickly concluded that she was possessed by the devil. She soon lost entirely the use of speech; and when she seemed to speak, every body that was present perceived that her voice was not her own, but that of the devil within her. In short, she was bewitched; and all the difficulty lay in determining who it could be that bewitched her. The nuns and the monks all demanded the magician's name, but the devil made no reply; for he knew they had no authority to ask questions. By the rules of witchcraft, when an evil spirit has taken possession, he may refuse to answer any questions asked him, unless they are put by a bishop, and to these he is obliged to reply. A bishop, therefore, was sent for, and now the whole secret came out: the devil reluctantly owned that he was a servant of the prior; that by his command he resided in his present habitation; and that, without his command, he was resolved to keep in possession. The bishop was an able exorcist; he drove the devil out by force of mystical arms; the prior was arraigned for witchcraft; the witnesses were strong and numerous against him, not less than fourteen persons being by who heard the devil speak Latin. There was no resisting such a cloud of witnesses; thé prior was condemned; and he who had assisted at so many burnings, was burned himself in turn. These were times, Mr. Rigmarole; the people of those times were not infidels, as now, but sincere believers!" — "Equally faulty with ourselves, they believed what the devil was pleased to tell them; and we seem resolved, at last, to believe neither God nor devil."

"After such a stain upon the convent, it was not to be supposed it could subsist any longer; the fathers were ordered to decamp, and the house was once again converted into a tavern. The king conferred it on one of his cast-off mistresses; she was constituted landlady by royal authority; and, as the tavern was in the neighborhood of the court, and the mistress a very polite woman, it began to have more business than ever, and sometimes took not less than four shillings a-day.

"But perhaps you are desirous of knowing what were the peculiar qualifications of women of fashion at that period; and in a description of the present landlady, you will have a tolerable idea of all the rest. This lady was the daughter of a nobleman, and received such an education in the country as became her quality, beauty, and great expectations. She could make shifts and hose for herself and all the servants of the family, when she was twelve years old. She knew the names of the four-and-twenty letters, so that it was impossible to bewitch her;

and this was a greater piece of learning than any lady in the whole country could pretend to. She was always up early, and saw breakfast served in the great hall by six o'clock. At this scene of festivity she generally improved good-humor, by telling her dreams, relating stories of spirits, several of which she herself had seen, and one of which she was reported to have killed with a black-hafted knife. From hence she usually went to make pastry in the larder, and here she was followed by her sweet-hearts, who were much helped on in conversation by struggling with her for kisses. About ten, miss generally went to play at hot-cockles and blindman's buff in the parlor; and when the young folks (for they seldom played at hot-cockles when grown old) were tired of such amusements, the gentlemen entertained miss with the history of their greyhounds, bear-baitings, and victories at cudgel-playing. If the weather was fine, they ran at the ring, or shot at butts, while miss held in her hand a riband, with which she adorned the conqueror. Her mental qualifications were exactly fitted to her external accomplishments. Before she was fifteen she could tell the story of Jack the Giant Killer; could name every mountain that was inhabited by fairies; knew a witch at first sight; and could repeat four Latin prayers without a prompter. Her dress was perfectly fashionable; her arms and her hair were completely covered; a monstrous muff was put round her neck, so that her head seemed like that of John the Baptist placed in a charger. In short, when completely equipped, her appearance was so very modest, that she discovered little more than her nose. These were the times, Mr. Rigmarole, when every lady that had a good nose might set up for a beauty; when every woman that could tell stories might be cried up for a wit." "I am as much displeased at those dresses which conceal too much, as at those which discover too much: I am equally an enemy to a female dunce, or a female pedant."

"You may be sure that miss chose a husband with qualifications resembling her own; she pitched upon a courtier equally remarkable for hunting and drinking, who had given several proofs of his great virility among the daughters of his tenants and domestics. They fell in love at first sight (for such was the gallantry of the times), were married, came to court, and madam appeared with superior qualifications. The king was struck with her beauty. All property was at the king's command; the husband was obliged to resign all pretensions in his wife to the sovereign whom God anointed, to commit adultery where he thought proper. The king loved her for some time; but, at length, repenting of his misdeeds, and instigated by his father confessor, from a principle of conscience, removed her from his levee to the bar of this tavern, and took a new mistress in her stead. Let it not surprise you to behold the mistress of a king degraded to so humble an office. As the ladies had no mental accomplishments, a good face was enough to raise them to the royal couch; and she who was this day a royal mistress, might the next, when her beauty palled upon enjoyment, be doomed to infamy and want.

"Under the care of this lady, the tavern grew into great reputation; the courtiers had not yet learned to game, but they paid it off by drinking; drunkenness is ever the vice of a barbarous, and gaming of a luxurious age. They had not such frequent entertainments as the moderns have, but were more expensive and more luxurious in those they had. All their fooleries were more elaborate, and more admired by the great and the vulgar, than now. A courtier has been known to spend his whole fortune at a single combat; a king to mortgage his dominions to furnish out the frippery of a tournament. There were certain days appointed for riot and debauchery, and to be sober at such times was reputed a crime. Kings themselves set the example; and I have seen monarchs in this room drunk before the entertainment was half concluded. These were the times, sir, when the kings kept mistresses, and got drunk in public; they were too plain and simple in those happy times to hide their vices, and act the hypocrite as now." "Lord, Mrs. Quickly!" interrupting her, "I expected to hear a story, and here you are going to tell me I know not what of times and vices; pr'ythee let me entreat thee once more to waive reflections, and give thy history without deviation."

"No lady upon earth," continued my visionary correspondent, "knew how to put off her damaged wine or women with more art than she. When these grew flat, or those paltry, it was but changing their names; the wine became excellent, and the girls agreeable. She was also possessed of the engaging leer, the chuck under the chin, winked at a double entendre, could nick the opportunity of calling for something comfortable, and perfectly understood the distinct moments when to withdraw. The gallants of those times pretty much resembled the bloods of ours; they were fond of pleasure, but quite ignorant of the art of refining upon it: thus a court-bawd of those times resembled the common, low-lived harridan of a modern bagnio. Witness, ye powers of debauchery! how often have I been present at the various appearances of drunkenness, riot, guilt, and brutality. A tavern is a true picture of human infirmity; in history we find only one side of the age exhibited to our view; but in the accounts of a tavern we see every age equally absurd and equally vicious.

Upon this lady's decease, the tavern was successively occupied by adventurers, bullies, pimps, and gamesters. Towards the conclusion of the reign of Henry VII. gaming was more universally practised in England than even now. Kings themselves have been known to play off, at primero, not only all the money and jewels they could part with, but the very images in churches. The last Henry played away, in this very room, not only the four great bells of St. Paul's cathedral, but the fine image of St. Paul, which stood upon the top of the spire, to Sir Miles Partridge, who took them down the next day, and sold them by auction. Have you then any cause to regret being born in the times you now live in, or do you still believe that human nature continues to run on declining every age? If we observe the actions of the busy part of mankind, your ancestors will be found infinitely more gross, servile, and even dishonest, than you. If, forsaking history, we only trace them in their hours of amusement and dissipation, we shall find them more sensual, more entirely devoted to pleasure, and infinitely more selfish.

"The last hostess of note I find upon record was Jane Rouse. She was born among the lower ranks of the people; and by frugality and extreme complaisance, contrived to acquire a moderate fortune: this she might have enjoyed for many years, had she not unfortunately quarrelled with one of her neighbors, a woman who was in high repute for sanctity through the whole parish. In the times of which I speak, two women seldom quarrelled that one did not accuse the other of witchcraft, and she who first contrived to vomit crooked pins was sure to come off victorious. The scandal of a modern tea-table differs widely from the scandal of former times; the fascination of a lady's eyes, at present, is regarded as a compliment; but if a lady formerly should be accused of having witchcraft in her eyes, it were much better, both for her soul and body, that she had no eyes at all.

"In short, Jane Rouse was accused of witchcraft, and though she made the best defence she could, it was all to no purpose; she was taken from her own bar to the bar of the Old Bailey, condemned, and executed accordingly. These were times, indeed! when even women could not scold in safety.

"Since her time the tavern underwent several revolutions, according to the spirit of the times, or the disposition of the reigning monarch. It was this day a brothel, and the next a conventicle for enthusiasts. It was one year noted for harboring whigs, and the next infamous for a retreat to tories. Some years ago it was in high vogue, but at present it seems declining. This only may be remarked in general, that whenever taverns flourish most, the times are then most extravagant and luxurious."

"Lord, Mrs. Quickly!" interrupted I, "you have really deceived me; I expected a romance, and here you have been this half-hour giving me only a description of the spirit of the times; if you have nothing but tedious remarks to communicate, seek some other hearer; I am determined to hearken only to stories."

I had scarce concluded, when my eyes and ears seemed opened to my landlord, who had been all this while giving me an account of the repairs he had made in the house, and was now got into the story of the cracked glass in the dining-room.

ON QUACK DOCTORS.

WHATEVER may be the merits of the English in other sciences, they seem peculiarly excellent in the art of healing. There is scarcely a disorder incident to humanity, against which our advertising doctors are not possessed with a most infallible antidote. The professors of other arts confess the inevitable intricacy of things; talk with doubt, and decide with hesitation: but doubting is entirely unknown in medicine: the advertising professors here delight in cases of difficulty; be the disorder ever so desperate or radical, you will find numbers in every street, who, by levelling a pill at the part affected, promise a certain cure without loss of time, knowledge of a bedfellow, or hinderance of business.

When I consider the assiduity of this profession, their benevolence amazes me. They not only, in general, give their medicines for half value, but use the most persuasive remonstrances to induce the sick to come and be cured. Sure there must be something strangely obstinate in an English patient who refuses so much health upon such easy terms! Does he take a pride in being bloated with a dropsy? does he find pleasure in the alternations of an intermittent fever? or feel as much satisfaction in nursing up his gout, as he found pleasure in acquiring it? He must; otherwise he would never reject such repeated assurances of instant relief. What can be more convincing than the manner in which the sick are invited to be well? The doctor first begs the most earnest attention of the public to what he is going to propose; he solemnly affirms the pill was never found to want success; he produces a list of those who have been rescued from the grave by taking it. Yet, notwithstanding all this, there are many here who now and then think proper to be sick: — only sick, did I say? there are some who even think proper to die! Yes, by the head of Confucius, they die! though they might have purchased the health-restoring specific for half-a-crown at every corner.

I can never enough admire the sagacity of this country for the encouragement given to the professors of this art; with what indulgence does she foster up those of her own growth, and kindly cherish those that come from abroad! Like a skilful gardener, she invites them from every foreign climate to herself. Here every great exotic strikes root as soon as imported, and feels the genial beam of favor; while the mighty metropolis, like one vast munificent dunghill, receives them indiscriminately to her breast, and supplies each with more than native nourishment.

In other countries the physician pretends to cure disorders in the lump; the same doctor who combats the gout in the toe, shall pretend to prescribe for a pain in the head; and he who at one time cures a consumption, shall at another give drugs for a dropsy. How absurd and ridiculous! this is being a mere jack of all trades. Is the animal machine less complicated than a brass pin? Not less than ten different hands are required to make a brass pin; and shall the body be set right by one single operator?

The English are sensible of the force of this reasoning; they have therefore one doctor for the eyes, another for the toes; they have their sciatica doctors, and inoculating doctors; they have one doctor, who is modestly content with securing them from bug bites, and five hundred who prescribe for the bite of mad dogs.

But as nothing pleases curiosity m e than anecdotes of the great, however minute or trifling, I must present you, inadequate as my abilities are to the s ject, with an account of one or two of those personages who lead in this honorable profession.

The first upon the list of glory is Doctor Richard Rock, F. U. N. This great man is short of stature, is fat, and waddles as he walks. He always wears a white three-tailed wig, nicely combed, and frizzled upon each cheek. Sometimes he carries a cane, but a hat never; it is indeed very remarkable that this extraordinary personage should never wear a hat; but so it is, a hat he never wears. He is usually drawn, at the top of his own bills, sitting in his arm-chair, holding a little bottle between his finger and thumb, and surrounded with rotten teeth, nippers, pills, packets, and gallipots. No man can promise fairer or better than he; for, as he observes, "Be your disorder never so far gone, be under no uneasiness, make yourself quite easy, I can cure you."

The next in fame, though by some reckoned of equal pretensions, is Dr. Timothy Franks, F. O. G. H. living in the Old Bailey. As Rock is remarkably squab, his great rival Franks is as remarkably tall. He was born in the year of the Christian era 1692, and is, while I now write, exactly sixty-eight years three months and four days old. Age, however, has no ways impaired his usual health and vivacity; I am told he generally walks with his breast open. This gentleman, who is of a mixed reputation, is particularly remarkable for a becoming assurance, which carries him gently through life; for, except Dr. Rock, none are more blessed with the advantages of face than Dr. Franks.

And yet the great have their foibles as well as the little. I am almost ashamed to mention it. Let the foibles of the great rest in peace. Yet I must impart the whole. These two great men are actually now at variance; like mere men, mere common mortals. Rock advises the world to beware of bog-trotting quacks: Franks retorts the wit and sarcasm, by fixing on his rival the odious appellation of Dumpling Dick. He calls the serious Doctor Rock, Dumpling Dick! Head of Confucius, what profanation! Dumpling Dick! What a pity, ye powers, that the learned, who were born mutually to assist in enlightening the world, should thus differ among themselves, and make even the profession ridiculous! Sure the world is wide enough, at least, for two great personages to figure in: men of science should leave controversy to the little world below them; and then we might see Rock and Franks walking together, hand in hand, smiling onward to immortality.

ADVENTURES OF A STROLLING PLAYER.

I AM fond of amusement, in whatever company it is to be found: and wit, though dressed in rags, is ever pleasing to me. I went some days ago to take a walk in St. James's Park, about the hour in which company leave it to go to dinner. There were but few in the walks, and those who stayed seemed by their looks rather more willing to forget that they had an appetite, than gain one. I sat down on one of the benches, at the other end of which was seated a man in very shabby clothes.

We continued to groan, to hem, and to cough, as usual upon such occasions; and, at last, ventured upon conversation. "I beg pardon, sir," cried I, "but I think I have seen you before; your face is familiar to me." "Yes, sir," replied he, "I have a good familiar face, as my friends tell me. I am as well known in every town in England as the dromedary, or live crocodile. You must understand, sir, that I have been these sixteen years merry-andrew to a puppet-show: last Bartholomew fair my master and I quarrelled, beat each other, and parted; he to sell his puppets to the pincushion-makers in Rosemary-lane, and I to starve in St. James's Park."

"I am sorry, sir, that a person of your appearance should labor under any difficulties." "O, sir," returned he, "my appearance is very much at your service: but, though I cannot boast of eating much, yet there are few that are merrier; if I had twenty thousand a year I should be very merry; and, thank the Fates, though not worth a groat, I am very merry still. If I have three-pence in my pocket, I never refuse to be my three half-pence; and, if I have no money, I never scorn to be treated by any that are kind enough to pay the reckoning. What think you, sir, of a steak and a tankard! You shall treat me now, and I will treat you again when I find you in the Park in love with eating, and without money to pay for a dinner."

As I never refuse a small expense for the sake of a merry companion, we instantly adjourned to a neighboring ale-house, and, in a few moments, had a frothing tankard, and a smoking steak, spread on the table before us. It is impossible to express how much the sight of such good cheer improved my companion's vivacity. "I like this dinner, sir," says he, "for three reasons; first, because I am naturally fond of beef; secondly, because I am hungry; and, thirdly and lastly, because I get it for nothing; no meat eats so sweet as that for which we do not pay."

He therefore now fell to, and his appetite seemed to correspond with his inclination. After dinner was over, he observed that the steak was tough; "and yet, sir," returns he, "bad as it was, it seemed a rump-steak to me. O the delights of poverty and a good appetite! We beggars are the very fondlings of Nature; the rich she treats like an arrant step-mother; they are pleased with nothing; cut a steak from what part you will, and it is insupportably tough; dress it up with pickles, and even pickles cannot procure them an appetite. But the whole creation is filled with good things for the beggar; Calvert's butt out-tastes champagne, and Sedgeley's home-brewed excels tokay. Joy, joy, my blood; though our estates lie no where, we have fortunes wherever we go. If an inundation sweeps away half the grounds in Cornwall, I am content: I have no land there: if the stocks sink, that gives me no uneasiness; I am no Jew." The fellow's vivacity, joined to his poverty, I own, raised my curiosity to know something of his life and circumstances; and I entreated that he would indulge my desire. "That I will," said he, "and welcome; only let us drink, to prevent our sleeping; let us have another tankard, while we are awake; let us have another tankard; for, ah, how charming a tankard looks when full!

"You must know, then, that I am very well descended; my ancestors have made some noise in the world, for my mother cried oysters, and my father beat a drum: I am told we have even had some trumpeters in our family. Many a nobleman cannot show so respectful a genealogy; but that is neither here nor there. As I was their only child, my father designed to breed me up to his own employment, which was that of a drummer to a puppet-show. Thus the whole employment of my younger years was that of interpreter to Punch and King Solomon in all his glory. But, though my father was very fond of instructing me in beating all the marches and points of war, I made no very great progress, because I naturally had no ear for music; so at the age of fifteen, I went and listed for a soldier. As I had ever hated beating a drum, so I soon found that I disliked carrying a musket also; neither the one trade nor the other was to my taste, for I was by nature fond of being a gentleman: besides, I was obliged to obey my captain; he has his will, I have mine and you have yours: now I very reasonably concluded, that it was much more comfortable for a man to obey his own will than another's.

The life of a soldier soon therefore gave me the spleen; I asked leave to quit the service; but, as I was tall and strong, my captain thanked me for my kind intention, and said, because he had a regard for me we should not part. I wrote to my father a very dismal, penitent letter, and desired that he would raise money to pay for my discharge; but the good man was as fond of drinking as I was (sir, my service to you), and those who are fond of drinking never pay for other people's discharges: in short, he never answered my letter. What could be done? If I have not money, said I to myself, to pay for my discharge, I must find an equivalent some other way; and that must be by running away. I deserted, and that answered my purpose every bit as well as if I had bought my discharge.

"Well, I was now fairly rid of my military employment, I sold my soldier's clothes, bought worse, and, in order not to be overtaken, took the most unfrequented roads possible. One evening, as I was entering a village, I perceived a man, whom I afterward found to be the curate of the parish, thrown from his horse in a miry road, and almost smothered in the mud. He desired my assistance: I gave it, and drew him out with some difficulty. He thanked me for my trouble and was going off; but I followed him home, for I loved always to have a man thank me at his own door. The curate asked a hundred questions; as, whose son I was; from whence I came; and whether I would be faithful. I answered him greatly to his satisfaction, and gave myself one of the best characters in the world for sobriety (sir, I have the honor of drinking your health), discretion and fidelity. To make a long story short, he wanted a servant, and hired me. With him I lived but two months; we did not much like each other; I was fond of eating, and he gave me but little to eat; I loved a pretty girl, and the old woman, my fellow servant, was ill-natured and ugly. As they endeavored to starve me between them, I made a pious resolution to prevent their committing murder; I stole the eggs as soon as they were laid; I emptied every unfinished bottle that I could lay my hands on; whatever eatable came in my way was sure to disappear: in short, they found I would not do; so I was discharged one morning, and paid three shillings and sixpence for two months' wages.

"While my money was getting ready, I employed myself in making preparations for my departure; two hens were hatching in an out-house; I went and took the eggs from habit, and, not to separate the parents from the children, I lodged hens and all in my knapsack. After this piece of frugality, I returned to receive my money, and, with my knapsack on my back and a staff in my hand, I bid adieu, with tears in my eyes, to my old benefactor. I had not gone far from the house, when I heard behind me the cry of "Stop thief!" but this only increased my despatch: it would have been foolish for me to stop, as I knew the voice could not be levelled at me. But hold, I think I passed those two months at the curate's without drinking; come, the times are dry, and may this be my poison if ever I spent two more pious, stupid months in all my life.

"Well, after travelling some days, whom should I light upon but a company of strolling players? The moment I saw them at a distance, my heart warmed to them: I had a sort of natural love for every thing of the vagabond order; they were employed in settling their baggage which had been overturned in a narrow way; I offered my assistance, which they accepted; and we soon became so well acquainted, that they took me as a servant. This was a paradise to me; they sung, danced, drank, ate, and travelled, all at the same time. By the blood of the Mirabels, I thought I had never lived till then; I grew as merry as a grig, and laughed at every word that was spoken. They liked me as much as I liked them; I was a very good figure, as you see; and, though I was poor, I was not modest.

"I love a straggling life above all things in the world; sometimes good, sometimes bad; to be warm to-day and cold to-morrow; to eat when one can get it, and drink when (the tankard is out) it stands before me. We arrived that evening at Tenterden, and took a large room at the Greyhound, where we resolved to exhibit Romeo and Juliet, with the funeral procession, the grave and the garden scene. Romeo was to be performed by a gentleman from the theatre royal in Drury-lane; Juliet, by a lady who had never appeared on any stage before; and I was to snuff the candles; all excellent in our way. We had figures enough, but the difficulty was to dress them. The same coat that served Romeo, turned with the blue lining outwards, served for his friend Mercutio; a large piece of crape sufficed at once for Juliet's petticoat and pall; a pestle and mortar, from a neighboring apothecary's, answered all the purposes of a bell: and our landlord's own family, wrapped in white sheets, served to fill up the procession. In short, there were but three figures among us that might be said to be dressed with any propriety; I mean the nurse, the starved apothecary, and myself. Our performance gave universal satisfaction: the whole audience were enchanted with our powers.

"There is one rule by which a strolling player may be ever secure of success; that is, in our theatrical way of expressing it, to make a great deal of the character. To speak and act as in common life, is not playing, nor is it what people come to see: natural speaking, like sweet wine, runs glibly over the palate, and scarce leaves any taste behind it: but being high in a part resembles vinegar, which grates upon the taste, and one feels it while he is drinking. To please in town or country, the way is, to cry, wring, cringe into attitudes, mark the emphasis, slap the pockets, and labor like one in the falling sickness; that is the way to work for applause; that is the way to gain it.

"As we received much reputation for our skill on this first exhibition, it was but natural for me to ascribe part of the success to myself; I snuffed the candles; and, let me tell you, that without a candle-snuffer, the piece would lose half its embellishments. In this manner we continued a fortnight, and drew tolerable houses: but the evening before our intended departure, we gave out our very best piece, in which all our strength was to be exerted. We had great expectations from this, and even doubled our prices, when, behold! one of the principal actors fell ill of a violent fever. This was a stroke like thunder to our little company: they were resolved to go, in a body, to scold the man for falling sick at so inconvenient a time, and that too of a disorder that threatened to be expensive. I seized the moment, and offered to act the part myself in his stead. The case was desperate; they accepted my offer; and I accordingly sat down with the part in my hand, and a tankard before me (sir, your health), and studied the character, which was to be rehearsed the next day, and played soon after.

"I found my memory excessively helped by drinking: I learned my part with astonishing rapidity, and bid adieu to snuffing candles ever after. I found that Nature had designed me for more noble employments, and I was resolved to take her when in the humor. We got together in order to rehearse, and I informed my companions, masters now no longer, of the surprising change I felt within me. Let the sick man, said I, be under no uneasiness to get well again; I'll fill his place to universal satisfaction: he may even die, if he thinks proper; I'll engage that he shall never be missed. I rehearsed before them, strutted, ranted, and received applause. They soon gave out that a new actor of eminence was to appear, and immediately all the genteel places were bespoke. Before I ascended the stage, however, I concluded within myself, that, as I brought money to the house, I ought to have my share in the profits. Gentlemen (said I, addressing our company), I do n't pretend to direct you; far be it from me to treat you with so much ingratitude; you have published my name in the bills with the utmost good-nature; and, as affairs stand, cannot act without me; so, gentlemen, to show you my gratitude, I expect to be paid for my acting as much as any of you, otherwise I declare off; I'll brandish my snuffers and clip candles as usual. This was a very disagreeable proposal, but they found that it was impossible to refuse it; it was irresistible, it was adamant: they consented, and I went on in king Bajazet: my frowning brows bound with a stocking stuffed into a turban, while on my captived arms I brandished a jack-chain. Nature seemed to have fitted me for the part; I was tall, and had a loud voice; my very entrance excited universal applause: I looked round on the audience with a smile, and made a most low and graceful bow, for that is the rule among us. As it was a very passionate part, I invigorated my spirits with three full glasses (the tankard is almost out) of brandy. By Alla! it is almost inconceivable how I went through it. Tamerlane was but a fool to me; though he was sometimes loud enough too, yet I was still louder than he; but then, besides, I had attitudes in abundance; in general, I kept my arms folded up thus upon the pit of my stomach; it is the way at Drury-lane, and has always a fine effect. The tankard would sink to the bottom before I could get through the whole of my merits: in short, I came off like a prodigy; and, such was my success, that I could ravish the laurels even from a surloin of beef. The principal gentlemen and ladies of the town came to me, after the play was over, to compliment me on my success: one praised my voice, another my person: Upon my word, says the squire's lady, he will make one of the finest actors in Europe; I say it, and I think I am something of a judge. Praise in the beginning is agreeable enough, and we receive it as a favor; but when it comes in great quantities we regard it only as a debt, which nothing but our merit could extort; instead of thanking them, I internally applauded myself. We were desired to give our piece a second time; we obeyed, and I was applauded even more than before.

"At last we left the town, in order to be at a horse-race some distance from thence. I shall never think of Tenterden without tears of gratitude and respect. The ladies and gentlemen there, take my word for it, are very good judges of plays and actors. Come, let us drink their healths, if you please, sir. We quitted the town, I say: and there was a wide difference between my coming in and going out: I entered the town a candle snuffer, and I quitted it a hero! — Such is the world — little to-day, and great to-morrow. I could say a great deal more upon that subject, something truly sublime, upon the ups and downs of fortune; but it would give us both the spleen, and so I shall pass it over.

"The races were ended before we arrived at the next town, which was no small disappointment to our company; however, we were resolved to take all we could get. I played capital characters there too, and came off with my usual brilliancy. I sincerely believe I should have been the first actor in Europe, had my growing merit been properly cultivated; but there came an unkindly frost which nipped me in the bud, and levelled me once more down to the common standard of humanity. I played Sir Harry Wildair; all the country ladies were charmed; if I but drew out my snuff-box, the whole house was in a roar of rapture; when I exercised my cudgel, I thought they would have fallen into convulsions.

"There was here a lady, who had received an education of nine months in London, and this gave her pretensions to taste, which rendered her the indisputable mistress of the ceremonies wherever she came. She was informed of my merits: every body praised me: yet she refused at first going to see me perform; she could not conceive, she said, anything but stuff from a stroller; talked something in praise of Garrick, and amazed the ladies with her skill in enunciations, tones and cadences. She was at last, however, prevailed upon to go; and it was privately intimated to me what a judge was to be present at my next exhibition: however, no way intimidated, I came on in Sir Harry, one hand stuck in my breeches, and the other in my bosom, as ususal at Drury-lane; but, instead of looking at me, I perceived the whole audience had their eyes turned upon the lady who had been nine months in London; from her they expected the decision which was to secure the general's truncheon in my hands, or sink me down into a theatrical letter-carrier. I opened my snuff-box, took snuff; the lady was solemn, and so were the rest. I broke my cudgel on Alderman Smuggler's back; still gloomy, melancholy all; the lady groaned and shrugged her shoulders. I attempted, by laughing myself, to excite at least a smile; but the devil a cheek could I perceive wrinkled into sympathy. I found it would not do; all my good-humor now became forced; my laughter was converted into hysteric grinning; and while I pretended spirits, my eyes showed the agony of my heart! In short, the lady came with an intention to be displeased, and displeased she was; my fame expired:—I am here, and —— the tankard is no more!"

RULES ENJOINED TO BE OBSERVED AT A RUSSIAN ASSEMBLY.

When Catharina Alexowna was made empress of Russia, the women were in an actual state of bondage; but she undertook to introduce mixed assemblies, as in other parts of Europe; she altered the women's dress by substituting the fashions of England; instead of furs, she brought in the use of taffeta and damask; and cornets and commodes instead of caps of sable. The women now found themselves no longer shut up in separate apartments, but saw company, visited each other, and were present at every entertainment.

But as the laws to this effect were directed to a savage people, it is amusing enough to see the manner in which the ordinances ran. Assemblies were quite unknown among them: the czarina was satisfied with introducing them, for she found it impossible to render them polite. An ordinance was therefore published according to their notions of breeding, which, as it is a curiosity, and has never been before printed that we know of, we shall give our readers.

I. The person at whose house the assembly is to be kept, shall signify the same by hanging out a bill, or by giving some other public notice, by way of advertisment, to persons of both sexes.

II. The assembly shall not be open sooner than four or five o'clock in the afternoon, nor continue longer than ten at night.

III. The master of the house shall not be obliged to meet his guests, or conduct them out, or keep them company; but though he is exempt from all this, he is to find them chairs, candles, liquors, and all other necessaries that company may ask for: he is likewise to provide them with cards, dice, and every necessary for gaming.

IV. There shall be no fixed hour for coming or going away; it is enough for a person to appear in the assembly.

V. Every one shall be free to sit, walk, or game, as he pleases; nor shall any one go about to hinder him, or take exception at what he does, upon pain of emptying the great eagle (a pint bowl full of brandy): it shall likewise be sufficient, at entering or retiring, to salute the company.

VI. Persons of distinction, noblemen, superior officers, merchants, and tradesmen of note, head-workmen, especially carpenters, and persons employed in chancery, are to have liberty to enter the assemblies; as likewise their wives and children.

VII. A particular place shall be assigned the footmen, except those of the house, that there may be room enough in the apartments designed for the assembly.

VIII. No ladies are to get drunk upon any pretence whatsoever, nor shall gentlemen be drunk before nine.

IX. Ladies who play at forfeitures, questions and commands, etc. shall not be riotous: no gentleman shall attemp to force a kiss, and no person shall offer to strike a woman in the assembly, under pain of future exclusion.

Such are the statutes upon this occasion, which, in their very appearance carry an air of ridicule and satire. But politeness must enter every country by degrees; and these rules resemble the breeding of a clown, awkward but sincere.

THE GENIUS OF LOVE:

AN EASTERN APOLOGUE.

THE formalities, delays, and disappointments, that precede a treaty of marriage here, are usually as numerous as those previous to a treaty of peace. The laws of this country are finely calculated to promote all commerce, but the commerce between the sexes. Their encouragements for propagating hemp, madder, and tobacco, are indeed admirable! Marriages are the only commodity that meets with none.

Yet, from the vernal softness of the air, the verdure of the fields, the transparency of the streams, and the beauty of the women, I know few countries more proper to invite to courtship. Here Love might sport among painted lawns and warbling groves, and revel amidst gales, wafting at once both fragrance and harmony. Yet it seems he has forsaken the island; and when a couple are now to be married, mutual love, or a union of minds, is the last and most trifling consideration. If their goods and chattels can be brought to unite, their sympathetic souls are ever ready to guarantee the treaty. The gentleman's mortgaged lawn becomes enamored of the lady's marriageble grove; the match is struck up, and both parties are piously in love — according to act of parliament.

Thus they who have a fortune, are possessed at least of something that is lovely; but I actually pity those that have none. I am told there was a time when ladies, with no other merit but youth, virtue, and beauty, had a chance for husbands, at least among the ministers of the church, or the officers of the army. The blush and innocence of sixteen was said to have a powerful influence over these two professions; but of late, all the little traffic of blushing, ogling, dimpling, and smiling, has been forbidden by an act in that case wisely made and provided. A lady's whole cargo of smiles, sighs, and whispers, is declared utterly contraband, till she arrives in the warm latitude of twenty-two, where commodities of this nature are found too often to decay. She is then permitted to dimple and smile, when the dimples and smiles begin to forsake her; and, when perhaps, grown ugly, is charitably intrusted with an unlimited use of her charms. Her lovers, however, by this time, have forsaken her; the captain has changed for another mistress; the priest himself leaves her in solitude to bewail her virginity, and she dies even without benefit of clergy.

Thus you find the Europeans discouraging love with as much earnestness as the rudest savage of Sofala. The Genius is surely now no more. In every region I find enemies in arms to oppress him. Avarice in Europe, jealousy in Persia, ceremony in China, poverty among the Tartars, and lust in Circassia, are all prepared to oppose his power. The Genius is certainly banished from earth, though once adored under such a variety of forms. He is no where to be found; and all that the ladies of each country can produce, are but a few trifling relics, as instances of his former residence and favor.

"The Genius of Love," says the eastern apologue, "had long resided in the happy plains of Abra, where every breeze was health, and every sound produced tranquillity. His temple at first was crowded, but every age lessened the number of his votaries, or cooled their devotion. Perceiving, therefore, his altars at length quite deserted, he was resolved to remove to some more propitious region; and he apprized the fair sex of every country, where he could hope for a proper reception, to assert their right to his presence among them. In return to this proclamation, embassies were sent from the ladies of every part of the world to invite him, and to display the superiority of their claims.

"And, first, the beauties of China appeared. No country could compare with them for modesty, either of look, dress or behavior; their eyes were never lifted from the ground; their robes, of the most beautiful silk, hid their hands, bosom, and neck, while their faces only were left uncovered. They indulged no airs that might express loose desire, and they seemed to study only the graces of inanimate beauty. Their black teeth and plucked eyebrows were, however, alleged by the genius against them; but he set them entirely aside when he came to examine their little feet.

"The beauties of Circassia next made their appear ance. They advanced, hand in hand, singing the most immodest airs, and leading up a dance in the most luxurious attitudes. Their dress was but half a covering; the neck, the left breast, and all the limbs, were exposed to view, which, after some time, seemed rather to satiate, than inflame desire. The lily and the rose contended in forming their complexions; and a soft sleepiness of eye added irresistible poignance to their charms; but their beauties were obtruded, not offered to their admirers; they seemed to give, rather than receive courtship; and the genius of love dismissed them, as unworthy his regard, since they exchanged the duties of love, and made themselves not the pursued, but the pursuing sex.

"The kingdom of Kashmire next produced its charming deputies. This happy region seemed peculiarly sequestered by nature for his abode. Shady mountains fenced it on one side from the scorching sun; and seaborne breezes, on the other, gave peculiar luxuriance to the air. Their complexions were of a bright yellow, that appeared almost transparent, while the crimson tulip seemed to blossom on their cheeks. Their features and limbs were delicate beyond the statuary's power to express; and their teeth whiter than their own ivory. He was almost persuaded to reside among them, when unfortunately one of the ladies talked of appointing his seraglio.

"In this procession the naked inhabitants of Southern America would not be left behind; their charms were found to surpass whatever the warmest imagination could conceive; and served to show, that beauty could be perfect, even with the seeming disadvantage of a brown complexion. But their savage education rendered them utterly unqualified to make the proper use of their power, and they were rejected as being incapable of uniting mental with sensual satisfaction. In this manner the deputies of other kingdoms had their suits rejected: the black beauties of Benin, and the tawny daughters of Borneo; the women of Wida with scarred faces, and the hideous virgins of Caffraria; the squab ladies of Lapland, three feet high, and the giant fair ones of Patagonia.

"The beauties of Europe at last appeared: grace was in their steps, and sensibility sat smiling in every eye. It was the universal opinion, while they were approaching, that they would prevail: and the genius seemed to lend them his most favorable attention. They opened their pretensions with the utmost modesty; but unfortunately, as their orator proceeded, she happened to let fall the words, house in town, settlement, and pin-money. These seemingly harmless terms had instantly a surprising effect: the genius, with ungovernable rage, burst from amidst the circle; and, waving his youthful pinions, left this earth, and flew back to those etherial mansions from whence he descended.

"The whole assembly was struck with amazement; they now justly apprehended that female power would be no more, since Love had now forsaken them. They continued some time thus in a state of torpid despair, when it was proposed by one of the number, that, since the real Genius of Love had left them, in order to continue their power, they should set up an idol in his stead; and that the ladies of every country should furnish him with what each liked best. This proposal was instantly relished and agreed to. An idol of gold was formed by uniting the capricious gifts of all the assembly, though no way resembling the departed genius. The ladies of China furnished the monster with wings; those of Kashmire supplied him with horns; the dames of Europe clapped a purse in his hand; and the virgins of Congo furnished him with a tail. Since that time, all the vows addressed to Love, are in reality paid to the idol; and, as in other false religions, the adoration seems more fervent where the heart is least sincere."

HISTORY OF THE DISTRESSES OF AN ENGLISH DISABLED SOLDIER.

No observation is more common, and at the same time more true, than that "one half of the world is ignorant how the other half lives." The misfortunes of the great are held up to engage our attention; are enlarged upon in tones of declamation; and the world is called upon to gaze at the noble sufferers: the great, under the pressure of calamity, are conscious of several others sympathizing with their distress; and have, at once, the comfort of admiration and pity.

There is nothing magnanimous in bearing misfortunes with fortitude when the whole world is looking on: men in such circumstances will act bravely even from motives of vanity: but he who, in the vale of obscurity, can brave adversity: who, without friends to encourage, acquaintances to pity, or even without hope to alleviate his misfortunes, can behave with tranquillity and indifference, is truly great; whether peasant or courtier, he deserves admiration, and should be held up for our imitation and respect.

While the slightest inconveniences of the great are magnified into calamities; while tragedy mouths out their sufferings in all the strains of eloquence — the miseries of the poor are entirely disregarded; and yet some of the lower ranks of people undergo more real hardships in one day, than those of a more exalted station suffer in their whole lives. It is inconceivable what difficulties the meanest of our common sailors and soldiers endure without murmuring or regret; without passionately declaiming against Providence, or calling on their fellows to be gazers on their intrepidity. Every day is to them a day of misery, and yet they entertain their hard fate without repining.

With what indignation do I hear an Ovid, a Cicero, or a Rabutin, complain of their misfortunes and hardships, whose greatest calamity was that of being unable to visit a certain spot of earth, to which they had foolishly attached an idea of happiness! Their distresses were pleasures compared to what many of the adventuring poor every day endure without murmuring. They ate, drank, and slept; they had slaves to attend them, and were sure of subsistence for life; while many of their fellow-creatures are obliged to wander without a friend to comfort or assist them, and even without a shelter from the severity of the season.

I have been led into these reflections from accidentally meeting, some days ago, a poor fellow, whom I knew when a boy, dressed in a sailor's jacket, and begging at one of the outlets of the town, with a wooden leg. I knew him to be honest and industrious when in the country, and was curious to learn what had reduced him to his present situation. Wherefore, after giving him what I thought proper, I desired to know the history of his life and misfortunes, and the manner in which he was reduced to his present distress. The disabled soldier, for such he was, though dressed in a sailor's habit, scratching his head, and leaning on his crutch, put himself into an attitude to comply with my request, and gave me his history as follows: —

"As for my misfortunes, master, I can't pretend to have gone through any more than other folks: for except the loss of my limb, and my being obliged to beg, I don't know any reason, thank Heaven, that I have to complain; there is Bill Tibbs, of our regiment, he has lost both his legs, and an eye to boot; but, thank Heaven, it is not so bad with me yet.

"I was born, in Shropshire; my father was a laborer, and died when I was five years old, so I was put upon the parish. As he had been a wandering sort of a man, the parishioners were not able to tell to what parish I belonged, or where I was born, so they sent me to another parish, and that parish sent me to a third. I thought, in my heart, they kept sending me about so long, that they would not let me be born in any parish at all; but at last, however, they fixed me. I had some disposition to be a scholar, and was resolved at least to know my letters; but the master of the workhouse put me to business as soon as I was able to handle a mallet; and here I lived an easy kind of a life for five years; I only wrought ten hours in the day, and had my meat and drink provided for my labor. It is true, I was not suffered to stir out of the house, for fear, as they said, I should run away; but what of that? I had the liberty of the whole house, and the yard before the door, and that was enough for me. I was then bound out to a farmer, where I was up both early and late; but I ate and drank well, and liked my business well enough, till he died, when I was obliged to provide for myself; so I was resolved to go and seek my fortune.

"In this manner I went from town to town, worked when I could get employment, and starved when I could get none; when happening one day to go through a field belonging to a justice of the peace, I spied a hare crossing the path just before me; and I believe the devil put it into my head to fling my stick at it: — well, what will you have on 't? I killed the hare, and was bringing it away in triumph, when the justice himself met me: he called me a poacher and a villain; and, collaring me, desired I would give an account of myself. I fell upon my knees, begged his worship's pardon, and began to give a full account of all that I knew of my breed, seed, and generation; but though I gave a very good account, the justice would not believe a syllable I had to say; so I was indicted at sessions, found guilty of being poor, and sent up to London to Newgate, in order to be transported as a vagabond.

"People may say this and that of being in jail; but, for my part, I found Newgate as agreeable a place as ever I was in in all my life. I had my bellyfull to eat and drink, and did no work at all. This kind of life was too good to last for ever; so I was taken out of pris n, after five months, put on board a ship, and sent off, with two hundred more, to the plantations. We had but an indifferent passage; for, being all confined in the hold, more than a hundred of our people died for want of sweet air; and those that remained were sickly enough, God knows. When we came ashore we were sold to the planters, and I was bound for seven years more. As I was no scholar, for I did not know my letters, I was obliged to work among the negroes; and I served out my time, as in duty bound to do.

"When my time was expired, I worked my passage home, and glad I was to see old England again, because I loved my country. I was afraid, however, that I should be indicted for a vagabond once more, so did not much care to go down into the country, but kept about the town, and did little jobs when I could get them.

"I was very happy in this manner for some time, till one evening, coming home from work, two men knocked me down, and then desired me to stand. They belonged to a press-gang: I was carried before the justice, and as I could give no account of myself, I had my choice left, whether to go on board a man of war, or list for a soldier. I chose the latter; and, in this post of a gentleman, I served two campaigns in Flanders, was at the battles of Val and Fontenoy, and received but one wound through the breast here; but the doctor of our regiment soon made me well again.

"When the peace came on I was discharged, and as I could not work, because my wound was sometimes troublesome, I listed for a landman in the East-India company's service. I here fought the French in six pitched battles; and I verily believe, that if I could read or write, our captain would have made me a corporal. But it was not my good fortune to have any promotion, for I soon fell sick, and so got leave to return home again, with forty pounds in my pocket. This was at the beginning of the present war, and I hoped to be set on shore, and to have the pleasure of spending my money; but the government wanted men, and so I was pressed for a sailor before ever I could set foot on shore.

"The boatswain found me, as he said, an obstinate fellow: he swore he knew that I understood my business well, but that I shammed Abraham, merely to be idle; but God knows, I knew nothing of sea-business, and he beat me without considering what he was about. I had still, however, my forty pounds, and that was some comfort to me under every beating; and the money I might have had to this day, but that our ship was taken by the French, and so I lost all.

"Our crew was carried into Brest, and many of them died because they were not used to live in a jail; but for my part, it was nothing to me, for I was seasoned. One night as I was sleeping on the bed of boards, with a warm blanket about me, for I always loved to lie well, I was awakened by the boatswain, who had a dark lantern in his hand. Jack, says he to me, will you knock out the French sentries' brains? I don't care, says I, striving to keep myself awake, if I lend a hand. Then follow me, says he, and I hope we shall do business. So up I got, and tied my blanket, which was all the clothes I had, about my middle, and went with him to fight the Frenchman. I hate the French because they are all slaves, and wear wooden shoes.

"Though we had no arms, one Englishman is able to beat five French at any time; so we went down to the door, where both the sentries were posted, and, rushing upon them, seized their arms in a moment, and knocked them down. From thence, nine of us ran together to the quay, and seizing the first boat we met, got out of the harbor and put to sea. We had not been here three days before we were taken up by the Dorset privateer, who were glad of so many good hands; and we consented to run our chance. However, we had not so much good luck as we expected. In three days we fell in with the Pompadour privateer, of forty guns, while we had but twenty-three; so to it we went, yard-arm and yard-arm. The fight lasted for three hours, and I verily believe we should have taken the Frenchman, had we but had some more men left behind; but unfortunately we lost all our men just as we were going to get the victory.

"I was once more in the power of the French, and I believe it would have gone hard with me had I been brought back to Brest: but, by good fortune we were retaken by the Viper. I had almost forgot to tell you, that in that engagement I was wounded in two places; I lost four fingers of the left hand, and my leg was shot off. If I had had the good fortune to have lost my leg and use of my hand on board a king's ship, and not aboard a privateer, I should have been entitled to clothing and maintenance during the rest of my life; but that was not my chance: one man is born with a silver spoon in his mouth, and another with a wooden ladle. However, blessed be God! I enjoy good health, and will forever love liberty and Old England. Liberty, property, and Old England forever, — huzza!"

Thus saying, he limped off, leaving me in admiration at his intrepidity and content; nor could I avoid acknowledging, that an habitual acquaintance with misery, serves better than philosophy to teach us to despise it.

ON THE FRAILTY OF MAN.

SUPPOSED TO BE WRITTEN BY THE ORDINARY OF NEWGATE.

MAN is a most frail being, incapable of directing his steps, unacquainted with what is to happen in this life; and perhaps no man is a more manifest instance of the truth of this maxim, than Mr. The. Cibber, just now gone out of the world. Such a variety of turns of fortune, yet such a persevering uniformity of conduct, appears in all that happened in his short span, that the whole may be looked upon as one regular confusion; every action of his life was matter of wonder and surprise, and his death was an astonishment.

This gentleman was born of creditable parents, who gave him a very good education, and a great deal of good learning, so that he could read and write before he was sixteen. However, he early discovered an inclination to follow lewd courses; he refused to take the advice of his parents, and pursued the bent of his inclination; he played at cards on the Sundays, called himself a gentleman, fell out with his mother and laundress; and, even in these early days, his father was frequently heard to observe, that young The. — would be hanged.

As he advanced in years, he grew more fond of pleasure; would eat an ortolan for dinner, though he begged the guinea that bought it; and was once known to give three pounds for a plate of green peas, which he had collected over-night as charity for a friend in distress; he ran into debt with every body that would trust him, and none could build a sconce better than he; so that, at last, his creditors swore with one accord that The. — would be hanged.

But, as getting into debt by a man who had no visible means but impudence for subsistence, is a thing that every reader is not acquainted with, I must explain that point a little, and that to his satisfaction.

There are three ways of getting into debt: first, by pushing a face; as thus, "You, Mr. Lustring, send me home six yards of that paduasoy, damme; — but hark'ye, do n't think I ever intend to pay you for it — damme." At this, the mercer laughs heartily, cuts off the paduasoy, and sends it home; nor is he, till too late, surprised to find the gentleman had said nothing but truth, and kept his word.

The second method of running into debt is called fineering; which is getting goods made up in such a fashion as to be unfit for every other purchaser; and, if the tradesman refuses to give them upon credit, then threaten to leave them upon his hands.

But the third and best method is called, "Being the good customer." The gentleman first buys some trifle, and pays for it in ready money; he comes a few days after with nothing about him but bank bills, and buys, we will suppose, a sixpenny tweezer-case; the bills are too great to be changed, so he promises to return punctually the day after, and pay for what he has bought. In this promise he is punctual; and this is repeated for eight or ten times, till his face is well known, and he has got, at last, the character of a good customer. By this means he gets credit for something considerable, and then never pays it.

In all this the young man, who is the unhappy subject of our present reflections, was very expert, and could face, fineer, and bring custom to a shop, with any man in England; none of his companions could exceed him in this; and his companions at last said that THE.— would be hanged.

As he grew old, he grew never the better; he loved ortolans and green peas, as before; he drank gravy-soup, when he could get it, and always thought his oysters tasted best when he got them for nothing, or, which was just the same, when he bought them upon tick; thus the old man kept up the vices of the youth, and what he wanted in power he made up in inclination; so that all the world thought that old THE. — would be hanged.

And now, reader, I have brought him to his last scene; a scene where, perhaps, my duty should have obliged me to assist. You expect, perhaps, his dying words, and the tender farewell of his wife and children; you expect an account of his coffin and white gloves, his pious ejaculations, and the papers he left behind him. In this I cannot indulge your curiosity: for, oh, the mysteries of fate! THE.— was drowned.

"Reader," as Hervey saith, "pause and ponder, and ponder and pause;" who knows what thy own end may be?

ON FRIENDSHIP.

THERE are few subjects which have been more written upon and less understood, than that of friendship. To follow the dictates of some, this virtue, instead of being the assuager of pain, becomes the source of every inconvenience. Such speculatists, by expecting too much from friendship, dissolve the connection, and by drawing the bands too closely, at length break them. Almost all our romance and novel writers are of this kind; they persuade us to friendship, which we find it impossible to sustain to the last; so that this sweetener of life, under proper regulations, is, by their means, rendered inaccessible or uneasy. It is certain, the best method to cultivate this virtue is by letting it, in some measure, make itself; a similitude of minds or studies, and even sometimes a diversity of pursuits, will produce all the pleasures that arise from it. The current of tenderness widens as it proceeds; and two men imperceptibly find their hearts filled with good-nature for each other, when they were at first only in pursuit of mirth or relaxation.

Friendship is like a debt of honor; the moment it is talked of, it loses its real name, and assumes the more ungrateful form of obligation. From hence we find, that those who regularly undertake to cultivate friendship, find ingratitude generally repays their endeavors. That circle of beings, which dependance gathers round us, is almost ever unfriendly; they secretly wish the terms of their connections more nearly equal; and, where they even have the most virtue, are prepared to reserve all their affections for their patron only in the hour of his decline. Increasing the obligations which are laid upon such minds, only increases their burden; they feel themselves unable to repay the immensity of their debt, and their bankrupt hearts are taught a latent resentment at the hand that is stretched out with offers of service and relief.

Plautinus was a man who thought that every good was to be brought from riches; and, as he was possessed of great wealth, and had a mind naturally formed for virtue, he resolved to gather a circle of the best men round him. Among the number of his dependants was Musidorus, with a mind just as fond of virtue, yet not less proud than his patron. His circumstances, however, were such as forced him to stoop to the good offices of his superior, and he saw himself daily among a number of others loaded with benefits and protestations of friendship. These, in the usual course of the world, he thought it prudent to accept: but, while he gave his esteem, he could not give his heart. A want of affection breaks out in the most trifling instances, and Plautinus had skill enough to observe the minutest actions of the man he wished to make his friend. In these he even found his aim disappointed; Musidorus claimed an exchange of hearts, which Plautinus, solicited by a variety of claims, could never think of bestowing.

It may be easily supposed that the reserve of our poor

proud man was soon construed into ingratitude; and such indeed, in the common acceptation of the world, it was. Wherever Musidorus appeared, he was remarked as the ungrateful man; he had accepted favors, it was said; and still had the insolence to pretend to independence. The event, however, justified his conduct. Plautinus, by misplaced liberality, at length became poor, and it was then that Musidorus first thought of making a friend of him. He flew to the man of fallen fortune, with an offer of all he had; wrought under his direction with assiduity; and, by uniting their talents, both were at length placed in that state of life from which one of them had formerly fallen.

To this story, taken from modern life, I shall add one more, taken from a Greek writer of antiquity: — Two Jewish soldiers, in the time of Vespasian, had fought many campaigns together, and a participation of danger at length bred a union of hearts. They were remarked through the whole army, as the two friendly brothers; they felt and fought for each other. Their friendship might have continued, without interruption, till death, had not the good fortune of the one alarmed the pride of the other, which was in his promotion to be a centurion under the famous John, who headed a particular part of the Jewish malcontents.

From this moment, their former love was converted into the most inveterate enmity. They attached themselves to opposite factions, and sought each other's lives in the conflict of adverse party. In this manner they continued for more than two years, vowing mutual revenge, and animated with an unconquerable spirit of aversion. At length, however, that party of the Jews, to which the mean soldier belonged, joining with the Romans, it became victorious, and drove John with all his adherents into the temple. History has given us more than one picture of the dreadful conflagration of that superb edifice. The Roman soldiers were gathered round it; the whole temple was in flames: and thousands were seen amidst them within its sacred circuit. It was in this situation of things, that the now successful soldier saw his former friend, upon the battlements of the highest tower, looking round with horror, and just ready to be consumed with flames. All his former tenderness now returned; he saw the man of his bosom just going to perish; and unable to withstand the impulse, he ran, spreading his arms, and cried out to his friend to leap down from the top, and find safety with him. The centurion from above heard and obeyed; and, casting himself from the top of the tower into his fellow-soldier's arms, both fell a sacrifice on the spot; one being crushed to death by the weight of his companion, and the other dashed to pieces by the greatness of his fall.

FOLLY OF ATTEMPTING TO LEARN WISDOM IN RETIREMENT.

Books, while they teach us to respect the interests of others, often make us unmindful of our own; while they instruct the youthful reader to grasp at social happiness, he grows miserable in detail; and, attentive to universal harmony, often forgets that he himself has a part to sustain in the concert. I dislike, therefore, the philosopher who describes the inconveniences of life in such pleasing colors, that the pupil grows enamored of distress, longs to try the charms of poverty, meets it without dread, nor fears its inconveniences till he severely feels them.

A youth who has thus spent his life among books, new to the world, and unacquainted with man but by philosophic information, may be considered as a being whose mind is filled with the vulgar errors of the wise; utterly unqualified for a journey through life, yet confident of his own skill in the direction, he sets out with confidence, blunders on with vanity, and finds himself at last undone.

He first has learned from books, and then lays it down as a maxim, that all mankind are virtuous or vicious in excess: and he has been long taught to detest vice and love virtue. Warm, therefore, in attachments, and steadfast in enmity, he treats every creature as a friend or foe; expects from those he loves unerring integrity; and consigns his enemies to the reproach of wanting every virtue. On this principle he proceeds; and here begin his disappointments: upon a closer inspection of human nature, he perceives that he should have moderated his friendship, and softened his severity; for he often finds the excellences of one part of mankind clouded with vice, and the faults of the other brightened with virtue; he finds no character so sanctified that has not its failings, none so infamous, but has somewhat to attract our esteem; he beholds impiety in lawn, and fidelity in fetters.

He now, therefore, but too late, perceives that his regards should have been more cool, and his hatred less violent; that the truly wise seldom court romantic friendship with the good, and avoid, if possible, the resentment even of the wicked; every moment gives him fresh instances that the bonds of friendship are broken if drawn too closely: and that those whom he has treated with disrespect, more than retaliate the injury: at length, therefore, he is obliged to confess, that he has declared war upon the vicious half of mankind, without being able to form an alliance among the virtuous to espouse his quarrel.

Our book-taught philosopher, however, is now too far advanced to recede; and though poverty be the just consequence of the many enemies his conduct has created, yet he is resolved to meet it without shrinking; philosophers have described poverty in most charming colors; and even his vanity is touched in thinking he shall show the world in himself one more example of patience, fortitude and resignation: "Come, then, O Poverty! for what is there in thee dreadful to the wise? Temperance, health, and frugality, walk in thy train; cheerfulness and liberty are ever thy companions. Shall any be ashamed of thee of whom Cincinnatus was not ashamed? The running brook, the herbs of the field, can amply satisfy nature; man wants but little, nor that little long. Come, then, O Poverty! while kings stand by, and gaze with admiration at the true philosopher's resignation."

The goddess appears; for Poverty ever comes at the call; but, alas! he finds her by no means the charming figure books and his own imagination had painted. As when an eastern bride, whom her friends and relations had long described as a model of perfection, pays her first visit, the longing bridegroom lifts the veil to see a face he had never seen before; but instead of a countenance blazing with beauty like the sun, he beholds deformity shooting icicles to his heart; such appears Poverty to her new entertainer: all the fabric of enthusiasm is at once demolished, and a thousand miseries rise upon its ruins; while Contempt, with pointing finger, is foremost in the hideous procession.

The poor man now finds that he can get no kings to look at him while he is eating: he finds that in proportion as he grows poor, the world turns its back upon him, and gives him leave to act the philosopher in all the majesty of solitude. It might be agreeable enough to play the philosopher, while we are conscious that mankind are spectators; but what signifies wearing the mask of sturdy contentment, and mounting the stage of restraint, when not one creature will assist at the exhibition? Thus is he forsaken of men, while his fortitude wants the satisfaction even of self-applause; for either he does not feel his present calamities, and that is natural insensibility; or he disguises his feelings, and that is dissimulation.

Spleen now begins to take up the man; not distinguishing in his resentment, he regards all mankind with detestation: and commencing man-hater, seeks solitude to be at liberty to rail.

It has been said, that he who retires to solitude is either a beast or an angel: the censure is too severe, and the praise unmerited; the discontented being, who retires from society, is generally some good-natured man who has begun life without experience, and knew not how to gain it in his intercourse with mankind.

LETTER,

SUPPOSED TO BE WRITTEN BY A COMMON-COUNCIL-MAN, AT THE TIME OF THE CORONATION.

SIR — I have the honor of being a common-council-man, and am greatly pleased with a paragraph from Southampton in yours of yesterday. There we learn that the mayor and aldermen of that loyal borough had the particular satisfaction of celebrating the royal nuptials by a magnificent turtle-feast. By this means the gentlemen had the pleasure of filling their bellies, and showing their loyalty, together. I must confess it would give me pleasure to see some such method of testifying our loyalty practised in this metropolis, of which I am an unworthy member. Instead of presenting his majesty (God bless him) on every occasion with our formal addresses, we might thus sit comfortably down to dinner, and wish him prosperity in a surloin of beef; upon our army levelling the walls of a town, or besieging a fortification, we might at our city-feast imitate our brave troops, and demolish the walls of a venison-pasty, or besiege the shell of a turtle, with as great a certainty of success.

At present, however, we have got into a sort of dry, unsocial manner of drawing up addresses upon every occasion; and though I have attended upon six cavalcades, and two foot-processions, in a single year, yet I came away as lean and hungry, as if I had been a juryman at the Old Bailey. For my part, Mr. Printer, I do n't see what is got by these processions and addresses, except an appetite; and that, thank Heaven, we all have in a pretty good degree, without ever leaving our own houses for it. It is true, our gowns of mazarine blue, edged with fur, cut a pretty figure enough, parading it through the streets, and so my wife tells me. In fact, I generally bow to all my acquaintance, when thus in full dress; but, alas! as the proverb has it, fine clothes never fill the belly.

But even though all this bustling, parading, and powdering, through the streets, be agreeable enough to many of us; yet, I would have my brethren consider whether the frequent repetition of it be so agreeable to our betters above. To be introduced to court, to see the queen, to kiss hands, to smile upon lords, to ogle the ladies, and all the other fine things there, may, I grant, be a perfect show to us that view it but seldom; but it may be a troublesome business enough to those who are to settle such ceremonies as these every day. To use an instance adapted to all our apprehensions; suppose my family and I should go to Bartholomew fair. Very well, going to Bartholomew fair, the whole sight is perfect rapture to us, who are only spectators once and away; but I am of opinion, that the wire-walker and fire-eater find no such great sport in all this; I am of opinion they had as lief remain behind the curtain, at their own pastimes, drinking beer, eating shrimps, and smoking tobacco.

Besides, what can we tell his majesty in all we say on these occasions, but what he knows perfectly well already? I believe, if I were to reckon up, I could not find above five hundred disaffected in the whole kingdom; and here we are every day telling his majesty how loyal we are. Suppose the addresses of a people, for instance, should run thus:—

"May it please your m——y, we are many of us worth a hundred thousand pounds, and are possessed of several other inestimable advantages. For the preservation of this money and those advantages we are chiefly indebted to your m——y. We are, therefore, once more assembled, to assure your m——y of our fidelity. This, it is true, we have lately assured your m——y five or six times; but we are willing once more to repeat what can't be doubted, and to kiss your royal hand, and the queen's hand, and thus sincerely to convince you, that we never shall do any thing to deprive you of one loyal subject, or any one of ourselves of one hundred thousand pounds." Should we not, upon reading such an address, think that people a little silly, who thus made such unmeaning professions? Excuse me, Mr. Printer: no man upon earth hath a more profound respect for the abilities of the aldermen and common-council than I; but I could wish they would not take up a monarch's time in these good-natured trifles, who, I am told, seldom spends a moment in vain.

The example set by the city of London will probably be followed by every other community in the British empire. Thus we shall have a new set of addresses from every little borough with but four freemen and a burgess; day after day shall we see them come up with hearts filled with gratitude, "laying the vows of a loyal people at the foot of the throne." Death! Mr. Printer, they will hardly leave our courtiers time to scheme a single project for beating the French; and our enemies may gain upon us, while we are thus employed in telling our governor how much we intend to keep them under.

But a people by too frequent use of addresses may by this means come at last to defeat the very purpose for which they are designed. If we are thus exclaiming in raptures upon every occasion, we deprive ourselves of the powers of flattery, when there may be a real necessity. A boy three weeks ago swimming across the Thames, was every minute crying out, for his amusement, "I 've got the cramp, I 've got the cramp:" the boatmen pushed off once or twice, and they found it was fun; he soon after cried out in earnest, but nobody believed him, and he sunk to the bottom.

In short, sir, I am quite displeased with any unnecessary cavalcade whatever. I hope we shall soon have occasion to triumph, and then I shall be ready myself, either to eat at a turtle-feast or to shout at a bonfire: and will either lend my faggot at the fire, or flourish my hat at every loyal health that may be proposed.

I am, sir, etc.

A SECOND LETTER,

SUPPOSED TO BE WRITTEN BY A COMMON-COUNCIL-MAN, DESCRIBING THE CORONATION.

Sir, — I am the same common-council-man who troubled you some days ago. To whom can I complain but to you? for you have many a dismal correspondent; in this time of joy my wife does not choose to hear me, because, she says, I'm always melancholy when she 's in spirits. I have been to see the coronation, and a fine sight it was, as I am told, to those who had the pleasure of being near spectators. The diamonds, I am told, were as thick as Bristol stones in a show glass; the ladies and gentlemen walked along, one foot before another, and threw their eyes about them, on this side and that, perfectly like clock-work. O! Mr. Printer, it had been a fine sight indeed, if there was but a little more eating.

Instead of that, there we sat, penned up in our scaffolding, like sheep upon a market-day in Smithfield; but the devil a thing I could get to eat (God pardon me for swearing) except the fragments of a plum-cake, that was all squeezed into crumbs in my wife's pocket, as she came through the crowd. You must know, sir, that in order to do the thing genteelly, and that all my family might be amused at the same time, my wife, my daughter, and I, took two-guinea places for the coronation, and I gave my two eldest boys (who by the by are twins, fine children) eighteen-pence a-piece to go to Sudrick fair, to see the court of the black King of Morocco, which will serve to please children well enough.

That we might have good places on the scaffolding, my wife insisted upon going at seven o'clock in the evening before the coronation, for she said she would not lose a full prospect for the world. This resolution, I own, shocked me. "Grizzle," said I to her, "Grizzle, my dear, consider that you are but weakly, always ailing, and will never bear sitting all night upon the scaffolding. You remember what a cold you got the last fast-day by rising but half an hour before your time to go to church, and how I was scolded as the cause of it. Besides, my dear, our daughter Anna Amelia Wilhelmina Carolina will look like a perfect fright if she sits up; and you know the girl's face is something at her time of life, considering her fortune is but small." "Mr. Grogan," replied my wife, "Mr. Grogan, this is always the case, when you find me in spirits; I do n't want to go, not I, nor I do n't care whether I go at all; it is seldom that I am in spirits, but this is always the case." In short, Mr. Printer, what will you have on 't? to the coronation we went.

What difficulties we had in getting a coach; how we were shoved about in the mob; how I had my pocket picked of the last new almanac, and my steel tobacco-box; how my daughter lost half an eye-brow, and her laced shoe in a gutter; my wife's lamentation upon this, with the adventures of a crumbled plum-cake; relate all these; we suffered this and ten times more before we got to our places.

At last, however, we were seated. My wife is certainly a heart of oak; I thought sitting up in the damp night-air would have killed her; I have known her for two months take possession of our easy chair, mobbed up in flannel night-caps, and trembling at a breath of air; but she now bore the night as merrily as if she had sat up at a christening. My daughter and she did not seem to value it a farthing. She told me two or three stories that she knows will always make me laugh, and my daughter sung me "the noon-tide air," towards one o'clock in the morning. However, with all their endeavors, I was as cold and as dismal as ever I remember. If this be the pleasures of a coronation, cried I to myself, I had rather see the court of King Solomon in all his glory, at my ease in Bartholomew fair.

Towards morning, sleep began to come fast upon me; and the sun rising and warming the air, still inclined me to rest a little. You must know, sir, that I am naturally of a sleepy constitution; I have often sat up at a table with my eyes open, and have been asleep all the while. What will you have on 't? just about eight o'clock in the morning I fell asleep. I fell into the most pleasing dream in the world. I shall never forget it; I dreamed that I was at my lord-mayor's feast, and had scaled the crust of a venison-pasty; I kept eating and eating, in my sleep, and thought I could never have enough. After some time, the pasty, methought, was taken away, and the dessert was brought in its room. Thought I to myself, if I have not got enough of venison, I am resolved to make it up by the largest snap at the sweet-meats. Accordingly I grasped a whole pyramid; the rest of the guests seeing me with so much, one gave me a snap, the other gave me a snap; I was pulled this way by my neighbor on my right hand, and that way by my neighbor on the left, but still kept my ground without flinching, and continued eating and pocketing as fast as I could. I never was so pulled and handled in my whole life. At length, however, going to smell to a lobster that lay before me, methought it caught me with its claws fast by the nose. The pain I felt upon this occasion is inexpressible; in fact, it broke my dream; when awaking I found my wife and daughter applying a smelling-bottle to my nose, and telling me it was time to go home; they assured me every means had been tried to awake me, while the procession was going forward, but that I still continued to sleep till the whole ceremony was over. Mr. Printer, this is a hard case, and as I read your most ingenious work, it will be some comfort, when I see this inserted, to find that —— I write for it too.

I am, sir, Your distressed humble servant,

L. GROGAN.

www.ingramcontent.com/pod-product-compliance
Lightning Source LLC
LaVergne TN
LVHW021241110826
845150LV00002B/372

* 9 7 8 1 4 2 5 5 6 1 5 7 4 *